Palgrave Critical Studies of Antisemitism and Racism

Series Editor
David Feldman
Birkbeck College—University of London
London, UK

Palgrave Critical Studies of Antisemitism and Racism considers antisemitism from the ancient world to the present day. The series explores topical and theoretical questions and brings historical and multidisciplinary perspectives to bear on contemporary concerns and phenomena.

Grounded in history, the series also reaches across disciplinary boundaries to promote a contextualised and comparative understanding of antisemitism. A contextualised understanding will seek to uncover the content, meanings, functions and dynamics of antisemitism as it occurred in the past and recurs in the present. A comparative approach will consider antisemitism over time and place. Importantly, it will also explore the connections between antisemitism and other exclusionary visions of society. The series will explore the relationship between antisemitism and other racisms as well as between antisemitism and forms of discrimination and prejudice articulated in terms of gender and sexuality.

More information about this series at
http://www.palgrave.com/gp/series/15437

Sol Goldberg · Scott Ury ·
Kalman Weiser
Editors

Key Concepts in the Study of Antisemitism

Editors
Sol Goldberg
University of Toronto
Toronto, ON, Canada

Scott Ury
Tel Aviv University
Tel Aviv, Israel

Kalman Weiser
York University
Toronto, ON, Canada

Palgrave Critical Studies of Antisemitism and Racism
ISBN 978-3-030-51657-4   ISBN 978-3-030-51658-1 (eBook)
https://doi.org/10.1007/978-3-030-51658-1

© The Editor(s) (if applicable) and The Author(s), under exclusive license to Springer Nature Switzerland AG 2021
This work is subject to copyright. All rights are solely and exclusively licensed by the Publisher, whether the whole or part of the material is concerned, specifically the rights of translation, reprinting, reuse of illustrations, recitation, broadcasting, reproduction on microfilms or in any other physical way, and transmission or information storage and retrieval, electronic adaptation, computer software, or by similar or dissimilar methodology now known or hereafter developed.
The use of general descriptive names, registered names, trademarks, service marks, etc. in this publication does not imply, even in the absence of a specific statement, that such names are exempt from the relevant protective laws and regulations and therefore free for general use.
The publisher, the authors and the editors are safe to assume that the advice and information in this book are believed to be true and accurate at the date of publication. Neither the publisher nor the authors or the editors give a warranty, expressed or implied, with respect to the material contained herein or for any errors or omissions that may have been made. The publisher remains neutral with regard to jurisdictional claims in published maps and institutional affiliations.

Cover credit: Peter Cripps/Alamy Stock Photo Design by eStudio Calamar

This Palgrave Macmillan imprint is published by the registered company Springer Nature Switzerland AG
The registered company address is: Gewerbestrasse 11, 6330 Cham, Switzerland

To our children
Odelya
Matan and Shira
Orly and Talia

Acknowledgments

This volume, the culmination of over five years of intellectual engagement and scholarly collaboration, would not be possible without the support and assistance of many parties. The editors would therefore like to express their profound gratitude for the invaluable financial and moral support provided by the following bodies and institutions: the Social Sciences and Humanities Research Council of Canada, the Canadian Embassy in Israel, the Israel and Golda Koschitzky Centre for Jewish Studies (York University), the Anne Tanenbaum Centre for Jewish Studies (the University of Toronto), the Stephen Roth Institute for the Study of Contemporary Antisemitism and Racism (Tel Aviv University), Tel Aviv University's Office of the Vice-President, and the Coburn Trust at the University of Toronto. We would also like to thank the members of our project steering committee who helped us conceive this volume—Professors Jonathan Judaken and Adam Teller. We recognize also the invaluable support provided by graduate student assistants, university staff members, and colleagues in convening highly stimulating project seminars and workshops in Tel Aviv and Toronto and a 2018 summer institute at York University dedicated to pedagogy about antisemitism. And, of course, we express our gratitude to the various authors whose contributions helped create a rich and diverse collection of essays. Finally, we wish to thank our spouses, without whose loving support and cooperation no scholarly achievements would be possible.

PRAISE FOR *KEY CONCEPTS IN THE STUDY OF ANTISEMITISM*

"This stimulating and useful book offers a fresh organizational approach to the multifaceted and often contentious field of the study of antisemitism. It brings together an impressive range of expertise and offers an interesting range of perspectives on the complexities, controversies and historical dynamics of antisemitism."
—Adam Sutcliffe, *Professor of European History, King's College London, UK*

"This book is the rarest of things: a handy reference work that is also intellectually challenging and methodologically innovative. Designed especially for the college classroom, the 22 essays in this volume offer substantive yet accessible overviews of major topics, not all of which are typically examined even in standard works on the subject. Written by leading scholars in the field, each entry cuts across boundaries of period, geography and discipline to produce fresh insights and perspectives. Amidst a spate of recent publications on antisemitism, Key Concepts stands out as a novel tool that will enhance our understanding of a complex and seemingly intractable phenomenon."
—Jonathan Karp, *Associate Professor in the History and Judaic Studies Department at Binghamton University, New York, USA*

"Finally, a comprehensive and innovative approach to a contested historical and political phenomenon. Instead of following the downtrodden path of a chronological narrative, the editors break up the topic up into well thought out Key Concepts, while the authors in turn provide fresh perspectives on a wide array of entangled topics that are essential for understanding anti-Semitism. Readable, insightful and provocative."
—Stefanie Schüler-Springorum, *Director, Center for Anti-Semitism Research, Technical University of Berlin, Germany*

Contents

1	**Introduction** Kalman Weiser	1
2	**Anti-Judaism** Jonathan Elukin	13
3	**Anti-Semitism (Historiography)** Jonathan Judaken	25
4	**Anti-Zionism** James Loeffler	39
5	**The Blood Libel** Hillel J. Kieval	53
6	**The Catholic Church** Magda Teter	65
7	**Conspiracy Theories** Jovan Byford	79
8	**Emancipation** Frederick Beiser	93
9	**Gender** Sara R. Horowitz	105

10	Ghetto Daniel B. Schwartz	121
11	The Holocaust Richard S. Levy	133
12	Jewish Self-Hatred Sol Goldberg	147
13	Nationalism Brian Porter-Szűcs	161
14	Nazism Doris L. Bergen	173
15	Orientalism Ivan Kalmar	187
16	Philosemitism Maurice Samuels	201
17	Pogroms Jeffrey S. Kopstein	215
18	Postcolonialism Bryan Cheyette	229
19	Racism Robert Bernasconi	245
20	Secularism Lena Salaymeh and Shai Lavi	257
21	*Sinat Yisrael* (Hatred of Jews) Martin Lockshin	273
22	Zionism Scott Ury	287

Works Cited	301
Index	331

Notes on Contributors

Frederick Beiser is Professor of Philosophy at Syracuse University, New York. He was born and raised in the United States but received his university education in the U.K. at Oriel and Wolfson Colleges, Oxford. Since 1980 he has held research fellowships in Germany, first as a Thyssen and then as a Humboldt fellow. He has taught at several American universities, including Harvard, Yale, the University of Pennsylvania, the University of Wisconsin, Madison, the University of Colorado, Boulder, and Indiana University, Bloomington. He is the author of *Hermann Cohen: An Intellectual Biography* (2018). In 2015 he received the Bundesverdienstkreuz from Joachim Gauck, the President of Germany, for his many books on German philosophy.

Doris Bergen is the Chancellor Rose and Ray Wolfe Professor of Holocaust Studies at the University of Toronto. She is the author or editor of five books, including *Twisted Cross: The German Christian Movement in the Third Reich* (1996) and *War and Genocide: A Concise History of the Holocaust* (2016). A Fellow of the Royal Society of Canada, Bergen was part of the team that designed the National Holocaust Monument in Ottawa, Canada. She serves on the Academic Committee of the United States Holocaust Memorial Museum in Washington, DC.

Robert Bernasconi is the Edwin Erle Sparks Professor of Philosophy and African American Studies at Penn State University. He is the author of two books on Heidegger (*The Question of Language in Heidegger's History of Being* and *Heidegger in Question*) and one on Sartre (*How to Read Sartre*). In addition, he has published numerous essays on the critical philosophy of race and on Hegel, Levinas, and Derrida, among others. He is the editor of three journals: *Critical Philosophy of Race*, *Levinas Studies*, and *Eco-Ethica*.

Jovan Byford is Senior Lecturer in Psychology at The Open University, UK. His research interests include the relationship between psychology and history, conspiracy theories, Holocaust memory, and antisemitism. He is the author of five books, including *Conspiracy Theories: A Critical Introduction* (2011) and *Denial and Repression of Antisemitism: Post-Communist Remembrance of the Serbian Bishop Nikolaj Velimirović* (2008). He also co-edited the book *Psychology and History: Interdisciplinary Explorations* (2014).

Bryan Cheyette is Chair in Modern Literature and Culture at the University of Reading, UK. He is the editor or author of eleven books, including *Ghetto: A Very Short Introduction* (2020), *Diasporas of the Mind: Jewish and Postcolonial Writing and the Nightmare of History* (2014), a Times Higher Book of the Year, and volume seven of *The Oxford History of the Novel in English* (2016). He writes regularly for *The Times Literary Supplement* and is currently working on *Testimonies: Slaves, Camps, Refugees*.

Jonathan Elukin is an Associate Professor in the history department at Trinity College, Hartford, Connecticut. He is the author of the monograph *Living Together, Living Apart: Rethinking Jewish-Christian Relations in the Middle Ages* (2013), and of numerous publications on antisemitism, including "Shylock, the Devil and the Meaning of Deception in *The Merchant of Venice*," *European Judaism* (2018), and "Post-Biblical Jewish History through Christian Eyes: Josephus and the Miracle of Jewish History in English Protestantism," in David Wertheim, ed., *The Jew as Legitimation: Jewish-Christian Relations beyond Antisemitism and Philosemitism* (2017).

Sol Goldberg is an Associate Professor (Teaching Stream) in the Department for the Study of Religion and the Anne Tanenbaum Centre for Jewish Studies at the University of Toronto. His teaching and research focus on philosophy of religion, Jewish philosophy, and theoretical issues in the study of antisemitism.

Sara R. Horowitz is Professor of Comparative Literature and Humanities at York University in Toronto. She is the author of *Voicing the Void: Muteness and Memory in Holocaust Fiction*, and served as the senior founding editor of the Azrieli Series of Holocaust Memoirs, Canada. She is the editor of *Lessons and Legacies, Volume X: Back to the Sources* (2012), and co-editor of the forthcoming *Shadows on the City of Lights: Jewish Post-War French Writing* and also of *Hans Günther Adler: Life,* Literature, Legacy (2016). In addition, she is the founding co-editor of the journal *KEREM: Creative Explorations in Judaism*.

Jonathan Judaken is the Spence L. Wilson Chair in the Humanities at Rhodes College. He has written, edited, or co-edited five books, including the monograph *Jean-Paul Sartre and the Jewish Question: Anti-antisemitism and the Politics of the French Intellectual* (2006), and the collections, *Race*

After Sartre: Antiracism, Africana Existentialism, Postcolonialism (2008) and *Naming Race, Naming Racisms* (2009). Most recently, he edited a roundtable issue of the *American Historical Review* titled, "Rethinking Anti-Semitism" (2018), and co-edited a special issue of the journal *Jewish History* on "Jews and Muslims in France Before and After *Charlie Hebdo* and Hyper Cacher" (2018). He is also a co-editor of *The Albert Memmi Reader* (forthcoming, 2020). He is currently completing a monograph entitled, *Critical Theories of Anti-Semitism: Confronting Modernity and Modern Judeophobia*.

Ivan Kalmar is Professor of Anthropology at the University of Toronto. Over his career, much of his work has focused on the image of Jews and Muslims in western cultural history. He is the author of *Early Orientalism: Imagined Islam and the Notion of Sublime Power* (2011) and co-editor of the volume, *Orientalism and the Jews* (2005). He has recently guest-edited a special issue of *Patterns of Prejudice* (2018) dealing with "Islamophobia in the East of the European Union," and a special issue on "Islamophobia in Germany: East/West" for the *Journal of Contemporary European Studies* (2020). He is writing a book on illiberalism in Central Europe for Bristol University Press.

Hillel J. Kieval is the Gloria M. Goldstein Professor of Jewish History and Thought at Washington University in St. Louis. His research interests range from pathways of Jewish acculturation and integration to the impact of nationalism and ethnic conflict on modern Jewish identities; and from cross-cultural conflicts and misunderstandings to the discursive practices of modern antisemitism. Among his publications are *The Making of Czech Jewry: National Conflict and Jewish Society in Bohemia, 1870–1918* (1988), *Languages of Community: The Jewish Experience in the Czech Lands* (2000), and, forthcoming, *Blood Inscriptions: Science, Modernity, and Ritual Murder at Europe's Fin de Siècle*.

Jeffrey Kopstein is Professor of Political Science at the University of California, Irvine. In his research, Professor Kopstein focuses on interethnic violence, voting patterns of minority groups, and anti-liberal tendencies in civil society, paying special attention to cases within European and Russian Jewish history. His co-authored book, *Intimate Violence: Anti-Jewish Pogroms on the Eve of the Holocaust* (2018) won the 2019 Bronisław Malinowski Award in the Social Sciences, given by the Polish Institute of Arts and Sciences of America for a book "of particular value and significance dealing with an aspect of the Polish experience."

Shai Lavi is Director of the Van Leer Jerusalem Institute and a Professor in the Faculty of Law at Tel Aviv University where he is also the co-director of the Minerva Center for the Study of End of Life. He earned his first and second degrees in law and sociology at Tel Aviv University and his doctorate in law at the University of California, Berkeley. His book on the end of life, *The Modern Art of Dying: A History of Euthanasia in the United States*, won the 2006 Sociology of Law Distinguished Scholarly Book Award of the American Sociological Association. He has been a visiting professor at Cornell University, the University of Toronto, Yeshiva University, and Humboldt University of Berlin.

Richard S. Levy has taught German history and the history of the Holocaust at the University of Illinois in Chicago since 1971. He is author of *The Downfall of the Anti-Semitic Political Parties in Imperial Germany* (1975), editor of *Antisemitism in the Modern World: An Anthology of Texts* (1991), *Antisemitism: A Historical Encyclopedia of Prejudice and Persecution*, 2 vols. (2005), and co-editor of *Antisemitism: A History* (2010). He has published twenty scholarly articles or chapters in anthologies. He co-founded and edited H-Antisemitism, an internet electronic discussion forum, from 1993 to 2004.

Martin Lockshin is University Professor Emeritus at York University in Toronto, where he has taught for over 40 years. He is the author of six books and many articles, mostly dealing with rabbinic literature, Jewish intellectual history, and Jewish Bible interpretation over the ages. He is particularly interested in the development of the school of *peshat* (plain interpretation of the Bible) in the Middle Ages, a phenomenon that occurred at more or less the same time in Jewish and Christian circles. He lives in Jerusalem.

James Loeffler is the Jay Berkowitz Professor of Jewish History at the University of Virginia, where he also serves as the Ida and Nathan Kolodiz Director of the Jewish Studies Program. His books include *Rooted Cosmopolitans: Jews and Human Rights in the Twentieth Century* (2018), which won the American Historical Association Rosenberg Prize in Jewish History and the Association for Jewish Studies Schnitzer Prize in Modern Jewish History. He is a co-editor of the *Association for Jewish Studies Review*.

Brian Porter-Szűcs is an Arthur F. Thurnau Professor of History at the University of Michigan-Ann Arbor. He is the author of *Poland and the Modern World: Beyond Martyrdom* (2014), *Faith and Fatherland: Catholicism, Modernity, and Poland* (2010), and *When Nationalism Began to Hate: Imagining Modern Politics in 19th Century Poland* (2000), which was recently translated into Polish. He is also co-editor of *Christianity and Modernity in East-Central Europe* (2010), and of *Negotiating Radical Change: Understanding and Extending the Lessons of the Polish Round Table Talks* (2000). In his current research project, he explores the history of economic thought and the origins of neoliberalism in the Polish People's Republic.

Lena Salaymeh is British Academy Global Professor in the Oxford School of Global and Area Studies, affiliated with Oxford's Middle East Centre, St Antony's College. She is a scholar of law and history, with specializations in

Islamic jurisprudence, Jewish jurisprudence, and critical research methods. Her scholarship on law and religion combines legal history and critiques of secularism. She was recently awarded a John Simon Guggenheim Fellowship and her book, *The Beginnings of Islamic Law* (2016), received the American Academy of Religion Award for Excellence in the Study of Religion. She has a PhD in Legal and Islamic History from the University of California, Berkeley and a JD from Harvard.

Maurice Samuels is the Betty Jane Anlyan Professor of French at Yale University, where he chairs the Judaic Studies Program and is the founding director of the Yale Program for the Study of Antisemitism. A recipient of the John Simon Guggenheim Fellowship, he is the author of four books, including *Inventing the Israelite: Jewish Fiction in Nineteenth Century France* (2010), *The Right to Difference: French Universalism and the Jews* (2016), and *The Betrayal of the Duchess* (2020), which tells the story of modern France's first antisemitic affair.

Daniel B. Schwartz is a Professor of Modern Jewish History at George Washington University, DC. He is the author of *The First Modern Jew* (2012), which won the 2012 Salo Baron Prize for best first book in Jewish studies and was a 2012 National Jewish Book Award finalist in the category of history. His most recent books are *Spinoza's Challenge to Jewish Thought: Writings on His Life, Philosophy, and Legacy* (2019) and *Ghetto: The History of a Word* (2019).

Magda Teter is a Professor of History and the Shvidler Chair of Judaic Studies at Fordham University, NY, and the author of *Jews and Heretics in Catholic Poland* (2005), *Sinners on Trial* (2011), *Blood Libel: On the Trail of An Antisemitic Myth* (2020) and many articles in English, Hebrew, Italian, and Polish. Teter's work has been supported by the John Simon Guggenheim Memorial Foundation, the Harry Frank Guggenheim Foundation, the Radcliffe Institute for Advanced Studies at Harvard University, and the Cullman Center for Scholars and Writers at the New York Public Library. She has served as the co-editor of the *AJS Review* and as the Vice-President for Publications of the Association for Jewish Studies.

Scott Ury is Senior Lecturer in Tel Aviv University's Department of Jewish History, where he is also Director of the Eva and Marc Besen Institute for the Study of Historical Consciousness and Senior Editor of the journal *History & Memory: Studies in Representation of the Past*. Previously, he was Director of Tel Aviv University's Stephen Roth Institute for the Study of Antisemitism and Racism. He is the author of *Barricades and Banners: The Revolution of 1905 and the Transformation of Warsaw Jewry* (2012), and co-editor of six volumes on various aspects of modern Jewish history including the recent Hebrew-language collection *Antisemitism: Historical Concept, Public Discourse* (2020).

Kalman Weiser is the Silber Family Professor of Modern Jewish Studies and the Associate Director of the Israel and Golda Koschitzky Centre for Jewish Studies at York University in Toronto, Canada. He specializes in Jewish history and the language and culture of Yiddish-speaking Jews. He is the author of *Jewish People, Yiddish Nation: Noah Prylucki and the Folkists in Poland* (2011), and co-editor of *Czernowitz at 100: the First Yiddish Language Conference in Historical Perspective* (2010) and also of the expanded and revised second edition of Solomon Birnbaum's *Yiddish: a Survey and a Grammar* (2015).

CHAPTER 1

Introduction

Kalman Weiser

This is a volume born of a common frustration, one that its co-editors first experienced when they independently began teaching university-level courses about antisemitism more than a decade ago. The academic study of antisemitism is a fascinating endeavor. It raises conceptual and methodological queries that transcend disciplinary boundaries and chronological eras. Its research literature is rich and contentious, examining thousands of years of recorded history through multiple theoretical lenses and at times from opposing ideological perspectives. In short, antisemitism is a subject that is wont to raise more questions than answers.

But antisemitism is not merely a topic of "academic" interest, a historically delimited phenomenon that can be approached with equanimity from the safe distance of the present. Sadly, as recent events demonstrate, manifestations of violence and hatred toward Jews continue to rear their ugly head, along with, and at times in conjunction with, other forms of intolerance and bigotry. Precisely those features that make studying the body of scholarship about antisemitism so engaging for the researcher—notably, its intellectual breadth, depth, and the often politicized nature of its controversies—also make teaching about it a formidable task, especially for the instructor attempting to strike a balance between the ideals of objective and engaged scholarship. The wide divergences in the cultural assumptions, political views, and moral intuitions that students bring to the classroom only magnify this challenge, which is likely to be felt now more than ever by instructors on today's politically charged campuses.

K. Weiser (✉)
York University, Toronto, ON, Canada
e-mail: kweiser@yorku.ca

Take, for example, the experience of two of this volume's three co-editors who teach undergraduate courses about antisemitism in metropolitan Canadian universities. Students are of diverse backgrounds in a multiethnic, multireligious city such as Toronto. While assertions of Jews' collective guilt for the crucifixion of Jesus still occasionally surface, most students are little inclined to announce adverse attitudes toward Jews. Rather, they frequently arrive in the classroom seeking insight into the Holocaust, often the only historical event focusing on Jews taught in the Canadian high school curriculum. Many are only remotely aware that the Nazis' brand of murderous Jew-hatred taps into a hoary tradition of anti-Jewish ideas and practices. Given the common North American understanding of Jews as foremost a faith community, students primarily conceive of antisemitism as a form of religious bigotry, one today restricted to the margins of respectable society in an ostensibly tolerant, multicultural country such as Canada. Jews are regularly perceived not as a minority group long subjected to forms of discrimination and intolerance but as part of a privileged white majority and consequently immune to or, in comparison with visible minorities, insignificantly affected by the hatred of contemporary racism. Students sometimes react with surprise or indignation when Jewish (and occasionally non-Jewish) classmates, even ones with little awareness of the Israeli–Palestinian conflict, feel insulted or threatened by imagery and rhetoric that periodically appears in anti-Zionist and anti-Israel campaigns that they deem inherently malicious, unjust, and prejudicial.

An entirely different reality faces the third co-editor, who teaches at an Israeli university with a largely Jewish student body. These students typically arrive in the classroom with a very different set of assumptions about the nature and history of antisemitism, as well as a different understanding regarding the historical relationship between its perpetrators and victims. Israeli students are the product of a state educational system that privileges an interpretation of antisemitism as an enduring theme in the millenniums-old history of the Jewish people. Indeed, providing a refuge from antisemitism is understood as part of the *raison d'être* for Israel's existence. For many Jewish students, antisemitism is a *sui generis* problem that has proven an existential threat to diasporic Jewish life from time immemorial, one to which Zionism has thus far provided the most effective response. Yet, many also see antisemitism as continuing to affect Jews everywhere—whether in the form of continued hostility toward Jews and Jewish communities outside Israel or as part of hostile campaigns seeking to delegitimize the State of Israel in the international sphere. Meanwhile, Palestinian citizens of Israel present in the same classroom seldom embrace Israel's founding narrative or recent legislative efforts to define it formally as a Jewish nation state. On the contrary, they commonly view themselves as the unjust victims rather than the beneficiaries of Zionism, which they understand as a discriminatory ethno-nationalist ideology. Their assumptions about the nature of antisemitism, its causes and manifestations, its entanglement with other forms of bigotry, and its relationship to Zionism are at times miles apart from those of many of their Jewish classmates. Together with some Jewish classmates, they define their opposition, whether to Zionism as a whole or to specific Israeli policies, not as motivated by anti-Jewish animus but as a strictly ethical protest meant to redress injustice.

Undoubtedly, such examples could be refined and multiplied to include other political contexts and demographic groups across the globe. Heightened sensitivity to social and political contexts, as well as cultural and political biases, is, however, not the only challenge awaiting the instructor. The task of teaching about antisemitism is rendered even more difficult by the paucity of suitable literature for use in the university classroom. Well-meaning but often simplistic or politically motivated narratives dominate offerings intended for students. Even the better textbooks available are hampered by the ambition to follow the phenomenon of Jew-hatred across vast temporal and territorial expanses for the benefit of students who often possess scant knowledge of either history or geography. In their quest for thoroughness, they necessarily support, wittingly or unwittingly, the historically questionable thesis of antisemitism as "The Longest Hatred," an uninterrupted but constantly evolving chain of Jew-hatred from antiquity until the present day (Wistrich 1992, 2010).

This view's popularity is perhaps not surprising in light of a long-standing tendency to treat antisemitism as merely the dark side of Jewish or modern European history. Indeed, the lion's share of textbooks and anthologies about antisemitism are produced by specialists in these fields. Vital contributions to the investigation of antisemitism from such varied disciplines as Religious Studies, Psychology, Sociology, Legal Studies, and Critical Race Theory have yet to be integrated systematically into the available literature directed at a student reader. Moreover, few graduate students in the Humanities or Social Sciences receive explicit training to conduct research or teach about antisemitism, either as a distinct phenomenon or in relation to other forms of racism and prejudice that require a wider, multidisciplinary framework.

The available literature directed at a student audience is, however, burdened by an even more fundamental challenge: the absence of a general scholarly consensus about the very definition and dimensions of the phenomenon under investigation. For centuries, theological justifications proved sufficient for religious thinkers—Jews, Christians, and Muslims—to account for Jew-hatred. Long before the introduction of "antisemitism" into any lexicon, Jewish communities used terms such as *Sinat-yisrael* (Jew-hatred) and *rishes* (evil) to express an antipathy they considered a well-nigh permanent, albeit lamentable, consequence of their status as the unique upholders of a sacred covenant with God and an unenviable reminder that they remained in exile from their ancient homeland. By the early nineteenth century, however, expectations concerning the inevitability of this hostility began to decline. At that time, many Jews began to undergo secularization and to abandon elements of their cultural particularity and social separateness, seeking to participate fully in the societies of European countries (and their colonial offshoots). The "Jewish Question," the question of whether Jews' integration into gentile societies was desirable and under what conditions, preoccupied thinkers across the continent. Ultimately, after much debate, most modernizing states had emancipated their Jewish populations by the twentieth century, spelling an end to most legal disabilities and their historic status as an autonomous "state within a state."

The term "Antisemitismus" (antisemitism) grew in popularity in the last third of the nineteenth century. It was then introduced in Germany as a term to designate both individual and organized political opposition to the Jews' rapid and unprecedented socioeconomic integration across European society following their civil and political emancipation. Its proponents—self-proclaimed Antisemites—wished to "turn back the clock," to limit or reverse what was perceived as Jews' illegitimate and threatening dominance in a number of professional and cultural fields. While some insisted that the term meant a secular and rational—rather than religious-based—opposition to Jews, one rooted in their purported racial foreignness as "Semites," it quickly spread across cultural and disciplinary borders to designate a variety of types of hostility toward them. Today, its veneer of pseudo-scientific sophistication stripped away, it serves as a catch-all phrase to describe virtually any act or attitude that targets Jews *qua* Jews (Engel 2009).

The thorough ambiguity of the term makes context all the more important in trying to define and identify incidents and aspects of antisemitism. Popular and humoristic quips defining antisemitism as hating Jews more than is "absolutely necessary" (ascribed to the British philosopher Isaiah Berlin, himself a Jew) or as "the socialism of fools" (usually attributed to the German socialist August Bebel) not only tell us much about the societies in which they originated. They also point to some of the fundamental questions contemporary scholars continue to explore in their attempts to understand the origins, nature, and definition of antisemitism. Does, for example, antisemitism constitute a rational phenomenon, a consequence of intergroup frictions between Jews and gentiles such as economic or political competition that is on par with those found between other human collectives? Is it a form of xenophobia, prejudice, or racism similar to others, *mutatis mutandis*? Or is it something exceptional, if not unique? If so, does this exceptionalism lie in some aspect(s) of Judaism, Jewish culture, or the Jews' character or nature? Or does it reside in non-Jews or their culture? Is it a psychological or social disorder that can be mitigated—perhaps even cured—through changes in theological interpretations, educational practices, or political, societal, and economic structures? Or is it an inescapable fate that will accompany the Jews for eternity?

Scholarly perspectives are in competition even over the very nature of antisemitism as a historical phenomenon, if indeed it constitutes a single phenomenon. Although some scholars take antisemitism to be an intrinsic feature of Western civilization with consistent features across time and space

(Wistrich 1992, 2010; Nirenberg 2013), it has recently been argued (Engel 2009; Judaken 2018) that the label is misapplied to a host of loosely similar but unrelated episodes involving "the Jews." In fact, these Jews often vary as much from context to context and in their self-understanding (e.g., from readily identifiable ultra-Orthodox Jews to people whose merely ancestral connection to Jews or Judaism does not show up in name, dress, behavior, or appearance) as do the antisemitic charges that they encounter (e.g., a "misanthropic clan," "rootless cosmopolitans," or a "financial cabal").

Many scholars active since the WWII era have viewed the Holocaust as the paradigmatic case of Jew-hatred. The centrality of the Holocaust in recent history has led many academics, explicitly or implicitly, to recognize patterns of antisemitism's continued malignancy in the present day by working backward from it, combing both the near and remote pasts in search of the factors that made conceivable the near total destruction of European Jewry. This privileging of the Nazi era and its depredations reinforces a tendency to view antisemitism within a teleological framework, one beginning with ancient tensions, continuing to medieval ghettos, and inexorably culminating in genocide. It also lends itself to a specific set of distortions, not the least of which is a "Germano-centric" model that lends preference to a modern, secular form of antisemitism as primarily a western and central European phenomenon that was "exported" into German-occupied territories in the context of World War II. Needless to say, such a model largely neglects indigenous factors and distinctive strains of hostility toward Jews—as well as often a larger degree of tolerance in various eras—present in eastern Europe, North Africa, and other regions.

Conventional surveys of antisemitism (e.g., Wistrich 1992; Laqueur 2006; Goldstein 2012) generally subscribe to a scheme that divides thousands of years of Jewish-gentile interaction into four broad chronological and conceptual periods. Like a physician studying the etiology of a disease, this approach commonly applies specialized terminology to designate distinctive strains of animus, their origins, and their manifestations. Accounts applying this periodization typically emphasize the decisive role played by Christianity in forging a new and enduring hostility toward Jews and Judaism while devoting significantly less attention to Jewish-Muslim encounters. Simultaneously, they note continuities and discontinuities in the transmission of anti-Jewish tropes since antiquity.

The first period, that of pagan Judeophobia in the Hellenistic world, is characterized by widespread ambivalence, with Jews and Judaism the subject of attraction and fascination, on the one hand, and fear and repulsion, on the other. Relying on scant documentation, scholars examine hostility toward Jews in places such as Roman-controlled Egypt and Palestine against the backdrop of competition for political privilege between rival populations and the religious and social exclusivity attributed to monotheistic Jews in a polytheistic world.

The second period, that of Christian anti-Judaism, emphasizes the emergence of a predominately theologically based enmity originating in the charge of Jews' collective responsibility for the cruelest (and most paradoxical) crime: the crucifixion of God descended to earth in human form to redeem a sinful humanity. With the ascent of Christianity, Jews in the medieval era are progressively demonized, morally and physically, in the popular mind and confined to ghettos in much of Europe. They are, however, not beyond redemption, for their legal and social abasement may be lifted once they recognize their theological error and embrace Jesus' messiahdom.

The ensuing period, that of modern antisemitism, is characterized by the replacement of religious explanations for Jews' nefarious character with secular ones over the course of the long nineteenth century. Especially significant in this era is the emergence of conspiracy theories alleging the existence of Jewish plots to subvert the traditional and wholesome norms of gentile society by cynically propagating such quintessentially modern ideologies as liberalism, capitalism, communism, and secularism in order to corrode the fabric of society and thereby facilitate world domination. Paradoxically, in an age when many acculturating Jews are becoming linguistically and physically indistinguishable from gentiles, modern scientific concepts are deployed to identify and biologically essentialize "the Jew." Not the Jew's beliefs but the Jew's immutable "racial" origin is now identified as the source of this perfidious nature. The collective expulsion of "the Jews" and ultimately their extermination is prescribed as an act of self-defense and vengeance for their misdeeds against humanity.

Finally, the last period, often called the "New Antisemitism," refers to the past two generations. Scholarship on this phenomenon points to a repackaging and integration of long-standing anti-Jewish tropes and motifs into campaigns against Zionism or Israel, a country widely understood as one that represents Jews everywhere. It conceives of contemporary antisemitism as no longer a primarily Christian or European problem but as a global affair, one that is embraced as much by radical Islamicists and self-styled progressives as by arch-conservatives and ethno-nationalists. According to this interpretation, representatives of both the Left and the Right—each for its own but sometimes overlapping reasons—see in Jews/Israel/Zionism the driving force behind the dark forces of racially oppressive colonialism and economically unjust and destructive globalization.

This widespread periodization becomes especially problematic when presented in single-author tomes, which seem invariably to reproduce the "lachrymose" narrative of Jewish history. The term, introduced by the seminal historian Salo W. Baron, refers to depictions of Jewish history as a long chain of at best intermittently mitigated persecution, expulsion, and legal inferiorization. The "all tragedy, all the time" approach often fails to situate the Jews' experience in the larger context of the societies in which they lived and to compare their status with those of other segments of the population. This approach no doubt derives much of its persuasiveness from the interpretative coherence it offers as well as from its confirmation of Jews' own collective memory as a persecuted people and subsequent self-fashioning. Baron was not one to trivialize antisemitism. But such an approach, he cautioned, is not only distorting but also lends itself to interpretations of Jewish collective experience that reinforce political commitments or agendas for social activism. Robert Wistrich's *A Lethal Obsession: Antisemitism from Antiquity to the Global Jihad*, a recent study by one of the central scholars of antisemitism, is perhaps the best illustration of these trends. While encyclopedic in scope, it offers a largely monolithic picture of both the culprits and victims of antisemitism. Jews are presented throughout as essentially unchanging in culture and behavior across space and time. Victims of prejudice and adverse circumstances until the advent of Zionism, Jews appear as passive objects rather than as agents engaged in dynamic social processes as well as in reinterpreting their own tradition and their relations with non-Jews in the light of new conditions.

Even books describing the specific constellation of causes producing "the changing face of antisemitism from ancient times to the present day" (as Walter Laqueur titled his 2006 monograph) argue that antisemitism continues to threaten Jewish life in much the same way as previously, its core logic and accusations assuming new guises and retooled for new circumstances as its focal point shifts from right-wing to left-wing political circles and from Christian or post-Christian societies to Muslim or Arab ones enflamed by decades of protracted conflict between Israel and the Palestinians. Books in this vein suggest that the dominant attitudes of non-Jews toward Jews have been consistently and universally hostile despite the diversity of interactions between the groups (and within the groups themselves)—so much so that some scholars refer to these works as representations of an "eternalist" school in the study of antisemitism (Judaken 2018).

In many senses, such pitfalls are, admittedly, difficult to avoid. By its very nature, the study of antisemitism emphasizes the negative aspects of attitudes and behavior toward Jews and Judaism while tending to neglect or ignore more benign or positive aspects of Jews' relations with non-Jews. Further, more dramatic expressions of anti-Jewish animus, such as those marked by demonization, extreme violence, or legal discrimination, overshadow the more routine manifestations of hostility or distaste for Jews and Judaism as well as the rather mundane daily interactions and exchanges that inform everyday life but do not make headlines. Lastly, the continuous focus on hostility toward Jews often relegates Jewish individuals and institutions to the sidelines of history and condemns them to the hapless role of historical victims rather than of historical agents.

* * *

The desire to address these intellectual dilemmas as well as the lack of suitable literature for both preparing instructors and teaching students is the inspiration for the present volume. *Key Concepts in the Study of Antisemitism* represents the culmination of a multiyear project generously sponsored by the Social Sciences and Humanities Research Council of Canada, York University's Israel and Golda Koschitzky Centre for Jewish Studies, the University of Toronto's Anne Tanenbaum Centre for Jewish Studies, and Tel Aviv University's Stephen Roth Institute for the Study of Contemporary Antisemitism and Racism. It is designed to improve the training of university faculty in teaching and research about antisemitism as well as other forms of prejudice and racism. The above critique notwithstanding, the volume acknowledges its debt to the existing body of literature and its authors, many of whom have conducted yeoman research or synthesized remarkable amounts of scholarship into digestible form. Since the study of antisemitism is too large and diffuse a field for any one person to master, *Key Concepts* is conceived as a collaborative, polyphonic work drawing on the strengths of individuals across a number of disciplines and with expertise in differing eras. While largely shaped by an anglophone tradition of scholarship, its contributors teach in diverse classroom settings in countries on three continents, offering them varied experiences that inform their approaches.

Key Concepts in the Study of Antisemitism is intended as both a reference work and a pedagogical tool for instructors teaching undergraduate and graduate courses about antisemitism and cognate topics at universities in North America, Europe, and Israel. It is also intended for researchers wishing to familiarize themselves with multidisciplinary, cutting-edge perspectives in its investigation. It unites twenty-one provocative essays by leading scholars in a variety of fields addressing the question of what relevance a given concept—such as Philosemitism, Racism, or Zionism—has for our understanding of antisemitism. The concepts explored in the volume were carefully chosen by the project's international steering committee to reflect best current practices in teaching and research about antisemitism, as well as to suggest potential directions for future scholarship. Each entry highlights the central problems, methodological or otherwise, that the study of its concept engenders. Many of the concepts, such as Anti-Zionism, Blood Libels, and the Catholic Church, are central to the academic discussion of antisemitism today and likely to appear on any course syllabus. Other concepts, such as Conspiracy Theories, Gender, Orientalism, Racism, and Self-Hatred indicate the wider significance of the study of antisemitism for the investigation of other forms of prejudice, hatred, and discrimination. They thus suggest new ways in which scholars might imagine courses within the broader contexts of the Humanities and Social Sciences that either feature some aspect of the complex phenomenon of antisemitism or include it because of its relation to other phenomena under investigation, such as the study of the Enlightenment, Nationalism, Postcolonialism, and Secularism.

Key Concepts in the Study of Antisemitism acknowledges the inherent complexity in identifying, describing, and explicating the phenomenon of antisemitism as well as the diversity of approaches to its investigation. It also recognizes that antisemitism cannot be understood in isolation, without considering the case of Jews in comparison with other groups or considering antisemitism in comparison with other forms of intergroup hostility and racism. In doing so, it aims to promote conversations across disciplinary, geographic, and thematic lines rather than to advocate a specific theoretical or analytical framework that unifies the study of antisemitism within a single field or imposes a self-contained, coherent narrative. Contributions to the volume employ an array of methods belonging to such diverse fields as critical theory, cultural and literary studies, intellectual and social history, legal studies, philosophy, political science, social psychology, and religious studies. The volume's modular, polyphonic approach gives primacy to concepts and the various ways that scholars utilize them without denying the paramount importance of either contexts or continuities.

To avoid many of the epistemological and pedagogical pitfalls described above (as well as others), *Key Concepts* is organized around specific concepts instead of chronology or geography. This organizational principle exploits the mobility of concepts, i.e., their potential applicability across time and space, permitting instructors the greatest latitude in the design of their research and teaching. Thus, for example, the entry on Pogroms examines anti-Jewish violence in Hellenistic Egypt, pre-expulsion Spain, and WWII-era Poland; that on Gender interrogates literary and popular media presentations in both modern Europe and North America; and the essay on Ghetto offers a genealogy of a term whose semantic field has been extended far beyond the context of a mandatory Jewish residential quarter to which it initially referred. This mobility does not mean, however, that the volume dismisses the importance of contextual nuance for understanding antisemitism. Indeed, some concepts, such as Nazism and Holocaust, are more closely tied to specific historical situations while others, such as Gender and Self-hatred, transcend chronology. However, it is our conviction that even those concepts that seem most time- or context-specific offer models and insights for illuminating other contexts. Thus, for example, the essay on Emancipation—a process that arises in the eighteenth and nineteenth centuries—can shed as much light on tensions surrounding Jews' citizenship in ancient Greek city-states as on contemporary debates about immigration and differential rights in twenty-first century societies. In many cases, the same concepts can thus be used to illuminate both the specifically Jewish and broader phenomena, helping students to understand both the universal and the particular in the experience of antisemitism.

In contrast with previous volumes or monographs commonly appearing on course syllabi, this volume is informed by the insight that there is neither a single way to think about antisemitism, nor an unambiguous, universally accepted definition of the term itself. This idea is reflected, for example, in the essay on the Historiography of Anti-Semitism, which treats modern definitions and explanations of the phenomenon. It explores ways in which scholars have grappled with these problems in their efforts to understand antisemitism both for its own sake and as a means to elucidate larger sets of questions about society. Further, while the editors recognize the importance of juridical efforts to define antisemitism for the purpose of curbing hate crimes, they remain skeptical that rigid definitions are conducive to scholarship, particularly about times and places other than the societies for which these laws are drafted. They have therefore not attempted to impose a unifying definition on the volume, allowing contributors to make use of terminology as they see fit as long as its meaning is made transparent to the reader.

The editors have also decided not to impose uniformity even in the case of the spelling of the very term (and its derivative forms) designating modern Jew-hatred: anti-Semitism or antisemitism. A lack of consistency between essays in this regard may prove disconcerting at times to the reader. But the editors deem this approach warranted in order not to conceal the various controversies surrounding the presence or absence of a hyphen whose stakes are far from insignificant. The morphology of the term suggests opposition to "Semitism," a vague concept in vogue in nineteenth-century Europe used to designate a mindset or traits associated with "Semites," a term that arose out of a nineteenth-century European philological tradition and its classification of cognate languages into families. Languages belonging to the Semitic family spoken chiefly in the Middle East and the Horn of Africa, such as Hebrew and Arabic, were often judged lacking in beauty and descriptive capacity in comparison with the Indo-Aryan (commonly referred to today as Indo-European) family of languages widely spoken in Europe, and speakers of Semitic languages (and even their presumed descendants who did not speak them) were often described as inherently inferior to "Aryans" or "Indo-Europeans." Some authors in this volume therefore eschew "Anti-Semitism," arguing that its use inadvertently lends credence to long discredited arguments about the essential otherness, racial or otherwise, of Jews. Moreover, they insist, the hyphenated term suggests, erroneously and perhaps also disingenuously, that Jews are not the exclusive target of this hatred since the philological class "Semites" includes other peoples as well. Others prefer hyphenating the word precisely to emphasize that the term has its origins in a tradition marking Jews, Arabs, and Muslims more broadly as sharing a common "Eastern" heritage and qualities that allegedly made them pernicious moral, theological, and political enemies of Europeans (Judaken 2018, pp. 1125–27). And, finally, some scholars may opt for a specific spelling more in keeping with the convention they first learned or the dictates of their Word Processor than out of acceptance of an argument about the history and nature of Jew-hatred. Given the contentious nature of the field as a whole, they may hold, no term will escape confusions, abuses, and ambiguities.

Contributing authors differ not only in their use of terminology and spelling but also in their fundamental approaches to concepts. Some employ a concept as a lens that analyzes reality or perceptions thereof. Thus, the authors of the essays on Conspiracy Theories and Ghetto, for example, do not question the essential existence of these phenomena or problematize their definitions but instead interrogate how and why they function. In contrast, other contributors treat concepts with a measure of skepticism, as ideological constructs whose genealogies need to be traced and implicit agendas exposed (e.g., the essays on Philosemitism, Racism, and Self-Hatred). Essays are also divided by whether they see antisemitism as a cause—as an explanation for something else (Anti-Judaism, which assesses the concept's use in addressing the nature of relations between Jews and non-Jews mainly in the pre-modern era)—or antisemitism as an effect—as what needs to be explained by something else (Nationalism). There are still other approaches to causality in the study of antisemitism reflected in the volume. The essay about Zionism, treated here separately despite itself being forged in the crucible of nineteenth-century European nationalisms, argues for an intimacy and perhaps an interdependency between antisemitism and certain strains of Zionist thought, in particular political Zionism. And, as the essay about Nazism demonstrates, some authors explicitly examine how phenomena can be mutually reinforcing or legitimating as, for example, how involvement in the legally sanctioned or obligatory persecution of Jews in Nazi Germany could inspire new or aggravate preexisting anti-Jewish sentiments and vice versa.

Key Concepts in the Study of Antisemitism aspires to be a selective, albeit essential, guide to the study of antisemitism. Essays can be read individually as the basis for a lesson or lecture that might appear on a wide range of syllabi. Alternately, they can be read in conjunction with other contributions to the volume and as a complement to additional sources. The essays are not conceived as encyclopedia entries, although they are organized alphabetically because this scheme is the most neutral way to order them. They do not follow a prescribed format or seek merely to summarize an existing body of knowledge. In each, the author was instructed not only to explain the relevance of a given concept for the study of antisemitism and to trace its history and major scholarly debates around it, but also to proffer an original argument that advances a particular perspective within the field, to point to avenues for further research, and to exemplify one of the diverse methods of investigation that scholars might employ in analyzing and applying any concept.

In considering how to make use of entries, either individually or in tandem, instructors designing courses and planning readings may wish to consider the following broad groupings of essays: entries focused on Jewish responses to antisemitism (Self-hatred, Zionism, Sinat Yisrael—that is, classic rabbinic understandings of Jew-hatred); entries focused on expressions of antisemitism (Ghetto, Nazism, Pogroms); entries that situate antisemitism in relation to other phenomena (Gender and Racism; and, in the case of the essays on Secularism and Orientalism, to Islamophobia as well); entries comparing discursive contexts and practices in which antisemitism appears (Anti-Zionism, the Catholic Church, Emancipation, Nationalism, Postcolonialism).

Like all other endeavors, the volume is admittedly incomplete. We hope, however, that it will still prove highly useful to scholars, students, and interested readers. The absence of essays specifically devoted to certain concepts widely considered indispensable to the study of antisemitism, e.g., Host Desecration or economic antisemitism, will surely disappoint some readers even if many of these concepts are discussed within the various essays in the volume. We trust that readers will appreciate what has been accomplished and be inspired to pursue further topics that were not included.

The volume's versatility reflects the way that the editors and members of the steering committee understand, and hope others will come to view, the study of antisemitism: it does not constitute an independent field of teaching and research to be monopolized by historians of modern Europe or the Jews, but rather an intersectional one whose significance and scope have often been misunderstood because of its scholarly isolation. With its unique emphasis, *Key Concepts in the Study of Antisemitism* thus aspires to re-situate the study of antisemitism at the crossroads of various fields of academic interest.

References

Engel, David. 2009. "Away from a Definition of Antisemitism. An Essay in the Semantics of Historical Description." In *Rethinking European Jewish History*, edited by J. Cohen and M. Rosman, 30–53. Oxford: Oxford University Press.

Goldstein, Phyllis. 2012. *A Convenient Hatred: The History of Antisemitism*. Brookline: Facing History & Ourselves.

Judaken, Jonathan. 2018. "Introduction." *American Historical Review* 123 (4): 1122–38.

Laqueur, Walter. 2006. *The Changing Face of Antisemitism: From Ancient Times to the Present Day*. Oxford: Oxford University Press.

Nirenberg, David. 2013. *Anti-Judaism: The Western Tradition*. New York: W. W. Norton.

Wistrich, Robert. 1992. *Antisemitism: The Longest Hatred*. New York: Pantheon Books.

Wistrich, Robert. 2010. *A Lethal Obsession: Anti-Semitism from Antiquity to Global Jihad*. New York: Random House.

CHAPTER 2

Anti-Judaism

Jonathan Elukin

In recent years, the term "anti-Judaism" has become an attractive alternative to anti-Semitism to characterize the hatred or persecution visited upon Jews in ancient, medieval, and early modern European societies (Nirenberg 2013). The term has at least challenged the primacy of "anti-Semitism," a word coined in nineteenth-century Europe and meant to express political opposition to the granting of citizenship to Jews in liberalizing European societies (Beller 2007). That word was very much a product of its time, for proponents of "anti-Semitism" in the nineteenth century were inspired by contemporary pseudoscientific racial ideas about the imagined biological inferiority of Jewish "Semites" relative to "Aryan" (white, Christian) Europeans. However, many Christians, particularly from rural and uneducated populations, were also still following the lead of the Catholic Church's traditional theological opposition to the Jews (Beller 2007, p. 16). Only a very few scholars have addressed the vexing issue of the survival of a premodern, religious anti-Judaism and its continuing role in modern anti-Semitism (Heschel 2011). While many scholars have been careful to invoke "anti-Semitism" only when describing what they believe to be a modern, racially engendered animus toward Jews, the word anti-Semitism now regularly appears in professional and popular accounts of Jewish history where it clearly refers to negative attitudes toward Jews in virtually any time or place. The routine use of the term has encouraged the acceptance of the idea of a permanent animosity to Jews, largely rooted in racial prejudice, beginning in the ancient world and continuing to the present day. That is why some scholars, sensitive to

J. Elukin (✉)
Trinity College, Hartford, CT, USA
e-mail: jonathan.elukin@trincoll.edu

the dangers of using the word anti-Semitism anachronistically, have embraced the new term, "anti-Judaism"; by doing so, they believe they can distinguish what they see as a *religiously* inspired, premodern theological animus toward Jews from a putative *racially* charged hatred that is particular to modernity. (Making a distinction between a premodern anti-Judaism and a modern anti-Semitism is also a way for some scholars to defend Christianity from responsibility for the racial ideology of Nazism.)

Such a terminological distinction, if accurate in reflecting social reality, should be helpful in achieving a fuller understanding of the history of hatred toward Jews. At the very least, fastidiousness about the definition and use of anti-Semitism is salutatory in that it reminds us that ideas of racial prejudice deriving from pseudoscientific categories in the nineteenth and twentieth centuries should not be applied willy-nilly to the ancient and medieval past. However, simply acting as a counterweight that tries to limit the indiscriminate use of the word anti-Semitism isn't enough to insulate the term anti-Judaism itself from criticism. We should not simply accept anti-Judaism as a preferable alternative to "anti-Semitism" simply because it provides what seems to be a way of thinking about anti-Jewish animus that goes beyond an anachronistic racial ideology. The increasing prevalence of the word anti-Judaism in both scholarly and popular writing about Jewish history demands that we scrutinize its origins, its underlying assumptions, and the ways the word itself shapes historical thinking and analysis.

It seems clear that the first scholars to use the term deployed it rather haphazardly in their own writing. All four of the scholars discussed below did pioneering work in exploring the origins of anti-Jewish animus in the Christian tradition. Taking a critical look at the appearance of the word anti-Judaism in their writing should not be understood as carping at their significant achievements, particularly when they were among the first to try to broaden our understanding of anti-Jewish animus by going beyond anti-Semitism. Aside from one instance by the last author we will consider, these scholars did not really reflect on the meaning or implication of the term anti-Judaism itself. It seemed an obvious alternative to anti-Semitism that emphasized the theological nature of hatred toward Jews.

Rosemary Reuther's *Faith and Fratricide: The Theological Roots of Anti-Semitism* (1974), was one of the first attempts to take Christian theological animosity to the Jews seriously; she indicted Christianity for preparing the way for the violent anti-Semitism of the twentieth century. Reuther argued that what she called anti-Judaism actually arose specifically from the theological dispute between Christians and Jews over the identity of Jesus as the messiah: "For Christianity, anti-Judaism was not merely a defense against attack, but an intrinsic need of Christian self-affirmation" (1974, p. 181). But she didn't restrict the use of anti-Judaism to a normative Christian context. She later used "anti-Judaism" to characterize pagan attitudes toward Jews (1974, p. 23). Like all the authors under consideration, she tried to come to grips with how anti-Judaism was related to anti-Semitism. She seemed to suggest that anti-Semitism itself somehow developed out of anti-Judaism: "there is no way to rid Christianity of its anti-Judaism, which constantly takes social expression in anti-Semitism, without grappling finally with its Christological hermeneutic itself" (1974, p. 116). However, the distinction that she drew between anti-Judaism and anti-Semitism became rather muddled, and at one point she seemed to abandon the idea of anti-Judaism altogether. "Rather, we must recognize Christian anti-Semitism as a uniquely new factor in the picture of antique anti-Semitism" (1974, p. 28).

A similar inconsistency can be found in John Gager's otherwise nuanced and insightful discussion in *The Origins of Anti-Semitism: Attitudes Toward Judaism in Pagan and Christian Antiquity*. While Gager rejected Reuther's larger indictment of early Christianity as exclusively anti-Jewish, his discussion emphasized that anti-Jewish sentiment in the early Church won out over more nuanced positions. Anti-Jewish ideology predominated because of an internal threat from what came to be understood as a Christian heresy, in particular the ideology promoted by Marcion in the second century. For Marcion, the Jesus known through Paul's letters was the true basis for Christianity and as a result he wanted to reject the Old Testament and its conception of God. Orthodox Christians, who saw themselves as the fulfillment of the prophecies of the Old Testament, responded by trying to shift the blame for the problematic aspects of the Old Testament onto the Jews themselves. There was nothing "wrong" with the Hebrew Bible or its God. It was the Jews who had distorted everything and should be rejected. This is the attitude that for Gager constitutes anti-Judaism: "In short, what emerges.... is a rekindling of traditional Christian anti-Judaism in which the full burden of Marcion's assault on the God of the Jews is deflected onto the Jews themselves" (1983, p. 164). Gager's subtle analysis falters when he argues that the "intensity of the [anti-Jewish] language clearly crosses the boundary between anti-Judaism and anti-Semitism" (1983, p. 164). He doesn't define the "traditional Christian anti-Judaism" then rekindled by the struggle against Marcion. How could something so central to Christianity's self-understanding as this underlying anti-Judaism remain dormant until triggered by the crisis with Marcion? The second problem is positing a transition from anti-Judaism to anti-Semitism that somehow seems to depend on the intensity of language against the Jews. Where is this so-called language boundary between anti-Judaism and anti-Semitism?

Heiko Oberman's erudite and impassioned *The Roots of Anti-Semitism: In the Age of Renaissance and Reformation*, which surveys attitudes toward Jews in the Reformation, makes a sophisticated attempt to differentiate between anti-Judaism and anti-Semitism. Oberman deploys anti-Judaism as a general term to describe the ideas of the Reformers about Judaism, but insists that these ideas about Jews do not make Protestant leaders anti-Semites because they did not think in terms of racial categories. As with Reuther and Gager, so too Oberman maintains that the response to the Jews could not be understood apart from internal Christian theological concerns. In

Oberman's understanding, Luther attacked the Jews because of his own theology of salvation: "The immediate target for this anti-Judaism was not the Jews at all, but rather a fundamental, and in those days, burning topic of the Reformation: the tension between the superficial expression of religious sentiment and the inner search for truth, between lighted candles and lighted hearts" (1984, p. 40). In other words, Luther originally thought of the Jews as tainted by the devil—just like popes, heretics, and, indeed, other Christians themselves—but also as still capable of saving themselves through the embrace of the true Christianity of the Reformation. Once the Jews seemed to reject the salvation offered by Luther, he turned on them, not, Oberman suggests, because they were Jews *qua* Jews or because of the nature of Judaism itself, but because they were another group who had succumbed to the devil. If the underlying motivation for Luther's attitudes toward Jews was his larger theological concern about salvation for all human beings, using the term anti-Judaism obscures, at least in part, the true dynamic of Luther's thinking. If the Jews had converted, then Luther's anger against the Jews would have dissipated. Would his anti-Judaism still exist at this point? Would it return to being dormant? A more complex process is at work in the way Luther's and other reformers' animosity to the Jews was driven by internal Christian theological pressures at specific historical moments, and the term anti-Judaism doesn't capture this more complicated reality. Yet, just as Reuther and Gager tried unsuccessfully to link anti-Judaism with anti-Semitism, Oberman concludes that once Luther came to believe that the Jews would not convert, then the "anti-Judaism inherent in Luther— and in the Christian faith as a whole—become[s] the plaything of modern anti-Semitism" (1984, p. 124). But is this larger Christian anti-Judaism the same or different from Luther's, which seemed to be so personal? And what does Oberman mean when he says that anti-Judaism became the plaything of anti-Semitism? Is it a necessary preparation for anti-Semitism? Can anti-Semitism exist without anti-Judaism?

Gavin Langmuir's important article, "Anti-Judaism as the Necessary Preparation for Antisemitism," in many ways helps refine some of the arguments found in Ruether, Gager, and Oberman. He at least offers a formal definition of anti-Judaism: "Anti-Judaism I take to be a total or partial opposition to Judaism—and to Jews as adherents of it—by people who accept a competing system of beliefs and practices and consider certain genuine Judaic beliefs and practices as inferior. Anti-Judaism, therefore, can be pagan, Christian, Communist, or what you will, but its specific character will depend on the character of the competing system" (1990, p. 57). There are several problems with the definition. What exactly does a partial opposition to Judaism mean? At what point do intellectual or cultural conflicts evolve into a systematic anti-Judaism? Is it possible to think of anti-Judaism as a distinct set of ideas that can exist apart from a specific time or place? Or if its specific character changes depending upon whichever group adopts an anti-Jewish position, how does anti-Judaism retain any kind of essential core of meaning? While Langmuir tries to refine the definition by asserting that "Christian anti-Judaism can be separated into three aspects: the doctrinal, the legal, and the popular," he seems to modify the centrality of anti-Judaism as a separate animating force by explaining Christian attacks on Jews as a result of specific changes in medieval society and individual psychoses (1990, p. 58). His portrait of the motivations for attacks on Jews makes it difficult to locate one specific ideological inspiration: "These projections of ritual murder, host desecration, and well-poisoning inevitably assumed a religious coloration, but in fact they owed more to tensions within the majority society and the psychological problems of individuals than to the real conflict between Christianity and Judaism. They were not a necessary or predictable result of anti-Judaism as a body of ideas but rather a social and psychological reaction to the institutionalization of the inferior minority in a rapidly developing society whose stresses increased dramatically at the end of the thirteenth century" (1990, p. 62). Moreover, Langmuir, like the others surveyed above, is equally vague on the relationship between anti-Judaism and anti-Semitism: "Henceforth and for centuries, however, anti-Judaism and antisemitism would coexist and could be mutually reinforcing" (1990, p. 62). Is he suggesting that anti-Semitism already exists in the medieval or early modern world? Does coexistence mean that both ideologies can be found in the same person or culture? How exactly can they reinforce each other if they are supposed to function in different times and with such different animating principles? In any event, seeing anti-Judaism as a separate, self-contained ideology leads Langmuir into the rather bizarre position of arguing that "to the extent that Christian anti-Judaism was responsible for making Jews an oppressed minority, it helped to create beliefs and attitudes that Christianity could not contain. They contaminated Christianity itself and were only generally condemned as unchristian in the second half of the twentieth century" (1990, p. 62). How can the idea of anti-Judaism contaminate Christianity if it evolved within it? (There is here, perhaps, a hint of trying to salvage some essential purity of Christianity).

In all four of these major scholars, there are recurring problems when trying to deploy anti-Judaism in a consistent and coherent fashion. If we are to use anti-Judaism at all, we ought to agree on what it means. Can we ever reach a scholarly consensus on its meaning? Does it mean specifically antagonism toward Judaism as a religion, or does it extend to animus toward Jews themselves? Does it condemn all aspects of Judaism or just certain elements that have come to seem intolerable to Christians?

The ambiguity and inconsistency of the term anti-Judaism in these foundational scholarly discussions masks an even more profound problem with the term, one that it shares with anti-Semitism. Although scholars may disagree about the precise meaning of the word, the structure of the term—like the word anti-Semitism—suggests that there is *one* kind of Judaism that generates one kind of negative sentiment about Judaism. The idea of a single Judaism has a long history inspired by internal Christian and Jewish priorities.

Jews and Christians both have investments in asserting the static nature of Judaism. For Jews, the survival of an essentially unchanging Judaism and the resilience of the Jewish people have been constant tropes of liturgy and historiography (Pianko 2015). The rabbinic movement itself was an effort to ground new ideas and practices in ancient revealed texts. Modern Jewish reformers look back to the past for evidence of dynamic or changing religious ideas to justify their own innovations. For those Christians who wished to displace Judaism and Jews and to promote Christianity as the true dispensation, it also made sense to see Judaism as unchanging, trapped at the moment of its rejection of Jesus. Catholics and Protestants alike tended to see contemporary Judaism of the post-biblical age as a relic of the past. Augustine famously argued that the Jews, essentially unchanged from the biblical period, were witnesses to the antiquity and authenticity of Christianized scripture. Some Protestants may have idealized the nature of Jewish government as a model for their own communities, but this Israelite commonwealth of the Bible was frozen in time. Anti-Judaism was thus predicated on this understanding of a monochromatic and unchanging Judaism. If Judaism were constantly changing, how could anti-Judaism survive as a coherent ideology?

The coherence and usefulness of anti-Judaism as a term and concept is undermined even more by the historical reality of social relations among Jews and Christians; history simply cannot sustain the idea of a monochromatic ideology of "anti" Judaism that controlled relations between Jews and gentiles, whether polytheists or Christians. Antipathy to the Jews as a group was very difficult to sustain in the multicultural world of late antiquity, particularly when Jews were longtime residents of late antique cities. In the end, thinking about relations between Jews and Christians in terms of anti-Judaism actually obscures rather than clarifies the dynamic between Jews and Christians. Even before the advent of Christianity, there is very little evidence of a coherent, ideological anti-Judaism in the ancient world that influenced the way Greeks or Romans thought about or treated Jews. Did any group of non-Jews before the advent of Christianity imagine themselves to have systematic negative attitudes toward Judaism that motivated violence against Jews or deeply felt animosity toward them? As Martin Goodman and Erich Gruen have recently demonstrated, most Greeks and Romans had only the vaguest notions of what Judaism was, and what they knew of it, they mostly found laughable or bizarre (Goodman 2007; Gruen 2002). The comments of Tacitus and others about the absurdity of circumcision, avoidance of pork, and other Jewish habits make it unlikely that their casual disparagement of Judaism could have led to a consistent, intense hatred of Jews. The infamous attack on Jews in Alexandria is perhaps the only example of popular violence against Jews in the ancient world. Was this violence the result of a pervasive "Judeophobia," as Peter Schäfer has argued (1997), or a product of local rivalries and frustrations particular to the Alexandrian context? Even if local Alexandrians had cultivated a particularly virulent distaste for Jews, it did not spread to other places, and Judaism qua Judaism was never the target. The Roman victories over the Jewish rebels had little to do with the content of Judaism or the nature of Jews themselves, and lots to do with rebellion against Roman political authority. It was about enforcing Roman authority and exploiting a military victory for internal Roman political needs (Goodman 2007, pp. 379–423). Even after the Jewish revolts, Jewish communities thrived throughout the Roman world of Late Antiquity. This fact suggests that whatever animosity against the Jews emerged during the revolts never succeeded in gaining a social foothold beyond the specific events of the rebellion. Whatever animosity had developed toward Jews, it did not become a pervasive ideology directed against Jews beyond moments of particular conflict. And, certainly, the negative attitudes toward Jews had very little to do with sustained opposition to Judaism itself. Second Temple and the evolving rabbinic Judaism was an epiphenomenon in the ancient world. It was barely a sustained and coherent ideology itself, let alone a movement calling forth a sustained and systematic ideology opposed to it.

The same is true to an even greater degree in early Christian attitudes toward Judaism, or at least toward the Jews who did not embrace Christianity. In the first place—and it's not quibbling–it doesn't really make sense to describe the attitudes of early Christians toward Jews as anti-Judaism per se. Those Jews who embraced Jesus did not see themselves in opposition to Judaism but rather as participating in its fulfillment. Gentiles of the early Christian communities at first likely shared that enthusiasm for Judaism, albeit with a messianic focus on Jesus. Many of the earliest Christians wished to continue the observances of Jewish law, with the added element of belief in Jesus as the messiah. They couldn't really express anti-Judaism without undermining their own claims to be the true Israelites. In fact, it is not "Judaism" itself that was the source of much gentile anxiety, but the Jews themselves—and much of that anxiety was the product of internal Christian conflicts, as we saw in the discussions above by Gager and Oberman. Increasingly for many early Christians, the people—that is the Jews—were the problem, not the religion they professed. For those Christians who sought the conversion of the Jews, the rabbis became the focus of antagonism for distorting the scriptural truth that would bring Jews to Christ. The rabbis had intentionally misunderstood the meaning of God's commandments so the Jews had lost the ability to see the spiritual truth of Scripture. Once people identifying as Christians began to withdraw or were harried out of local Jewish communities, there was an increased alienation from what Jews did or believed. But even for Paul, who first articulated this approach, it was not so much a sense of the danger of Judaism but rather its irrelevance after Jesus that shaped his thinking about salvation. Indeed, the observance of the law, in one generous reading of Paul, was restricted to Jews but not in itself demonized. To be sure, the New Testament, which reflected at least in part some of the attitudes of various early Christian communities, contained language criticizing the Jews for rejecting Jesus and indicting various Jewish elites for stage-managing the crucifixion. To what extent these ideas were internalized by individual Christians in a growing and dynamic network of communities increasingly removed from what was becoming rabbinic Judaism remains a very open historical question.

But such uncertainty reminds us that we don't have a clear view of what the range of early (or later) Christians actually thought about Judaism. Certainly, their behavior doesn't suggest a unified and cohesive ideology that demonized the Jews. It is easy to assume a neat divide between the opposing religious communities, but it has become increasingly clear that communities of early Christians and Jews interacted more intimately and in nuanced ways that remind us to look beyond the rhetoric of community leaders. The clear social divide between early Christians and Jews may have come much later under pressure of Christian imperial authority (Schwartz 2004). At that time, as well in post-Constantine Christianity, the anti-Jewish rhetoric of imperial laws is often bound up with animosity toward pagans and heretics. The persecuting language of the laws seems less specifically focused on Judaism per se, than on any opposition to Christian orthodoxy. Early Christians such as Chrysostom, who felt most threatened by the popularity of Late Antique Jewish communities, seemed more concerned with the failings of early Christians than with the nature of Judaism itself. Even Christians who might have harbored real animosity toward Jews were generally restrained by Augustine's famous manifesto about the need to preserve the Jews as witnesses to the authenticity and antiquity of Christianity. The survival of the Jews as a people mattered as long as they fulfilled the basic task of preserving Hebrew Scriptures and were themselves evidence of God's judgment. Individual Jews seemed to be considered a regular and unremarkable part of the late antique world. At least in Augustine's community, the identity of a Jew involved in a court case went unremarked (Fredriksen 2008, pp. 313–14).

One might assume that a singular anti-Judaism crystallized in the Middle Ages. But that assumption ignores the more complicated social reality of medieval Europe (Elukin 2007; Malkiel 2009). By trying to classify all negative Christian attitudes toward Jews under one rubric, we distort the complicated and fluid nature of Christian thinking about Jews in medieval and premodern Europe. The existence of Jewish communities (or at least small groups of Jews) in many locations in the medieval world is powerful evidence that most medieval Christians tolerated the presence of Jews in their towns. Most of these Jewish communities thrived and allowed for the development of the rich culture of medieval *Ashkenaz*. Jews accommodated themselves to the tension between quasi-tolerance and idiosyncratic violence. There is a fundamental disconnect between description and reality in using a totalizing word like anti-Judaism to capture the feelings of Christians who lived and worked with Jews for generations.

Even some of the violence directed against Jews might be difficult to categorize solely under a rubric of anti-Judaism. To be sure, some of the fantasies of child murder associated with the blood libel accusations asserted that the Jews killed Christian children as part of ritual preparations for Passover. In that sense, a perverted kind of Judaism could be held responsible, although the animus was usually directed at evil Jews. At the same time, some Christians recognized that Jewish religious law made these accusations ludicrous. But the Jews were accused of many other things that could not be ascribed to a specific religious commandment. How is well-poisoning related to the nature of Judaism or any of its ritual commandments? The violence in Spain in 1392 and the later expulsion seem to have had more to do with a post-Crusade national or even proto-racial purity (or class warfare in urban settings) than with a generalized animosity toward Judaism. While the expulsion seems to have been triggered by increasing concerns that *conversos* were being drawn back to Judaism, it seems as if the phenomenon was explained by continued associations with Jewish friends and family rather than a vaguer sense of the power of the religion's hold on former Jews.

Perhaps there is an even more fundamental issue to be addressed in trying to understand the utility of the term anti-Judaism. Why do we assume that there was one consistent Christian identity that produced the same attitudes toward Jews? Where do we find this stable, authentic, and monochromatic Christianity? We have already seen the differences among leading Christian thinkers. Surely religious culture and identity varied enormously across space and time in medieval and early modern Europe. It is thus unreasonable to imagine that popular attitudes toward Jews and Judaism would have remained stable. The definition of medieval and early modern Christianity itself presents the first challenge. Do we mean the official theology of the Church? The attitudes and ideologies of the clergy? The opinions and behaviors of the laity? Whichever way we define Christianity, we can be sure that it was very different in the ninth century than it would be in the twelfth or even later in the fifteenth century. With the advent of the Reformation, trying to identify a common Christian ideology becomes infinitely more difficult. Moreover, Christian identities also varied widely according to time and place. No doubt people living in a cosmopolitan city in Spain thought about Christianity and behaved as Christians in ways very different from peasants in a village in France or Germany. How can we then make any constructive generalizations about a monochromatic "Christian" attitude toward Jews? The anti-Jewish attitudes that manifested themselves in Christian Europe came from a wide variety of Christian cultures and identities (Elukin 2015).

The Manichean quality of "anti-Judaism" ultimately obscures the much more complicated entanglement of Christianity and Judaism that transcended simple persecution and animus. A great deal of Christian thinking about Judaism was not "anti" in any one-dimensional sense. Christians appropriated aspects of Judaism and Jewish history in order to advance their own particular theological or political agendas. For example, Christians throughout late antiquity and the Middle Ages accused their theological or political enemies of Judaizing, that is, indicting them for displaying putative Jewish characteristics as a way to defame them. What often looked like anti-Jewish expressions were dramas about internal Christian issues that relied upon Jewish actors. Many of the tales of Jews stealing or stabbing the Eucharist, for example, ended with them converting when they saw a vision of a child in the Eucharist or when they witnessed a bleeding Host. The Jews thus became unwilling actors in a drama driven by contemporary Christian needs to reinforce belief in the real presence of God in the Eucharist (Rubin 2004). Even the portraits of Jews with distorted features and clothing in crucifixion scenes did not originally express prejudice toward Jews as individual human beings in the Middle Ages. They were actually symbols in an internal Christian dialogue about the nature of Jesus' physical body. Christian artists distorted Jews' features to make Jews stand out in the depictions of the Crucifixion. These Jews were meant to represent contemporary Christians who seemed reluctant to embrace Jesus' physicality. They, like the Jews, mocked the crucified Christ (Lipton 2014). In a similar vein, Christians may have used the Jews as an outlet for their own anxieties about the financial and legal nature of Christian culture. Christians could displace that anxiety by condemning Jews as usurers and Judaism as legalistic. Even some actual physical attacks on Jews had double meanings, or an underlying meaning. Often when different elements in a town or kingdom persecuted the Jews, it was a way to strike at powers, such as a king or local lord, who stood behind the Jews. Think, for example, of the attacks on English Jews as a way for indebted knights to strike at the kings who ultimately held the debts owed to the Jews.

A wide range of evidence from the medieval and early modern periods supports the very complicated role that Jews and Judaism played in Christian imagination. Anti-Judaism is simply too one-dimensional to serve as an effective description of Christian attitudes. Does anti-Judaism have any meaning in describing the putative autobiography of a medieval Jewish convert to Christianity, which actually allowed the Christian author to attack his rival monastic order (Schmitt 2013)? Does it help us understand the sophisticated retellings or commentaries on the destruction of Jerusalem which allowed medieval and early modern Christians to work out contemporary issues of identity and politics (Groves 2015; Vincent 2013)? Does it help us understand the Huguenot historian, Jacques Basnage, who attacked Catholics with an extended critique of rabbis in his famous history of the Jews (Elukin 1992)? Does anti-Judaism really capture the multivalent attitudes toward Jews that led Protestants to understand the miraculous survival of the Jews in exile after the destruction of Jerusalem as a rational miracle that demonstrates God's power (Elukin 2017)? Does anti-Judaism help us to understand how Christian authors looked to Jewish characters such as Shylock or Daniel Deronda to explore subjects such as salvation and identity that went beyond the concern with Jews and Judaism (Elukin 2018)? Does anti-Judaism accommodate those Christians in the Renaissance who turned to Jewish teachers to learn Hebrew, rabbinic readings of Scripture, and the mystical texts of the *kabbalah* in order to discover Christian revelation? Does anti-Judaism capture the thinking of Protestants, particularly during the conflicts of the seventeenth century, who saw in Israelite history models for contemporary religious or political practices? They validated aspects of Judaism even as they appropriated them and turned them to their own purposes (Grafton and Weinberg 2011; Guibbory 2010; Shalev 2014). The term anti-Judaism obscures, distorts, or marginalizes all of these episodes of appropriation.

A fuller portrait of Christian attitudes toward Jews in the ancient, medieval, and early modern worlds requires a more nuanced and critical approach to the term anti-Judaism. The problems and inconsistencies discussed above should not deter scholars from trying to develop a vocabulary that reflects historical reality more accurately. Scholars need a way to describe the persistent animus toward Jews throughout history, for the continuation of negative ideas about Jews should not be lost by disaggregating each moment of hatred. The survival of anti-Jewish tropes and the almost biological mutation of hatred toward Jews in many modern Christian and Islamic cultures—or in post-religious liberal contexts with a focus on Israel—is itself a crucial historical phenomenon. However, just as we must not lose sight of the larger, historical network of negative ideas about Jews, so too we must not fail to acknowledge the differences and changes in attitudes toward Jews from context to context. We therefore need not just a term, but rather a whole terminology, that enables scholars to explore the conceptual and historical continuities and discontinuities identified in this essay. Anti-Judaism may be part of this terminology; but it certainly should not be the whole of it. Trying to understand and write about the history of hatred toward Jews thus remains an ongoing challenge.

References

Beller, Steven. 2007. *Antisemitism: A Very Short Introduction.* Oxford: Oxford University Press.
Elukin, Jonathan. 1992. "Jacques Basnage and *The History of the Jews:* Polemic and Allegory in the Republic of Letters." *Journal of the History of Ideas* 53: 603–31.
Elukin, Jonathan. 2007. *Living Together, Living Apart: Rethinking Jewish-Christian Relations in the Middle Ages.* Princeton: Princeton University Press.
Elukin, Jonathan. 2015. "Christianity and Judaism; Christians and Jews." In *The Routledge History of Medieval Christianity 1050–1500*, edited by R. N. Swanson. London: Routledge.
Elukin, Jonathan. 2017. "Post-Biblical Jewish History Through Christian Eyes: Josephus and the Miracle of Jewish History in English Protestantism." In *The Jew as Legitimation: Jewish-Gentile Relations Beyond Antisemitism and Philosemitism*, edited by David J. Wertheim, 103–16. Cham, Switzerland: Palgrave Macmillan.
Elukin, Jonathan. 2018. "Shylock, the Devil and the Meaning of Deception in *The Merchant of Venice.*" *European Judaism* 51 (2): 44–51.
Fredriksen, Paula. 2008. *Augustine and the Jews: A Christian Defense of Jews and Judaism.* New York: Doubleday.
Gager, John. 1983. *The Origins of Anti-Semitism: Attitudes Toward Judaism in Pagan and Christian Antiquity.* New York: Oxford University Press.

Goodman, Martin. 2007. *Rome and Jerusalem: The Clash of Ancient Civilizations*. New York: Vintage.
Grafton, Anthony, and Joanna Weinberg. 2011. *"I Have Always Loved the Holy Tongue:" Isaac Casaubon, The Jews, and a Forgotten Chapter in Renaissance Scholarship*. Cambridge, MA: Harvard University Press.
Groves, Beatrice. 2015. *The Destruction of Jerusalem in Early Modern English Literature*. Cambridge: Cambridge University Press.
Gruen, Erich S. 2002. *Diaspora: Jews Amidst Greeks and Romans*. Cambridge, MA: Harvard University Press.
Guibbory, Achsah. 2010. *Christian Identity, Jews, and Israel in Seventeenth-Century England*. Oxford: Oxford University Press.
Heschel, Susannah. 2011. "Historiography of Antisemitism Versus Anti-Judaism: A Response to Robert Morgan." *Journal for the Study of the New Testament* 33 (3) (March): 257–79.
Langmuir, Gavin. 1990. "Anti-Judaism as the Necessary Preparation for Antisemitism." In *Toward a Definition of Antisemitism*, 57–62. Berkeley: University of California Press.
Lipton, Sara. 2014. *Dark Mirror: The Medieval Origins of Anti-Jewish Iconography*. New York: Metropolitan Books.
Malkiel, David. 2009. *Reconstructing Ashkenaz: The Human Face of France-German Jewry, 1000–1250*. Stanford: Stanford University Press.
Nirenberg, David. 2013. *Anti-Judaism: The Western Tradition*. New York: W. W. Norton.
Oberman, Heiko. 1984. *The Roots of Anti-Semitism: In the Age of Renaissance and Reformation*. Translated by James I. Porter. Philadelphia: Fortress Press.
Pianko, Noam. 2015. *Jewish Peoplehood: An American Innovation*. New Brunswick: Rutgers University Press.
Reuther, Rosemary. 1974. *Faith and Fratricide: The Theological Roots of Anti-Semitism*. New York: The Seabury Press.
Rubin, Miri. 2004. *Gentile Tales: The Narrative Assault on Late Medieval Jews*. Philadelphia: University of Pennsylvania Press.
Schäfer, Peter. 1997. *Judeophobia: Attitudes Toward the Jews in the Ancient World*. Cambridge, MA: Harvard University Press.
Schmitt, Jean-Claude. 2013. *The Conversion of Herman the Jew: Autobiography, History and Fiction in the Twelfth Century*. Translated by Alex J. Novikoff. Philadelphia: University of Pennsylvania Press.
Schwartz, Seth. 2004. *Imperialism and Jewish Society: 200 B.C.E. to 640 C.E.* Princeton: Princeton University Press.
Shalev, Eran. 2014. *American Zion: The Old Testament as a Political Text from the Revolution to the Civil War*. New Haven: Yale University Press.
Vincent, Nicholas. 2013. "William of Newburgh, Josephus, and the New Titus." In *Christians and Jews in Angevin England: The York Massacre of 1190, Narratives and Contexts*, edited by Sarah Rees Jones and Sethina Watson, 57–90. Woodbridge: Boydell.

CHAPTER 3

Anti-Semitism (Historiography)

Jonathan Judaken

Seminal aspects of the approach to studying anti-Semitism were laid in the years between the Dreyfus Affair (1894–1906) and the rise of Nazism and the Holocaust (1933–1945). In this period, the first scholarly monographs on the subject appeared and many key concepts and narratives to explain anti-Semitism emerged. The earliest historians of the subject sought to debunk long-enduring myths about Jews, along with the widely accepted idea that Jews were a distinct race. Following World War I, new studies began to focus on the links between nationalism and anti-Semitism and to consider the dynamics of group formation against outsiders. The rise of the Nazis led to the first critical histories of anti-Semitism that insisted that anti-Semites, not Jews, were the proper objects of study for these scholars. But it was World War II and the Holocaust that was the major crucible shaping the study of anti-Semitism, initiating some of the key debates that persist in the field. Some examined the specific contextual forces that engendered Nazism, while others sought its causes in the deep recesses of Christian culture or even in an ostensibly eternal hatred of Jews within the West. Disputes emerged about differences between religious and racial anti-Semitism, medieval and modern forms, and the exceptionality as opposed to the comparability of anti-Semitism to other forms of racism. These contentious issues remain central to the historiography today. This chapter examines the shaping influence of these early studies.

J. Judaken (✉)
Rhodes College, Memphis, TN, USA
e-mail: judakenj@rhodes.edu

1880–1918: POLITICAL ANTI-SEMITISM AND ITS HISTORY

Perhaps the earliest monograph opposing anti-Semitism was published in 1893 by Henri Jean Baptiste Anatole Leroy-Beaulieu (1842–1912), *Israel Among the Nations: A Study of the Jews and Antisemitism* (1895), a counter to the Pope of French anti-Semitism, Édouard Drumont, who had helped to stoke the Dreyfus Affair. But Bernard Lazare's 1894 *Anti-Semitism: Its History and Causes* is the most enduring work of this formative period. Indeed, it was the first overarching history of the topic. But despite his Thucydidean proclamation promising "to write neither an apology nor a diatribe, but an impartial study in history and sociology" (1995, p. 7), Lazare's book reflects the biases of an assimilated French Jew of the period. "[T]he general causes of antisemitism have always resided in Israel itself," he wrote, "and not in those who antagonized it" (1995, p. 8). Phrases such as these led Drumont to praise the book as the only one by a Jew worth reading. Other anti-Semites lauded the work as well. What Lazare objected to was his perception of a narrow ritualism in Judaism and the rabbinic tradition of the Talmud as a form of religious obscurantism. Some of Lazare's theses about the causes of anti-Semitism thus dovetailed with the long history of anti-Jewish discourse. But his analysis of the evolution of modern anti-Semitism out of Christian anti-Judaism made the work the most comprehensive early study.

Several other studies appeared during the Dreyfus Affair, but to gauge some of their tendencies, let's consider Lucien Wolf's long entry on "Anti-Semitism" published in the *Encyclopaedia Britannica* in 1910–1911. Wolf's essay was animated by the conviction that anti-Semitism sensu stricto was a modern phenomenon, coterminous with the circumstances in which the word itself was popularized in Germany around 1880 as part of the bid to politicize it. Demonstrating this conviction, Wolf surveyed the political struggles of the concluding quarter of the nineteenth century and the early years of the twentieth century in Germany, Russia, Rumania, Austro-Hungary, and France. He emphasized the development of industrial and commercial capitalism in each place, alongside the power of the bourgeoisie.

But adopting the liberal script that one finds in many of the early historians of anti-Semitism, Wolf also highlighted and worried about the role of Jews within the economy and culture. Jewish "concentration" within the bourgeoisie, with "the bulk of them" flocking "to the financial and the distributive (as distinct from the productive) fields of industry to which they had been confined in the ghettos" (1910), alongside their crowding into the professions, including medicine, law, and journalism together with their pronounced role within modern art, literature, and science, made Jews visible targets for those railing against modernity. Once the great depression of the nineteenth century ended (1873–1896), however, anti-Semitism also abated. Wolf's convictions were Whiggish. He believed that anti-Semitism was a bygone relic that rested upon the phantasm of race. Wolf thus cautioned in his conclusion that Zionism only stoked the fire of anti-Semitism since it accepted its two core convictions: nationalism and race. His concern for the future lay more decidedly in the oppression of Jews in Eastern Europe, since it would result in the masses of *Ostjuden* pouring over the borders into the West, which meant renewable fodder for ignorant and superstitious elements.

In the period from the Dreyfus Affair through the eve of World War I, a literature on anti-Semitism began to emerge that surveyed the phenomenon as a response to the crises of modernity. These early analysts ascribed many causes to anti-Semitism, but often coalesced in blaming Jews and especially their ostensible religious dogmatism as the core source of the problem. They all depicted certain types of Jews as responsible for the opprobrium and oppression that was their fate.

1918–1933: The Radicalization of Anti-Semitism and Early Theories to Explain It

The unprecedented death and destruction of World War I, alongside the rise of ethno-nationalism and the redrawing of the European map, vitalized a more intensely paranoid, conspiratorial form of anti-Semitism. New historical works that emerged in this context often focused on how a new exclusionary nationalism mingled with anti-Semitism to target the Jewish minority.

Felix Goldmann's (1882–1934) *The Essence of Anti-Semitism* (1920) expressed this new anxiety, as did Ismar Freund's primer on Jew-hatred, *Jew Hate: A Contribution to History and Psychology* (1922). Fritz Bernstein's 1926 *Jew Hate as a Sociological Problem* (1951) insightfully captures this new era of scholarship, as Bernstein develops in some detail Goldmann's suggestion that Jew-hate is a special case of the general group antagonism directed against a weak minority. Since Jews are widely dispersed, this enmity is likewise prevalent in many places, Bernstein maintained. Since the process is not rational, apologetics evident in works like Freund's, which insist that Jews generally do not conform to the stereotypes that deride them, are fruitless. Jewish behavior has nothing to do with anti-Jewish perceptions, writes Bernstein: "The Gentiles' hate against us causes them to interpret our every action unfavorably and then to infer the existence of unfavourable qualities" (1951, p. 71).

To explain the mechanisms of anti-Jewish contempt, Bernstein analyzes group identity and formation through the prejudices groups develop against vulnerable minorities. Writes Bernard Praag in his Introduction to the 1951 edition of the work, "in doing so, Bernstein is probably the first who attempts to sketch a general theory of social groups and conflicts between groups." In his final chapter, Bernstein applies this to the specifics of the Jewish experience. Doing so, he gives a Zionist spin to a psychoanalytic theory of projection. Bernstein maintains that group formation depends upon stereotyped thinking. When groups feel frustration or suffer, "the urge to direct and discharge unfriendly feelings against someone appears to be *primary*" (1951, p. 12). Since we avoid targeting family, friends, and those upon whom we are dependent, contempt must be deflected outside this immediate circle. This is the psychic process that defines group formation, which latches onto convenient biological, geographic, cultural, and socioeconomic identifiers and demarcates boundaries by coding enemies and constantly bolstering an ideology that offers a sense of social purpose. Our hostile feelings are consequently discharged upon outsiders, preferably weaker groups. Prejudice is a primal instinct according to Bernstein. Jews will therefore be targets wherever they remain a minority. Contrary to Lucien Wolf, Bernstein's solution therefore entails a need for a Jewish state. For Bernstein, Zionism is the only possible way to derail group enmity against the Jews by consolidating the minority into its own country.

A year after Bernstein's study, Kurt Wawrzinek's dissertation, *The Emergence of German Anti-Semitic Parties* (1927), became the first historical monograph on the German anti-Semitic movement. The same year, the most renowned writer on the topic in this period, Arnold Zweig (1867–1968), published *Caliban or Politics and Passion: Attempt at Human Group Afflictions Demonstrated in Anti-Semitism* (1927), his own Freud-inspired projection theory accounting for group dynamics in the etiology of anti-Semitism. The following year, the title of Samuel Blitz's *Nationalism: A Cause of Anti-Semitism* (1928) summarized not only his argument, but encapsulated the key theme of studies in the interwar years, showing that it preoccupied not only German scholars of the era.

1933–1938: The Rise of the Nazi Party and the Critical Historiography of Anti-Semitism

Nazi accession to power magnified a critical historiography not much evident in prior approaches, since now writers stopped blaming Jews or insisting that they change and began to focus on diagnoses of the anti-Semites as the cause of the problem. Early innovators included James Parkes, most importantly in his 1934 *magnum opus*, *The Conflict of the Church and the Synagogue: A Study in the Origins of Anti-Semitism* (1969), along with Hugo Valentin, whose subtitle clearly indicates a turn in the literature, *Anti-Semitism: Historically and Critically Examined* (1936).

Clergyman James Parkes was a hugely influential early scholar of anti-Semitism. The author of dozens of books and 329 total publications, he stands as a key historiographical pioneer. In Tony Kushner's words, "Parkes reversed the causality of Jew hatred. It was the fault of Christians that Jews were persecuted and reviled. To Parkes this was a deep stain on the reputation of his faith and the only response was for Christians to combat anti-semitism wherever they found it" (2005, p. xi). In *The Conflict of the Church and the Synagogue*, Parkes made two key interventions. First, he castigated earlier works for their apologetic rather than critical tenor. His second move was really groundbreaking, since he sought to show that it wasn't anything in Judaism, but rather early Christianity that laid the foundations for the long history of anti-Semitism.

Parkes maintained that anti-Semitism was a passion play in three acts: from the Gospels to Charlemagne, the theological anti-Semitism of the first three centuries was then abetted by Roman Law; the second act followed up through the Reformation; and the third act, the modern period, was "still upon the stage" (1969, p. 371). Explicitly arguing against racial and economic accounts of the foundations of anti-Semitism, he insisted instead that its underpinnings were religious: "the main responsibility must rest upon the theological picture created in patristic literature of the Jew as a being perpetually betraying God and ultimately abandoned by Him" (1969, p. 375). In this way, Parkes, who was trained as a pastor, not only established the groundwork for a series of studies that followed but shifted the terms of the discussion, which began to explore how Greco-Roman and especially Christian culture laid the foundations for modern anti-Semitism. Cecil Roth, a doyen of Jewish studies in Britain, continued Parkes' revisionism with his essay, "The Medieval Conception of the Jew: A New Interpretation" (1938) that also located the origins of anti-Semitism in Christian culture. Parkes' and Roth's arguments were documented extensively in Jacob Rader Marcus' classic anthology of source material, *The Jew in the Medieval World* (1938), which came out the same year.

Valentin's critical history, *Antisemitism*, had come out two years earlier, offering a long-term survey going all the way back to antiquity before taking apart the key myths of Nazi anti-Semitism. Valentin's conclusion is not dissimilar to a point made first by Lazare but abetted by several of the interwar works we have considered: "Antisemitism is merely a special case of the hatred of foreigners," he declares (1936, p. 19). The critical turn in his conclusion echoes Fritz Bernstein and Arnold Zweig:

> The view widely prevalent in Jewish and non-Jewish circles that by acting in this way or that the Jews might have been able to avert Antisemitism is based on an illusion. For it is not Jews who are hated, but an imaginary image of them, which is confounded with the reality, and the Jews' actual 'faults' play a very unimportant part in the matter....In fact it is not at all certain that Antisemitism would be weakened to any extent if the Jews were to consist exclusively of angels in human form. (1936, p. 305)

Anti-Semitism is not amenable to "facts or arguments" since it is a form of scapegoating, which will continue so long as Jews remain a religious, national, and racial minority, or until humanity develops a sense of solidarity above these notions, Valentin averred.

Historical Approaches During and After the Second World War

World War II gave rise to several important works seeking to explain Nazism as the most radical form of historical anti-Semitism. These pitted the assessment that Nazi anti-Semitism was a unique product of the separate path of German modernity (i.e. what is called in German the *Sonderweg* thesis) against a viewpoint that contended that Hitlerism was a radicalization of an eternalist, European tradition of anti-Jewish contempt.

Rohan Butler's *The Roots of National Socialism, 1783–1933* (1941) was an early exemplar of explanations of Nazi anti-Semitism that located Nazism as a product of German modernity: "[T]hat line of thought which leads from Herder to Hitler is traditionally and typically German," explained Butler (1941, p. 283). Franz Neumann's *Behemoth: The Structure and Practice of National Socialism* (2009), first published in 1942 and then expanded in 1944, combined his foundational analysis of the Nazi state with a *Sonderweg* argument about German anti-Semitism. He understood that a racial ethno-nationalism was "deeply embedded in the history of German thought" (2009, p. 104). Going back further than Butler, in what became a popular trajectory, he traced this lineage from Luther to Hitler. But he nonetheless insisted that "[a]lthough Anti-Semitism was nowhere so actively propagated as in Germany, it failed to strike root in the population"—least of all among the worker's movement, which "remained immune from it" (2009, p. 110).

To account for this audacious claim, Neumann distinguished between non-totalitarian anti-Semitism and hard-core Nazi totalitarian ideology, which identified Jews with "the incarnation of evil in Germany" (2009, p. 122). Pre-totalitarian anti-Semitism, Neumann suggested, appealed to religious anti-Judaism, but even more powerfully spoke to economic, social, and political discontent. It was an "outlet for resentment" expressing the gripes of the older and newer middle classes dislocated by capitalist modernity. Modernity was personified by Jews, explains Neumann:

> The modern theater, atonal music, expressionism in painting and literature, functional architecture, all these seemed to constitute a threat to the conservatives whose cultural outlook was basically rural, and who thus came to identify the city and its culture, it economics, and its politics with the Jew. (2009, p. 123)

So rather than a fundamental outlook, anti-Semitism was a screen and Jews a scapegoat that masked deeper social forces that the Nazis manipulated when useful.

When Neumann revised his book for a second publication in 1944, he added an appendix with a section titled "Anti-Semitism." The tone of the writing is totally different, since he now knew that he had erred in his earlier analysis. Neumann flatly rejected "the scapegoat theory according to which the Jews are used as scapegoats for all evils of society." Instead, he advanced "the spearhead theory of Anti-Semitism," arguing that the Jews are "guinea pigs" for an "all-comprehensive terrorist machine. The denunciation of bolshevism, socialism, democracy, liberalism, capitalism as Jewish, together with the planned extermination of the Jews," served to foster a totalitarian society that persecuted all groups that were not subservient to the Nazi system (2009, pp. 550–52). Anti-Semitism was consequently the spearhead for a broader totalitarian assault on democracy. This became the most prominent explanation of Nazi anti-Semitism during the Second World War.

While Neumann's focus in his *Behemoth* was on the Nazi state, his Frankfurt School colleague Paul Massing's straightforward historical analysis of the preamble to Nazi anti-Semitism in *Rehearsal for Destruction: A Study of Political Anti-Semitism in Imperial Germany* (1949) built on Wawrzinek's 1927 dissertation. Massing located German anti-Semitism within the German pathway through modernity from Jewish emancipation to World War I: "Anti-Semitism was inextricably tied to German nineteenth-century nationalism; its destructive nature derived from the peculiar social and political crises through which Germany struggled," wrote Samuel Flowerman in introducing the work (1949, p. xiii). According to Massing's version of the *Sonderweg* thesis, the failure of Germany to institutionalize bourgeois liberalism on the Western model combined with class tensions in shaping Germany's Imperial era anti-Semitism.

Eva Reichmann's *Hostages of Civilisation* (1949) built on interwar studies, melding the insights of sociologists about the role of Jewish minorities within Gentile society with psychoanalytic intuitions. These were inserted into a *Sonderweg* argument about how Germany's special path placed it between West and East as it negotiated the crises of modernity. Germany's rapid industrialization and late unification under the militarism and bureaucratic order of Prussia combined with slackening moral constraints to make Jews a fitting target for those frustrated and left behind by modernizing tendencies, whose "root lies in this anomaly of the German national consciousness," allowing "people to hate with a good conscience and still to feel morally superior" (1949, pp. 63, 166–67).

The *Sonderweg* analyses of Butler, Neumann, Massing, and Reichmann were countered by an eternalist narrative that emerged in the same period. These were works attuned to the fury of the Holocaust that sought its roots in a deeper history of Jews in the West. Three important examples demonstrate this tendency that picked up the thread laid down by Parkes and Roth as the Nazi assault peaked.

Koppel S. Pinson (1904–1961) was a professor of history at Queens College, CUNY and Executive Editor of the journal *Jewish Social Studies* when he pulled together *Essays on Antisemitism* in 1942, bringing out a revised and enlarged edition in 1946. The volume comprised a set of "analytical studies" that explored the underlying reasons for anti-Semitism alongside a collection of "historical and regional studies" from the Hellenistic-Roman world forward. If the compendium stressed continuity, then Salo Baron's Foreword emphasized the unprecedented nature of Nazi anti-Semitism. The tone of many of the articles was filled with dismay, penned as they were amid the destruction of European Jewry, most emphatically Zevi Diesendruck's essay "Antisemitism and Ourselves." A professor of philosophy at Hebrew Union College, Diesendruck maintained that Nazi anti-Semitism finally revealed anti-Semitism in its nakedness. His analysis that anti-Semitism is "unique, unsubsumable, and irrational" just as much as it is "inevitable and immutable" (1946, p. 47) has consequences for how to fight it. He believed that endeavors like those of the Anti-Defamation League, the French *Alliance Israélite Universelle*, and other communal organizations were hopeless because they operate on enlightenment principles, suggesting that persuasion and knowledge can alleviate the problem.

The work of Joshua Trachtenberg concurred with Diesendruck's analysis. Trachtenberg was a congregational rabbi, a leader of American Labor Zionism, and author of two major works on Jews in medieval Europe: *Jewish Magic and Superstition* in 1939 and his masterpiece, *The Devil and the Jews* in 1943. Trachtenberg had shown in his first study that the image of the Jew was associated with sorcery and magic. This was the basis for why Jews were accused of ritual murder, well-poisoning, and spreading disease, itself a product of the association of Jews with the work of the Devil that "permeated every layer of Christian society," he augured in his second work (1983, p. 217). During the height of the Holocaust what Trachtenberg sought to establish was that the "figure of the 'demonic' Jew, less than human, indeed, antihuman," "the Jew as an alien, evil, antisocial…creature, essentially subhuman" was "the creation of the medieval mind" (1983, p. xiv).

Trachtenberg's study helped lay the tracks for the post-Holocaust eternalist history of anti-Semitism that was influenced by the narrative of political Zionism:

> [The Jew] is the archenemy of Western civilization. He is alien, not to this or that land, but to all Western society, alien in his habits, his pursuits, his interests, his character, his very blood. Wherever he lives he is a creature apart. He is the arch-degenerate of the world, infecting its literature, its art, its music, its politics and economics with the subtle poison of his insidious influence, ripping out its moral foundation stone by stone until it will collapse helpless in his hands. This is his final goal: to conquer the world, to refashion it in his craven image, enslave it to his own alien ends. (1983, p. 3)

Trachtenberg maintained that the demonizing of Jews over the long history of Western culture made Judeophobia different from other forms of racial bias "in expression and intensity" (1983, p. xv). He rejected materialist accounts of anti-Semitism or other rationalist explanations of "psychological xenophobia that rejects 'difference' and resents minority cultures as a result of economic and social frictions" (1983, p. 2). He also rejected arguments about propaganda techniques that focused on scapegoats as a means to deal with social tensions.

Instead, Trachtenberg clearly read history backward from Nazi propaganda to the medieval world. "'Medieval' defines not a chronological but a mental epoch," he insisted (1983, p. 5). While dressed in the modern idiom of scientific anti-Semitism, the same medieval mental habits were what predominated among the masses: "The era of rationalism and liberalism made no difference—it passed the masses by unnoticed. Not until medieval habits of thought—and the social conditions in which they flourish—have been uprooted will there be a difference" (1983, p. 219).

The third example of an eternalist approach, suggested by Parkes and Roth in the 1930s and developed by Diesendruck and Trachtenberg in the 1940s, was penned by Jules Isaac (1877–1963). In 1943, under the Nazi jackboot in Vichy France, Isaac began a series of works that located the origins of anti-Semitism within Christian teachings. These included *Jesus and Israel* (written between 1943–1946), *Genèse de l'Antisémitisme*, and his primer, *The Teaching of Contempt*, whose title became shorthand for the problem he illuminated. He focused on core myths in Christianity, most toxically the deicide charge whereby Jews are identified as Christ killers. This hostile slur morphed into other anti-Jewish Christian myths. They were the key vector of Judeophobia that undergirded the abandonment of the Jews during the Holocaust. Ultimately, Isaac's publications and interfaith work were a precursor to the changes in Catholic theology distilled in *Nostra Aetete* (1965), which had an impact on changing the doctrine of other Christian churches as well.

THE HOLOCAUST: THE GENESIS OF THE MAJOR THEORIES FOR EXPLAINING ANTI-SEMITISM

The rise of the Nazi regime and the ensuing genocide occasioned not only key narratives but also a golden age in theorizing anti-Semitism. The psychoanalysis of Sigmund Freud, the Critical Theory of the Frankfurt School, the application of social science and sociology by scholars like Talcott Parsons, the existentialism of Jean-Paul Sartre, and the philosophically inflected history of Hannah Arendt have had an enduring effect on how scholars understand the underlying motives and factors that contribute to anti-Semitism.

Sigmund Freud offered a series of suggestions about the psychic sources of Judeophobia in his earlier writings that he brought together in *Moses and Monotheism*, first published in 1939. In the work, he discussed the Oedipal relationship between the "religion of the father" (Judaism) and the "religion of the son" (Christianity). He connected his analysis of circumcision provoking a fear of castration anxiety with the claim of Jewish chosenness as a font of anti-Semitism. He also evoked the notion of the "narcissism of minor differences" that he maintained leads to rigid group identification. Developing these psychoanalytical insights, Freud proposed that anti-Semitism was the product of seething resentment at Jews by Christians, who were first converted by the sword in the name of the New Testament narrative that was a set of stories about Jews. Christians unconsciously begrudged Jews for being the source of the civilizational moral precepts contained in the New Testament—ideals to which all assent but that prove difficult for individuals to uphold given their instinctual drives.

Freud's analysis inspired Maurice Samuel's now-forgotten account of anti-Semitism, *The Great Hatred* (1940). Samuel hammered home his thesis that "Christophobia" was the underlying cause of anti-Semitism: "Jews are loathed as the Christ-givers, the creators or representatives of the non-force principle in human relations," he thundered. The Catholic intellectual Jacques Maritain would pick up on Samuel's formulation of Freud's thesis, giving his theory a distinctly Christological spin in his interventions against anti-Semitism during the Second World War.

Another effort was the massive collection, *Jews in a Gentile World: The Problem of Anti-Semitism* (1942), edited by Isacque Graeber and Steuart Henderson Britt. The volume assembled eighteen sociologists, anthropologists, psychologists, political scientists, economists, and historians. There was arguably no more important essay in the collection than Parsons' "The Sociology of Modern Anti-Semitism" (1942), since he brought together several classical sociological theories in developing his analysis. Parsons maintained that anti-Semitism results from the social breakdown unleashed by modernization: urbanization, industrialization, the instability of the economy, the increasing heterogeneity and mobility of the population, the debunking of traditional values and ideas, the expansion of popular education and modern mass means of communication. These all result in the large-scale incidence of "anomie" in Western society. Parsons argued that anomie results in social and psychological insecurity, frustration, and resentment, often expressed as aggression. The more heightened the anxiety, the more "free floating" the aggression. In these circumstances, people act out this frustration and insecurity on a symbolic object and Parsons held, following Max Weber, that Jews were particularly apt targets given their history. As exemplified by Parsons' contribution, the social scientific bent in *Jews in a Gentile World* made it an innovative contributor to these debates.

The leading lights of the Frankfurt School were also busy throughout World War II developing their contribution to understanding anti-Semitism by bringing together Weber's sociology, Marxism, and psychoanalysis. Their greatest collective product was the *Studies in Prejudice* series. Its most ambitious volume was a collaborative work led by Theodor Adorno, *The Authoritarian Personality*.

Institutionally, *The Authoritarian Personality* was a joint undertaking of the Berkeley Public Opinion Study and the Institute of Social Research, combining Berkeley's experimental and empirical academic social psychology with the Frankfurt School's sociological, psychoanalytic, and philosophical bent. They sought to identify the roots of fascist and anti-Semitic personalities. The authors proposed that by examining a series of traits and measuring responses to a series of questions on the F-Scale—where the F stood for fascist—it would be possible to determine an individual's tendency toward fascism, and the correlated anti-Semitism, xenophobia, and authoritarianism. Although some of the methodology in the work received criticism, it had an enormous impact on the types of studies conducted by social psychologists following its publication.

The Frankfurt School's more speculative theoretical intervention was Max Horkheimer's and Theodor Adorno's *Dialectic of Enlightenment* (2000). Originally published in 1947, with the concluding segment on the "The Elements of Anti-Semitism" added in 1949, Horkheimer and Adorno consider anti-Semitism within the development of Western rationality and the administered society of modernity. They argue that Western rationality is dialectically entwined with myth in the domination of nature. They trace this from ancient Greece through the Enlightenment and into the mass culture of modernity. Against this long-term theoretical and historical backdrop, they conclude with a discussion of eight intertwined elemental theses about the underlying causes of anti-Semitism that are unified by their socio-psychoanalytic approach, with Freud's theory of projection at its heart.

Unlike the Frankfurt School, Sartre's major analysis of anti-Semitism preferred existential psychoanalysis to a Freudian-inspired model. *Anti-Semite and Jew* was published in 1946 and since then it has remained a forceful examination of Jewish subjugation, explored as a dialectic between Self and Other. In French discussions, it became the ur-text to postwar debates about anti-Semitism and the Jewish condition. For Sartre, the key drivers are anxiety and alienation, but his understanding is existential, not psychoanalytic or Marxist. Anxiety is the affective sense of human freedom that results from the responsibility to define oneself through choices effected in action. The key claim of *Anti-Semite and Jew* is that anti-Semites are men of "*mauvaise foi*" (bad faith or self-deception) who avoid anxiety and deny freedom by fleeing the responsibility to make meaning out of the situations in which they find themselves. Instead, anti-Semites justify all their choices by blaming a purportedly degenerate Jewish Other for the decadence and decay they believe must be eliminated to redeem the world.

Hannah Arendt offered her interactionist account of modern anti-Semitism partly as a response to her unfavorable assessment of Sartre's existentialism as well as the Frankfurt School's socio-psychoanalytic approach. Arendt's magnum opus, *The Origins of Totalitarianism* ([1951] 1973), is a triptych: she begins with the development of anti-Semitism in Western and Central Europe that she then connects to colonial imperialism, and ultimately to both Nazi and Soviet totalitarianism. She insists that totalitarianism was a new form of political rule, transcending the traditional concepts of tyranny, despotism, and dictatorship. She thus rethinks the paradigm of totalitarianism, explaining how National Socialism and Marxism were linked by using terror in the service of an ideology that worked to control the masses. Total domination was realized in the camps, which were different from prior penal colonies, religious persecutions, or slavery.

Accounting for modern anti-Semitism within this process, Arendt insisted that it was categorically different from Christian anti-Judaism. She explicitly derided the notion of "eternal anti-Semitism." Modern anti-Semitism could only be explained historically by accounting for the role of the Jews in the development of modernity. "Modern anti-Semitism," she asserted, "must be seen in the more general framework of the development of the nation-state, and at the same time its source must be found in certain aspects of Jewish history and specifically Jewish functions during the last centuries" ([1951] 1973, p. 9). Arendt's historicist turn would help to launch the dominant approach to analyzing anti-Semitism, as historians became the key interpreters of the underlying causes of anti-Semitism rather than social scientists or philosophers. After Arendt, the field of anti-Semitism became more specialized, which is why all the historiographic essays that exist tracing regional or national histories begin in this epoch.

Conclusion

As this essay has shown, the first historical monographs on anti-Semitism emerged with the rise of anti-Semitism as a political movement in the 1880s, and more specifically with the Dreyfus Affair in France (1894–1906) when they reached a zenith. But these initial efforts often still blamed Jews and Judaism for their persecution and understood Jewishness within a racial optic. They insisted that if Jews changed their habits, their oppression would end. The settlement of the Peace of Paris after World War I shifted the discussion to how race and nation were intertwined in the context of the formation of new nation-states and to exploring how groups defined themselves against targeted Others.

Only with the rise of the Nazis, however, did scholars begin explicitly to turn attention from the object of hatred (i.e. Jews) to the subject who hates (i.e. anti-Semites). Historians and social theorists began to focus on explaining why anti-Semites targeted Jews and why this mattered to the populations that acted on this ideology. This turn was the beginning of the critical historiography on anti-Semitism. At the same time, during the 1940s the classical theories about the causes of anti-Semitism arose, as the core explanatory frameworks for anti-Semitism developed directly in response to the Holocaust. Nazi anti-Semitism came to form a template for all forms of Judeophobia. A narrative of the eternal hatred of Jews within the West also became prominent.

In the 1950s, as decolonization and the Civil Rights movement geared up, social theorists and philosophers turned their attention more exclusively to anti-Black racism, leaving historians as the primary scholars on the topic of anti-Semitism. The field expanded and began to splinter. A proliferation of studies emerged, most often focused on individual regions, countries, or key figures that contributed to a historiography of subfields. The best work continued to rethink earlier conceptualizations of anti-Semitism. Existing historiographies thus often start their overviews in the 1950s or 1960s (Brown 1994, pp. 249–328; Pulzer 2005) because of their focus on national or regional histories of anti-Semitism. A historiographic survey of the field's emergence, its early development, and the intellectual and social factors in response to which its underlying concepts and narratives were formed has thus been a lacuna in the study of anti-Semitism. This overview attempts to fill this gap.

References

Arendt, Hannah. (1951) 1973. *The Origins of Totalitarianism*. San Diego: Harcourt Brace Jovanovich.
Bernstein, Peretz Fritz. 1951. *Jew Hate as a Sociological Problem*. New York: Philosophical Library.
Blitz, Samuel. 1928. *Nationalism: A Cause of Anti-Semitism*. New York: Bloch Publishing.
Brown, Michael, ed. 1994. *Approaches to Antisemitism: Context and Curriculum*. New York: American Jewish Committee.
Butler, Rohan. 1941. *The Roots of National Socialism, 1783–1933*. London: Faber and Faber.
Diesendruck, Zevi. 1946. "Antisemitism and Ourselves." In Pinson 1946, 41–48.
Flowerman, Samuel. 1949. Introduction to *Rehearsal for Destruction: A Study of Political Anti-Semitism in Imperial Germany*, by Paul Massing, xiii–xiv. New York: Harper.
Freund, Ismar. 1922. *Der Judenhaß: Ein Beitrag zu seiner Geschichte und Psychologie*. Berlin: Philo Verlag.
Goldmann, Felix. 1920. *Vom Wesen des Antisemitismus*. Berlin: Philo Verlag.
Horkheimer, Max, and Theodor W. Adorno. 2000. *Dialectic of Enlightenment*. New York: Continuum.
Kushner, Tony. 2005. Foreword to *Campaigner Against Antisemitism: The Reverend James Parkes, 1896–1981*, edited by Colin Richmond and Tony Kushner. Portland: Vallentine Mitchell.
Lazare, Bernard. 1995. *Antisemitism: Its History and Causes*. Lincoln: University of Nebraska Press.
Leroy-Beaulieu, Anatole. 1895. *Israel Among the Nations: A Study of the Jews and Antisemitism*. Translated by Frances Hellman. London: W. Heinemann.
Massing, Paul. 1949. *Rehearsal for Destruction: A Study of Political Anti-Semitism in Imperial Germany*. New York: Harper.
Neumann, Franz. 2009. *Behemoth: The Structure and Practice of National Socialism, 1933–1944*. Chicago: Ivan R. Dee.
Parkes, James William. 1969. *The Conflict of the Church and the Synagogue: A Study in the Origins of Antisemitism*. New York: Atheneum.

Parsons, Talcott. 1942. "The Sociology of Modern Anti-Semitism." In *Jews in a Gentile World: The Problem of Anti-Semitism*, edited by Isacque Graeber and Steuart Henderson Britt, 101–122. New York: Macmillan.

Pulzer, Peter. 2005. "Third Thoughts on German and Austrian Anti-Semitism." *Journal of Modern Jewish Studies* 4 (2) (July): 137–78.

Reichmann, Eva. 1949. *Hostages of Civilisation: The Social Sources of National Socialist Anti-Semitism*. Westport: Greenwood.

Roth, Cecil. 1938. "The Mediaeval Conception of the Jew: A New Interpretation." In *Essays and Studies in Memory of Linda R. Miller*, edited by Israel Davidson, 171–90. New York: Jewish Theological Seminary of America.

Samuel, Maurice. 1940. *The Great Hatred*. New York: Alfred A. Knopf.

Trachtenberg, Joshua. 1983. *The Devil and The Jews: The Medieval Conception of the Jew and Its Relation to Modern Anti-Semitism*. Philadelphia: Jewish Publication Society.

Valentin, Hugo. 1936. *Anti-Semitism: Historically and Critically Examined*. New York: Viking.

Wolf, Lucien. 1910–1911. "Anti-Semitism." In *Encyclopaedia Britannica*, vol. 2, 11th ed., 134–46. Cambridge: Cambridge University Press.

Zweig, Arnold. 1927. *Caliban, oder Politik und Leidenschaft: Versuch über die menschlichen Gruppenleidenschaften dargetan am Antisemitismus*. Potsdam: Kiepenhaeuer.

CHAPTER 4

Anti-Zionism

James Loeffler

Of all the keywords frequently included in the modern lexicon of antisemitism, "anti-Zionism" may be the most resistant to conceptual analysis. This is not merely, as one might expect, because of the heated political debates that attend the subject today in connection with the Israeli–Palestinian conflict. Rather, the challenge to any conceptualization of anti-Zionism and its connection to antisemitism derives from the slippery semantics that characterize the relationship between the two terms. Is anti-Zionism an ideological offshoot of antisemitism? Or is it a wholly distinct political concept that only intersects with antisemitism intermittently like a Venn diagram? Is it a matter of degree or category?

These are not simple questions to answer. Nor is this merely a matter of academic hair-splitting. For instance, in response to concerns about increased confrontations and intimidation directed at Jewish students on American college campuses, the U.S. Congress recently drafted the Anti-Semitism Awareness Act of 2019. This law, intended to provide (in the context of the 1964 U.S. Civil Rights Act) an authoritative "definition of anti-Semitism for the enforcement of Federal antidiscrimination laws concerning education programs or activities" (U.S. Congress 2019, p. 1), relies on the U.S. State Department official statement of 2010, which, in turn, lists four criteria to identify "anti-Semitic conduct that is couched as anti-Israel or anti-Zionist" and "discriminatory anti-Israel conduct that crosses the line into anti-Semitism" (U.S. Congress 2019, pp. 4–5). The 2010 definition concludes, however, with a crucial caveat: "However, criticism of Israel similar

J. Loeffler (✉)
University of Virginia, Charlottesville, VA, USA
e-mail: james.loeffler@virginia.edu

to that leveled against any other country cannot be regarded as anti-Semitic" (U.S. Department of State 2010, p. 1). By implication, what anti-Zionism is can only be decided comparatively. It is thus not exclusively the *content* of anti-Zionist ideology that determines whether it is antisemitic, but the *context* in which criticism occurs.

Context is, of course, the hallmark of modern historicism. Yet when it comes to anti-Zionism, historians have shown a surprising reluctance to fully historicize the term. Rather than see its broader meaning as context-dependent, scholars have typically posited fixed, ahistorical definitions of anti-Zionism, then proceeded to track how the concept converges and diverges over time with antisemitism. Some even speak of a borderline across which the two become one permanently. The historian's task then becomes, sometimes explicitly and other times implicitly, to pinpoint that relationship.

This yardstick approach arguably has its virtues. It allows for cases to be compared, for the relative size and intensity of anti-Zionism to be traced through time, and for linkages to causal drivers to be sought in the form of historical events. But in the final analysis, this yardstick approach fails to establish *how* antisemitic and anti-Zionist ideologies interact and shape one another through time. That is because it rests on an ahistorical assumption that anti-Zionism possesses a static character that reveals itself in discrete episodes. Few scholars would allow such a position vis-à-vis the history of antisemitism. Indeed, it is an axiom in scholarly histories of antisemitism that a context-dependent phenomenon must be viewed as dynamic and subject to constant change. Yet anti-Zionism rarely if ever receives a similar form of critical historical analysis. As a result, while the historical past is constantly invoked today in some cases to justify anti-Zionist politics and in others to critique anti-Zionism on grounds of deeper linkages to antisemitism, history itself is flattened out in a most ahistorical way.

In this essay, I begin with a methodological critique of this predominant approach before proposing an alternative method of analysis focused on several main strands in anti-Zionism's intellectual genealogy. Doing so promises a better understanding of the specific origins of anti-Zionism as a distinct, self-conscious ideology without reducing it to an essentialist definition. Furthermore, mapping such a historical genealogy allows us to see how the concept of anti-Zionism is repeatedly linked to antisemitism—though not in the ways many might assume. For even a preliminary examination of the usage of the term "anti-Zionism" and its morphological variants across the twentieth-century world yields a surprising result. The entanglement of the two terms is less a by-product of later historical contingencies such as the establishment of the State of Israel, the Nakba, or the Six-Day War than it is a defining condition of their relationship from the outset. The meanings of the two words have not converged or diverged so much as evolved together, in dialectical fashion, from the early twentieth century down to the present.

* * *

Historians have long debated the question of continuity and discontinuity in the history of antisemitism. But there is little question that the appearance of a specific neologism "anti-Semitism" in the 1870s marked a turning point. The word itself served to consolidate a wide array of anti-Jewish stereotypes and ideological prejudices, some deep-rooted and others unique to the modern period, into a self-conscious ideology of anti-Jewish animus. A new word signified a new idea. What, then, of the history of the term "anti-Zionism"? Curiously enough, there have been no systematic scholarly attempts to track its appearance. This is not for lack of interest in the subject itself. The nexus of antisemitism and anti-Zionism in Arab, Islamic, Communist, and radical Left politics has received extensive scrutiny. But "anti-Zionism" as a catch-phrase, let alone a theoretical concept, has resisted such inquiry. Why is this the case?

The common explanation is that in contrast to a complex form of ideological hatred such as antisemitism, "anti-Zionism" simply constitutes a generic opposition to the Zionist movement and the State of Israel. Unlike antisemitism, then, anti-Zionism is not even a fully formed ideology but a reflexive political position. While premodern anti-Judaism and anti-Jewishness morphed over time into "anti-Semitism," or even more plainly, "antisemitism," opposition to Zionism remained merely "*anti*-Zionism" (Miller 2000, p. 1).

Just because antisemitism has a singular semantic history, however, it does not follow that anti-Zionism has none. If antisemitism arguably risks being *over*-theorized in contemporary scholarship, anti-Zionism remains strangely *under*-theorized (Engel 2009). This is true even in the quarters where much ink is spent in writing the putative history of anti-Zionism. A case in point is the dominant scholarship of the late historian Robert Wistrich. In his publications on the subject from the 1970s through to posthumous works, Wistrich time and again revisited the range of anti-Zionist and antisemitic political expressions in European and Middle Eastern society. Yet in spite of his continual insistence on the deep, continuous blurring of the lines between antisemitism and anti-Zionism, he never offered any historical definition of the latter term. In fact, he stressed that it was not even an ideology per se. Anti-Zionism, in his estimation, consisted merely of political antagonism directed toward Zionism. Such a position "may not always have been anti-Jewish in origin and intention," claimed Wistrich, and it only acquired antisemitic significance when it fell "into the established groove of an endemic antisemitism that has been a central feature of civilization for more than two millennia" (1985, p. 22). The study of anti-Zionism for Wistrich, then, remained little more than an exercise focused on measuring when political rhetoric becomes antisemitic.

Other scholars have proffered more nuanced historical accounts of certain varieties of anti-Zionist expression throughout the twentieth century (Penslar 2006; Myers 2006; Eisenberg 1998). Yet to date there have been no broad synthetic historical accounts as there have long been in the case of antisemitism. The reason seems to be an underlying assumption shared across a broad swathe of these historians that anti-Zionism does not possess its own independent history. An elementary political position is only an extension of other ideologies, such as Arab nationalism or Communism. Antisemitism, by contrast, is often viewed as a complex, freestanding ideology. Talk of a convergence between the two at some point after 1948 or 1967 or 1991 or 2001 then comes to mean simply when anti-Zionism acquires antisemitic overtones or undertones. The term itself remains a rigid descriptor; only its relationship to antisemitism changes.

The virtue of this approach is that it allows for a typological analysis of ideas, images, and attitudes regardless of the declared intent behind such expressions. Just as we would not measure racism only by those who call themselves racist, we naturally do not restrict the study of anti-Zionism to those who employ the term as a self-description. The problem with a yardstick approach, however, is that it merely replicates a model of ideas without sufficiently scrutinizing the language that carries the concepts. Semantic shifts matter. Historical analysis of anti-Zionism requires mapping its lexical appearance across various cultures, countries, and contexts—and its changing relationship to the term "antisemitism." Only once we have achieved that can we contemplate writing a proper history of anti-Zionism. What follows is a preliminary genealogical inquiry into the interaction between these two ideas in three key contexts: Anglo-American Jewish anti-Zionism, Arab anti-Zionism, and Communist anti-Zionism.

* * *

It is often observed that the first anti-Zionists were those Jewish opponents of the Zionist movement, which made its appearance in the final two decades of the nineteenth century. Some traditionalist Jewish religious leaders in Europe and the Middle East viewed its stated aims as incompatible with Jewish beliefs regarding the Jews' historical exile and the arrival of the messianic era (Wistrich 1996). At the same time, many Western Jewish liberal religious and lay leaders opposed the political implications of defining Jews as a distinct ethnic nation with an international politics of its own (Wistrich 1998; Laqueur 1971; Cohen 1951). Finally, some Sephardic Jewish elites in the Ottoman Empire worried on a more practical level that the Zionist aspirations for Palestine would jeopardize Jews' legal and social position in Ottoman society (Campos 2011, pp. 210–17). What united all of these early critics was a view of Zionism as a deviation from a normative form of Judaism, along with a shared belief that Zionism would trigger still more antisemitism.

Concerned primarily about the risk Zionism posed to Jews, early anti-Zionist Jewish publicists tended to present their ideas as corrections to an ideational error in the context of an intramural conversation among Jews rather than as a formal ideological doctrine. The Anglo-Jewish journalist and diplomat Lucien Wolf, for instance, described himself in a 1904 article as "a convinced and uncompromising anti-Zionist." Yet he declined to formulate a systematic definition of his views. It sufficed to point out all the faults in Zionist thought and to reassert alternative ideals of Jewishness: "The real Jewish Nationalism, the only true Zion," Wolf argued, was a prophetic ideal of "lofty toleration and real universalism" (1904, pp. 1, 21). He depicted Zionism as a false doctrine that would only stimulate more antisemitism rather than defeat it. Anti-Zionism signaled a return to some imagined ideals of a purer universalist religion of Judaism that would coincidentally further the cause of Jewish self-definition as Europeans—and prevent antisemitism. To explain "Why I Am an Anti-Zionist," American Rabbi Emanuel Schreiber wrote a series of articles in 1921 attacking Zionist assumptions about historical progress: "The whole structure, yea the very foundation of Zionism is based on Pessimism, hopelessness and despair" (1921a, p. 12). Zionist schemes for solving the Jewish Question of Europe via emigration were not only foolish and impractical, but played right into the hands of the antisemites: "Ever since the inception of Zionism the anti-Semites of the whole world hailed the Zionist movement as the best thing that could have happened to the non-Jews" (1921b, p. 11).

The success of the Zionist movement in securing the Balfour Declaration in 1917 and beginning to grow a formal Jewish polity in British Mandatory Palestine produced an important change in political discourse among Zionism's Jewish opponents. Increasingly in the 1920s and 1930s, British and American Jewish critics discarded the appellation "anti-Zionist" in favor of the self-designation "non-Zionist" (Knee 1977; Shimoni 1986). To date, there has been no systematic study of "non-Zionism" as distinguished from "anti-Zionism." Scattered evidence and local case studies suggest, however, that the phrase crystallized in Jewish parlance as a crucial mediating term between other forms of anti-Zionism and Zionism. By 1940, for instance, the leaders of the American Jewish Committee (AJC), a leading communal organization, could still reject the Zionist movement's language of political nationalism yet voice support for the basic Zionist aim of Jewish territorial sovereignty in Palestine. "A very sharp distinction must be drawn between *Zionism*, defined as a movement to secure in Palestine the right for Jews to settle and establish a Jewish community or perhaps eventually even a state," wrote AJC executive director Morris Waldman in 1940, "and, on the other hand, *Jewish nationalism*, which is the view that all Jews, wherever they may be, belong to the Jewish nation and have a right to establish the counterpart of a national government with branches in the various countries in which Jews live" (quoted in Loeffler 2018, p. 187). After 1948, AJC leader Jacob Blaustein likewise repeatedly emphasized in his dealings with U.S. officials and Arab diplomats that he was "neither a Zionist nor an anti-Zionist, but a non-Zionist" (quoted in Loeffler 2018, p. 190). These and other similar-minded Jewish leaders readily accepted and openly supported Israel, even as they continued to recoil from its nationalist implications for the broader global politics of Jewish collective identity.

This trend of non-Zionism developed in part thanks to the crystallization of a new strident ideology of Jewish anti-Zionism. The central organization in this process, the American Council for Judaism, founded in 1943, departed from its forebears in asserting that Zionism was not just a threat to ideals of Jewish emancipation or non-political identity. Nor was anti-Zionism but a misapprehension of the ideals of Judaism. Rather it was its polar opposite. As ACJ founder Rabbi Elmer Berger wrote in 1957, earlier Jewish anti-Zionists had never successfully delineated their ideology, leaving Jews without a proper definition of "what anti-Zionism really is." It was now the task of his organization to take up that charge (Berger 1960, p. 5).

The ACJ's own definition consisted of three crucial points that would also mark subsequent iterations of Jewish anti-Zionism. First, Berger insisted on a sharp distinction between Judaism and Zionism: "[T]he principle that Judaism is a religion—not a nationalism—is the basis of the anti-Zionism of the American Council for Judaism" (1957, p. 11). From a heretical deviation from classical Judaism, Zionism was now defined as its very *antithesis*. The second component of this new ideology was a preemptive insistence that "anti-Zionists are neither anti-Jewish nor anti-Semitic" (Berger 1957, p. 27). Because of the newfound centrality of the Jewish state to global Jewish identity in the wake of the Holocaust, any Jewish anti-Zionist faced self-evident pressure to explain why fellow Jews would attack a Jewish country. Finally, Berger and his colleagues stressed that Zionism was not only the cause of antisemitism but *itself* a form of antisemitism. To illustrate this argument, the ACJ expended considerable effort across the 1950s and 1960s to secure legal rulings and policy statements from U.S. State Department officials and legal experts to the effect that Zionism constituted a form of state-sponsored legal discrimination on the basis of race and religion *against* American Jewish citizens (Mallison 1962–1963; Coleman 1964).

The ACJ never grew beyond its status as a small, fringe organization in the American Jewish communal landscape. Nonetheless, its rhetoric resonated more broadly in the work of later twentieth-century American Jewish intellectuals such as Daniel Boyarin and Judith Butler. These thinkers categorized Zionism as a gross historical deviation from the more authentic traditions of diaspora Judaism; for them anti-Zionism represented not only a principled ideological opposition to Zionism but a necessary ethical move to define a contemporary Jewish radical politics (Cooper 2015).

This same emphasis on anti-Zionism as essential to a latter-day Jewish politics reveals itself in the platform of the contemporary American group, Jewish Voice for Peace. Founded in 1996, this organization self-consciously situates itself in a long historical tradition of "anti-Zionist Jews" ("Our Approach"). Jewish Voice for Peace "unequivocally opposes Zionism" not only because of Israel's "racist" harm to Jews and non-Jews alike ("Our Approach"), but in order to fulfill a pressing political imperative in the name of solidarity. "[I] t is important that JVP is a Jewish group," they write, because "Israel claims to be acting in the name of the Jewish people, so we are compelled to make sure the world knows that many Jews are opposed to their actions. There are often attempts to silence critics of Israel by conflating legitimate criticism with anti-Semitism" ("FAQ"). Acknowledging the controversial debates over the line between antisemitism and anti-Zionism, in other words, they seek to use their Jewishness to shield other non-Jewish forms of anti-Zionism from charges of antisemitism.

* * *

A similar complex dynamic between anti-Zionism and antisemitism has long featured prominently in Arab anti-Zionism. As far back as the 1890s, Arab leaders in Ottoman Palestine expressed reservations about the new Zionist immigration and land purchases. Then, in the context of the young Turk Revolution of 1908, rhetorical flourishes of explicit anti-Zionism began to appear among local Arab nationalist leaders. From the outset, the question of the borderline between political opposition to Zionism and the taboo of antisemitism surfaced in commentaries. In his famous 1911 speech in the Ottoman parliament, for instance, Jerusalem notable Ruhi Al-Khalidi denounced the Zionists for a religiously inspired plot to create "a Jewish kingdom having Jerusalem as its centre" (quoted in Beska 2016, p. 187). While he argued that Zionism posed a grave political danger to the Ottoman Empire, he preemptively defended his own rhetoric from charges of anti-Jewish prejudice. "Just as I am an anti-Zionist," declared Al-Khalidi, "I am not an anti-Semite, which is proved by the letters sent here by the rabbi of Izmir and other rabbis who oppose Zionism" (quoted in Beska 2014, p. 59; cf. Fishman 2011, pp. 111–12). Self-conscious attempts to decouple anti-Zionism from antisemitism by reference to Jewish anti-Zionists would emerge as a staple of Arab political rhetoric for the next hundred years (Gribetz 2017).

A second characteristic of early Arab anti-Zionism was an impulse to preempt accusations of antisemitism by deconstructing the terms "Jew" and "Semite." In the immediate aftermath of World War I, Arab nationalist intellectuals seeking a rhetorical trope to delegitimize Jewish political claims to territorial nationhood in Palestine began to voice their own Semitic racial theory. In his 1921 *The Case Against Zionism*, for instance, the director of the Arab National League in the United States, Habib Katibah, wrote, "The predominant race in Palestine is the Semitic race; so whatever may be said about the opposition of the Palestinians to Zionism, it is not anti-Semitism" (1921, p. 16). To be an Arab anti-Zionist, in other words, meant to attack Zionism, often in flagrantly ideological terms, while strenuously disavowing any bias against Judaism and its adherents (Loeffler 2018, pp. 160–61).

To be sure, not all Arab anti-Zionists took this tack. In the 1930s and 1940s, the increasingly Islamist rhetoric of the Mufti Amin al-Husseini in Palestine and the Muslim Brotherhood in Egypt frequently collapsed the rhetorical distinctions between Jews and Zionists, anti-Zionism and anti-semitism (Herf 2006). The Arab League's diplomatic rhetoric in the 1940s and 1950s likewise blurred the line between Zionists, Jews, and Israelis. Yet strikingly, many Muslim and Arab diplomats in the 1960s and 1970s continued to offer a distinction between antisemitism and anti-Zionism in international diplomatic fora. Likewise, in its 1968 charter the Palestinian Liberation Organization combined an attack on Zionism as "racist and fanatic in its nature, aggressive, expansionist, and colonial in its aims, and fascist in its methods" with a renunciation of all "discrimination of race, color, language, or religion," and an assertation that all "Jews who normally had resided in Palestine" before 1917 are "considered Palestinians," and welcome to remain, since Judaism "is a religion… not an independent nationality" (PLO 1968).

That entanglement persists even today. The revised 2017 Charter of the Palestinian group Hamas, the Islamic Resistance Movement, departs from its earlier rhetoric of "a struggle against the Jews" and "Israel, Jews, and Judaism" as the evil enemies of "Islam and Muslim people" (Hamas [1988] 2004) to a position of explicitly disavowing antisemitism: "Hamas rejects the persecution of any human being or the undermining of his or her rights on nationalist, religious or sectarian grounds. Hamas is of the view that the Jewish problem, anti-Semitism and the persecution of the Jews are phenomena fundamentally linked to European history and not to the history of the Arabs and the Muslims" (2017). Scholars have questioned how much this rhetorical distinction is merely a propagandistic tactic in Arab and Muslim politics, then and now. But the entanglement undoubtedly reflects a longer, more complicated ideological continuity in Arab anti-Zionist discourse worthy of further study.

* * *

If anti-Zionism first appeared in parallel in smaller Jewish circles and in Arab politics, developing down through the twentieth century, it spread into a global ideology thanks to the platforms and prestige of global Communism. In explaining the origins of this phenomenon, historians have often been hard pressed to reconcile two contradictory facts. On the one hand, Marxist revolutionary socialism evinced a deep hostility to Zionism and Jewish nationhood from the 1890s onward. Lenin canonized this position in his early speeches and writings against the Jewish Labor Bund, in which he elevated Zionism into a unique form of bourgeois nationalism that threatened the revolutionary cause. For their part, too, the Jewish Labor Bund developed a political philosophy of "doikeyt," or "here-ness," centered on a symbolic rejection of Zionism's telos of migration out of Europe and back to Zion. On the other hand, the early Soviet authorities did not immediately move to demonize Zionism as they did religious Judaism and even Jewish Bundism. Soviet Zionism existed in a state of semi-legal legitimacy up through the end of the 1920s (Galili and Morozov 2006, pp. 6–9). Even then, Zionism itself provoked little direct comment from Soviet ideologues. More crucially, Stalin chose to recognize and arm the State of Israel in 1948. Yet he did so at the very moment of inception of the Soviet policy of anti-Cosmopolitanism. That sweeping ideological campaign against Westernism and Jewishness collapsed the difference between the two, as well as between "Jews" and "Zionists," accusing all of a secretive world plot against Communism on behalf of Western, especially United States, interests. It led to the show trials and execution of the leading Jewish intellectuals of the Soviet Union, and inspired a half-decade of antisemitic state terror before Stalin's death in 1953 (Frankel 1991; Gitelman 1990; Brent and Naumov 2004).

Despite the anti-Cosmopolitan campaign, it was only in the early 1960s, in the context of the Cold War and the rising anti-colonial movement, that the Soviets began to export a distinct ideology of anti-Zionism. This policy change emerged out of a more aggressive orientation toward the growing ties between Israel, West Germany, and the United States and sensitivity to the Soviet regime's own internal antisemitism problem. This new propaganda campaign focused in part on the United Nations and the debates over racism, human rights, and international law. There, Soviet spokesmen denounced Zionism as a racist ideology, akin to Nazism, while at the same time vocally denouncing antisemitism. Typical of this process was a 1964 UN speech on human rights, in which the Soviet representative called for international legal action to ensure the "speedy eradication [of] antisemitism, Zionism, Nazism, neo-Nazism and all other forms of the policy and ideology of colonialism, national and race hatred and exclusiveness" (quoted in Loeffler 2018, pp. 252–53).

This pattern of pairing antisemitism with Zionism continued and intensified in both Soviet and Arab political rhetoric in the aftermath of the Six-Day War in 1967. Soviet writings regularly equated Zionism directly with the practice of "genocide" in Palestine, while also stressing the need to combat the "virus of antisemitism." Soviet anti-Zionism adopted and expanded the claim that Zionism itself was an intrinsically racist ideology. In the aftermath of the 1975 UN GA Resolution 3379, in which the UN General Assembly voted to label Zionism a form of racism, Soviet propagandists increasingly spoke of racism as *the* core animating principle of Zionism. Thus in 1981 V. A. Semeniuk wrote that in its very essence, Zionism privileges Jews over non-Jews and is thus "a form of racism and racial discrimination" (p. 35) that "exploits antisemitism to justify its own existence" (p. 58). In an attempt to forestall criticism, Soviet officials frequently employed Jewish spokespeople as mouthpieces for anti-Zionist rhetoric (Korey 1989).

Beyond inverting Zionism from a response to antisemitism into antisemitism itself, the other main feature of this Communist anti-Zionism doctrine was to expand "Zionist" and "anti-Zionist" from derogative terms linked narrowly to the Arab–Israeli conflict and the debates over Zionism into larger, free-floating signifiers in a transnational radical Left discourse regarding globalization and the United States. This trend found a parallel expression in Communist Poland, East Germany, and other parts of the Communist Empire. There, anti-Zionism developed into a specific ideological discourse that fused new and old tropes, domestic politics and foreign policy into a larger ideology that demonized Zionism and Jewishness alike (Stola 2000; Dahlmann 2013; Herf 2016).

* * *

The expiration of global Communism and the launch of a formal Israeli–Palestinian peace process led many in the 1990s to anticipate the end of anti-Zionism, if not antisemitism. Yet already in the same decade some scholars began to speak of a new ideological surge that permanently fused antisemitism and earlier overlapping strains of anti-Zionism, along with extremist Islamic theology, into a potent new anti-Jewish ideology. Whatever it had been in the past, wrote Yehuda Bauer in 1990, anti-Zionism has become de facto antisemitic, since the assimilation of classically antisemitic tropes into the stock vocabulary and imagery of anti-Zionism had effected an irreversible change: "[Today's] anti-Zionists are, whether they realize it or not, antisemites" (1990, p. 208). While historians differ strongly on Bauer's conclusions about a decisive convergence between anti-Zionism and antisemitism, scholars are increasingly sensitive to the fundamental blurring of terminological and conceptual boundaries in contemporary political discourse.

This new trend has produced debates around the question of whether it is possible to make ontological distinctions between antisemitism and anti-Zionism (Freedland 2004; Wistrich 2016). Anti-Zionists and their critics each invoke history—of Zionism, anti-Zionism, and antisemitism—to justify their positions and explain what is and is not antisemitic. Yet in spite of this intense interest, there have still been precious few attempts to historicize these terms in relation to one another. Instead, most contemporary discourse gestures at the past only to center its disputes about present-day intent and effect. If this might be seen as a hyper-qualitative approach, a parallel phenomenon of hyper-quantification has also emerged of late. This policy-driven research takes the form of attempts to perfect the correct measurement of antisemitism and anti-Zionism in the global arena. Organizations ranging from American and Israeli academic institutions to the Anti-Defamation League in the United States and the Institute for Jewish Policy Research in the United Kingdom have focused extensively on mapping local and global antisemitism using quantitative polling methods. The European Antisemitism Survey and ADL Index of Antisemitism, for instance, stress precise tracking and extensive measurement of antisemitic acts and attitudes across countries. Much of this cataloging play influential roles in shaping political and legislative debates about anti-Zionism and antisemitism in Europe and the United States. It has produced a set of statistics that are cited at regular intervals to explain the rise in antisemitism and anti-Zionism, and the ties between them. Yet rarely is this discussion accompanied by larger contextualization or longitudinal analysis.

To be sure, measurement has its place. But without a baseline understanding of the deeper contextual questions about entanglements, convergences, and divergences in the histories of antisemitism and anti-Zionism, it is likely to remain a sterile science that documents without explanation and provokes without critical reflection. As this chapter has aimed to demonstrate, a fuller inquiry into anti-Zionism needs to begin with a more precise calibration of the terms in question across various contexts, especially in non-English-speaking cultures. The growth of networks and the migration of keywords and calques between disparate contexts is a second, vital step to take. Most of all, such an inquiry will have to engage with the proliferation of related terms that often mediate between the dialectical poles of antisemitism and anti-Zionism, yet which receive even less scholarly scrutiny, among them "non-Zionist," "anti-Israel," and "pro-Israel."

In the end, an incessant drive to measure the intensity of contemporary anti-Zionism and catalogue its antecedents will yield little insight absent a proper historical reconstruction of the evolution of the term itself (Volkov 2006, 2011). That exercise will require grappling with the constant historical interplay between anti-Zionism and antisemitism, even as the meanings accruing to both words have inevitably changed throughout time. Measurement and definition are crucial tools of the historian. Without contextualization, however, we risk forever finding the subject as we expect to find it, rather than applying the powerful lens of history to realize the distance between the present and the past.

Acknowledgements I thank Lila Corwin Berman, Ari Joskowicz, Mira Sucharov, and the editors of this volume for their incisive comments and suggestions.

References

Bauer, Yehuda. 1990. "Antisemitism and Anti-Zionism—New and Old." In *Anti-Zionism and Antisemitism in the Contemporary World*, edited by Robert Wistrich, 195–208. London: Palgrave.

Berger, Elmer. 1957. *Judaism or Jewish Nationalism: The Alternative to Zionism*. New York: Bookman Associates.

Berger, Elmer. 1960. "The Old Wolf—In Sheep's Clothing." *Issues* 14 (2) (Spring): 5–7.

Beska, Emanuel. 2014. "Political Opposition to Zionism in Palestine and Greater Syria: 1910–1911 as a Turning Point." *Jerusalem Quarterly* 59: 54–67.

Beska, Emanuel. 2016. "The Anti-Zionist Attitudes and Activities of Ruhi al-Khalidi." In *Arabic and Islamic Studies in Honour of Ján Pauliny*, edited by Zuzana Gažáková and Jaroslav Drobný, 181–203. Bratislava: Comenius University.

Brent, Jonathan, and Vladimir Naumov. 2004. *Stalin's Last Crime: The Plot Against the Jewish Doctors, 1948–1953*. New York: Harper Collins.

Campos, Michelle. 2011. *Ottoman Brothers: Muslims, Christians, and Jews in Early Twentieth-Century Palestine*. Stanford: Stanford University Press.

Cohen, Naomi Wiener. 1951. "The Reaction of Reform Judaism in America to Political Zionism (1897–1922)." *Publications of the American Jewish Historical Society* 40 (4) (Spring): 361–94.

Coleman, Clarence. 1964. "U.S. Rejects the 'Jewish People' Concept." *Issues* 18 (6) (Fall–Winter): 2–6.

Cooper, Julie. 2015. "A Diasporic Critique of Diasporism: The Question of Jewish Political Agency." *Political Theory* 43 (1): 80–110.

Dahlmann, Hans-Christian. 2013. *Antisemitismus in Polen 1968: Interaktionen zwischen Partei und Gesellschaft*. Osnabrück: Warsaw GHI.

Eisenberg, Ellen. 1998. "Beyond San Francisco: The Failure of Anti-Zionism in Portland, Oregon." *American Jewish History* 86 (3) (September): 309–21.

Engel, David. 2009. "Away from a Definition of Antisemitism. An Essay in the Semantics of Historical Description." In *Rethinking European Jewish History*, edited by J. Cohen and M. Rosman, 30–53. Oxford: Oxford University Press.

Fishman, Louis. 2011. "Understanding the 1911 Ottoman Parliament Debate on Zionism in Light of the Emergence of a 'Jewish Question.'" In *Late Ottoman Palestine: The Period of Young Turk Rule*, edited by Yuval Ben-Bassat and Eyal Ginio, 103–23. New York: I.B. Tauris.

Frankel, Jonathan. 1991. "The Soviet Regime and Anti-Zionism: An Analysis." In *Jewish Culture and Identity in the Soviet Union*, edited by Yaacov Ro'i and Avi Beker, 310–54. New York: New York University Press.

Freedland, Jonathan. 2004. "Is Anti-Zionism Anti-Semitism?" In *Those Who Forget the Past: The Question of Anti-Semitism*, edited by Ron Rosenbaum, 422–37. New York: Random House.

Galili, Ziva, and Boris Morozov. 2006. *Exiled to Palestine: The Emigration of Zionist Convicts from the Soviet Union, 1924–1934*. London: Frank Cass.

Gitelman, Zvi. 1990. "The Evolution of Soviet Anti-Zionism: From Principle to Pragmatism." In *Anti-Zionism and Antisemitism in the Contemporary World*, edited by Robert Wistrich, 11–25. London: Palgrave.

Gribetz, Jonathan. 2017. "The PLO's Rabbi: Palestinian Nationalism and Reform Judaism." *Jewish Quarterly Review* 107 (1): 90–112.

Hamas. (1988) 2004. "The Covenant of the Islamic Resistance Movement." In *Israel in the Middle East*, edited by Itamar Rabinovich and Jehuda Reinharz, 2nd ed., 430–37. Waltham: Brandeis University Press.

Hamas. 2017. *A Document of General Principles and Policies*. http://hamas.ps/en/post/678/a-document-of-general-principles-and-policies.

Herf, Jeffrey. 2006. "Convergence: The Classic Case. Nazi Germany, Anti-Semitism and Anti-Zionism during World War II." *Journal of Israeli History* 25 (1) (March): 63–83.

Herf, Jeffrey. 2016. *Undeclared Wars with Israel: East Germany and the West German Far Left, 1967*. Cambridge: Cambridge University Press.

Katibah, Habib Ibrahim. 1921. *The Case Against Zionism*. New York: Palestine National League.

Knee, Stuart. 1977. "Jewish Non-Zionism in America and Palestine Commitment, 1917–1941." *Jewish Social Studies* 39 (3) (Summer): 209–26.

Korey, William. 1989. "The Soviet Public Anti-Zionist Committee: An Analysis." In *Soviet Jewry in the 1980s: The Politics of Anti-Semitism and Emigration and the Dynamics of Resettlement*, edited by Robert Freedman, 26–50. Durham: Duke University Press.

Laqueur, Walter. 1971. "Zionism and its Liberal Critics, 1896–1948." *Journal of Contemporary History* 6: 161–82.

Loeffler, James. 2018. *Rooted Cosmopolitans: Jews and Human Rights in the Twentieth Century*. New Haven: Yale University Press.

Mallison, W. Thomas, Jr. 1962–1963. "Zionist-Israel Claims on 'The Jewish People' Are Unconstitutional." *Issues* 16 (7) (Winter): 2–14.

Miller, Rory. 2000. *Divided Against Zion. Anti-Zionist Opposition in Britain to a Jewish State in Palestine, 1945–1948*. London: Frank Cass.

Myers, David N. 2006. "Can There Be a Principled Anti-Zionism? On the Nexus between Anti-Historicism and Anti-Zionism in Modern Jewish Thought." *Journal of Israeli History* 25 (1): 33–50.

Penslar, Derek. 2006. "Antisemites on Zionism: From Indifference to Obsession." In *Israel in History. The Jewish State in Comparative Perspective*, 112–29. London: Routledge.

PLO (Palestinian Liberation Organization). 1968. *The Palestinian National Charter: Resolutions of the Palestine National Council July 1–17*. The Avalon Project: Documents in Law, History, and Diplomacy. http://avalon.law.yale.edu/20th_century/plocov.asp.

Schreiber, Emanuel. 1921a. "Why I Am an Anti-Zionist." *Bnai Brith Messenger*, June 3, 12.

Schreiber, Emanuel. 1921b. "Why I Am an Anti-Zionist." *Bnai Brith Messenger*, September 30, 11.

Shimoni, Gideon. 1986. "From Anti-Zionism to Non-Zionism in Anglo-Jewry, 1917–1937." *Jewish Journal of Sociology* 28 (1) (June): 19–47.

Stola, Dariusz. 2000. *Kampania antysyjonistyczna w Polsce, 1967–1968*. Warsaw.

U.S. Congress. 2019. *Anti-Semitism Awareness Act of 2019*. S 852. 116th Cong., 1st sess. Introduced in Senate March 14. https://www.congress.gov/bill/116th-congress/senate-bill/852/text.

U.S. Department of State. 2010. "Defining Anti-Semitism." https://www.state.gov/s/rga/resources/267538.htm.

Volkov, Shulamit. 2006. "Readjusting Cultural Codes: Reflections on Anti-Semitism and Anti-Zionism." *Journal of Israeli History* 25 (1) (March): 51–62.

Volkov, Shulamit. 2011. "Tenu'a be-ma'agal: Heker ha-antishemiut mi-Shmuel Etinger u-hazara." *Tsiyon* 76 (3): 369–79.

Wistrich, Robert. 1985. *Anti-Zionism as an Expression of Antisemitism in Recent Years*. Jerusalem: Shazar Library, The Institute of Contemporary Jewry, Vidal Sassoon International Center for the Study of Antisemitism, The Hebrew University of Jerusalem.

Wistrich, Robert. 1996. "Zionism and Its Religious Critics in fin-de-siècle Vienna." *Jewish History* 10 (1) (Spring): 93–111.

Wistrich, Robert. 1998. "Zionism and Its Jewish 'Assimilationist' Critics (1897–1948)." *Jewish Social Studies* 4 (2) (Winter): 59–111.

Wistrich, Robert, ed. 2016. *Anti-Judaism, Antisemitism, and Delegitimizing Israel*. Lincoln: University of Nebraska Press.

Wolf, Lucien. 1904. "The Zionist Peril." *Jewish Quarterly Review* 17 (1) (October): 1–25.

CHAPTER 5

The Blood Libel

Hillel J. Kieval

I begin this investigation into the blood libel—also known as the ritual murder accusation—by looking at perception and the production of knowledge in societies, in particular, the ways in which received knowledge is applied to situations in the present. One prism through which members of Christian societies in medieval and early modern Europe understood the Jewish populations alongside whom they lived was provided by attitudes and beliefs that derived from their own storehouse of knowledge—transmitted through homily, sermon, and popular discourse—in which New Testament narratives of the Passion of Christ figured prominently. According to these stories, Jews in the time of Jesus opposed his divine mission, sought to block God's revelation, and, ultimately, conspired to have Jesus tried and executed by the Roman authorities in Judea. In their demands for retribution and their passive or active involvement in the Messiah's suffering, ancient Jews had assumed the role of enemies of God—but also that of instruments of the divine will. Centuries later members of Christian communities in Europe came to regard Jews in their own day as continuing to play a central role in the ongoing drama of salvation. Of course, to perceive the world in this way was to engage in a type of mythical thinking, by which I mean, implicitly connecting everyday experience to mythical, or sacred, time. In this uniting of past, present, and future, the Jew whom one encountered on the street, in the marketplace, or leaving the synagogue, could be indistinguishable from his or her mythical twin.

H. J. Kieval (✉)
Washington University, St. Louis, MO, USA
e-mail: hkieval@wustl.edu

© The Author(s) 2021
S. Goldberg et al. (eds.), *Key Concepts in the Study of Antisemitism*, Palgrave Critical Studies of Antisemitism and Racism, https://doi.org/10.1007/978-3-030-51658-1_5

Myth, however, was not the only prism through which Jews were encountered. In most situations, and for long stretches of time, concrete social interactions between Christians and Jews overshadowed the impulse to impose a mythical perspective on reality. But there were periods when deep engagement with symbol and myth altered—indeed distorted—the relationship between the two groups. England and France in the twelfth century and the Holy Roman Empire in the thirteenth and fourteenth centuries—when classic formulations of the blood libel took shape—are cases in point. The first recorded story of a "ritual murder" carried out by Jews on a Christian victim, patterned after New Testament precedents, relates to the disappearance and apparent murder of a Christian boy in the English city of Norwich in 1144, although it was not produced in the narrative form before 1150. The classic document, *The Life and Passion of William of Norwich*, was written by the Benedictine monk Thomas of Monmouth over a period of some twenty years, beginning with his arrival in Norwich six years after the disappearance and death of the boy William. Thomas' main motivation in producing his narrative appears to have been to establish William as a Christian martyr and to promote the Norwich Cathedral as a destination for Christian pilgrims. His *Life and Passion of William of Norwich* contained nearly all of the motifs found in the classic accounts of Jewish ritual murder: the youthful innocence of the victim, the description of the crime itself as a compulsive reenactment of the crucifixion of Jesus, the enthusiasm and bloodthirstiness of the perpetrators, and the numerous miracles that the martyr performed after his death (Langmuir 1990b; Rubin 2014).

As Miri Rubin points out, Thomas does not accuse any Jewish individual per se of the kidnapping and killing of young William; rather, the murder is presented as a *group* crime "of a cruel and inventive nature" (2014). Finally, Thomas' own inventiveness leads him to introduce an additional theme, which will come to occupy a central role in subsequent narratives of ritual criminality, eventually establishing a link to modern antisemitism: transnational conspiracy. He introduces the character of a fellow monk, a Jewish convert to Christianity, by the name of Theobald, who confesses to the narrator a secret: the Jews, Theobald explains, believe that they can never return to their ancestral homeland without offering up a Christian child for sacrifice. Placing the center of the international conspiracy in Narbonne (a city in the south of France, but identified by Thomas as "Spain"), Theobald explains that the leaders and rabbis of the Jews meet annually to decide where, among all the places in which Jews live, a Christian is to be taken and killed (Rubin 2014, pp. xxiii–xxiv). Thomas' account was likely copied and distributed among a number of Benedictine monasteries in England, in places such as Gloucester and Bury St. Edmunds, where similar complaints against Jews soon followed (Gloucester in 1168; Bury St. Edmunds in 1181).

The power of this document is all the more unusual in that no trial was ever held for the murder of William of Norwich, and no Jews were ever arrested, punished, or killed. A murder trial did take place in Norwich in

1150, but *it* involved the murder of a Jewish banker by a Christian knight who was in debt to him. E. M. Rose, the author of a recent study on the origins of the blood libel in medieval Europe, points out that the knight's Bishop, William Turbe, who defended him before the royal court in London, argued that it was in fact not his client, but the slain banker—as well as the entire Jewish community—who should be on trial, charged with the murder of young William (2015, pp. 80–82). It was in the aftermath of this trial that Thomas of Monmouth set about composing his own account. But Bishop Turbe's words to the court provide evidence for the presence in Norwich of an *oral* tradition, which attributed the death of William to a Jewish ritual conspiracy, well before Thomas of Monmouth set quill to parchment.

It was in the same year, 1150, that the boy William began to appear in numerous visions and effect miracles. Within two decades, his fame would spread over both sides of the English Channel, stimulated at least in part by a fundraising tour, led by Bishop Turbe, to collect monies for the rebuilding of the Norwich Cathedral, in which young William's relics were displayed. This renewed publicity of William's martyrdom may have been one of the key factors behind repeated accusations of Jewish ritual murder that emerged in the years following 1170, in places such as Blois (France) in 1171; Fulda (Holy Roman Empire) in 1235; and Lincoln (England) in 1255. What Thomas' written account did provide was a crucial vehicle for the accusation's transmission—over impressive distances and to various settings—producing what would become a cohesive, influential, and much imitated, narrative account.

In the case of little Hugh of Lincoln (1255), the tragic discovery of the body of a nine-year-old boy, drowned in a well, was transformed explicitly into a tale of sacrifice and martyrdom in which Jewish conspiracy and the compulsion to reenact the torture and crucifixion of Christ assumed central roles. "They beat him till blood flowed," wrote the thirteenth-century historian Matthew Paris, "they crowned him with thorns, derided him, and spat upon him" (Kieval 1994, pp. 55–56).

The Fulda case (1235), the first to emerge in the Holy Roman Empire, is noteworthy for introducing to ritual murder discourse the theme of what some modern historians have come to call "ritual cannibalism," the claim that, in addition to kidnapping and murdering Christian children, Jews also consumed, in some way, their bodies, usually by drinking their blood (Langmuir 1990a). In the case of Fulda, members of the Jewish community were accused of murdering five brothers, collecting their blood, and consuming it for its alleged medicinal properties. Later accusations added other uses for blood, often drawn from popular beliefs about medicine and magic. An accusation from Tyrnau (Trnava) in 1494, for example, offered four different reasons for this gruesome practice: the blood of a Christian child was a well-known remedy for "the wound of circumcision"; when put into food, it could act as an aphrodisiac; it could ease the menstrual flow (in both Jewish women *and* Jewish men); and Jews were commanded annually to shed Christian blood in sacrifice to God. Interestingly, the one theme that people commonly associate with the blood libel today—that Jews use blood as an ingredient in the preparation of Passover *matzot* (unleavened bread)—was not always present in premodern accusations. It does appear, nevertheless, to have had its origins in Europe in the thirteenth century.

The introduction of the increasingly dominant image of Jewish consumption of the blood of Christian children has moved a number of modern historians—notably Gavin Langmuir—to argue that there were, in fact, two distinct accusations against Jews: ritual murder, in which Jews reenacted the torture and crucifixion of Jesus; and the blood libel, which held that Jews committed the murders in order to consume the blood of their victims in the fulfillment of Jewish ritual (Langmuir 1990b). Other scholars argue that the distinction was not always clearly drawn and that, in any event, blood featured prominently in both types of anti-Jewish narrative. A related issue that divides historians concerns the question of why the medieval accusation emerged in the first place: Why the twelfth and the thirteenth centuries? Why first in England and then in France and the Empire? And why this particular form of myth?

A number of historians—among them E. M. Rose, Miri Rubin, and Robert Stacey—have taken note of the fact that the increased attention that pious Christians paid to recapitulating the suffering and crucifixion of Christ developed in the context of the First and Second Crusades (1096–1099 and 1147–1149) (Rose 2015; Rubin 2014). Indeed, the years immediately preceding and following the disastrous Second Crusade seem to have provided the critical matrix linking contemporary political and military affairs not only to Christian sacred narrative—at the center of which stood the figure of the captive and suffering Messiah—but to local tragedies as well. In other words, the answer to the question why a mythical interpretation of child killings (or even the invention of such killings) would have been compelling to contemporary observers may lie in the general power and circulation of this particular paradigm in European society at the time. Israel Jacob Yuval has provocatively suggested that it was, in fact, Jewish resistance to the violence of the First Crusade—which, famously, featured murder/suicides of entire families—that first planted the suggestion in the minds of Christian onlookers that Jews were capable of (perhaps, prone to?) murdering children (2006, pp. 144–204).

One of the strengths of Yuval's thesis is that it eschews the notion that medieval Jews were passive and powerless in the face of Christian hostility toward them; on the contrary, Jews and Christians had engaged in mutual—and mutually referential—polemical discourse since late antiquity. Its weaknesses, however, are several: Christian accounts of Jewish ritual murder from the twelfth and thirteenth centuries do not mention Jewish behavior during the First Crusade; the classical accusation, moreover, connects more closely to the Second Crusade; and it emerged in England and not in the Rhineland, the site of the murder/suicides of 1096. Yuval points to an accusation of murder (if not ritual murder) that occurred in Würzburg during the early months of the Second Crusade, in 1147, as having, in fact, predated both the trial of 1150 and Thomas of Monmouth's written account of William of Norwich. But, as we have seen, an oral tradition of Jewish ritual murder had already begun to take shape in Norwich; moreover, attention must be paid to the immediate context of the violence committed against Jews in this period—the psychological and military preparation for the Second Crusade. The distinguished Rabbi Jacob Tam, attacked in his home region of Champagne, wrote in his account of the incident that his attackers claimed that they were taking vengeance on the Jews for "inflicting wounds on Christ."

Yuval's suggestions concerning the origins of the blood libel help to turn our attention to another important question: do actual Jewish behaviors matter in the production of ritual murder accusations? Gavin Langmuir famously argued that what he called "antisemitism" was to be distinguished, first and foremost, from conflictual relations and everyday hostility by virtue of the fact that its messages about Jews were fanciful or, to use his word, "chimerical." They were products of the Christian imagination, born of cultural and psychological conflicts within Christian society, and did not reflect actual social, economic, and political interactions between Christians and Jews. In his view, both the blood libel and the ritual murder accusation answered psychological needs deep within the dominant Christian community (1990c).

For Langmuir the critical moment in the shift from the ritual murder accusation to the blood libel came with the debates within the Church on the nature of the Eucharist, and the consolidation of what would become the orthodox position on *transubstantiation*—the doctrine that holds that the *real* substances behind the consecrated bread and wine in the Eucharist are the body and blood of Christ—which developed in the first decades of the thirteenth century. In his view, knowledge that Jews themselves, the enemies of Christ, felt compelled to prepare their own consecrated bread with the blood of an innocent Christian child somehow allayed the doubts and anxieties that Christians felt toward their own doctrine and practice. Other scholars, such as the folklorist Alan Dundes, have directed a more psychoanalytically informed analysis at the blood libel. Dundes suggests that the Eucharist service—whatever its interpretation—is "an act of blatant cannibalism," which engendered in Christians strong feelings of guilt. It was through a process of what he calls *projective inversion* ("in which A accuses B of carrying out an action which A really wishes to carry out him or herself") that such feelings were allayed (1991).

What both types of psychological explanation share is their focus on the ritual behavior of medieval Christians as the locus of narrative formulations—and attacks—regarding Jews. They agree that it is not to any specific Jewish behaviors that one should turn in explaining the meaning and function of the blood libel, but to theological conflicts and psychological anxieties that were present in the Christian societies that produced this narrative. If Dundes' borrowing from the Freudian conceptual arsenal might seem formulaic, Langmuir's more capacious reading has the advantage of blending high-minded theological disagreements, intra-communal social conflict, and ritual theory. He says relatively little, however, about the much more obvious connection between "theological anxiety" and social accusation that is to be found in the charge of Host desecration. This accusation, which has been analyzed extensively by Miri Rubin in her book *Gentile Tales*, held that Jews (often with the help of unwitting Christians) sought to acquire consecrated hosts and subject them to various forms of physical torture. Hosts that were subjected to such acts of violence would bleed profusely, sometimes fly toward heaven, or maintain their form even when subjected to fiery ovens, thereby confirming their status as comprising, substantively, the body of Christ. The Host desecration accusation, which crystalized in Paris in 1290, spread eastward to the Holy Roman Empire and—in the sixteenth and seventeenth centuries—to the Polish–Lithuanian Commonwealth, where it joined in Counter-Reformation battles against Protestants and other heretics (Rubin 2004).

An alternative to a purely psychological reading of blood libels and ritual murder accusations in their premodern contexts might, instead, apply ritual or narrative theory to this conflictual encounter. Christopher Ocker recommends an approach that connects the ritual murder accusation to the growing Christian identification with what he calls the "subjectivity of Christ" (1998). From this perspective, one can view the accusation as the incorporation of contemporary Jews into a metahistorical sacred narrative; Jews of the twelfth, thirteenth, or fourteenth century are assigned roles in a sacred drama of which they may have been only vaguely aware. Such a phenomenon can be seen as a form of ritual reenactment in which Jews assume the role of unknowing—or unwilling—participants. Similarly, I think, with the blood libel itself, Jews are invited, as it were, to celebrate the Eucharist, but through a kind of ritual inversion, demonically mirroring the proper rite and, thereby, acknowledging its salvific truth and effect. Both forms of ritual collaboration involve a degree of psychological violence directed at Jews, as they are extracted against their will from their real-life contexts and assigned roles in an ahistorical drama—sometimes with lethal, real-life consequences.

Blood libels and ritual murder accusations took shape, of course, in concrete historical settings. And it is to the political institutions, economic and social relations, and cultural practices of these settings to which one must turn in order to discover the precise ways in which an accusation might work itself out. The changing political relations between the English monarchy and the Jews, for example, helps to explain why in 1144 no Jews were tried or convicted for the murder of William of Norwich, while in Lincoln in 1255 nineteen Jews were executed. In the middle of the twelfth century, the Jews of England enjoyed the direct protection of the king, to whom they paid significant taxes; and it was the king's sheriff in Norwich who heard the original complaints about the Jews, which he apparently did not consider credible. By the middle of the thirteenth century, in contrast, Henry III had sold his regalian rights to his brother, and hence was no longer receiving income from the Jews. He did reserve the right to confiscate their property, however, if they were convicted of a crime. During a royal visit to Lincoln, Henry intervened directly in the case, ordering the execution of one Copin—the main suspect—in Lincoln, and the arrest of ninety Jews, to be held in the Tower of London; eighteen of these were later hanged. The Jews of Blois, meanwhile, lived under the control, not of the king of France, but of the local duke, Thibault V, who lent his full support to the accusation of ritual murder. The duke had fallen upon hard times economically, was in direct competition with both his brother, the Duke of Champagne (where Jewish life thrived), and King Louis VII. Medieval Jewish tales speak of a Jewish mistress and a jealous wife, but more likely it was the combination of economic strain, political competition, and religious belief that induced Thibault to arrest, condemn, and brutally execute over thirty Jews.

In the Holy Roman Empire of the late middle ages, accusations of ritual murder appeared hand in hand with the growing economic and political strength of imperial cities and towns. They often accompanied efforts by city councils to challenge princely political control, to achieve the status of royally chartered free cities, and, in the process, to demand from royal or princely authority the right to exclude Jews from the polity. Accusations of Jewish ritual murder in such places as Endingen (1470), Trent (1475), Regensburg (1470–1476), and Freiburg (1504) ended in most instances with the execution of the accused (or their death under torture); the conversion or expulsion of the remaining Jewish communities; and the consolidation of Christian civic solidarity at home. As Ronnie Po-chia Hsia notes, however, the flood of accusations, trials, and expulsions that swept across southwestern Germany on the eve of the Reformation soon confronted a formidable cultural repudiation. The Reformation's own learned and moral discourses concerning ritual, belief, and religious truth produced what might be called a "disenchanting" of Christian culture in Central and Western Europe, which, in the process, relegated the charge of Jewish ritual murder to the sphere of disreputable knowledge—disdained by learned elites though perpetuated in popular culture (Hsia 1988). Andreas Osiander (1498–1552), a leading reformer in Nüremberg, wrote a strident critique of the blood libel in the aftermath of a case that unfolded in the Hungarian town of Bazin/Pösing in 1529, in which thirty Jews were arrested, among them the community's rabbi and his children. All were burned at the stake; the remaining Jews were expelled from the city. The boy, of whose murder the Jews were accused, was eventually found alive.

Among the reasons cited by Osiander in his refutation of the reality of Jewish ritual murder was the fact that Mosaic law over and over forbids the shedding of innocent blood; that the Jewish dietary laws, in fact, forbid the consumption of any blood, even that of kosher animals; that Jews believe in eternal life and would certainly avoid infanticide in order to achieve salvation; and, regarding the suggestion that Jews needed the blood of children to heal themselves of diseases inflicted by God, he wrote: "I say this is in many ways contrary to God's Word, against nature and human reason, because if God were to punish them with a special disease, no human could heal it." Hsia reminds us that the Protestant Reformation inaugurated a period of critical reception of all manner of Catholic belief and practice—miracles, pilgrimages, Marian devotion, and the veneration of saints—as well as a fundamental challenge to the validity of the eucharistic doctrine of transubstantiation, which had provided the symbolic scaffolding on which the plausibility of the blood libel had rested (1988, pp. 136–62).

For the most part, ritual murder and host desecration accusations did not enter Poland–Lithuania until the sixteenth century, their number and frequency rising sharply with the formal introduction of the Counter-Reformation in the 1560s. Historians differ as to the precise number of cases that occurred as well as to the ultimate motives that lay behind them. Magda Teter has situated early modern trials against Jews for sacrilege against the Host within the broader context of Counter-Reformation struggles over the meaning of the sacred during a time of religious and political upheaval. It appears that between 1540 and 1790 between eighty and one hundred ritual murder accusations were serious enough to have left behind a historical record.

Sandomierz, in the Kingdom of Poland, was the site of two major blood libels at the turn of the seventeenth and eighteenth centuries (1698 and 1710–1713). In the latter case, it was Stefan Żuchowski (1666–1716)—parish priest, archdeacon, and town inquisitor—who instigated and organized the criminal investigation. Żuchowski, who had been appointed commissioner for Jewish affairs by the synod of the Cracow diocese in 1711, is thought to have taken a personal interest in the question of Jewish ritual murder in the aftermath of the first Sandomierz trial and went on to publish two books on the subject that proved extremely influential in the Kingdom of Poland in later decades.

In the 1710–1713 Sandomierz case, Jan Serafinowicz, a convert from Judaism who served as a witness for the prosecution, broke from all historical precedent in testifying to the court that Jews did, in fact, perform ritual murder on Christian children. He also seems to have been the author of a manuscript filled with "evidence" supporting the blood libel, which became a handbook of sorts for prosecutors and eventually was summarized in a book, *Złość żydowska* (Jewish Malice), and published in 1758 by Gaudenty Pikulski, a Catholic priest. The engagement of Bishop Kajetan Sołtyk with followers of the messianic pretender Jakob Frank provided another, more dramatic occasion in which former or dissenting Jews would step forward to attest to the "truth" of the charge that Jews used Christian blood for ritual purposes. In the aftermath of a public disputation in Kamieniec-Podolski in 1757, Sołtyk sought to exploit the propagandistic potential of the Frankists, who were styling themselves "Contra-Talmudists." He instigated another public disputation, which took place in Lwów in September 1759, in which they asserted that the Talmud teaches that Jews require Christian blood and that whoever believes in the Talmud is bound to follow this teaching. Deeply concerned about the flurry of ritual murder accusations in Poland, the Council of the Four Lands (*Va'ad arbaaratzot*) sent three emissaries to the Vatican between 1754 and 1761 to appeal to the Pope for protection. In 1758 Pope Benedict XIV ordered an investigation into the matter and charged Lorenzo Ganganelli, councilor of the Holy Office of the Inquisition—and later Pope Clement XIV—to prepare a report on the commission's work. Ganganelli's report reviewed the major accusations of Jewish ritual murder since the thirteenth century and concluded that the blood libel was indeed a calumny, of which Jews and Judaism were innocent.

In countries that lay to the west of Poland–Lithuania, the Protestant Reformation, reforms in legal procedure, and, eventually, the spread of Enlightenment rationalism combined to cast aspersion and doubt on ritual murder and host desecration accusations generally, relegating them to the intellectually suspect categories of popular superstition and legend. Relatively few trials were prosecuted on these charges in Western and Central Europe from the mid-sixteenth to the mid-nineteenth century. In Poland–Lithuania, however, a similar delegitimizing process would not take place before the end of the eighteenth century, the product of two, related, cultural developments: the spread of Enlightenment ideas among magistrates and officials; and the abolition of torture in criminal investigations in 1776. The result would be the virtual elimination of ritual murder trials during the last quarter of the century. In the Russian empire—following the partitions of Poland—significant reforms to the criminal code did not occur until the 1860s, and trials against Jews for ritual murder did take place from time to time. One notable example can be found in the Belarusian town of Velizh in 1823–1824. That case elicited the surprising intervention of the Tsar Alexander I, who inaugurated a formal imperial investigation that stretched until 1835 before finally ending in the acquittal of all Jews accused (Avrutin 2018).

The consensus of respectable opinion in Europe regarding the blood libel may have met its match with the famous Damascus Affair, which broke out in 1840. At the center of this episode was a ritual murder investigation in the predominantly Muslim Ottoman empire that began with the disappearance and presumed murder of a Capuchin monk named Father Thomas, but which soon mushroomed into a major international incident—involving the governments of France, Britain, Egypt, and Austria—and which nearly escalated into a serious military conflict. The theory that a kidnapping and ritual murder had been committed came from within the city's Christian community; the French diplomatic mission in Damascus became involved in the investigation because the Franco-Turkish Concession Treaty of 1740 had put the Ottoman Empire's Roman Catholic clergy under the protection of France.

The Damascus affair bore characteristics of *both* the medieval and the modern blood libel. As in premodern times, confessions were extracted from suspects through the use of torture (indeed some of those arrested died as a result); local authorities, including the French consul, appeared to accept the traditional blood accusation at face value as true, or at least plausible. At the same time, the imperial protector of the Jews, the Ottoman Sultan, responded in the traditional manner, issuing a *firman* (edict) condemning the charge. And, as in most premodern cases, the judicial proceedings did not culminate in a formal trial but rather took the form of prolonged interrogations (again, under torture) punctuated by various delays until higher authorities called an end to them.

The case also exhibited more modern features. These included the dissemination of purportedly neutral—though highly exploitative—coverage of the ritual murder accusation in mass circulation newspapers in England, France, and Germany (including *The Times* of London); the entanglement of the affair in nineteenth-century international diplomacy and competition; and the political mobilization of Jewish communities across Europe to achieve justice for their coreligionists. Damascus thus occupies a curiously indeterminate position in the history of the ritual murder accusation: it was both a European and a non-European event; a product of medieval religious understandings as well as of nineteenth-century *Realpolitik*; a marker of both the premodern political status of Jews as a dependent and subservient minority and of the transition to the politics of emancipation in which Jews became citizens of the modern state bestowed with equal political rights. In its investigative and juridical procedures, however, Damascus was a throwback to the past (Frankel 1997).

During the last two decades of the nineteenth century and the first decade and a half of the twentieth—following a hiatus of close to three hundred years—accusations against Jews for the crime of ritual murder proliferated through much of Central Europe and as far east as the Russian empire. One turn-of-the-century observer, combing largely through German and Austrian newspapers, detailed no fewer than 128 public accusations of Jewish ritual murder during the years 1881–1900. The spate of modern accusations actually increased as the nineteenth century drew to a close. According to a Jewish defense organization based in Berlin, no fewer than 79 "*bona fide*" ritual murder accusations were leveled against Jews between 1891 and 1900—primarily in Austria-Hungary, Germany, and Bulgaria. Not surprisingly, the vast majority of these claims of Jewish ritual murder may never have gone beyond rumor mongering or sensational reporting in the mass media. It is conceivable that dozens of accusations were followed up by criminal investigations of varying duration and intensity. Remarkably, four Central and East European states—Germany, Austria, Hungary, and Russia—chose formally to prosecute Jewish defendants at six public trials between 1879 and 1913, thereby breaking with a long-standing tradition of skeptical neutrality on the part of the state.

The trials in question took place in Kutaisi (Russian Georgia, 1879); Tiszaeszlár (Hungary, 1882–1883); Xanten (Germany, 1891–1892); Polná (Austrian Bohemia, 1899–1900); Konitz (Germany/West Prussia, 1900–1901); and Kiev (Russian Ukraine, 1911–1913). Each of the trials received extensive coverage and publicity both at home and abroad, but three appear to have generated the most discussion in the foreign press: Tiszaeszlár, because it was the first modern prosecution in Central Europe and, as such, elicited widespread questioning of the compatibility of ritual murder discourse and modern culture; Polná, because it coincided with the Dreyfus affair in France, was implicated in the heated national controversy between Germans and Czechs, and, finally, featured a dramatic intervention on the Jewish defendant's behalf by Tomáš Masaryk, a leader of the progressive wing of the Czech national movement who would go on to become the first president of independent Czechoslovakia; and Kiev—the Beilis affair—because it seemed to epitomize to the western world both the backwardness of Imperial Russia and the hopelessness of its oppressed Jewish population.

It would be mistaken, however, to view the ritual murder trials of modern Europe as a return to medieval superstition. In each of the states in question, prosecutors and ministry officials conducting formal criminal investigations and, eventually, prosecuting the Jewish defendants in open trial tried to maintain their identity as scientifically trained, bureaucratic rationalists. Their cases also relied to a large extent on the opinions of a variety of expert witnesses—including physicians, forensic scientists, criminologists, theologians, and academic scholars of Judaism—whose testimony appeared to provide the modern ritual murder accusation an aura of scientific respectability. Far from being a throwback to the middle ages, the modern ritual murder trial was, in fact, a product of post-Enlightenment politics, fears, and conventional wisdoms. It succeeded for as long as it did because it was articulated through the idioms of scientific discourse and rationality.

Eventually, the very sources of authority on which the modern proceedings rested began to undermine the credibility of the ritual murder accusation. A case in point can be found in the Polná affair, in which Leopold Hilsner stood accused of the murder of Anežka Hrůzová, a nineteen-year-old peasant woman from a neighboring village. The prosecution had built its case on what it claimed to be a foundation of forensic evidence: a sweep of the crime scene; blood on the trousers of the defendant; and a medical autopsy of the victim's corpse. At the same time, it left open the question of motive—a void quickly filled by local rumor, the daily press, and the attorney who represented the victim's family in court. Yet when the medical faculty at the Czech University in Prague re-did the forensic examinations and publicized their results, which were highly critical of the original findings, the high court in Vienna ordered a retrial for the defendant. That Hilsner was also to be convicted of murder at his second trial, and sentenced once more to death, indicates the depth of public antipathy toward him as an individual and of societal suspicions of Jews as a whole. But the ritual murder accusation in its modern form—and the willingness of state agents to prosecute trials on its basis—was to have a finite lifespan. Outside the realm of Nazi rhetoric, the ritual murder accusation would not survive as a political weapon, or even as a viable object of social knowledge, beyond the First World War (Kieval, forthcoming).

The question remains as to what the political and cultural meanings of the modern ritual murder accusation were. What was it saying about the world in which one lived? Why was it an attractive or compelling belief to those people who held it? A partial answer would be the following: the modern accusation of Jewish ritual murder functioned politically as a rhetorical assault on the recently completed emancipation of the Jews of Central Europe and on the liberal state that acknowledged the legal equality of the Jewish religion. Proponents of the accusation claimed to have discovered precisely in the religious culture of the Jews the code that proved their unsociability and, hence, their disqualification from the political category of citizen and the social category of neighbor. The cultural meanings of the accusation were bleaker still. It articulated a new sense of danger and threat stemming from the social effects of modern life, located in the secret proclivities of the recently emancipated Jews, and inscribed on the mutilated bodies of their victims.

References

Avrutin, Eugene M. 2018. *The Velizh Affair: Blood Libel in a Russian Town*. New York: Oxford University Press.

Dundes, Alan. 1991. "The Ritual Murder or Blood Libel Legend: A Study of Anti-Semitic Victimization Through Projective Inversion." In *The Blood Libel Legend: A Casebook in Anti-Semitic Folklore*, edited by Alan Dundes, 336–76. Madison: University of Wisconsin Press.

Frankel, Jonathan. 1997. *The Damascus Affair: "Ritual Murder," Politics, and the Jews in 1840*. Cambridge: Cambridge University Press.

Hsia, Ronnie Po-chia. 1988. *The Myth of Ritual Murder: Jews and Magic in Reformation Germany*. New Haven: Yale University Press.

Kieval, Hillel J. 1994. "Representation and Knowledge in Medieval and Modern Accounts of Jewish Ritual Murder." *Jewish Social Studies: History, Culture, Society* 1 (1): 52–72.

Kieval, Hillel J. Forthcoming. *Blood Inscriptions: Science, Modernity, and Ritual Murder in Fin de Siècle Europe*. Philadelphia: University of Pennsylvania Press.

Langmuir, Gavin. 1990a. "Ritual Cannibalism." In *Toward a Definition of Antisemitism*, 263–81. Berkeley: University of California Press.

Langmuir, Gavin. 1990b. "Thomas of Monmouth: Detector of Ritual Murder." In *Toward a Definition of Antisemitism*, 209–236. Berkeley: University of California Press.

Langmuir, Gavin. 1990c. "Toward a Definition of Antisemitism." In *Toward a Definition of Antisemitism*, 311–352. Berkeley: University of California Press.

Ocker, Christopher. 1998. "Ritual Murder and the Subjectivity of Christ: A Choice in Medieval Christianity." *Harvard Theological Review* 91 (2) (April): 153–92.

Rose, E. M. 2015. *The Murder of William of Norwich: The Origins of the Blood Libel in Medieval Europe*. Oxford: Oxford University Press.

Rubin, Miri. 2004. *Gentile Tales: The Narrative Assault on Late Medieval Jews*. Philadelphia: University of Pennsylvania Press.

Rubin, Miri. 2014. Introduction to *The Life and Passion of William of Norwich*, by Thomas of Monmouth. Translated and edited by Miri Rubin. London: Penguin Books.

Yuval, Israel Jacob. 2006. *Two Nations in Your Womb: Perceptions of Jews and Christians in Late Antiquity and the Middle Ages*. Berkeley: University of California Press.

CHAPTER 6

The Catholic Church

Magda Teter

The fiftieth anniversary of the Declaration "Nostra Aetate" issued at the II Vatican Council was celebrated internationally in 2015 by both Jewish and Catholic communities. There was much to celebrate for the Declaration was a milestone in Jewish-Catholic relations, spurring a new era of dialogue and rapprochement between the two communities. But 2015 also marked the eight-hundredth anniversary of another major council in the history of the Catholic Church—the IV Lateran Council. Like Vatican II, the IV Lateran, while dealing with pressing issues for the Church at the time, also included Jews in its deliberations, with no less pivotal results. The last four canons of the Council were devoted to Jews, and the most (in)famous was Canon 68, which sought to mark off "Jews and Saracens," that is Jews and Muslims, from Christians. Though there is no direct link between the 1215 canon and the Nazi decision to apply badges for the conquered and degraded populations, including Jews, both anniversaries offer symbolic bookmarks in the history of Jewish-Catholic relations. One symbolizes Church triumphalism and oppression of Jews, the other reconciliation and atonement following the horrors of the Second World War.

As with all symbolic markers, the two anniversaries also obscure the complexity of the long history of Jewish-Christian relations in general, and Jewish-Catholic relations in particular. Very often modern scholars of Jewish-Christian relations tended to focus on anti-Jewish sentiments, and study those relations within the context of the history of antisemitism, rarely seeing Jews as historical actors. Already in 1934, James Parkes, troubled

M. Teter (✉)
Fordham University, New York City, NY, USA
e-mail: mteter@fordham.edu

by the contemporary outburst of antisemitism, viewed "the conflict of the Church and the Synagogue" since antiquity as the "origins of antisemitism" (1969). Parkes studied classic Christian texts and laws to point to religious rather than economic roots of antisemitism, noting that "nowhere is the general term 'Jew' coupled with any term of economic significance, and nowhere do we find cases of economic hostility or maladjustment between the Jews of a locality and their neighbors" (1969, p. 372). Indeed, Parkes noted that evidence shows that Jews "in the east as well as in the west ... lived on good terms with their neighbors." What Parkes was hinting at was tension between the *theological* (or hermenutical) Jew, encountered in theological texts, and *historical* Jews, encountered in daily life. These historical encounters challenge common assumptions of distinctions between premodern and modern periods, between anti-Judaism and antisemitism. Inclusion of Jews as historical actors complicates the often theoretical approaches to antisemitism, which emerges as a disembodied, almost mythical, indeed, even "irrational," force—the "longest hatred."

But focus on *texts* to demonstrate continuity and transformation of anti-Jewish sentiments obscures the social dimension of history. To be sure there are distinctions between premodern anti-Jewish sentiments and modern antisemitism. For one, the term "antisemitism" was coined only in 1879 by Wilhelm Marr, precisely because there emerged something new that needed a new name. This modern antisemitism was grounded in modern racial theories and spurred by the development of nation states that granted or considered granting Jews equality before the law. In premodern religious anti-Judaism, conversion could erase "Jewishness" and along with it the social and legal distinctions between Jews and Christians. In the modern period, racial antisemitism no longer allowed that.

Also significant, scholarly debates about antisemitism have been predicated on the understanding of modernity as a period of Jewish social integration, with modern antisemitism as a backlash to that social and political integration, implying that there was less social integration in the premodern period. Reading the classical texts and laws along with evidence of historical relations between Jews and Christians reveals a complex historical reality, blurring the sharp boundaries between the modern and premodern periods. On the one hand, premodern Jewish-Christian relations offer a more complex view of premodern anti-Jewish sentiments, on the other, the continuity of the religious dimension of Christian attitudes toward Jews in the modern period becomes obvious.

The Theological Jew

The sketches of what would shape the theological Jew began to emerge already in the writings of Paul; the writings of early Christian church fathers elaborated on these themes and created a framework for the theological understanding of Jews in Christian society to be embraced by medieval and early modern popes. To justify his new theology grounded in faith not law, Paul called Jesus' followers "the children of the promise"; they were like the younger son of Abraham, Isaac. And though Jews traced their lineage to Isaac and saw him as a Jewish Patriarch, in Paul's new interpretation Jews were "the children according to flesh," like Ishmael, the elder son of Abraham "by a slave woman" (Gal. 4, and Rom. 9). Paul extended his interpretation also to another pair of biblical brothers, Jacob and Esau. In his Epistle to Romans, while discussing the mysteries of God's election, Paul used a fateful phrase: "The elder shall serve the younger" (Rom. 9:12, citing Gen 25:23), a phrase that would have real-life consequences in the subsequent centuries of Jewish-Christian relations.

Centuries later the story of Jacob and Esau more explicitly referred to Jews and Christians. After Christianity had already become the religion of the empire, Augustine of Hippo (354–430) understood the phrase "the elder shall serve the younger" to mean "that the older people of the Jews was destined to serve the younger people, the Christians" (*de Civitate Dei* 16:35). Augustine also elaborated on the notion of the "carnality" of Jews as shaped by Paul's description of Jews as "children of the flesh." Esau, according to Augustine, could not control his carnal cravings and sold his birthright for a bowl of lentils. For Augustine the biblical trope of brothers helped explain the relationship between Jews and Christians, and Christ and the Jews. The troubled relationship between the first brotherly pair, Cain and Abel, also proved powerful. For Augustine, Abel's murder was the prefiguration of Christ's death. But it was what followed the killing that would help Augustine frame Jews in the figure of Cain. Commenting on the biblical verse "And the Lord God set a mark upon Cain, lest any one finding him should slay him," Augustine wrote:

> It is a most notable fact that all the nations subjugated by Rome adopted the heathenish ceremonies of the Roman worship, while the Jewish nation, whether under pagan or Christian monarchs has never lost the sign of their law, by which they are distinguished from all other nations and peoples. No emperor or monarch who finds under his government the people with this mark kills them, that is, makes them cease to be Jews, and as Jews to be separate in their observances, and unlike the rest of the world. Only when a Jew comes over to Christ, he is no longer Cain.... (*Contra Faustum*, 12:13)

Augustine elaborated on the command not to harm Jews when explaining the Jews' dispersion. "Jews who killed him and refused to believe in him," Augustine wrote, bore witness "by the evidence of their own Scriptures ... for us that we have not fabricated the prophecies about Christ" (*de Civitate Dei* 18:46; Psalm 59-11). Though Jews "did not believe in our Scriptures, their own Scriptures are fulfilled in them, while they read them with blind eyes." The Jews' testimony, he continued, was supplied for the Christians' "benefit by their possession and preservation of those books," and their dispersion "among all nations, wherever the Christian Church spreads. ... Hence the prophecy in the Book of Psalms: 'Do not slay them, lest at some time they forget our Law; scatter them by your might.'" All in all, according to Augustine, Jews were guilty of killing Jesus, but like Cain they should not be harmed, for they had a theological purpose for the Christian Church. As "enemies" they bore "important testimony" by preserving the Scriptures and serving as "a great confirmation of our faith" so that "the believing Gentiles cannot suppose these testimonies to Christ to be recent forgeries; for they find them in books held sacred for so many ages by those who crucified Christ, still venerated by those who daily blaspheme Him" (*Contra Faustum*, 16:21). Indeed, "The unbelief of the Jews has been made of signal benefit to us so that those who do not receive these truths in their hearts for their own good nonetheless carry in their hands, for our benefit the writings in which these truths are contained." The unbelief of the Jews, Augustine continued, "increases rather than lessens the authority of these books; for this blindness it itself foretold. They testify to the truth by their not understanding." Jews, therefore, were theologically necessary for Christians, just as they were during Christ's passion.

POPE INNOCENT III TURNS TO AUGUSTINE

Augustine's teachings remained in the domain of theology until they resurfaced in a new context later in the Middle Ages, providing a new theological framework for Church legislation and other official declarations about Jews that sought to enforce the Jews' degraded status "of servitude," while still protecting them physically. It is here that the theological Jew, who Paul and Augustine invented, meets the historical Jew, flesh and blood, in a tense encounter.

The early medieval popes relied on Roman law to formulate their positions on Jews. Change came in the era of the Crusades. During the First Crusade in 1096, Jews were brutally attacked by the crusaders marching through Europe. Many were killed, forcefully converted, or died at their own hands to avoid being baptized (Eidelberg 1996). So when in the 1140s the Second Crusade rolled, Jews sought protection from Church officials. Pope Eugenius III reissued the bull *Sicut Judaeis*, which had first been issued in 1120 by Pope Calixtus II (Grayzel 1962). And though no text of this version survived, one by Pope Alexander III (1159–1181) does, and it articulates but basic protection of Jews grounded in Roman law and earlier papal pronouncements (Grayzel 1962, p. 252). It was the abbot of Cluny, Bernard of Clairvaux, responding to anti-Jewish crusader violence who used Augustine to provide theological justification for the protection of Jews (Chazan 1980, p. 103). Bernard admonished the crusaders that "the Jews are not to be persecuted, killed, or even put to flight." The Scriptures, he argued, demand that. "Ask anyone who knows the Sacred Scriptures what he finds foretold of the Jews in the Psalm. 'Not for their destruction do I pray.'... The Jews are for us the living words of Scripture, for they remind us always of what our Lord suffered. They are dispersed all over the world so that by expiating their crime they may be everywhere the living witnesses to our redemption...." Jews were not to be killed because "when the time is ripe all Israel shall be saved.... If the Jews are utterly wiped out, what will become of our hope for their promised salvation, their eventual conversion?" Jews were both witnesses to Christian "redemption" and necessary for the final salvation.

But it was Pope Innocent III who began to draw heavily on theological arguments presented by Augustine for legal purposes. Several of his documents became part of the Canon Law, and formed a backbone for the long-standing Church policies concerning Jews. When reissuing *Sicut Iudaeis*, also called *Constitutio pro Iudaeis*, Pope Innocent III changed the preamble and applied Augustine's language in a legal context. "Although the Jewish perfidy," Innocent wrote, "is in every way worthy of condemnation, nevertheless because through them the truth of our own faith is proved, they are not to be severely oppressed by the faithful" (Grayzel 1933, pp. 92–95). "Thus, the Prophet says, 'Thou shalt not kill them, lest at any time they forget thy law,' or more clearly stated," explained the pope, "thou shall not destroy the Jews completely, so that the Christians should never by any chance be able to forget Thy Law, which though they themselves fail to understand it, they display in their book to those who understand." Jews, Innocent reaffirmed, had a place in Christianity, albeit limited, to preserve their Scriptures "for those who understand" them.

Innocent III introduced an equivocation about protecting Jews. Jews should not be destroyed "completely" (*omnino*) or harmed "without the judgment of the authority of the land" (*sine judicio potestatis terre*); they should be allowed to celebrate their festivals and observe their rites without disturbance; and their cemeteries should not be desecrated. But this protection was "only" for those Jews "who have not presumed to plot against the Christian faith." This equivocation opened doors for a withdrawal of assurances of protection from Jews.

In his statutes about Jews, Innocent III's language was sterner than that of his predecessors. He called Jews Jesus' "crucifiers" and demanded that their social position be diminished. In 1205 in his letter to King Philip Augustus of France, he invoked Cain's crime, the biblical figures of Hagar and Sarah, and hope for Jews' conversion, noting that "though it does not displease God, but is even acceptable to Him that the Jewish dispersion should live and serve under Catholic kings and Christian princes until such time as their remnant shall be saved," still it was "offensive" that the princes preferred "the sons of the crucifiers, against whom to this day the blood cries to the Father's ears, to the heirs of the Crucified Christ," and "Jewish slavery to the freedom of those whom the Son freed, as though the son of a servant could and ought to be an heir along with the son of the free woman" (Grayzel 1933, pp. 104–9). At issue was Jews' social position in France. They appear to have been prosperous, had Christian servants and nurses, and built a new synagogue near a church. Moreover, they seem to have received, against the statutes of the III Lateran Council, extraordinary treatment in French courts, where "Christian witnesses are not believed against [Jews], while [Jews] are admitted to testimony against Christians." Worried that "through them [Jews] the name of God" would be blasphemed, and "Christian liberty become less than Jewish servitude," the pope urged the king to "restrain Jews from their presumptions." Reiterating the message in his letter to the archbishop of Sens and the bishop of Paris, Pope Innocent III wanted to prohibit Jews "strictly" from having Christian servants "lest the children of a free woman should be servants to the children of a slave" (Grayzel 1933, pp. 114–5). In his many letters and bulls, Innocent repeatedly used the phrase "Jewish servitude," letting the discrepancy over historical Jewish status stand in stark contrast to the theological Jew, the "elder brother" who should be serving the younger.

To be sure, Paul's and Augustine's comparison of Jews to the "children of a slave woman" and their use of the biblical phrase that "the elder shall serve the younger" were implicit even in early medieval synodal and Roman imperial legislation that forbade Jews from holding Christian slaves or public office. But Pope Innocent III's language connected the legal message more tightly to Augustine's tropes. If earlier much of the anxiety over Christians serving Jews was about Jews converting their Christian slaves, or later servants, to Judaism, for Innocent III the question increasingly, and crucially, became that of social status—Jews should not be above Christians. To be sure, Innocent also expressed anxiety over conversion of Christian servants to Judaism; he did so in language contrasting "the grace of freedom" of Christianity with the "shame of slavery" in Judaism—thus once more juxtaposing social status and theology.

If submitting to or serving Jews brought shame to lay Christians, how much more shameful it was when involving priests. Writing to the Archbishop of Compostella and the bishops of Leon in northern Iberia, Innocent III railed against clergy being "forced not only to beg but even to do menial labor and serve the Jews, to the shame of the Church and all Christendom" (Grayzel 1933, pp. 90–91). Jews were to be a permanently subjugated group until they converted.

That anxiety over status spilled over to questions of daily contact, including food and drink. Jewish laws of kashrut prohibited Jews from eating animals slaughtered by Christians, and demanded that parts of the animals slaughtered by Jews be disposed of, which often meant selling them to Christians, who were not bound by these laws. This practice was interpreted as a slight to Christians. "Another scandal of no mean consequences is created by them," wrote Innocent III to the Count of Nevers in 1208 (Grayzel 1933, pp. 126–31). While Jews "shrink from eating as unclean (*immudis*) the meat of animals killed by Christians, yet, they obtain it as a privilege from the favor of the princes to give the slaughtering of the animal over to such who cut the animals according to the Jewish rite, and then take of them as much as they desire, and offer the leavings (*residuo*) to the Christians." If that were not enough, "no less detestable" was what they did with wine, the pope complained. Jews "shod in linen boots" tread the wine and "having extracted the purer wine in accordance with the Jewish rite, they retain some for their own pleasure, and the rest, the part which is abominable to them, they leave to the faithful Christians." And, as if to add insult to injury, "now and again, the sacrament of the blood of Christ is performed" with this wine.

Jews were aware that their laws of kashrut caused tensions and tried to accommodate that. Medieval rabbinic responsa provide evidence of how Jews coped with these issues. For example, the medieval halakhic work *Or zaru'a* discusses a question raised about the validity of the ritual slaughter of an animal when a Jewish slaughterer was accompanied in the act of the slaughter by a Christian butcher [*akum*], who "applied his knife to the neck of the cow" as soon as the Jewish butcher completed the slaughter. Rabbi Meshullam, whom *Or Zaru'a* quotes, ruled that his practice was permitted (*Or Zaru'a* vol. I, no. 478). Social connections, including collaborations—like the one mentioned in *Or Zaru'a*—and even friendships between Jews and non-Jews disturbed the theological order that was beginning to take shape in law, interpreted as "insolence." Complaints about these actual, close, sometimes perhaps too close, relations between Jews and Christians were behind the four canons of the IV Lateran Council, which sought to constrain the status of the Jews. Within the context of the IV Lateran Council, reforming and ordering Christendom, the canons were meant to articulate the proper social order between Christians and non-Christians, particularly Jews, but also Saracens, as Muslim were then called. This is especially true of canon 68, which sought to mark off Jews and Saracens from Christians.

Theological Ideas of Jewish Servitude and Historical Reality

By the sixteenth century, theological ideas of Jewish servitude in Christianity had become deeply ingrained, clashing with historical reality. In 1555, Pope Paul IV began his now infamous bull, *Cum Nimis Absurdum*, saying that "it is absurd and improper that Jews, whose own guilt has consigned them to perpetual servitude, under the pretext that Christian piety receives them and tolerates their presence should be ingrates to Christians, so that they attempt to exchange the servitude they owe to Christians for dominion over them" (Stow 1977, pp. 294–98). The pope then enumerated "the insolence" into which Jews "have erupted": dwelling "side by side with Christians," and "near their Churches with no distinct habit to separate them," even erecting homes in "the more noble sections and streets of the cities, holdings, and territories, where they dwell"; owning "fixed property"; and employing "nurses, housemaids, and other Christian servants." The pope also charged them with "perpetrating many other things in ignominy and contempt of the Christian name."

Drawing on centuries-old Christian teachings about Jews' theological role, the pope acknowledged that "the Roman Church tolerates the Jews in testimony of the true Christian faith and so that they, led by the piety and kindness of the Apostolic See, should at length recognize their errors, and make all haste to arrive at the true light of the Catholic faith." For this reason, to remedy the contrast in social status between the theological Jew and the historical Jew, the pope enacted laws that would lessen the status of the Jews in society to reflect the theological ideal. "Thereby," the pope announced, Jews should "agree that, as long as they persist in their errors, they should recognize through experience that they have been made slaves, while Christians have been made free through Jesus Christ, God, and our Lord." It was "iniquitous," the pope emphatically added, "that the children of the free woman should serve the children of the maid servant."

The bull included fifteen clauses, many of which reiterated existing canon law, with the first one establishing segregated Jewish quarters that by the 1580s would become known as ghettos (Stow 1992; Ravid 1992). Other clauses reiterated the marking on the Jews, the prohibition to hire Christian servants, working on Sundays, socializing with Jews, and added clauses regulating Jewish-Christian economic interactions. While the bull was quickly implemented in Rome and the Papal States, it was much slower to be implemented elsewhere, and in some Catholic areas, it was never implemented at all—the historical conditions simply did not allow for the theological status to hold.

THE HISTORICAL JEW(S)

Despite clear theological framing about the legal position of Jews in Christian society, Christians, both the laity and clergy, engaged, as both Jewish and Christian sources from all periods attest, in close social and professional relations with Jews. The twelfth-century rabbi Meshullam ben Jacob discussed a case of two Jews who "were partners in the management of the affairs of the bishopric of Narbonne" (Meshullam, no. 32). In other countries and other periods, too, despite the Jews' theological degradation, relations between Jews and Christians, and even the clergy, were not necessarily adversarial. In Poland, for example, in the second half of the seventeenth century parishioners of a town not far from Poznań complained against their priest (AAwP, Dep. Testium XV, 75v–76). The priest, according to the parishioners' main complaint, was apparently abusive, insulting townspeople, abusing parish finances, but he also socialized with Jews, especially with Jewish women, with whom he liked to dance, causing even some male Jews to complain to the authorities.

Because Jews were central to the economy of the Polish-Lithuanian Commonwealth, Catholic clergy, despite prohibitions in church law, welcomed Jews into their possessions and engaged in business relationships with them, causing outrage among higher Church officials. On December 3, 1749 a parish priest in the small town of Gawłuszowice, near Mielec in Małopolska, was punished by an episcopal court for not expelling a Jewish lease-holder of a brewery in the village of Niekurza, belonging to the Church, despite previous orders to do so (AKM, Acta Ep 90, fol. 271). Another example shows a Jew from Nowy Korczyn, a town near Cracow, who held the lease of a brewery in a nearby village Chańcza that belonged to the Cistercian monastery (AKM, Acta Ep 90, fol. 275). The bishop's decree admonished the Jew, Abram Józefowicz, not to take up leases of ecclesiastical properties or do anything prohibited by canon law in the future, under the penalty of arrest, which would have required cooperation with secular authorities. It also ordered him to give up the lease of the brewery in Chańcza. Whether Abram left or not remains unknown. Further instances of business relations between Jews and Catholic clergy can be found in the *takkanot vaad arba' arazot*, the ordinances of the Council of Four Lands, which often list communal expenses. Among them we find payments resulting from debts owned by Jews to the Jesuits and Dominicans (Halpern 1945, takkanah 639). Such close business relations between Jews and Christians led Pope Benedict XIV to issue his encyclical letter *A Quo Primum* in 1751 condemning the prominent role Jews played in Poland-Lithuania. The encyclical draws from the earlier papal documents, building on the idealized social position of Jews and outlining the laws current Jewish-Christian relations in Poland violated.

As in the previous papal constitutions and encyclicals, the theological Jew, in his idealized, subordinate position within the Christian body, clashed with the historical Jew of everyday life. Benedict XIV, admittedly not a historian but an expert in canon law, praised earlier bishops for their effectiveness in regulating Jewish-Christian interactions, not realizing that the synodal pronouncements he praised for preventing Poland from "being contaminated by Jewish faithlessness," not only did little to prevent such interactions but could appear as evidence for their existence. Indeed, as the pope himself noted, "Christians and Jews lived in the same cities and towns" (1847, p. 297). Despite the laws so praised by the pope, the reality was—not surprisingly—quite different. And Church officials reported that to Rome on a regular basis.

In 1556, a year after Pope Paul IV issued his bull *Cum Nimis Absurdum* establishing the ghetto in Rome, Luigi Lippomano, at the time the papal nuncio to Poland and a figure later mentioned by Benedict XIV in *A Quo Primum*, reported the impossibility of implementing the premise of *Cum Nimis Absurdum*. "I have received a copy of the bull that His Holiness has issued against the Jews," Lippomano wrote. "And may it please God that one could implement it here, but I see no chance because they have so many favors that it is astonishing, and all these Lords Palatines are their manifest defenders.... Money is enough to change everything [*Basta che gli danari giocano per tutto*]" (Wojtyska 1993, pp. 276–77). The implementation of the bull was impossible, not only because Jews had defenders, but also because of the nature of Jewish settlement in Poland. Still, Polish bishops, especially in the late seventeenth and in the eighteenth centuries, frequently reissued statutes regulating Jewish-Christian interaction and economic relations.

A few decades after Lippomano's letter, a Polish writer, Sebastian Miczyński, also complained with hostility that "Jews are so loved by some Lords [and] enjoy so much freedom that whatever they come to desire [*pokuszą*], they [eventually] get. They hold in control arrendas, tolls, duties, salt mines [*żupy*], mills, and taverns" (1618, p. 25). Though Miczyński's work may be discounted as polemical, his frustration was shared by more prominent and respectable figures. In 1636, for example, the papal nuncio to Poland, Marius Filonardi, wrote to Cardinal Antonio Barberini, the Camerlengo of the Sacred College of Cardinals: "The Jews, who in these parts [of the country] are more powerful and richer and much favored than elsewhere, have effectively secured a permit to establish homes and businesses in Masovia [in violation of the 1527 decree *de non tolerandis judaeis*], which is [one] of the main provinces of the Kingdom and which till now had remained free of this kind of commerce, [and they] are in such favor with His Majesty, not only among the heretics with whom they plot against Catholics [*sono d'intelligenza contri i cattolici*] but also among many Christian Senators" (quoted in Chynczewska-Hennel 2003, pp. 187–88). Jews, whom Filonardi called "bloodsuckers" [*sanguesughe*], were "in such favor" because they could offer credit to the nobles and the King during the Diets. And similar complaints continued to be voiced by other Church officials well into the eighteenth century.

Both archival sources and prescriptive legal texts demonstrate a constant tension between theology and historical reality. But the sharp language and frequent anti-Jewish statements and laws indicate precisely the opposite—complex, often amicable, relations between Jews and Christians, and even between Jews and the Catholic clergy. They show Jews closely integrated into society to the ire of religious leaders familiar with theologically inflected laws and norms.

The theological Jew did not disappear with "modernity," remaining a powerful concept; so, too, did the tension between the historical and theological. Indeed, when Theodor Herzl met with Pope Piux X in January 1904, seeking the Vatican's support for the state he was hoping to establish for Jews in Palestine, the pope explained his lack of support for the Jewish cause on theological grounds. "We cannot support this movement. We cannot impede Jews from going to Jerusalem, but we cannot support it" (Herzl 1960, pp. 1601–5). Jerusalem's soil "was sanctified by the life of Jesus Christ. As the head of the Church, I cannot tell you otherwise. Jews did not recognize our Lord, therefore we cannot recognize the Jewish people." Though the pope was not pleased with the fact that at the time Jerusalem was under Turkish control, he could not accept the idea of Jerusalem in Jewish hands, for "either Jews will cling to their faith and continue to await the Messiah, who for us, has already appeared. In this case, they will be denying the divinity of Jesus and we cannot help them. Or else, they will go there without religion, and then we can be even less favorable to them." Although "the Jewish religion was the foundation of our own," the pope said, "it was superseded by the teachings of Christ, and we cannot concede it any further validity. The Jews, who ought to have been the first to acknowledge Jesus Christ, have not done so to this day." In Pius X's words, the bitterness over the Jews' rejection of Christ was still palpable, and Judaism and Jews continued to be seen as a negation of Christianity. But even in this conversation the tension between the theological and the real historical Jews was obvious. Pope Pius X recalled the Jews of Mantua and his relations with them while he lived in the city, and commented on his usual, amicable interactions with Jews: "I have always been on good terms with Jews. Only the other evening two Jews were here to see me. After all, there are other bonds than those of religion: courtesy and philanthropy. These we do not deny to the Jews." But Catholics prayed for Jews "to be enlightened." And so, the pope said, "if you come to Palestine and settle your people there, we shall have churches and priests ready to baptize all of you." Religion, in Pope Pius X's view, was what divided Jews and Christians—daily encounters by-passed that, but ultimately, conversion was the most desired outcome.

THEOLOGY AND ANTISEMITISM IN MODERN TIMES

Until recently, the Church had not abandoned the theological Jew and its hope for the Jews' conversion. It was that hope for conversion that made the Church uncomfortable with racial antisemitism. In 1928, the Sacred Congregation of the Holy Office condemned antisemitism on the basis of theology and tradition: "The Catholic Church habitually prays for the Jewish people who were the bearers of the Divine revelation up to the time of Christ; this, despite, indeed, on account of their spiritual blindness." The Apostolic See "has protected this people against unjust oppression and, just as every kind of envy and jealousy among the nations must be disapproved of, so in an especial manner must be that hatred which is generally termed antisemitism." Racial antisemitism as embodied by the Nazi regime was particularly troubling, and Pope Pius XI responded in 1937 with "Mit Brendenner Sorge." Still, seeking to protect its own interests, the Church remained ambivalent. In September 1938, for example, during his meeting with Belgian pilgrims, Pius XI emphasized that it was not possible for Christians "to take part in antisemitism." But he allowed for people "to defend themselves, to adopt measures of protection against that which threatens their legitimate interests."

That same year, Pius XI commissioned the drafting of an encyclical "Humani generis" to address more explicitly the question of racism and antisemitism (Passelecq and Suchecky 1997, pp. 246–59). The text condemned placing race "on the pedestal," acknowledging that the "struggle for racial purity ends up being uniquely the struggle against Jews," and recalling that the Church repeatedly condemned persecution of the Jews, "especially when they wear the mantle of Christianity." "Humani generis" offered "a vigorous condemnation of antisemitism and racism wherever these doctrines lift their heads." The encyclical was as equivocal as Pius XI's statement to the Belgian pilgrims; it condemned racial antisemitism, but affirmed "the true nature, the authentic basis of the social separation of the Jews from the rest of humanity." The "so-called Jewish question," the encyclical asserted, is "not one of race, or nation, or territorial nationality, or citizenship in the state. It is a question of religion and, since the coming of Christ, a question of Christianity."

Unable to break from the long tradition, the encyclical noted Jews' rejection of the "promised" savior, who "was violently repudiated, and condemned as a criminal by the highest tribunals of the Jewish nation, in collusion with the pagan authorities who held the Jewish people in bondage. Ultimately, the Savior was put to death." "Humani generis" expressed hope for Jewish conversion, and reminded the faithful that "the hour and manner of the return of the Jewish people as a whole to their Father's house in the Church of Christ remains God's secret." Christians are advised to look "forward to the day when again Jew and Gentile will be united in their Father's house, and to pray earnestly for the hastening of its coming."

The encyclical was never published, Pope Pius XI died, Pius XII became a new pope, and soon World War II broke out. But its existence demonstrates that the highest Church officials felt compelled to address the rise of modern, racial, and increasingly violent antisemitism, while struggling with the legacy of their own tradition of seeing Jews through a theological lens shaped by early Christian writers, seeing Jews as "bearers of Divine revelation," and thus worthy of protection and of prayers for conversion, but still responsible for Jesus' death.

The value of public pronouncements and condemnations is often largely ceremonial. It is unlikely that, had it been made public, the encyclical "Humani generis" would have stemmed the hatred and violence against Jews and prevented the unprecedented act of destruction and violence that left more than two-thirds of European Jews dead, with many Catholics participating in the atrocities. Though millions of other Europeans suffered and died during World War II, the unprecedented targeting of Jews for total destruction meant that after the war many Christians, Protestant and Catholic, began to reexamine Christian teachings about the Jews. New dialogue was opened up with Jewish leaders who provided guidance from the Jewish side. The result was the declaration "Nostra Aetate," issued in 1965.

"Nostra Aetate" contained traditional, theologically loaded language, and said nothing about living Judaism. But, by calling for "mutual understanding and respect" and "fraternal dialogue," the declaration did shift the tone of Jewish-Catholic relations, the theological framework, and redefined the relationship between Jews and the Church. The Church was no longer standing next to the blinded and dejected *Synagoga*; it was now engaging with the *Synagoga* as an equal partner. Although, according to "Nostra Aetate," the Church still remained "the new people of God," the Jew was no longer an enemy of Christianity to be rejected. With "Nostra Aetate," an era of mutual dialogue and understanding as well as openness began. The shift in theology now emphasized not servitude but partnership and respect.

To be sure, "Nostra Aetate" did not eliminate antisemitism, and some of the theological issues that have plagued Jewish-Christian relations for centuries will likely never be resolved, though the latest declaration of the Vatican Commission for Religious Relations with the Jews issued in December 2015 addresses many of them. Still, at least for now, the tension between the historical and theological Jew has lessened significantly—the two sides are partners in dialogue.

References

AAwP (Archiwum Archidiecezjalne w Poznaniu). Dep. Testium XV, 75v–76.
AKM (Archiwum Kurii Metropolitalnej). Kraków, Acta Episcopalia 90.
Benedict XIV, Pope. 1847. *Benedicti XIV Pont. Opt. Max. olim Prosperi Cardinalis de Lambertinis Bullarium.* 17 vols. Vol. 3/1. Prati: Typographia Aldina.
Chazan, Robert. 1980. *Church, State, and Jew in the Middle Ages.* New York: Behrman House.
Chynczewska-Hennel, Teresa. 2003. *Marius Filonardi (1635–1643).* Vol. 1, *Acta Nuntiaturae Polonae.* Cracow: Academia Scientiarum et Litterarum Polona.
Eidelberg, Shlomo. 1996. *The Jews and the Crusaders: the Hebrew Chronicles of the First and Second Crusades.* Hoboken: KTAV Publishing House.
Grayzel, Solomon. 1933. *The Church and the Jews in the XIIIth Century: A Study of Their Relations During the Years 1198–1254.* Philadelphia: The Dropsie College.
Grayzel, Solomon. 1962. "The Papal Bull *Sicut Judaeis.*" In *Studies and Essays in Honor of Abraham A. Neuman,* edited by Meir Ben-Horin, Bernard D. Weinryb, and Solomon Zeitlin, 243–80. Leiden: Brill.
Halpern, Israel. 1945. *Pinkas va'ad arba aratzot.* Jerusalem: Mosad Bialik.
Herzl, Theodor. 1960. *The Complete Diaries of Theodor Herzl.* Edited by Raphael Patai. 5 vols. New York: Herzl Press.
Miczynski, Sebastian. 1618. *Zwierciadło Korony Polskiey.* Cracow: Máciej Jedrzeiowczyk.
Parkes, James William. 1969. *The Conflict of the Church and the Synagogue: A Study in the Origins of Antisemitism.* New York: Atheneum.
Passelecq, Georges, and Bernard Suchecky. 1997. *The Hidden Encyclical of Pius XI.* New York: Harcourt Brace.
Ravid, Benjamin. 1992. "From Geographical Realia to Historiographical Symbol: The Odyssey of the Word 'Ghetto.'" In *Essential Papers on Jewish Culture in Renaissance and Baroque Italy,* edited by David B. Ruderman, 373–85. New York: New York University Press.
Stow, Kenneth. 1977. *Catholic Thought and Papal Policy, 1555–1593.* New York: Jewish Theological Seminary Press.
Stow, Kenneth. 1992. "The Consciousness of Closure: Roman Jewry and Its *Ghet.*" In *Essential Papers on Jewish Culture in Renaissance and Baroque Italy,* edited by David Ruderman, 386–400. New York: New York University Press.
Wojtyska, Henryk Damian. 1993. *Aloisius Lippomano (1555–1557).* Vol. 3/1, *Acta Nuntiaturae Polonae.* Rome: Institutum Historicum Polonicum Romae.

CHAPTER 7

Conspiracy Theories

Jovan Byford

INTRODUCTION

Any attempt to understand antisemitism and its persistence in modern society would be incomplete without engagement with the topic of conspiracy theories. This is because much of contemporary antisemitism takes the form of a conspiracy theory. Animosity toward Jews is today seldom expressed in terms of the demeaning stereotypes that defined racial antisemitism in the past, or as routine "dislike" of Jews or disapproval of their culture or religion. Instead, the biggest "fault" of Jews in the eyes of antisemites worldwide is their alleged possession of considerable wealth, power, and influence, which they use to control democratic governments, international organizations, financial institutions, media corporations, and cultural establishments. For those affiliated with the far-right, Jews represent an omnipotent force with almost supernatural powers, intent on the destruction of independent nations and the creation of a secular, Jewish-controlled, New World Order. Sections of the Left, on the other hand, see Jewish elites as united in a powerful Israel/Zionist/Jewish lobby that pulls the strings of western politics and controls the mass media.

The connection between antisemitism and conspiracy theory manifests itself also in another, possibly less obvious, way. The idea of Jewish power persists as a latent motif in a sizeable proportion of contemporary conspiracy culture. Of course, not all conspiracy theories are necessarily antisemitic; there are many that, while being farfetched and ludicrous, are, at least in terms of ethnic or religious prejudice, relatively harmless. In fact, since the end of WWII, exponents of conspiracy theories, especially those with mainstream

J. Byford (✉)
The Open University, Milton Keynes, UK
e-mail: jovan.byford@open.ac.uk

© The Author(s) 2021
S. Goldberg et al. (eds.), *Key Concepts in the Study of Antisemitism*, Palgrave Critical Studies of Antisemitism and Racism, https://doi.org/10.1007/978-3-030-51658-1_7

pretentions, have often sought to distance themselves from the idea of a specifically Jewish plot. The most common arch-villains of contemporary conspiracy theories are organizations such as the Bilderberg Group, or vague entities such as the "creators of the New World Order," or the shadowy elite within the American establishment. Yet, discernible within many of these contemporary, seemingly non-antisemitic conspiracy narratives, are worrying, and often very subtle, allusions to Jewish involvement. This means that just as conspiracy theories are an important dimension of contemporary antisemitism, so antisemitism remains a regrettable, and persistent, ingredient of the conspiracy culture.

In this chapter, we will explore the longstanding connections between conspiracy theories and antisemitism and why the two phenomena are so inextricably and unavoidably linked. We will start by looking at what conspiracy theories are and where they come from.

What Are Conspiracy Theories?

The term "conspiracy theory" describes explanations which presume that a historical or political event (or series of events) occurred as a consequence of a carefully worked out plan, plotted in secret by a small group of powerful individuals. Although such explanations may focus on different conspiratorial bodies—the Illuminati, Jews, Communists, the US government, etc.—they are permeated by the same fundamental claim: there is "an occult force operating behind the seemingly real, outward forms of political life" (J. M. Roberts 1974, pp. 29–30), and visible reality is no more than an illusion, a smokescreen that conceals the sinister machinations of some powerful, secretive, and menacing cabal.

But conspiracy theories involve more than just the claim that events in history are the outcome of collusion or a secret, and evil, plot. Conspiracy theories are complex and alluring stories, characterized by a common rhetorical style. Anyone who has had the opportunity to engage with conspiracy theories about 9/11, the COVID-19 pandemic, or the machinations of the Bilderberg group, the Illuminati, or Jews will be struck by the fact that they often sound remarkably alike. Tales of conspiracy—regardless of whether expounded in Washington, London, Moscow, Tehran, or Beijing or of whether they purport to explain a war, a political assassination, a disease, or a financial crisis—are marked by a distinct thematic configuration, narrative structure, and explanatory logic. When describing the conspirators, their nefarious plan, and the means of mass manipulation through which they keep their endeavors secret, or when presenting evidence to substantiate the conspiracy claims, conspiracy theorists resort to a number of recurring motifs and tropes (see Byford 2011). American historian Richard Hofstadter (1967) referred to the common features of the conspiracy theory as markers of a distinct explanatory or rhetorical "style" which he chose to call "paranoid." He employed the term style, "much as a historian of art might speak of the baroque or the mannerist style.

It is, above all, a way of seeing the world and of expressing oneself" (p. 4). For similar reasons, conspiracy theories are said to constitute a distinct culture that encompasses a system of knowledge, beliefs, values, and practices shared by communities of people around the world (Barkun 2006).

The uniformity of the conspiracist "style" of rhetoric can be shown to persist over time. The language of contemporary conspiracy culture bears a close resemblance to that found in the writings of nineteenth- and twentieth-century conspiracy theorists; it draws on the same armory of arguments and tropes and, as we shall see, writers today will often recognize the enduring relevance of the work of their predecessors. This thread of continuity that runs through conspiracy theories is sufficiently robust to make it possible to speak of a tradition of explanation (Billig 1978, 1987) made up of a corpus of ideas, arguments, "facts," "revelations," and "proofs" pertaining to the alleged world plot, which have accumulated over time, and which are reused, refined, expanded, and applied to new circumstances by successive generations of conspiracy theorists.

Where Do Conspiracy Theories Come From?

When tracing the origins of the conspiracy tradition, it is tempting to look back either to the stories of plots and intrigues that defined the real-life politics and religious mythology of ancient Athens and Rome, or at the "cloak and dagger" political culture of the medieval and early modern periods. One might also seek the origins of specifically antisemitic conspiracy theories in the medieval Christian anti-Jewish demonology which perceived Jews as Christ-killers, sorcerers, poisoners of wells, and murderers of children (Trachtenberg 1983). In other words, it sometimes seems that conspiracy theories are as old as human society itself.

But conspiracy theories of the kind discussed in this chapter are of more recent origin. They date back to the late eighteenth century, when, shortly after the French Revolution, a number of authors such as John Robison and Augustin Barruel wrote lengthy treatises attributing the causes of this dramatic historical event to the machinations of secret societies, including the Freemasons and the Illuminati. These post-revolutionary conspiracy theories differed from those that existed beforehand in several important ways. Until then, tales of political conspiracy were confined to fairly specific intrigues and plots among powerful figures of the day, who were said to be motivated by financial or political gain. By contrast, the conspiracy theory about the French Revolution was preoccupied with the actions of mysterious secret societies whose composition, political character, and modus operandi were shrouded in mystery (Cubitt 1989). More importantly, conspirators were no longer seen as working for personal benefit. The alleged plot was not limited either temporally by the length of the conspirators' term of office, political career, or life, or spatially by their finite sphere of influence. The Illuminati plot was seen as timeless, and had the destruction of the social order and established way of life as its ultimate aim. Conspiracy became seen as the motive force in history, accounting for any event, past, present, or future.

Up until the middle of the nineteenth century, most conspiracy theories focused on the machinations of secret societies, especially the Illuminati and the Freemasons. Occasionally, writers alluded to these organizations as "puppets manipulated by Jews" (cited in von Bieberstein 1977), but this view was not dominant. This changed around the 1850s, when the wave of liberal reform in Europe led to the granting of full citizenship and property rights to Jews. The emancipation of the Jewish community provoked a bitter reaction across the continent, especially from conservative forces. Nationalist writers and publishers, or traditionally conservative clerical authorities in Germany, France, Russia, and elsewhere, turned their attention to Jews as the ultimate sinister force that pulls the strings of politics. They mistakenly and tendentiously concluded that, because Jews benefited from the values of liberalism, secularism, and the Enlightenment, they must have been instrumental in their creation and dissemination (Poliakov 1974).

Antisemitic conspiracy theories which emerged in the middle of the nineteenth century drew on many of the medieval stereotypes about Jews, and as such continued the longer tradition of anti-Jewish demonology which permeated Christianity throughout the Middle Ages. Yet they also modernized the medieval anti-Jewish tropes, adapting them to the modern age of secular politics. For instance, in the Middle Ages, Jews were seldom seen as a malign force in their own right; they were despised and feared as the "spawn of Satan," his agents on earth, and "a diabolic beast fighting the forces of truth and salvation with Satan's weapon" (Trachtenberg 1983, p. 18). By contrast, in the world of nineteenth-century political conspiracy theory, Jews became the would-be masters, a source of secular power that used money, influence, and arcane knowledge to subvert traditional values and institutions, promote atheism, and turn people into slaves. Nevertheless, traces of the medieval myths persist even in contemporary conspiracy culture, in the form of the obsession with the conspirators' esoteric, occult powers, which they supposedly use to manipulate the masses. For instance, radio show host and conspiracy theorist Alex Jones mixes the motif of the financial and political influence of secret societies, Wall Street, or the "military industrial complex" with the claims of ritualistic "human sacrifices" and satanic practices, which echo the medieval blood libel myth.

The notion of a Jewish quest for world domination occupied a central place in conspiracy theories for almost a hundred years, from the mid-nineteenth to the mid-twentieth century. Its popularity peaked in the 1920s, in the aftermath of the Russian Revolution. Anxieties provoked by the threat of communism made the public in Europe, North America, and elsewhere in the world susceptible to the conspiracist notion that turmoil in Russia in 1917, just like the French Revolution and the events in-between, was orchestrated by a network of clandestine forces, among which Jews played a prominent role. The popularity of these theories is best illustrated by the success of the *Protocols of the Elders of Zion*, the notorious antisemitic pamphlet and proven forgery, which supposedly revealed the aims of the ongoing Jewish plot, and outlined the means by which world domination was to be achieved. Originally published in Russia in 1903, the *Protocols* was later translated into most languages of the world and millions of copies were sold. In the period between 1920, when it acquired international fame, and the defeat of Nazism in 1945, the *Protocols* was outsold worldwide only by the Bible (Cohn 1967).

After WWII, however, the prominence of antisemitic conspiracy theories diminished. Once the Holocaust made it impossible to champion the idea of a Jewish conspiracy with the same degree of openness as before (Poliakov 1974; Billig 1978), attention was turned to the maneuverings of organizations such as the Council on Foreign Relations or the Bilderberg Group (Lipset and Raab 1978; Billig 1978). In many ways, conspiracy theorists returned to their roots and created a twentieth-century variant of the secret society mythology, with some new protagonists, but old aims and methods. This post-war transformation illustrates well the fluid and dynamic quality of conspiracy theories that accounts for their persistence. Because purveyors of conspiracy theories have always been surrounded by skeptics and subjected to criticism and ridicule, anticipating and reacting to potential or actual charges of irrationality, paranoia, or prejudice has become an essential feature of any conspiracy narrative. This drives the conspiracy tradition of explanation to evolve, so as to remain pertinent, and politically acceptable, in response to changing social and political circumstances.

The Thread of Antisemitism

At first sight, a distinction can be made between the New World Order-style conspiracy theories of the kind one encounters in high-street bookshops or on syndicated radio shows and the openly antisemitic ones which, at least in the West, are today largely confined to the margins. The former have a more "reasonable" appearance and they do not identify an ethnic group as being in control of organizations plotting world domination. In fact, most conspiracy theorists with mainstream pretensions—e.g., Allen (1972), Robertson (1991), and Marrs (2000)—go out of their way to distance themselves from antisemitism, arguing that those who continue to peddle the notion of Jewish conspiracy are only discrediting the important task of exposing the "real" would-be rulers of the world.

However, while it might be possible to make a theoretical distinction between the two sorts of conspiracy theory, in practice the boundaries can be blurred. The conspiracy theorist is operating in an ideological space with a long antisemitic legacy that cannot be easily discarded (Byford and Billig 2001). This legacy usually resurfaces when the conspiracy theorist seeks to situate the present political situation in a broader historical context.

The past is an essential feature of any conspiracy theory. It would be implausible for a conspiracy theorist to argue that a present-day plot is historically isolated. For example, one cannot convincingly claim that until the Bilderberg group was founded in 1954, things happened by chance, while since then everything has been the result of a conspiracy. Or that the 9/11 attacks as "the mother of all conspiracies" was a singular, unprecedented event. A conspiracy theory is a view of the world not only as it is at present, but also as it always was. Specific plots need to be, and invariably are, imagined as links in a longer chain of conspiracies.

When locating current plots and schemes within the centuries-long line of conspiratorial activity, conspiracy theorists seldom set out to write the history of the conspiracy from scratch. Instead, they draw on the work of other conspiracy theorists: they refer to, cite, and quote established sources within the conspiracy culture. This reliance on the work of other conspiracy theorists is not the result of intellectual laziness or lack of creativity. It is necessitated by the conspiracy theory's inherent problem with proof. Writers of conspiracy material are accountable for the claims they make, yet, by definition, they deal with imperfect evidence: they are concerned with knowledge that is inherently secret and that the most powerful forces in the world are, supposedly, working hard to suppress. Conspiracy theorists can, therefore, never offer incontrovertible proof for their claims. As was stated in an editorial published in the 1970s in the British far-right publication *Spearhead*, "if such a degree of proof was available, there would no longer be a conspiracy" (cited in Billig 1978, p. 309).

To address the tricky issue of evidence, conspiracy writers tend to interpret the world around them through the work of other conspiracy theorists, past and present, and invoke their authority as a substitute for direct proof. After all, the main criterion for a successful conspiracy theory is its acceptance by the wider community of conspiracy enthusiasts, who will judge it by, among other things, an author's apparent knowledge of the canonical works of the genre. This tendency to regurgitate old arguments and tropes and apply old ideas to new circumstances is why conspiracy theories so often sound alike.

This feature of conspiracy theories is important in relation to conspiratorial antisemitism. As was already noted, between the mid-nineteenth century and the end of WWII, antisemitism was the dominant motif in conspiracy theories. Much of the conspiracist literature of that period, but also about that period, revolves around the idea of a Jewish conspiracy. This means that, when authors today reflect on the history of the plot—a task that, as we have seen, requires them to recognize the relevance of past conspiracies and past conspiracy theories—they invariably come into contact with the antisemitic legacy of the conspiracy culture. A couple of tropes ubiquitous in contemporary conspiracy literature will be used to illustrate the links between the seemingly non-prejudicial conspiracy theories and their less palatable, more antisemitic variants.

The first trope concerns the causes of the Russian Revolution of 1917. It is today virtually impossible to find an elaborate account of the conspiracy theory that does not allude to the hidden causes of the revolution and allege that a group of American bankers bankrolled Bolshevik revolutionaries. This motif is regarded as common sense by leading conspiracy theorists (Jim Marrs, Pat Robertson, David Icke, Alex Jones, etc.) and among contributors to countless conspiracy websites worldwide.

At first sight, there is nothing antisemitic about the claim that American bankers financed the Bolsheviks. Those who make it will seldom present it as a Jewish conspiracy, or even discuss the identity of the bankers involved. However, a different picture emerges when one examines more closely the sources for this claim. For instance, in Jim Marrs' bestselling book, *Rule by Secrecy* (2000), the five-page section in which the true origins of the Russian Revolution are "exposed" includes citations of seven sources, mostly books by other conspiracy theorists. Among them is the today largely forgotten work *Czarism and the Revolution* by Arsene de Goulévitch (1962). Marrs identifies de Goulévitch as a particularly important source, given that, as a Russian, he was an eyewitness to "the early days of Bolshevism" (Marrs 2000, p. 192). What Marrs omits, however, is that de Goulévitch—his key "witness"—was a White Russian general and antisemitic campaigner who fled to Paris after the revolution, where he campaigned against "Jewish propaganda." His book *Czarism and the Revolution*, originally published in French in the 1930s, attracted interest from far-right circles in the US and Britain after a translation was published in California in 1962 (see Billig 1978). In de Goulévitch's writing (unlike in Marrs'), the revolution is presented as the complot by Jewish bankers. In fact, the main source for de Goulévitch's claims, which Marrs indirectly reproduces, was the writings of Boris Brasol, the man who brought the *Protocols of the Elders of Zion* to the United States.

Marrs is by no means an exception when it comes to citing such discredited sources. In the writings of most other popular conspiracy theorists of today, one is never far away from de Goulévitch and other exponents of the kind of antisemitism that writers are so keen to avoid being associated with. Even when *Czarism and the Revolution* is not quoted from directly, there is a reference to some other work in which the book is cited. One only needs to follow the paper trail, and usually not for long.

The second example is the ubiquity of the Rothschild family in conspiracy narratives. Ever since the nineteenth century, the Rothschilds, who combined Jewishness, financial wealth, and international connections, have been the epitome of the international Jewish conspiracy (Barkun 2006). The family name continues to feature in conspiracy narratives to the present day, although many writers of the post-1945 era have tended to play down their importance or avoid emphasizing their Jewishness.

For example, in the works of Jim Marrs (2000) or David Icke (1999), the "Rothschild organization," is seen as the pinnacle of the world plot and the sinister force behind various international organizations and secret societies. Similar obsession with the Rothschilds is apparent in Pat Robertson's conspiracy classic, *The New World Order* (1991). For the most part, the emphasis tends to be on their wealth, business acumen, and good connections, rather than their Jewishness. And yet, there are other, much wealthier and better-connected families that are completely overlooked by conspiracy theorists. So, what makes the Rothschilds so "unique"? The answer lies in their history, namely, the Rothschild family's supposed involvement, in the eighteenth century, with a German Masonic lodge. Because of this link with freemasonry, the Rothschilds embody the connection, essential to contemporary conspiracy theories, between two sources of nefarious power: secret societies and wealthy bankers (Robertson 1991). Also, their continuing wealth and influence epitomizes the persistence of the conspiracy across centuries. Crucially, the "revelation" about the Rothschilds and their longstanding role in the conspiracy is not a discovery of contemporary theorists: they lifted it directly from the book *World Revolution* (1921) by the British author Nesta Webster, where the same argument is presented to connect not the Freemasons and "high finance," but the Illuminati and Jews. Webster herself "borrowed" the claim from German nineteenth-century antisemitic conspiracy theorists (von Bieberstein 1977).

These examples are representative of a pattern that permeates contemporary conspiracy culture. They illustrate how, while portraying itself as a more reasonable and sound explanation of history and politics, the present-day secret society mythology is in fact a continuation and refinement of a tradition of explanation with a legacy of antisemitism.

Whenever attention is drawn to the presence, in contemporary conspiracy literature, of such antisemitic motifs, coded references, or innuendos, debate tends to revolve around the issue of intent and whether the authors in questions are "antisemitic." And yet, it could be argued that at issue here is not the antisemitic dispositions or intentions (or the lack thereof) of individual conspiracy theorists, but the consequence of their work. By recognizing the relevance of antisemitic works of the past and by perpetuating their message (albeit often in a coded or veiled form), the seemingly "reasonable" conspiracy theories ensure the persistence of antisemitic themes and the motif of Jews as a source of sinister influence. In other words, conspiracy theories, because of their internal logic, organization, and approach to evidence, and because of the way in which they are written and transmitted, find it hard to escape their own disreputable ideological and intellectual history and so remain susceptible to corruption by antisemitism.

Antisemitic Conspiracy Theories and the Left

The conspiracy theories discussed so far have been propagated by authors aligned, for the most part, with the right-wing of politics. However, recent years have witnessed an increased awareness of a seemingly new brand of conspiratorial antisemitism propagated by sections of the Left. The phenomenon, often referred to as "left-wing antisemitism" or "anti-Zionism," is defined by the fact that, ostensibly, the central objects of disparagement and animosity are not Jews as such, but Israel as the Jewish state (e.g., Hirsh 2017). Within this view, Israel is a source of uniquely harmful influence in the world: its actions, and even its very existence, are believed to be an expression of a singularly iniquitous nationalist ideology (Zionism), which is racist, imperialist, expansionist, and tyrannical. What is more, the apparent failure by the international community to deal with Israel is attributed to the disproportionate political and financial power of pro-Israel interest groups, particularly in the West.

Before moving on to discuss antisemitism on the Left in more detail, a note of clarification is necessary. For decades, many of Israel's policies have come under sustained criticism from individuals and organizations on different sides of the political spectrum. The state of Israel and its government have often, and quite legitimately, been called to account for the violations of the rights of Israeli Palestinians, the continuing occupation and blockade of Gaza, the building of Jewish settlements on occupied territories, the use of military force that many argue is disproportionate, lacklustre commitment to a two-state solution, and so on. Criticism of Israel is, therefore, not in and of itself either "antisemitism" or "anti-Zionism." Israel can, and should be, held up to the same standard as any other state in the world.

However, within sections of the Left, the censure of Israel is sometimes tarnished with the kind of language, and imagery, typically associated with right-wing antisemitism. As David Cesarani notes, the definitive crossing of the boundary between legitimate criticism of Israel and antisemitism occurs at the point where it "intentionally or unintentionally uses or echoes long-established anti-Jewish discourse, characterising Jews inside Israel or in the Jewish diaspora as singularly wealthy, powerful, conspiratorial, treacherous and malign" (2004, p. 72). In other words, when the argument is embellished with the motifs of a Jewish conspiracy.

The conspiracist element of Left antisemitism is most obvious in discussions about the existence and the machinations of what has become known as the Israel/Zionist/Jewish lobby. A common assumption of left-wing anti-Zionist critique is that Israel pursues the oppression of the Palestinians with unwavering political, military, and financial support from the governments of the United States and to a lesser extent Britain, because the latter are in the grip of the menacing and all-powerful pro-Israel lobby. When the sinister influence of "the Lobby" is discussed in the context of US politics, the focus of attention is principally on organizations which campaign for the interests of the American Jewish community and Israel, such as the American Israeli Public Affairs Committee (AIPAC), the Anti-Defamation League (ADL), or the American Jewish Committee (AJC). These are, indeed, highly influential and effective pro-Israel advocacy groups, albeit with somewhat different agendas and ways of functioning, which operate openly, transparently, and in accordance with US law. Yet in some of the criticism, a "slippage" (Fine 2006) or what Richard Hofstadter (1967) called "a leap of the imagination" occurs, whereby disparate organizations come to be seen as parts of a single, unified, all-powerful conspiratorial body, which uses its virtually unlimited financial resources to purchase political influence on an unprecedented scale and control the government, the media, and academia, and whose loyalty lies with Israel, rather than the country in which they operate.

A particularly notable example of the Lobby thesis is John Mearsheimer's and Stephen Walt's essay "The Israel Lobby" (2006), subsequently expanded into a 500-page book *The Israel Lobby and U.S. Foreign Policy* (2007). This much-quoted work has been instrumental in publicizing—and, because of the authors' academic credentials, legitimizing—the view that the Israel lobby drives US foreign policy. Although the authors explicitly distanced themselves from antisemitic conspiracy theories when they stated that the Lobby is not engaged "in a conspiracy of the sort depicted in tracts like the *Protocols of the Elders of Zion*," they nevertheless suggested that pro-Israel organizations, as a unified, and malign force, have a "stranglehold on Congress," exercise undue influence on public debate and popular opinion, "police academia," and work against America's national interest (Mearsheimer and Walt 2006). Their suggestion that Jewish individuals or groups were instrumental in taking the US to war in Iraq is particularly problematic, as it echoes the rhetoric that has been used by antisemites to scapegoat Jews since at least the First World War (Hirsh 2017).

The motif of "the Lobby" is present on the British left too. In 2002, the British Labour Party MP Tam Dalyell stated that Tony Blair's foreign policy was "unduly influenced by a cabal of Jewish advisers" (Brown and Hastings 2003). Ten years later, Jeremy Corbyn, a fellow MP and leader of the Labour Party between 2015 and 2020, called for an inquiry into the influence of "pro-Israel lobbying groups" on the British government. He went as far as to suggest that the influence of "the Lobby" goes "to the heart of what's going on in the Home Office and the way the government makes decisions" (Bright 2012). During the 2017 General Election campaign, a pro-Corbyn group based in Bristol displayed a giant banner depicting Prime Minister Theresa May wearing Star of David earrings (Clark 2017).

Large sections of the Left, while highly critical of Israel, downplay the role of "the Lobby." Noam Chomsky, for example, has dismissed the insinuation that America's support for Israel is attributable to the "effectiveness of the American Jewish community in political life and in influencing opinion" (1983, p. 13) on the grounds that such a view overestimates the role of political pressure groups. In fact, ever since the Vietnam War, when the conflict in the Middle East came to be viewed through the lens of the broader critique of American interventionism and "imperialism," a much more prevalent view within left-wing thought has been that Israel is America's stooge, not the other way around. So, how and why does the view of Israel as America's "colony" morph, within sections of the political left, into the claim that those whose loyalty is ultimately with Israel control the levers of power in countries like the United States or Britain?

The presence of antisemitic motifs in left-wing writing cannot be explained in terms of the continuities within the conspiracy tradition that, as we have seen, are so easily discernible in the literature of the Right. Exegeses of "the Lobby" theory of American politics, such as the aforementioned examples, do not situate the machinations of AIPAC within a longer history of (Jewish) conspiracy. The likes of the Rothschilds are not identified as the precursors of "the Lobby," and early twentieth-century classics of antisemitic conspiracy theories do not feature in the references or footnotes.

Instead, conspiracy tradition has a subtler and indirect influence. The century-long dominance of conspiratorial antisemitism has left behind it a rich inventory of images, motifs, and tropes about Jewish financial power and questionable loyalty. Although largely ostracized from polite conversation and the mainstream of politics, this antisemitism nevertheless circulates in public discourse and colors the perceptions of events involving Jews. Thus, any discussion that involves Jews and political influence is vulnerable to the resurfacing of the "underground repertoire of stereotypes, instinctively understood by both the utterer and the recipient," and their almost subliminal influence. The "antisemitic atmosphere" on the Left is therefore sustained not through a whole-scale endorsement of the conspiracy tradition, but by "the drip-drip-drip of argument, coded and implicit, clothed in allusion and wrapped in innuendo, always with a pre-emptive disavowal of any antisemitic intent" (Pulzer 2003, p. 101).

This contamination by antisemitic motifs should not occur so easily, however. Left-wing thought is marked by a long tradition of opposition to racism and a standing commitment to equality and social justice. Its contemporary exponents should therefore be more resistant to ideas traditionally peddled by their ideological opponents. And yet, among many critics of "the Lobby," this sensitivity is lacking.

The reason for this lies in the fact that the Lobby narrative contains within it a premise which is essential to the overall conspiracy thesis, but which also suppresses the immunity to antisemitic tropes. It is the premise that antisemitism is less of a social problem, or threat, than the *accusation* of antisemitism, which "the Lobby" uses to silence opponents and de-legitimize criticism of Israel (Hirsh 2017). Mearsheimer and Walt (2006), for instance, called the "charge of antisemitism" one of the Lobby's "most powerful weapons," used to manipulate public opinion and pursue its agenda. In the UK too, it has become commonplace for anyone on the Left called to book for an antisemitic remark to claim victimhood of "the Lobby's" disingenuous smear campaign.

Thus, by persuading their audience, and, importantly, also themselves, that the moral standpoint from which their arguments can be criticized has been consciously imposed by "the Lobby"—and is therefore an essential part of its sinister method—writers can pre-empt, destabilize, and render unfounded any criticism of their ideological position. This places the Lobby theory of politics beyond moral reproach, removes the taboo surrounding antisemitism, and reinforces the believers' conviction in the absolute truth of their views. The belief that everything, including the definition of what is acceptable, is manipulated by the sinister "Lobby" shields this worldview from the effects of disconfirming evidence, but also makes it vulnerable to the malign influence of antisemitic motifs and stereotypes rooted in the conspiracy tradition.

Conclusion

The continuing presence of antisemitic motifs in conspiracy theories propagated by the Right and the theorizing about the machinations of the Israel/Zionist/Jewish Lobby by sections on the political left are not unrelated phenomena. In sharing the motif of a Jewish plot, conspiracy theories propagated on both sides of the political spectrum are locked in a relationship of mutual reinforcement. A number of writers on the far-right of American politics have greeted the writing on "the Lobby" as a long-awaited vindication of their views and have embraced it as a convenient source of legitimacy (Hirsh 2007). For instance, in 2006, David Duke, the white supremacist and former leader of Ku Klux Klan praised Mearsheimer and Walt's essay on the Lobby as proof that his theories about a Jewish conspiracy have been correct all along (Lake 2006). At the same time, by persevering with their often-subtle allusions to the Jewish conspiracy, writers on the Right (many of whom claim to be pro-Israel) continue to keep alive the gamut of stereotypes, motifs, and tropes which will occasionally seep into the discourse of the Left, especially in response to events in the Middle East. This cooperation across the traditional ideological divides has already produced the "routine stereotype" of twenty-first-century antisemitism, namely, the claim about the Jewish/Zionist influence behind the neoconservative elite in the United States and its deicison to take America to war in Iraq. This motif is so prevalent today, on both sides of the political spectrum, that it is threatening to become as robust a feature of conspiracy culture as is the idea about Jewish origins of Bolshevism (Cesarani 2004).

Finally, understanding the link between conspiracy theory and antisemitism explored in this chapter is important because it sheds light on the complex causal relationship between the two phenomena. It is often assumed that antisemitic conspiracy theories are a manifestation or rationalization of a more basic or profound feeling of animosity and hatred toward Jews. However, as I have tried to show, this is not necessarily the case. The idea of a Jewish plot can, and often does, emerge as an unintended consequence of the endorsement of the conspiracy theory, a tradition of explanation and a way of seeing the world that has, for reasons examined in this essay, failed to exorcise the ghost of antisemitism from its past.

References

Allen, Gary. 1972. *None Dare Call It Conspiracy*. Rossmoor: Concord Press.
Barkun, Michael. 2006. *A Culture of Conspiracy: Apocalyptic Visions in Contemporary America*. Los Angeles: University of California Press.

Billig, Michael. 1978. *Fascists: A Social Psychology of the National Front.* London: Academic Press.
Billig, Michael. 1987. "Anti-Semitic Themes and the British Far Left: Some Social-Psychological Observations on Indirect Aspects of the Conspiracy Tradition." In *Changing Conceptions of Conspiracy*, edited by C. F. Graumann and S. Moscovici. New York: Springer-Verlag.
Bright, Martin. 2012. "Jeremy Corbyn Calls for Inquiry on 'Pro-Israel Lobby.'" *The Jewish Chronicle*, April 19. https://www.thejc.com/news/uk-news/jeremy-corbyn-calls-for-inquiry-on-pro-israel-lobby-1.32916.
Brown, Colin, and Chris Hastings. 2003. "Fury as Dalyell Attacks Blair's 'Jewish Cabal.'" *Daily Telegraph*, May 4. http://www.telegraph.co.uk/news/uknews/1429114/Fury-as-Dalyell-attacks-Blairs-Jewish-cabal.html.
Byford, Jovan. 2011. *Conspiracy Theories: A Critical Introduction.* Basingstoke: Palgrave Macmillan.
Byford, Jovan, and Michael Billig. 2001. "The Emergence of Antisemitic Conspiracy Theories in Yugoslavia During the War with NATO." *Patterns of Prejudice* 35 (4): 50–63.
Cesarani, David. 2004. *The Left and the Jews/The Jews and the Left.* London: Labour Friends of Israel.
Chomsky, Noam. 1983. *The Fateful Triangle: The United States, Israel and the Palestinians.* Boston: South End Press.
Clark, Natasha. 2017. "Labour Poster Row." *The Sun*, June 7. https://www.thesun.co.uk/news/3746401/labour-supporting-banner-showing-theresa-may-wearing-star-of-david-earrings-removed-after-complaints-of-anti-semitism.
Cohn, Norman. 1967. *Warrant for Genocide: The Myth of the Jewish World Conspiracy and the Protocols of the Elders of Zion.* London: Secker & Warburg.
Cubitt, G. 1989. "Conspiracy Myths and Conspiracy Theories." *Journal of the Anthropological Society of Oxford* 20 (1): 12–26.
Fine, Robert. 2006. "The Lobby: Mearsheimer and Walt's Conspiracy Theory." www.EngageOnline.org.uk, March 21. https://engageonline.wordpress.com/2006/03/21/the-lobby-mearsheimer-and-walts-conspiracy-theory-robert-fine.
Goulévitch, Arsene de. 1962. *Czarism and the Revolution.* Hawthorn: Omni Publications.
Hirsh, David. 2007. *Anti-Zionism and Antisemitism: Cosmopolitan Reflections.* Vol. 1 of *Yale Initiative for the Interdisciplinary Study of Antisemitism Working Papers*. New Haven: Yale University.
Hirsh, David. 2017. *Contemporary Left Antisemitism.* London: Routledge.
Hofstadter, Richard. 1967. *Paranoid Style in American Politics and Other Essays.* New York: Vintage Books.
Icke, David. 1999. *The Biggest Secret.* Ryde, Isle of Wight: David Icke Books.
Lake, E. 2006. "David Duke Claims to Be Vindicated by a Harvard Dean." *The New York Sun*, March 20. http://www.nysun.com/national/david-duke-claims-to-be-vindicated-by-a-harvard/29380/.
Lipset, Seymour Martin, and Earl Raab. 1978. *The Politics of Unreason: Right-wing Extremism in America, 1790–1977.* Chicago: University of Chicago Press.
Marrs, Jim. 2000. *Rule by Secrecy: The Hidden History That Connects the Trilateral Commission, The Freemasons and the Great Pyramids.* New York: Harper Collins.

Mearsheimer, John, and Stephen Walt. 2006. "The Israel Lobby." *London Review of Books* 28 (6) (March 23): 3–12.
Mearsheimer, John, and Stephen Walt. 2007. *The Israel Lobby and U.S. Foreign Policy.* New York: Farrar, Straus and Giroux.
Poliakov, Leon. 1974. *The History of Antisemitism.* 4 vols. London: Routledge & Kegan Paul.
Pulzer, Peter. 2003. "The New Antisemitism, or When Is a Taboo Not a Taboo?" In *A New Antisemitism?: Debating Judeophobia in 21st-century Britain,* edited by Paul Iganski, Barry Alexander Kosmin, and Geoffrey Alderman. London: Profile.
Roberts, John Morris. 1974. *The Mythology of the Secret Societies.* St Albans: Paladin.
Robertson, Pat. 1991. *The New World Order.* Dallas: Word Publishing.
Trachtenberg, Joshua. 1983. *The Devil and The Jews: The Medieval Conception of the Jew and Its Relation to Modern Anti-Semitism.* Philadelphia: Jewish Publication Society.
von Bieberstein, Johannes Rogalla. 1977. "The Story of Jewish-Masonic Conspiracy: 1776–1945." *Patterns of Prejudice* 11 (6): 1–21.
Webster, Nesta. 1921. *World Revolution: The Plot Against Civilization.* London: Constable.

CHAPTER 8

Emancipation

Frederick Beiser

All discussions of antisemitism involve, implicitly or explicitly, the concept of emancipation. The reasons for this are very simple: the so-called "Jewish question" was essentially the question whether emancipation was justified. Should the Jews be emancipated? If so, under what conditions? And to what extent? Modern antisemitism, as an intellectual attitude, can be defined by its answers to these questions. The antisemite maintains that emancipation is not justified, or that it is so only under very restricted conditions.

Nowhere were these questions investigated with more vigor and rigor, and for a longer period of time, than in Germany. The Jewish question preoccupied intellectuals in Germany for more than a century, beginning in 1781 and not ending until 1933. The de facto achievement of emancipation in 1871, when Kaiser Wilhelm I proclaimed the full equality of all citizens regardless of their religion, did not end the discussion of the Jewish question. By 1873 the reaction against emancipation began; and by 1879 the "Berlin movement" was born, marking the rise of modern antisemitism. After that, the discussion of the rights and wrongs of emancipation did not cease until 1933. It stopped then for all too tragic reasons, of which we are all very familiar.

Because the discussion of the Jewish question was so intense and protracted in Germany, and because Germany was the land in which the fate of European Jewry was eventually decided, I will focus in this essay on the concept of emancipation as it was discussed in Germany. I will consider only the major philosophical issues in this discussion. I make no attempt to provide a complete historical survey.

F. Beiser (✉)
Syracuse University, Syracuse, NY, USA
e-mail: fbeiser@syr.edu

The concept of emancipation has ancient roots going back to the Roman Republic.[1] The Latin etymology of the verb "*emancipare*" is "*e manu capere*," which literally means to take from the hand. Originally, emancipation referred to the legal act by which the *pater familias* set his son free from paternal authority so that he was legally responsible for his own actions. Later the word was also applied to the legal act by which the master set free his slave. Since the son or slave was regarded as property, emancipation was also understood as releasing or surrendering what one owned. *Mancipium* (literally, what one had in hand) was the abstract noun for someone's possession or right of ownership. Hence "*emancipare*" also had connotations of releasing or surrendering property.

This sense of emancipation—releasing someone from servitude or bondage—had a long history which persisted until the beginning of the eighteenth century. However, in the beginning of the early modern era (ca. the sixteenth century), there began a marked shift in its meaning that only became widespread in the late eighteenth and early nineteenth centuries. The verb was originally *transitive* in meaning, referring to the act by which the father or master liberated his son or slave; but it gradually acquired a *reflexive* meaning, so that one freed or emancipated oneself. Now the slave or servant emancipated himself; he did not receive emancipation from the master. In estatist society of the early modern era this reflexive meaning originally had a pejorative connotation: it was what rebellious subjects or servants did when they took too much liberty for themselves and flaunted their stations in society. But when the legitimacy of that society came into question in the later eighteenth century, the reflexive meaning acquired a positive connotation. To emancipate oneself was to free oneself from illegitimate rule, to throw off unjust bondage. Emancipation was not the illegitimate act of rebellious servants or slaves; it was the legitimate act of liberating oneself and claiming what one was due. Emancipation thus acquired the connotation of *self*-emancipation.

In the wake of the July revolution of 1830, the word "emancipation" became a shibboleth of the new revolutionary age. The goal of revolution was for the people to emancipate themselves, to free themselves from the despotism and privileges of the old estatist society. Emancipation lost its reference to the act of a single person; it was now applied to whole peoples or nations who would free themselves. Now emancipation became the goal of a whole historical epoch. Heinrich Heine, writing in 1828, used the term to characterize his whole age: "What is the great task of our time? It is emancipation. Not merely of the Irish, the Greeks, Frankfurt Jews, Westindian blacks and similar oppressed peoples, but of the whole world, especially Europe…" (1981, p. 376). In a similar fashion Karl Rosenkranz, a neo-Hegelian philosopher,

---

[1] This account of the etymology of the word is taken from four sources: Rürup (1975), Greiffenhagen (1972), Schulz (1913), and Koselleck and Grass (1975). The most thorough account is that of Koselleck and Grass.

wrote ten years later: "Every age creates its own special term for the eternal interests of spirit...In our day it is the thought of freedom. The act by which the enslaved becomes free is emancipation" (quoted in Koselleck and Grass 1975, p. 167).

"Emancipation" was imported into Germany around the second decade of the nineteenth century, when it was used frequently in political discussions and parliamentary debates (Rürup 1975). The word has no direct German equivalent. The closest German analogue is *Befreiung*, which literally means liberation, though this lacks the political connotations of emancipation. Some conservatives thought the foreign term to be unbearably trendy and tendentious, the preferred moniker of leftists who wanted to taunt the establishment. It is noteworthy that the term occurs most commonly in a specific context in Germany: discussions about the emancipation of the Jews. The British wrote about the emancipation of the Irish; the Americans debated the emancipation of the slaves; and the Germans discussed the emancipation of the Jews.

The discussion of emancipation in Germany revolved around three major issues. First, is emancipation a legitimate demand? Second, if it is legitimate, under what conditions, or to what extent, should it be granted? Third, what is the justification for the demand of emancipation? What moral or political basis does it have? Is it based on abstract principles of natural right? Or should it be founded on principles of utility alone?

It might seem that the inspiration for discussion of emancipation in Germany came from the French Revolution. On September 28, 1791, the French National Assembly abolished all civil restrictions imposed on Jews and granted them full citizenship. The Assembly reasoned that the rights of man and the citizen, which it had declared August 26, 1789, should apply to everyone without exception. The action of the National Assembly became the hope for almost all the Jews of Germany. Their claim to emancipation rested upon the French Declaration of the Rights of Man. If everyone deserved these rights simply as a human being, then Jews could not be excluded from them. These rights were universal and categorical, imposing unconditional obligations on all authorities to recognize them; no longer, then, were rights a grant or gift laid down by some prince.

As inspiring and influential as the acts of the National Assembly were, they do not mark the beginning of the discussion of emancipation in Germany. That discussion began a few years earlier, before the French Revolution, and even a few months before the Edict of Toleration of Joseph II of Austria. According to common consensus, the first statement of the case for emancipation was made by Christian Wilhelm Dohm in his *Ueber die bürgerliche Verbesserung der Juden*, which was first published in 1781. Dohm's work has been subject to much revisionist scrutiny in recent years, but it still holds the title, even among his critics, for starting the modern discussion of the Jewish question. It has been pointed out that Dohm did not expressly use the concept of emancipation in making his case for greater civil equality (Katz 1964, pp. 14–16); and it has been argued that he did not have the modern concept of natural rights, which would oblige the state to grant rights to all Jews on par with German non-Jews (Rose 1992, pp. 70–79). Both these points are correct, to some degree, but they should be themselves subject to careful revision. Although Dohm did not use the *word* "emancipation," he still used the *concept* because he argued for liberating Jews from civil restrictions and for granting them greater civil equality. That is an argument for emancipation in substance, if not in words. It is incorrect that Dohm did not have the concept of natural rights, that he conceived rights only as a gift or privilege granted by the state. Dohm appeals to the concept of natural rights several times in his argument (1781, pp. 24, 162, 275, 278), and it is fair to say that his whole case would collapse without them. Nevertheless, it is true that much of Dohm's argument on behalf of emancipation does not appeal directly to natural rights but to the advantages accruing to the state should it grant its Jews equality.

Dohm's revisionist critics are correct in pointing out the limitations of his case in behalf of emancipation. Dohm's main argument for emancipation was that it is in the interests of the state to grant civil equality to the Jews, because having more citizens, and having them engaged in useful occupations, increases the general prosperity of the state. His argument is therefore fundamentally utilitarian, presupposing notions of prosperity and welfare. This limitation of his argument has much to do with Dohm's audience: the Prussian government, which would not have smiled upon notions of equal rights. Dohm was also clear that the Jews should be granted equal rights only upon certain conditions: namely, that they assume all the burdens of Prussian citizenship, which include not only paying taxes but also doing military service. Dohm was explicit that Jews who refuse military service should be not only denied equal rights but also expelled from the state (1781, p. 242).

The great innovation of Dohm's argument was that emancipation should *precede* the moral improvement of the Jews. Moral improvement should follow emancipation and should not be a condition of it. Jews should be granted civil equality, Dohm contended, even though many of them were believed to have objectionable moral characteristics, viz. they were mercenary and lacked manners. They had such a moral character, he claimed, simply because they had lived under oppression. Hence Jewish character could never be a reason for denying civil equality. Nevertheless, Dohm conceded that granting civil equality still *ultimately* depended on the moral improvement of the Jews. If they proved "stubborn and stiff necked" even after emancipation, the case for their emancipation would be lost; the rights granted to them should be revoked.

After the French Revolution, Dohm's argument seemed unduly cautious and conservative. The Declaration of the Rights of Man seemed to make the case for Jewish emancipation self-evident and imperative. The general trend of history, despite occasional retreats and relapses, seemed to move ineluctably in the direction of emancipation. One of the most brilliant spokesmen for emancipation in the post-revolutionary age was Gabriel Riesser (1806–1863), who argued in a dazzling manifesto that the Jews deserved emancipation simply as a natural right (1831a). For him, the case for emancipation was simple and self-evident. The natural rights of man, as declared by the French National Assembly, applied to the Jews like everyone else, and they prohibited all discrimination against minorities on grounds of religion. Those who wanted to maintain the old *Sondergesetze*, which laid down special, legal restrictions on Jews, were not only irrational but reactionary, vainly attempting to buck the course of history. There could be no question, as far as Riesser was concerned, of making emancipation conditional, of granting the Jews equal rights only if they "improved morally," or only if they performed certain services and gave certain benefits to the state. The demand of emancipation was categorical: even if the Jews provided no such benefits, they still deserved equal civil rights simply because they were human beings. Dohm's demand for the self-improvement of the Jews was simply beside the point and unnecessary.

We are today all the children of Gabriel. We too believe that the case for emancipation is self-evident, based upon certain basic human rights. Someone who opposes emancipation, therefore, seems like a benighted and prejudiced reactionary, a misguided defender of a medieval order. But history demands that we be more cautious here, that we examine impartially the opposite viewpoint. For many early nineteenth-century writers, Jewish emancipation was extremely controversial, and it was equally self-evident to them that governments should *not* emancipate the Jews. It would be a mistake to brand these thinkers reactionaries and obscurantists, as some of them were progressive and even approved the ideals of the revolution.

To understand their position, we do well to consider a work written in reaction to Riesser's, H. E. G. Paulus' *Die Jüdische Nationalabsonderung* (1831). Paulus argued that the entire case for emancipation was deeply flawed because it began from one false premise: that the Jews are citizens. The Jews are not *Staatsbürger*—citizens of the state—but they are *Schützbürger*—protected residents. Their legal status in Germany was that of resident aliens; and just as resident aliens—e.g., Frenchmen or Englishmen living in Germany—do not have the right to vote or to hold public office, neither should the Jews have such rights. The fact that the Jews had lived in Germany for centuries gave them no rights of citizenship because they were still only foreigners, residents without the rights of citizenship. What made the Jews foreigners, despite living so long in Germany, and despite even speaking and acting like Germans, is that their first loyalties were to the Israelite state. The whole argument for the separation of church and state, of which liberals were so fond, simply did not apply to Judaism, which was a political as much as a religious doctrine. It was a fundamental tenet of Judaism, as a religion, that each Jew should forever remain loyal to the state of Israel, and that he should work toward its restitution. This should be always his first duty, to which obedience to the state in which he happened to live should be subordinated. So, given that the Jews were only resident foreigners, whose duty was to another state, it was absurd to emancipate them. This would be like granting Frenchmen and Englishmen who are resident in Germany the right to vote and to hold office. No one thought that this should happen to French and English residents; they should think the same with regard to the Jews. The fact that the Jewish state no longer existed, the fact that it was crushed by the Romans centuries ago, was irrelevant; in their hearts, the Jews pined for the restitution of Israel; they were citizens of that potential, future state and not of Germany. Thus Paulus articulated a theme that many opponents of emancipation had already used, and would continue to use in later years: the state within the state. The case for emancipation seemed stranded on the beach of dual citizenship or divided loyalty.

It was kindness on the part of providence that granted Riesser the opportunity to reply to Paulus' argument. He made full use of it in another brilliant tract, his *Vertheidigung der bürgerlichen Gleichstellung der Juden* (*Defense of the Civil Equality of the Jews*) (1831b), which he wrote in a few days in a fit of indignation. Riesser granted Paulus' principle that no one could be a citizen of two states or obey two sovereigns (1831b, p. 38). But he asked where the other state was in this case. It did not even exist. The Jews could not be considered mere foreign residents for the simple reason that there was no other country in which they had their home. "We are not immigrants but we are born here; and because we are born here we have no claim to a home anywhere else; we are Germans or we are homeless" (1831b, p. 39).

Riesser's argument did not completely bury the dual loyalty theme, which would continue to play a major role in arguments against emancipation. Although the Jewish state did not exist, Paulus still claimed that it held its place in the Jewish heart and imagination. Riesser's reassurances that the great majority of Jews no longer believed in the restitution of the Jewish state also could not convince someone like Paulus, who could protest that this left the orthodox out of account. The favorite reply to such reassurances was that, even if they were true, they only went to show that the great majority of contemporary Jews were not *good* Jews. The good Jew—the truly believing Jew—knew that his ultimate loyalties lay not with Germany but with Israel. Here we can begin to resolve the apparent paradox that the antisemites preferred orthodox to reformed Jews: the orthodox seemed to confirm their stereotypes and validated their argument.

Although there were flaws in Riesser's argument, he was still right about one very important thing: the direction of history. History was on Riesser's side, because it was moving toward "the March revolution," the revolution of 1848, which renewed the call for the Rights of Man. Article V of the New Constitution, worked out by the Frankfurt Parliament in 1848, seemed to guarantee all the freedoms necessary for complete emancipation. §14 gave every German freedom of faith and conscience; §16 stated explicitly that enjoyment of civil or political rights should not be conditioned or limited by religious confession; and §17 abolished the state church. For good measure,

§137 of Article II declared that all citizens should be equal before the law and that public office should be open to all. It was no accident that one of the major figures behind this legislation was none other than Gabriel Riesser, who was the vice-president of the Frankfurt Parliament.

The debate about emancipation after 1848 concerns less whether there should be emancipation than the conditions under which it should be given. That there should be emancipation was now accepted by many, either because they were resigned to the course of history or because they saw the rights of man as fundamental to the modern state. But the crucial question was then how far, or to what extent, the Jews should be emancipated? It was widely accepted by liberals, and even many conservatives, that they should have *civil* equality, i.e., equal protection before the law; but it was hotly disputed whether they should be given *political* equality, i.e., the right to vote, to hold political office, and to have government employment.

Much of the debate about the conditions for emancipation revolved around the question of integration or assimilation. If Jews are to have equal civil and political rights, to what extent should they become like their fellow citizens culturally or socially? That there should be some degree of integration everyone agreed, Jew and non-Jew alike; but the question was again to what extent or to what degree. The debate was vague and slippery not least because the concepts of integration and assimilation were rarely defined. Integration or assimilation was usually understood as an amalgam of political, cultural, and moral characteristics. To be well-integrated or assimilated meant to be a *good* German, of course. But what was that? What did a Jew have to do to be such a person? There was something of a consensus among Jew and non-Jew. First, the Jew had to speak good German, as opposed to Yiddish or *Judendeutsch*, which was regarded as a vulgar dialect. Second, he had to be equitable or fair in his social and economic dealings with non-Jews, never slighting, cheating, or exploiting them and never offering more favorable terms to Jews. This was important since Jews were widely suspected of cheating and exploiting Gentiles; many antisemites claimed that the Talmud allowed Jews to cheat Gentiles. Third, the Jew had to be patriotic, putting Germany before other countries in matters of international politics. This too was very important, because Jews were also suspected, because of their international financial connections, of supporting the enemy. Fourth, the Jew had to accept his fair share of public burdens, both in war and peace; in other words, he had to pay taxes and serve in the military. Fifthly and finally, the Jew had to be modest, never placing himself above the Gentile because of wealth, social status, or education. This was a reason for special offense on the part of Gentiles, who resented upwardly mobile Jews. The "uppity Jew," the parvenu Semite, became a favorite theme of social satire. It was indeed no accident that Adolf Stöcker, the firebrand preacher of the 1880s, gave his first antisemitic speech on the theme of how Jews should be more modest (1880).

It was remarkable how many Jewish champions of emancipation agreed to these conditions; even such a stalwart spokesman as Gabriel Riesser accepted them. Many of these authors admitted that the abuses of usury on the part of Jewish lenders were damaging the cause of emancipation and should be controlled. Ultra-orthodox Jews who wished to minimize contact with Gentiles were often regarded as an embarrassment to the cause of emancipation. Even such a moderate orthodox Jew as Heinrich Graetz found himself shunned by his liberal colleagues.

The greatest sticking point in discussions about assimilation or integration was religion. Was it necessary to be a Christian to be a good German? Or could one be a Jew and still a good German? There were three possible positions on this question. The *conservatives* insisted that an important condition of civil and political rights should be membership in one of the Christian churches, so that a Jew could be a full citizen only if he or she converted. The *liberals* argued that no such condition was necessary, that civil rights and duties were independent of a person's religion, which had to do with matters of private conscience. Finally, the *radicals* claimed that emancipation was completely incompatible with religion, that freedom and equality in the new age meant abolishing religion because *all* religious affiliation, whether Christian or Jewish, was only another form of servitude.

The conservative position is the most difficult for many of us to understand today. Those who defend the necessity of Christian membership in the state seem to harken back to the medieval era, those dark days where the ideal was the unity of state and church. But here again it is necessary to examine the arguments given by the advocates of the Christian state viz., Friedrich Stahl (1858) and Constantin Frantz (1844). Far from being medieval, their conception of the state was the product of much more recent developments: German nationalism and the romantic tradition.

The champions of the Christian state were believers in the ideal of community, according to which there should be unity among the citizens of the state. The more unity in the state, the more its citizens have in common, the stronger and happier the state. What citizens should have in common is language, culture, history, and, last but not least, religion. There was no greater source of unity in the state than religion precisely because it concerned the innermost values and beliefs of the citizen. To allow religious sects apart from the public religion, then, was only to invite disunity and discord. To the advocates of the Christian state, the liberal doctrine of the separation of church and state was a drastic mistake. The problem with this doctrine, they argued, is that it treated religion as if it were solely a matter of individual conscience, as if it had no importance or implications for one's actions in the public or political world. If the state remained completely outside the religious sphere, as the liberal doctrine insisted, the state deprived itself of its most important support and foundation. A stable and secure state required that its citizens obeyed the law not only in their actions but also in their heart and soul. What more powerful force was there for forming heart and soul than religion?

Given such an ideal of the state, it should be clear that the devotees of the Christian state could grant emancipation only upon one condition: conversion. Jews who refused to convert would have to be tolerated—none of them advocated expulsion—but they could not be given the full rights of citizenship. They could have at best *civil* equality, which gave them equal protection of life, liberty, and property before the law, but they could not have *political* equality, which made them co-legislators in the state, and which gave them the right to hold offices and public positions. According to the terminology of the time, they could have "passive" but not "active" citizenship.

The liberal response to the Christian state, which was put forward most eloquently and vehemently by Riesser (1831a, pp. 9–10; 1831b, pp. 11–14), was to point out what a flimsy and artificial remedy lay in conversion. Conversion invited hypocrisy. If professing belief was a necessary condition for full citizenship, and if only full citizenship was connected with certain advantages, then people would join the church for those reasons and not because they really believed in its doctrines. The conservatives failed to heed the fundamental reason for a separation of church and state: that conscience cannot be compelled. If conscience is forever free, then there is no remedy but separation of church and state. Allowing different forms of belief in the state is a sheer necessity, one which any healthy state has to acknowledge.

The radical standpoint, which is best represented by Bruno Bauer (1843), Karl Marx (1844), and the young Wilhelm Marr,[2] held that emancipation means the abolition of all religion, which is a form of human alienation. The case for Jewish emancipation is therefore null and void, because it means allowing the Jews their own special form of religion when the ideal state should have no religion at all. The case for the emancipation of the Jews was tantamount to asking for special privileges and rights, which no group should have in a completely free and equal society. Paradoxically, the radical standpoint came together with the conservative one in denying the Jews any special rights and privileges as a minority religion. It was perhaps no accident that, in the case of Bauer and Marr, such radicalism eventually transformed into a vehement antisemitism.

In addition to these three positions, there was another, more radical and extreme than any of them, that rejected emancipation entirely because it disputed the very possibility of integration. This was the standpoint of racism. It maintained that a Jew has the character that he does not because of his education but because of his race or ethnic origin. That character was obnoxious, because it was grasping, egoistic, and competitive. Conversion was not an option, therefore, because once a Jew, always a Jew; there was no point in putting a Christian veneer on a rotten substance.

---

[2] In his early days Marr was a radical spokesman for the ideals of the Young Germany movement (1846). Later he argues, much like Bauer, that the ideal of human emancipation means that there cannot be any specifically Jewish emancipation (1862, p. 5).

The racist attack on emancipation was first put forward by Eugen Dühring,[3] who challenges our preconceptions of antisemitism as an irrational ideology for the simple reason that Dühring was the most rationalist philosopher of his age. Though a lone voice when the antisemitism controversy began in the late 1870s, Dühring eventually attracted a large following among disaffected youth. Some of the leading antisemitic spokesmen of the 1880s—Max Liebermann von Sonnenberg, Heinrich Nordmann, Moritz Busch, and Ernst Henrici—also became racists in Dühring's footsteps. It is one of the terrible ironies of history that the most extreme standpoint— one rejected by the great majority of opponents of emancipation before the 1880s—finally became the new orthodoxy under Nazi rule. Under those conditions, all discussions of emancipation finally came to their bitter and horrible close after 1933.

In the 1880s, in response to the Russian pogroms and persistent antisemitic agitation in Germany, the debate about emancipation took on a new direction. The question now was from *whom* should come emancipation, from the government of the lands in which Jews resided or from the Jews themselves? In other words, should emancipation come from top down or from bottom up? Frustrated by the slow pace of reform, angered by the persistent gap between legal and social emancipation, and worried by the prospect of future persecution, many Jews argued that they would have to take matters into their own hands and to organize themselves to defend and lobby for the cause of emancipation. One of the most important organizations behind this self-emancipation movement was the *Centralverein deutscher Staatsbürger jüdischen Glaubens*, which was formed in 1893.[4] The *Centralverein* prosecuted antisemites in the courts, fought antisemitic candidates in elections, and wrote against antisemitic literature. Their activities were inspired by the belief that Jewish self-defense was the best road to integration and acceptance in German national life. Another very different approach to self-emancipation came from the Zionists, first and foremost among them Leon Pinsker ([1882] 1975) and Theodor Herzl ([1896] 1993). They were responding to the same events as liberal Jews—persistent persecution and prejudice, the growth of antisemitic parties, the growing popular reaction against emancipation—but they drew a very different conclusion: that antisemitism is ineradicable and that integration is illusory. If the Jew were truly to emancipate himself—if he were to cease to be the victim of intolerance and prejudice—then the only alternative for him was emigration and the formation of a national Jewish homeland somewhere in the Americas or in Palestine. Thus the debate about emancipation eventually evolved into a question about the merits of Zionism.

---

[3] Dühring first put forward a moderate version of his views (1875, pp. 243–46, 391–94). The more mature and extreme exposition of his views is in his *Die Judenfrage als Racen-, Sitten- und Culturfrage* (1881).

[4] On the *Centralverein*, see Schorsch (1972).

A careful study of the emancipation debate in Germany shows the paramount importance of bracketing notions of antisemitism as a pathology or prejudice. We need to examine impartially and thoroughly the reasons the antisemites gave for their attitudes. While these reasons were often not good reasons, *even from their contemporary standpoint*, we still need to know them to understand antisemitic attitudes. Historical understanding demands that we examine all standpoints in a debate from within, from the perspective of the participants themselves. This often shows that what appears to be prejudice and pathology is more a mixture of insight, error, and confusion. Although from our contemporary perspective antisemitism seems to be irrational, the interests of reason demand that we demonstrate this, that we examine impartially the arguments given by the antisemites. Only when we know how and where they falter we can claim that the history of antisemitism belongs to the history of prejudice and pathology.

References

Bauer, Bruno. 1843. *Die Judenfrage*. Braunschweig: Friedrich Otto.
Dohm, Christian Wilhelm. 1781. *Ueber die bürgerliche Verbessung der Juden*. Berlin: Friedrich Nicolai.
Dühring, Eugen. 1875. *Cursus der Philosophie als streng wissenschaftlicher Weltanschauung und Lebensgestaltung*. Leipzig: Koschny.
Frantz, Constantin. 1844. *Ahasverus oder die Judenfrage*. Berlin: Wilhelm Hermes.
Greiffenhagen, M. 1972. "Emanzipation." In *Historisches Wörterbuch der Philosophie*, edited by Joachim Ritter, vol. 2, 448–49. Basel: Schwabe.
Heine, Heinrich. 1981. "*Reisebilder*." In *Sämtliche Schriften*, edited by Klaus Briegleb, vol. 4. Frankfurt: Ullstein.
Herzl, Theodor. (1896) 1993. *The Jewish State: An Attempt at a Modern Solution of the Jewish Question*. London: Henry Pordes.
Katz, Jacob. 1964. "The Term 'Jewish Emancipation': Its Origin and Historical Impact." In *Studies in Nineteenth-Century Jewish Intellectual History*, edited by Alexander Altmann, 1–26. Cambridge, MA: Harvard University Press.
Koselleck, Reinhart, and Karl Grass. 1975. "Emanzipation." In *Geschichtliche Grundbegriffe*, edited by Otto Brunner, Werner Consze, and Reinhart Koselleck, vol. 2, 153–97. Stuttgart: Ernst Klett Verlag.
Marr, Wilhelm. 1846. *Das junge Deutschland in der Schweiz*. Leipzig: Verlag von Wilhelm Journay.
Marr, Wilhelm. 1862. *Der Judenspiegel*. Fünfte Auflage. Hamburg: Selbstverlag des Verfassers.
Marx, Karl. 1844. Review of *Die Judenfrage*, by Bruno Bauer. *Deutsch-Französische Jahrbücher* 1: 182–214.
Paulus, H. E. G. 1831. *Die Jüdische Nationalabsonderung nach Ursprung, Folgen und Besserungsmitteln*. Heidelberg: C.F. Winter.
Pinsker, Leon. (1882) 1975. "Auto-Emancipation: An Appeal to His People by a Russian Jew." In *Road to Freedom: Writings and Addresses*. Westport: Greenwood Press.

Riesser, Gabriel. 1831a. *Ueber die Stellung der Bekenner des Mosaischen Glaubens in Deutschland.* Altona: Johann Friedrich Hammerich.

Riesser, Gabriel. 1831b. *Vertheidigung der bürgerlichen Gleichstellung der Juden gegen die Einwürfe des Herrn Dr. H.E.G. Paulus.* Altona: Johann Friedrich Hammerich.

Rose, Paul. 1992. *German Question/Jewish Question: Revolutionary Antisemitism from Kant to Wagner.* Princeton: Princeton University Press.

Rürup, Reinhard. 1975. "Emanzipation—Anmerkungen zur Begriffsgeschichte." In *Emanzipation und Antisemitismus*, 126–32. Göttingen: Vandenhoeck & Ruprecht.

Schorsch, Ismar. 1972. *Jewish Reactions to German Anti-Semitism, 1870–1914.* New York: Columbia University Press.

Schulz, Hans. 1913. "Emanzipation." In *Deutsches Fremdwörterbuch*, vol. 1, 170–71. Straßburg: Trübner.

Stahl, Friedrich Julius. 1858. *Der christliche Staat.* Zweite durchgesehene Auflage. Berlin: Oehmigke.

Stöcker, Adolf. 1880. *Das moderne Judenthum in Deutschland, besonders in Berlin.* Berlin: Verlag von Wiegandt und Grieben.

CHAPTER 9

Gender

Sara R. Horowitz

JEWS AND GENDER

Ideas about gender—about what men and women are and do—are deeply enfolded in the images and narratives that comprise the discourse of antisemitism. Because representations of Jews are inevitably gendered, it would be impossible to understand fundamental aspects of the mechanisms of antisemitism in modernity without considering its intersections with gender and sexuality. In cultural and political discourse, notions of gender and race function together as important signifiers of otherness and outsiderness, especially in the context of evolving ideas about the modern citizen. Both the external discourse *about* Jews and the internal discourse *among* Jews rely, either implicitly or explicitly, on gendered tropes—recurring patterns of images about sexual difference, identity, and practice. These gendered Jewish figures include effeminate, weak, and passive men; aggressively greedy and rapacious men; domineering and suffocating women; and materialistic, frigid, and manipulative women. In the popular imagination, gender difference and Jewish difference become intertwined, the one fueling, challenging, or justifying the other.

Although they initially followed separate trajectories, the theoretical and critical conversations about gender and about antisemitism bear on one another in important ways. By now, the significance of gender as a crucial component of cultural analysis has been well established. Introduced first by feminist studies and enriched by gender and queer studies, using gender as a category of analysis entails examining the actual and imagined experiences

S. R. Horowitz (✉)
York University, Toronto, ON, Canada
e-mail: srh@yorku.ca

and perceptions of sexuality and sexual difference, the ways cultures understand these differences, and the ways political and social structures organize them. Analyzing a culture's concepts of gender also serves as a portal to understanding power relations more broadly. Ideas about women's biology and role, or about normative and deviant masculinity, for example, convey cultural anxieties about citizenship, belonging, exclusion, stability, and change. In other words, what we talk about when we talk about gender are live tensions at the heart of a culture's vision of itself.

Similar observations, of course, have been made about the place of "the Jew" in Western discourse. Particularly as modern liberal culture opens itself up to the social and political integration of Jews, ideas about what Jews are and do circulate in both popular and intellectual discussions. On one level, these ideas address whether and how Jews might be integrated into modern culture. On another level, they function as a fulcrum for engaging vexing issues of values, civilization, and power, and changing cultural values. Discussions of the signification of gender and of Jews overlap, then, because they gesture in parallel ways: they are about a particular subject—the place of women, or homosexuals, or Jews, in modern culture—but they also serve as organizing metaphors through which modern Western culture maps out its own inner continuities and instabilities. Taken together, the scholarly and theoretical discourses of gender and of antisemitism shed light on one another because discourses of the other generally follow similar parameters.

In the popular discourse, discussions of "the Jew," of women, and of masculinity in modernity are all part of a more far-reaching conversation about citizenship, privilege, and power—a conversation fraught with anxieties about integrity, dissolution, belonging, exclusion, change, and destabilization. In the European context on the edge of liberalization, the idea of the citizen is connected with the notion of a normative heterosexual masculinity; the citizen is imagined as male, white, and Christian. As social norms begin to change and the rights of citizenship are extended to those previously excluded, the inclusion of the racialized or gendered other disrupts existing structures of power and privilege. In response, misogyny, homophobia, and antisemitism work together to defend what is perceived as a threatened body politic: each bias fuels and legitimates the other.

This linking of perceived social destabilization with images of the other is not only a phenomenon of a dominant culture whose borders have become more porous. As Jews negotiate a growing openness to full social and political participation, Jewish anxieties about insider and outsider status and the complicated pulls of assimilation and continuity create an internal dynamic that absorbs the conversations about Jews by others into a conversation by Jews about themselves. First in Europe, then in North America, this inner dynamic generates a set of feminized stereotypes that reproduce both antisemitic and misogynistic tropes as part of a complicated means to work through anxieties about (male) Jewish identity. Here, too, ideas about gender, racial, and religious difference mutually buttress one another, drawing on a similar emotional charge and reproducing cultural norms.

The Gendered Citizen

To probe the intersecting ideas about Jews and gender, a fruitful place to begin is with the French Revolution of 1789, so central to the Enlightenment project and the emancipation of both Jews and women in European culture. The integration of both Jews and women emerge out of Enlightenment ideals about human and social perfectibility. Not without great opposition, French liberals argued for according the full rights of citizenship to France's native Jews, starting a modern movement that spread to Germany, and eventually to other European nations. These same ideals shaped North American ideas about citizenship, human rights, nation, and difference. At the same time that the Jewish question was on the table, French intellectuals debated the rights of women. In uncannily similar terms, Jews and women were both seen as deeply flawed, possessing characteristics that had been used to justify their exclusion from full social and political participation in French culture. Jews, for example, were viewed as materialistic, manipulative, and physically and morally weak. As a category, "the Jew" most often signified Jewish men, who were frequently described as being like women. Women were seen as childlike, overly emotional, superstitious, and resistant to the rational thought so central to Enlightenment notions of progress. But new ideas about education and social improvement argued that those negative characteristics were not indelibly attached to the Jew or to woman, but might be ameliorated under proper conditions. In other words, it was precisely the exclusion of Jews and of women from the advantages of education, economic opportunity, and cultural integration that created their negative characteristics.

In the debates about citizenship and emancipation emerging from the French Revolution, both the woman's question and the Jewish question were articulated with ambivalence. Denis Diderot, for example, expressed compassion for woman's unequal legal status, blaming much of female limitations on social institutions that treat women like "imbecile children." But Diderot ultimately wondered whether women could ever attain the rationality and emotional control necessary for responsible citizenship; he suspected that some aspects of women's intellectual inferiority may be innate rather than the product of social norms, and equivocated about their suitability for citizenship ([1772] 1927). By contrast, his contemporary, Choderlos de Laclos, saw women's negative characteristics as a product of limited educational and social opportunities, and argued that "natural woman" was man's equal, and that the dissolution of social and legal barriers would enable women to think as rationally and morally as men ([1793] 1903). Debates about the status of the Jew followed similar parameters. For example, in an address now famous for articulating the terms by which liberal democracies would regard the presence of the other and of minority cultures, Count Stanislas de Clermont-Tonnerre insisted that for the French Republic to be consistent with its own principles of equality and human rights, it must grant equal rights to French Jews. But he was careful to delineate the terms under which that could occur. "The Jews should be denied everything as a nation, but granted everything as individuals. ... . they must constitute neither a state, nor a political corps, nor an order; they must individually become citizens. ... The existence of a nation within a nation is unacceptable to our country" (quoted in Berkovitz 1989, p. 71). This formulation, which came to be understood as the standard for Jewish integration in modern liberal Europe (as well as North America), rested on a clearly drawn boundary between private and public life. It associated private and public space, respectively, with personal and national identity. Thus, the private Jew—the only kind of "Jew" deemed acceptable—was relegated to domestic space—that is to say, to the space traditionally troped as female. The "public" Jew, the citizen, was not a Jew at all but a Frenchman. At its most inclusive and liberal, the argument on behalf of extending greater opportunities for education and cultural participation to both women and Jews saw their potential to become good French citizens. Put simply, French women would become more like French men, and French Jews would become more like Frenchmen.

Of course, this very formulation highlights the imagined identification of Frenchness with maleness. As Judith Surkis notes in her discussion of modernity in France, "the citizen became sexed" (2006, p. 2). Other scholars have also noted that, from the French Revolution onward, a notion of normative masculinity was integral to the modern concept of the ideal citizen, undergirding the idea of nation. And the same could be said of other European cultures, as they experienced a move to liberal democracy. Hence, Jay Geller terms European bourgeois society "an exclusively masculine order" (1992, p. 243). This gendering of citizenry provides the grounding for individual and national identity as well as for social orders and political institutions. As Sandrine Sanos observes: "The self was not an abstract entity, but a gendered notion that involved delineating the proper masculinity of the French citizen in a social order underpinning the nation" (2013, pp. 27–28).

At moments of rapid social change or crises of instability, anxieties about the state of the nation become expressed through metaphors about the male body under assault. Mary Louise Roberts has outlined ways in which images of the modern woman and the mother that arose in France during the first quarter of the twentieth century offer an "accessible way to discuss the meaning of social and cultural change" (1994, p. 4). And, as Joan Scott noted in an influential essay about employing gender as a category of analysis, how cultures understand the bodily differences of sexuality must be seen as "a primary way of signifying relations in power" (1986). Gender, then, functions as a concrete way to talk about charged ideas: social change, cultural meaning, moral order, and democratization—indeed, the very survival of civilization.

Women and Jews, then, faced uncannily similar impediments to full integration and raised similar cultural anxieties. In her ground-breaking *Gender and Assimilation in Modern Jewish History*, Paula Hyman traces some of the ways in which gender was implicated in modernity, emancipation, and the actualization of the Enlightenment project. Hyman refers to the "coincidence of antisemitism and misogyny" (1995, p. 137), a connection arising because both Jews and women, in making a claim for equality and full citizenship rights, challenged the old order, which she aptly characterizes as a "nostalgic and antimodern vision of a smoothly functioning, non-egalitarian, hierarchical social order in which subordinate groups (like women and Jews) knew their place" (1995, p. 137). I suggest that not only did women and Jews raise comparable anxieties in the dominant culture, but that in the evolving discourse about the other, categories such as race and gender undergo the same dynamics and become symbolically interchangeable. Misogyny and antisemitism emerge out of similar cultural struggles, as Hyman observes. But in addition, and more fundamentally, they gesture to imaginary (or constructed) categories whose boundaries blur, and whose terms depend on one another. Judith Butler refers to this as "interarticulations" of "vectors of power"—categories that "require and deploy one another for the purpose of their own articulation" (1993, p. 18).

Thus, Jewish difference is implicated with gender difference. Both differences are perceived as rooted essentially in the body, but have far-reaching implications regarding intellectual, emotional, and moral qualities. Zygmunt Bauman introduced the term "allosemitism" to connote the ubiquitous "practice of setting the Jews apart as people radically different from all others, needing separate concepts to describe and comprehend them and special treatment in all or most social intercourse" (1998, p. 143).[1] Bryan Cheyette employs the term "semitic discourse," rather than antisemitism and philosemitism, to signify a discourse about Jews wherein a "protean instability or ambivalence" is the one consistent aspect of the Jew as a cultural signifier (2003, p. 433). This conviction of the Jew's radical and essential otherness is a precondition of antisemitism, and melds with the more visible essentialism of gender difference. Thus, the masculinity of the Jewish man is always put to question. For example, in turn-of-the-century Austria, Otto Weininger's influential 1903 treatise, *Sex and Character*, insists on the "homology of Jew and woman" (2005, p. 309). These parallel constructs build on stereotypes of women and of Jews as non-reflective, non-moral beings, ruled by desire and incapable of transcendence. For Weininger, woman's character is biologically over-determined by her gender. Jews are "like women" (2005,

---

[1] As Bauman notes, the term "allosemitism" was coined by the Polish Jewish literary historian Artur Sandauer.

p. 320)—effeminate and similarly limited. In the European imagination, circumcision reinforces the feminization of Jewish men. It is seen as a form of displaced castration that renders Jewish men genitally other as women are genitally other. While the Jewish tradition sees the sign of circumcision as the sacred covenant made visible, the European tradition sees in it the essential unassimilability of the Jew, both the emblem and the cause of persecution.[2] Through European eyes, then, the absence of the foreskin is difference made visible: inextricably connected to gender and just as innate.

By the late nineteenth century, racialist thinking had permeated the discourse of antisemitism. Locating Jewish degeneracy in the body of the Jew diverged from Enlightenment ideas about amelioration and assimilation through education, but picked up on the anxieties about essential Jewish difference. The racialized Jew was not so much educable as indelibly marked. As Sander Gilman (1985) and others have observed, the racialized other is linked with sexual deviance. In a range of often contradictory stereotypes, the Jewish male was portrayed as being both more and less than a "real" man. In the European imagination, the Jew was venal, lusty, and rapacious, with an excessive sexual appetite that posed a threat to an orderly society and to cultural purity. George Mosse describes the image of the Jew in nineteenth- and twentieth-century Germany as "short legs, a greedy and sensual corpulence" (1964, p. 140). And, at the same time, the Jew was effeminate, weak, and womanish. In either case, his presence posed a danger to the body politic of liberal society. Gilman points to the association of Jewish men and hysteria, a psychological diagnosis linked literally with the physiology of women (1991, p. 63). Jay Geller reminds us of the association of the presumed Jewish odor—the *foetor Judaicus*—with menstruation (1992, p. 243). While images of "the Jewess" also circulated in European culture—mostly as an eroticized, exotic other—it was the image of the Jewish man that resonated most powerfully and most threateningly in the European imagination. By excess or inadequacy, the maleness of the Jew was at odds with the imagined masculinity of the ideal European citizen. Gender, of course, is not a static category but one in ongoing cultural reorganization. Similarly, Jewish manhood was repeatedly redefined against (and as distinct from) masculine normativity, whatever parameters that normativity assumed. In debates about progress and social change, discussion about the civic participation of the Jew was always about Jews and, at the same time, about something else: social stability, national identity, cultural values, and other issues at the heart of how cultures think about themselves and their survival and perpetuation. As Geller comments, "…to allow the unmanned or the unmanly into the public sphere – was in turn to question the legitimacy of the entire order" (1992, p. 243). For social conservatives resistant to the sea change wrought by modernity,

---

[2] In another context, Sander Gilman (1997) observes that Europeans criticized circumcision as a sign of Jewish self-isolation, and at the same time, as a biological and naturally occurring (that is, racial) aspect of embodied Jewish difference.

Jews stood for unwanted social upheaval. As Weininger put it, "the spirit of modernity is Jewish, wherever one looks at it" (2005, p. 299). In examining the social dynamics surrounding the Dreyfus Affair in France at the turn of the century, for example, Christopher Forth places the terms of the public debate in the broader context of a suspicion of "deficient manhood" and the non-Frenchness of French Jews (2004, p. 22). Expressions of the ways that cultures understood sexual difference merged with the ways that cultures understood racial difference, and, indeed, difference more broadly.

The promise and process of Jewish emancipation in liberal cultures did not merely produce a set of gendered signifiers. It had a profound effect on the gendered organization of the lives of actual Jews. Hyman and others have documented the ways in which the embourgeoisement of Jewish society opened doors for male success and fuller participation in civic life, but, ironically, restricted and impoverished the lives of women—spiritually and psychologically, if not materially. For example, in analyzing the memoirs of Belorussian-born Pauline Wengeroff, Shulamit Magnus claims that Wengeroff's experiences map the effects of late nineteenth- and early twentieth-century westernization on Jewish households, and particularly on Jewish women. Wengeroff grew up in a religiously devout household and married a Hasidic Jew who later abandoned traditional Judaism. Because he saw Jewish observance as an impediment to social mobility, he pressured his wife to give up even private, domestic religious practices, such as keeping kosher and observing the sabbath. Although she struggled against her husband, she eventually gave in. In her memoirs, she grieves the loss of religious life. Wengeroff understood her personal predicament as representative of a wider social phenomenon. As Magnus points out, Wengeroff portrays her "personal tragedy as characteristic of broader processes in modernizing Jewish society, in which… upwardly aspiring husbands coerced more traditional wives to abandon observance" (1995, p. 185).

Moreover, the promise of emancipation and integration often did not live up to expectations. According to Hyman, "it is fair to state that prevailing cultural attitudes towards Jews in the very societies they were eager to join were generally disparaging" (1995, p. 136). Even when materially successful, Jews failed to attain a social stature commensurate with their economic class. To gain social acceptance, Jewish men frequently insisted that their households more closely resemble the European bourgeois household. Magnus notes that husbands often insisted that their wives cease working for income, in contrast with the social habits in Jewish communities where "women in all classes of Jewish society, including the wealthy, had always been economically active" (1995, p. 186). This served to increase men's control over the inner workings of their households, and over the management of domestic space. One might say that, paradoxically, as Jewish men worked to integrate themselves more fully into western society and to more closely resemble their non-Jewish counterparts, and as they secularized and claimed greater cultural freedom, they imposed greater restrictions on the lives of Jewish women.

The Emergence of the Jewish Woman

Just as the liberal citizen was implicitly conceptualized as masculine, the European discourse about the place of "the Jew" imagined a male Jew. Antisemitic tropes highlighted his disparity from the masculine norm. One consequence of the frequent troping of the Jewish man as female was that the Jewish woman virtually disappeared from the public conversation. However, under the altered social conditions and norms of North America, different gendered Jewish images developed. The European trope of the effeminate Jewish male crossed the Atlantic and circulated in the popular imagination. Its flipside—the aggressive, rapacious Jewish man—endured as well, especially in the context of business. But it was largely displaced elsewhere by American racialized stereotypes of the overly sexualized African-American man. But in America, new antisemitic figures gained currency—ones that were mediated through representations of Jewish women. In addition to the ways that non-Jewish Americans saw the Jew, an internal-gendered Jewish discourse developed negative stereotypes of the Jewish woman. These female tropes began with the immigrant experience, and continue into the present. The waves of immigration from eastern and central Europe at the turn of the century often included single men and unaccompanied married men entering the United States alone to lay down roots and collect enough economic resources to bring their families. Perhaps for this reason, in internal Jewish discourse, immigrant Jewish women often came to stand for the Old World. Jewish men frequently had the opportunity to acculturate to American mores, learning English, adopting American dress, and shedding religious practices, before sending for wife and family. Dressed in old-world garb, their hair covered by the kerchiefs or wigs mandated by religious practice, newly arrived wives at Ellis Island often struck the men who had arrived only a few years earlier as shabby and too outwardly Jewish. It was often said that the river bottom at ports of entry along the Hudson River were covered with wigs that men had unceremoniously ripped of the heads of their wives even before bringing them home. Viewed with a mixture of nostalgia and revulsion, these newly arrived Jewish immigrant women came to symbolize both a mythic purity of remembered Jewish life in the shtetl that was lost in the New World, and the outwardly Jewish traits that impeded social mobility. These complicated and contradictory symbolic meanings that acclimatizing Jews projected on to one another have been captured and critiqued by American Jewish fiction writers of the first half of the twentieth century, such as Abraham Cahan (1896) and Anzia Yezierska (1920).

To more established Jews who had reached the United States in earlier waves of immigration, and who viewed themselves as Americanized, a feared association with the immigrants who filled the teeming tenements of the Lower East Side threatened their own sense of belonging. Repudiating what they saw as vulgar shtetl habits—such as talking loudly, poor hygienic habits, and flashy clothing—columns in the Yiddish and Anglo-Jewish press offered far-reaching advice directed primarily at women (Joselit 2001). Single women, in particular, came under scrutiny for impropriety. Young immigrant women who hoped to advance economically, educationally, or intellectually attempted self-consciously to erase traces of the Jewish ghetto from their demeanor. Anzia Yezierska's memoir exemplifies this dynamic. Born between 1880 and 1885 in Płońsk, a Russian-Polish village near Warsaw, Yezierska arrived in the United States with her family in the early 1890s. In describing her experience attending university, Yezierska recollects feeling radically out of place. She contrasted her own brightly colored clothing with the conservatively stylish outfits of other women students. This contrast in dress was an emblem of a larger difference in self-expression and self-presentation. Even more than their mode of dress, Yezierska envied her classmates' more reserved way of speaking. Desperately wanting to integrate into American intellectual circles, she struggled to modulate her speech—subdued tone, hands still—in contrast to the more histrionic modes of expression that typified the Lower East Side. She was especially self-conscious in her conversations with educational philosopher John Dewey, who mentored her. Ironically, it was precisely what he viewed as her passionate expressiveness, hand gestures and all, that attracted him to Yezierskia. He saw her as vibrant and outspoken, in markedly favorable contrast to the reserved women of his own social circles. Although her novels and short stories of Jewish women's immigrant life in New York brought her initial success, even a stint as a Hollywood scriptwriter—she was lauded as an authentic voice of the tenements, a Cinderella of the sweatshops—by the 1940s, she was seen by the American mainstream as well as within the Jewish community as "too Jewish." Her writing offended both immigrant and Americanized Jews who felt publicly mocked and exposed (Yezierska 1932, 1950, 1979; S. Horowitz 2006).

Although Yezierska was unusual in her intellectual ambition and writerly achievement, the Jewish traits that made her uneasy were precisely those criticized in young immigrant Jewish women of her generation: personal ambition and lack of reserve in speech and dress. In the drive to fit in and Americanize, young Jewish women came to stand for a range of visible or imagined habits that marked immigrants as Jewish and impeded their social and economic mobility. Termed "ghetto girls," Jewish immigrant women, whose work in factories and shops provided them with disposable income, were criticized for their loud clothing and makeup, and for their selfish materialism. Even as the immigrant experience and the Lower East Side tenements receded into the past, the image of the brash ghetto girl remained a potent symbol for Jewish anxieties of exclusion in America (Prell 1999, pp. 21–57; Joselit 2001). These female stereotypes originated within the Jewish community but circulated beyond it. For example, the 1947 film *Gentleman's Agreement*, based on Laura Z. Hobson's novel of the same name, probes the phenomenon of genteel antisemitism in postwar America. In it, journalist Skylar Philip Green determines to write an exposé of antisemitism by posing as a Jew. He conducts a social experiment: if nothing about him were to change, would people treat him differently if they believed him to be Jewish? The film's premise minimizes differences between Jewish and non-Jewish men. For instance, Green muses on his resemblance to his friend Dave Goldman, a Jewish American who has just returned from active combat duty in the U.S. Army. "Dark hair, dark eyes, sure so does Dave. So do a lot of guys who aren't Jewish. No accent, no mannerisms. Neither does Dave." But, as the film has it, Jewish women—in contrast to Jewish men—have distinct characteristics. Green's secretary, Elaine Wales, confesses to him that she is secretly Jewish. She reveals that when looking for a job, she received no response to the many letters of application sent out under her own, recognizably Jewish, name, Estelle Walovsky. But when she sent out an identical letter to her current employer, this time under an assumed name that masked her Jewishness, she was hired. When Green realizes that his company has no known Jews on staff, he places an ad in the newspaper for a secretary, explicitly inviting people of all religious backgrounds to apply. Surprisingly, Wales/Walovksy objects. She warns that the ad would attract the "wrong type" of Jew—one who wears loud clothing and "too much rouge." She fears that the presence of the "wrong type" of Jewish woman will reflect badly on Jewish women like her, who can pass. "It's no fun being the fall guy for the kikey ones," she tells Green. The fluid identification of Green with Goldman and Goldman's military service breaks with older tropes of the Jewish man as unmanly, weak, and indelibly different. The fears of Green's secretary, however, indicate the enduring resonance of the more recent stereotype of the Jewish woman as materialistic and vulgar—characteristics once linked with stereotypes of Jewish men.

The older European tropes of Jewish men—greedy, effeminate, immoral, vulgar—never disappear. In the second half of the twentieth century, they permeate popular American culture, surfacing, for example, in the neurotic nebbish of Woody Allen's comic films in the 1960s and 1970s, or the character of Miles Silverberg, the neurotic twenty-something executive producer in the 1990s comedy series *Murphy Brown*. Together with newer stereotypes of Jewish women that gain currency in the new world, these images become part of an internal dynamic through which Jews negotiate their place in America. As Riv-Ellen Prell astutely observes, "Jews became Americans through their use of stereotypes of one another as men and women and intimates as surely as they did through work, education, and the transformation of Judaism..." (1999, p. 20). There is an extensive body of work that unpacks the coalescence of antisemitism and misogyny in North American stereotypes of the second half of the twentieth century. Developed as an internal set of signifiers, late twentieth-century stereotypes such as the Jewish mother and the Jewish American Princess (or JAP) evolve from the earlier image of the "ghetto girl." Like the older European stereotypes of the Jewish male, these newer images use gendered negative associations—this time with Jewish women—to contend with ongoing anxieties within the Jewish communities. These newer stereotypes are seen as a means to mediate the continued presence of antisemitism notwithstanding the promise of American tolerance. Through such stereotypes, Jewish men project onto Jewish women the unwanted characteristics associated with Jews generally—such as pushiness, greed, and materialism. These feminized stereotypes are also seen as an expression of the ambivalent pull of Jewishness: the simultaneous fears of being deemed too Jewish and of losing one's Jewish identity. Hyman observes that Jewish men "responded to their disparagement in cultures influenced by antisemitism by creating negative stereotypes of Jewish women" (1995, p. 134). As Jewish men experienced both the possibility and limitations of success in America, as they responded to the promise and the threat of full integration and assimilation, as well as to their own desire both to give up and to maintain Jewish identity in a more open culture, they ascribed to women a suffocating parochialism, a sense of entrapment by an inherited tradition. We can see this in the portrayal of Jewish women in Philip Roth's early fiction, such as *Goodbye Columbus* and *Portnoy's Complaint*, and in Woody Allen's early films, such as *Annie Hall* and *Radio Days*.

As many literary scholars have pointed out, mid-twentieth-century fiction and film by and about Jewish men expressed a repudiation of the Jewish woman and a search for what came to be called "the ultimate *shiksa* (gentile woman)." This dynamic served as a metaphor (and a means) to solidify social belonging in America. In the 1972 film *Heartbreak Kid*, for example, Jewish Lenny abandons Lila, his plump, sloppy, sunburned Jewish wife while honeymooning in Miami Beach to pursue the beautiful and wealthy WASP Kelly, played by the willowy blonde model Cybill Shepherd. By the end of the twentieth century, Jewish women come to exemplify outmoded strategies for Jewish continuity. Jewish mothers, wives, and girlfriends are seen as preventing their sons, husbands, and boyfriends, as Rachel Josefowitz Siegel observes, "from achieving the American male-defined goals of autonomy and independence.… She is the scapegoat, the recipient of all ambivalent feelings… toward the Jewish presence" (1986, p. 254). In a trenchant analysis of the stereotype of the JAP, Prell has noted her non-productivity and voracious consumption that tax male energy. The JAP's overweening (if sometimes misguided) concern with her own beauty and with attracting a wealthy Jewish man is linked with her own lack of sexual desire or pleasure (Prell 1990). Radiating outward from the Jewish community into the larger North American culture through humor, literature, and popular culture, these stereotypes continue the melding of misogyny and antisemitism. Depicted as the parvenu, the nouveau riche whose material acquisition cannot confer social legitimacy, in popular culture the JAP comes to signify the thwarted social aspirations of the Jew (G. Spencer 1989; Schnur 1987; Alperin 1989; Beck 1991, 1992; Lamb 1989; Rothbell 1986).

THE JEWISHNESS OF THE JEWISH WOMAN

The burgeoning resources of feminist theory offer a set of methodological tools to critique the misogyny that undergirds the popular representation of Jewish women. But feminist studies often perpetuated antisemitic discourse. Susannah Heschel, for example, has traced the ways that feminist critiques often explain modern sexism as a direct inheritance of the Jewish roots of Christianity, an unwanted inheritance that came to western culture through the Old Testament. In essence blaming Judaism for the endurance of sexism, such critiques, Heschel notes, perpetuated older ideas of Judaism as patriarchal and authoritarian, in contrast to the more benevolent promise of Christianity. Most disturbingly, Heschel points to the equation made by some German feminists of Jewish patriarchy with National Socialism. "German woman emerge not as responsible for Nazism, but as victims of it and, by extension, as victims of Judaism" (1995, p. 136). As feminist theory developed in America, the critical practices of women of color offered promising models to help unpack the imbrication of sexism and antisemitism that fueled the circulation of such images in American and American Jewish culture. Like women of color who noted that they suffered the consequences of being both black and female in a racist and sexist society, Jewish women also observed that they experienced a sense of being an outsider twice-over. Moreover, women of color saw their situation as compounded by misogyny among men of color, just as Jewish women complained of misogyny on the part of Jewish men. Many Jewish studies scholars in the latter quarter of the twentieth century, developing a set of critical practices for the emergent subfield of Jewish women's studies, drew on the scholarship and activism regarding women of color. Moreover, Jewish feminist scholars identified with their critique of feminist theory. Women of color argued that feminist theory that emerged from the feminism of white women did not adequately grasp their cultural position and was inflected with the racism of American culture (Carby 1988; Collins 1990). However, in viewing the situation of Jewish women in America, many feminists of color saw them simply as white women, perhaps among the more privileged and least conscious of their privilege.[3]

In the current millennium, the popular discourse on Jews, Jewishness, and Jewish identity genders the images of Jews that circulate in contemporary culture in ways that connect to a much earlier discourse on Jewish separateness, sexuality, and unassimilability. As Daniel Iskowitz observes, twenty-first-century American films simultaneously exhibit both "'too much' Jewishness" and "'not enough' Jewishness" (2006, p. 237), still negotiating the tensions of Jewishness and Americanness through gendered images.

---

[3] For example, in calling for a coalition of women of oppressed minorities, Chicana critic Gloria Anzaldúa explicitly excluded Jewish women. She upbraids the "white Jewishwomen" in her seminar for feeling that they "'belonged' more to the women-of-color group than they did to the white group" (1990, p. xx).

In contemporary American culture, both the older tropes of Jewish male difference and the newer tropes of Jewish female difference still have currency. In both scholarship and popular culture, the unmanliness of the Jewish man is often posited both as a threatening social deviance and as a virtue. A recent guide to dating and marrying Jewish men, for example, *Boy Vey! The Shiksa's Guide to Dating Jewish Men*, illustrates the endurance of gendered antisemitic tropes into the twenty-first century, even under radically shifting understandings of gender, ethnicity, and race. The *Guide* acknowledges that Jewish men are different than others, initially casting such difference in positive—one might say philosemitic—terms, seeing them as more emotionally open, more communicative, more involved with family, less in need of imposing machismo on women, and less disturbed by strong women than are other men (Grish 2005). Still, the sexuality of the Jewish man is described as deviating from the norm. Non-Jewish women, the *Guide* warns, cannot know "what to expect from his sex drive" (p. 5), will find his secondary sex characteristics abnormal—"more body hair than a yak" (p. 74)—and will struggle with his deeply engrained miserliness. The author suggests that non-Jewish women are more appealing to Jewish men because Jewish woman are self-absorbed and overly concerned with professional success and material wealth—traits that echo the attributes of the JAP. Deemed repellant in Jewish women, these attributes are precisely what the *Guide* finds desirable in the Jewish male—for example, "professional drive" and an appreciation of women who "nudg[e] him up the corporate ladder" (S. Horowitz 2008). The image of the JAP underlies the reality TV show, *Princesses: Long Island*, and resonates with the character of Carrie Bradshaw, as played by the Jewish Sarah Jessica Parker, on the comic series *Sex and the City*.

Some critics argue that by the new millennium, Jewish stereotypes have been debunked in American popular culture. Samantha Baskind (2007), for example, points to the subversion of Jewish stereotypes in movies like *Keeping the Faith* (2000) and *Meet the Fockers* (2004). Indeed, Joel and Ethan Coen's film *A Serious Man* (2009), Larry David's television series *Curb Your Enthusiasm* (2000–present), and Amazon's video series *The Marvelous Mrs. Maisel* (2017–present) play self-consciously with well-established stereotypes and stock figures. Other critics, however, see the endurance of traditional gendered Jewish stereotypes well into the first quarter of the twenty-first century. Notwithstanding the greater diversity in representations of Jews in popular culture, David Reznik argues against the view that America has entered a "postracial age" where gendered Jewish stereotypes have diminished currency. Rather, he observes, "traditional American Jewish stereotypes from twentieth-century film actually persist quite prevalently on the big screen today" (2016, p. 2), tracing examples of the Jewish mother, the princess, the neurotic effeminate man, and the greedy "scumbag." And we are only beginning to assess the influence of internet productions on the evolution of popular culture. How such images will morph under current progressive and regressive political forces remains to be seen.

REFERENCES

Alperin, Mimi. 1989. "JAP Jokes: Hateful Humor." *Humor: International Journal of Humor Research* 2 (4): 412–16.
Anzaldúa, Gloria. 1990. *Making Face, Making Soul = Haciendo Caras: Creative and Critical Perspectives by Women of Color.* San Francisco: Aunt Lute Foundation.
Baskind, Samantha. 2007. "The Fockerized Jew?: Questioning Jewishness as Cool in American Popular Entertainment." *Shofar* 25 (4): 3–17.
Bauman, Zygmunt. 1998. "Allosemitism: Premodern, Modern, Postmodern." In *Modernity, Culture and the Jew*, edited by Bryan Cheyette and Laura Marcus. Stanford: Stanford University Press.
Beck, Evelyn Torton. 1991. "Therapy's Double Dilemma: Anti-Semitism and Misogyny." In *Jewish Women in Therapy: Seen But Not Heard*, edited by Rachel Siegel and Ellen Cole, 19–30. New York: Haworth Press.
Beck, Evelyn Torton. 1992. "From 'Kike' to 'JAP': How Misogyny, Antisemitism and Racism Construct the "Jewish American Princess." In *Race, Class, and Gender: An Anthology*, edited by Margaret L. Anderson and Patricia Hill Collins, 88–95. Belmont: Wadsworth.
Berkovitz, Jay R. 1989. *The Shaping of Jewish Identity in Nineteenth-Century France.* Detroit: Wayne State University Press.
Butler, Judith. 1993. *Bodies That Matter: On the Discursive Limits of "Sex."* New York: Routledge.
Cahan, Abraham. 1896. *Yekl: A Tale of the New York Ghetto.* New York: D. Appleton.
Carby, Hazel. 1988. "It Jus Be's Dat Way Sometime: The Sexual Politics of Women's Blues." In *Gender and Discourse*, edited by Alexandra D. Todd and Sue Fisher. Norwood: Ablex Publishing.
Cheyette, Bryan. 2003. "Neither Excuse Nor Accuse: T.S. Eliot's Semitic Discourse." *Modernism/Modernity* 10 (3) (September): 431–37.
Collins, Patricia Hill. 1990. *Black Feminist Thought: Knowledge, Consciousness, and the Politics of Empowerment.* New York: Routledge.
Diderot, Denis. (1772) 1927. "On Women." In *Dialogues*, translated by Francis Birrell. London: Routledge.
Forth, Christopher. 2004. *The Dreyfus Affair and the Crisis of French Manhood.* Baltimore: Johns Hopkins University Press.
Geller, Jay. 1992. "(G)nos(e)ology: The Cultural Construction of the Other." In *People of the Body: Jews and Judaism from an Embodied Perspective*, edited by Howard Eilberg-Schwartz, 243–62. Albany: SUNY Press.
Gilman, Sander. 1985. *Difference and Pathology: Stereotypes of Sexuality, Race, and Madness.* Ithaca: Cornell University Press.
Gilman, Sander. 1991. *The Jew's Body.* New York: Routledge.
Gilman, Sander. 1997. "Decircumcision: The First Aesthetic Surgery." *Modern Judaism* 17: 201–10.
Grish, Kristina. 2005. *Boy Vey! The Shiksa's Guide to Dating Jewish Men.* New York: Simon Spotlight Entertainment.
Heschel, Susannah. 1995. "Configurations of Patriarchy, Judaism, and Nazism in German Feminist Thought." In *Gender and Judaism: The Transformation of Tradition*, edited by T. M. Rudavsky, 135–54. New York: New York University Press.

Horowitz, Sara R. 2006. "Anzia Yezierska." In *Jewish Women: A Comprehensive Historical Encyclopedia*, edited by Paula Hyman and Dalia Ofer, compact disc. Jerusalem: Shalvi Publishing.

Horowitz, Sara R. 2008. "Lovin' Me, Lovin' Jew: Gender, Intermarriage, and Metaphor." In Lassner and Trubowitz 2008, 196–216.

Hyman, Paula. 1995. *Gender and Assimilation in Modern Jewish History: The Roles and Representation of Women*. Seattle: University of Washington Press 1995.

Iskowitz, Daniel. 2006. "They All Are Jews." In *You Should See Yourself: Jewish Identity in Postmodern American Culture*, edited by Vincent Brook, 230–52. New Brunswick: Rutgers University Press.

Joselit, Jenna Weissman. 2001. *A Perfect Fit: Clothes, Character and the Promise of America*. New York: Henry Holt.

Laclos, Choderlos de. (1793) 1903. *De l'éducation des femmes*. Paris: Vanier.

Lamb, Lynette. 1989. "JAP Jokes Are Nothing to Laugh At: Why Should Jewish Women Take the Rap for Our Materialistic Culture?" *Utne Reader*, May/June.

Magnus, Shulamit. 1995. "Pauline Wengeroff and the Voice of Jewish Modernity." In *Gender and Judaism: The Transformation of Tradition*, edited by T. M. Rudavsky, 181–90. New York: New York University Press.

Mosse, George. 1964. *The Crisis of German Ideology: Intellectual Origins of the Third Reich*. New York: Grosset & Dunlap.

Prell, Riv-Ellen. 1990. "Rage and Representation: Jewish Gender Stereotypes in American Culture." In *Uncertain Terms: Negotiating Gender in American Culture*, edited by Faye Ginsburg and Anna Lowenhaupt Tsing, 248–68. Boston: Beacon Press.

Prell, Riv-Ellen. 1999. *Fighting to Become Americans: Assimilation and the Trouble Between Jewish Women and Jewish Men*. Boston: Beacon Press.

Reznik, David. L. 2016. *New Jews: Race and American Jewish Identity in 21st Century Film*. London: Routledge.

Roberts, Mary Louise. 1994. *Civilization Without Sexes: Reconstructing Gender in Post-War France, 1917–1927*. Chicago: University of Chicago Press.

Rothbell, Gladys. 1986. "The Jewish Mother: Social Construction of a Popular Image." In *The Jewish Family: Images and Reality*, edited by Steven Cohen and Paula Hyman. New York: Holmes & Meier.

Sanos, Sandrine. 2013. *The Aesthetics of Hate: Far-Right Intellectuals, Antisemitism, and Gender in 1930s France*. Stanford: Stanford University Press.

Schnur, Susan. 1987. "Blazes of Truth: When Is a JAP Not a Yuppie?" *Lilith* 17 (Fall): 10–11.

Scott, Joan W. 1986. "Gender: A Useful Category of Historical Analysis." *The American Historical Review* 91 (December): 1053–75.

Siegel, Rachel Josefowitz. 1986. "Anti-Semitism and Sexism in Stereotypes of Jewish Women." *Women and Therapy* 5 (2–3): 249–57.

Spencer, Gary. 1989. "An Analysis of JAP-Baiting Humor on the College Campus." *International Journal of Humor Research* 2: 329–48.

Surkis, Judith. 2006. *Sexing the Citizen: Morality and Masculinity in France, 1870–1920*. Ithaca: Cornell University Press.

Weininger, Otto. 2005. *Sex and Character: An Investigation of Fundamental Principles*. Translated by Ladislaus Lob. Bloomington: University of Indian Press.

Yezierska, Anzia. 1920. *Hungry Hearts*. Boston: Houghton Mifflin.
Yezierska, Anzia. 1932. *All I Could Never Be*. New York: Brewer, Warren and Putnam.
Yezierska, Anzia. 1950. *Red Ribbon on a White Horse*. New York: Scribner.
Yezierska, Anzia. 1979. *The Open Cage: An Anzia Yezierska Collection*. New York: Persea.

CHAPTER 10

Ghetto

Daniel B. Schwartz

Nothing would seem more elementary than the relevance of the ghetto to the study of antisemitism, and vice versa. More than any other term, "ghetto" is synonymous with the forced segregation and concentration of Jews from medieval Christian Europe to the Nazi Holocaust, and as such would appear to be an obvious addition to any volume of key concepts of antisemitism.

On closer examination, however, the relationship between the idea of the ghetto and antisemitism is exceedingly complex and on many points contested. Few would dispute that there is a connection, but consensus on the nature of that connection is elusive. Some disagreement on this score can be attributed to a notable indistinctness in the use of the word "ghetto," which, over time, came to be applied to coercive and voluntary Jewish quarters alike, and even more generally to a period or mentality in Jewish history—the "medieval" or "premodern"—as much as to a material place. Yet, debate also exists with respect to narrower understandings of the ghetto that would limit the concept to communities that were, as one influential model holds, compulsory, segregated, and enclosed (Ravid 1992).

Any attempt to relate the ghetto to antisemitism, another famously ambiguous concept, must contend with what are essentially moving targets. In general, though, a few basic questions have traditionally informed discussion of this relationship. First, as mentioned, there is the issue of definition: what do we mean when we use the term "ghetto," and what do we mean by "antisemitism"? A second issue concerns the nature and sources of the outside pressure involved in the establishment of ghettos: namely, to what extent can

D. B. Schwartz (✉)
George Washington University, Washington, DC, USA
e-mail: dbs50@gwu.edu

antisemitism be said to be a decisive cause of this pressure, and if it is critical, what form does this antisemitism take? Next, there is the matter of determining the relative weight of external versus internal motivation in ghettoization. Is outside force an indispensable factor that effectively creates or at least strongly conditions Jewish spatial separation? Or, does it tend to ratify a de facto separatism that already exists or would come into being spontaneously even without such pressure? Is it antisemitism that causes the ghetto, or the ghetto that causes antisemitism? Finally, there is the matter of whether the original ghettos of early modern Italy and Central Europe and the ghettos of Nazi-occupied Eastern Europe share more than a terminological identity: are these examples of Jewish spatial segregation similar enough to warrant designation by the same word or so distinct in their purpose and underpinnings as to call for a different label entirely?

In what follows, I offer a genealogy of the concept of the Jewish ghetto, with a focus on the nuances of its relationship to antisemitism. The bulk of the essay is a discussion of different perspectives on the germaneness of antisemitism to the establishment of ghettos in the fifteenth and sixteenth centuries, though I briefly take up the revival of mandatory ghettos for Jews by the Nazis during the Holocaust toward the end. In a nutshell, this piece seeks to caution against a tendency in some of the more recent research to minimize the part played by antisemitism in the genesis of Jewish ghettos. In the case of the pre-emancipation ghettos in particular, such revisionism is often part of a larger pushback against what Salo W. Baron famously labeled the "lachrymose theory of pre-Revolutionary Jewish woe" (1928, p. 526)—a pushback that is, in general, historiographically necessary and salutary, but can be taken to excess. While we now have a much richer understanding of the range of practical and ideological motivations that contributed to the founding of enforced Jewish quarters, of the diversity of meanings imputed to them, and of the different functions they served, this should not obscure the degree to which anti-Jewish ideas, beliefs, images, frames, and anxieties influenced, and were in turn influenced by, the rise of ghettos. Antisemitism may not have been, in all or even most cases, a sufficient cause of the creation of Jewish ghettos; it was, however, a necessary one.

The Rise of Ghettos

While the etymology of the word "ghetto" has long been debated and even today remains contested by some, most agree that its roots lie in Venice and here solely in geographic happenstance—the fact that the island on the northern edge of the city to which the Jews of Venice were restricted in 1516 was already known as the *Ghetto* (or *Geto*) *Nuovo*. "Ghetto" itself is thought to derive from the verb *gettare*, meaning to pour or to cast, which would evoke the copper foundries that had once occupied the site. *Il Ghetto* was, initially, simply the proper name for the mandatory and exclusive Jewish district of Venice, bearing a significance somewhat like that of later territorial designations elsewhere (to wit, the "Lower East Side" in New York City), which acquired a Jewish connotation due to its large and predominantly Jewish population toward the turn of the twentieth century. And it probably would have remained as such were it not for Pope Paul IV's 1555 bull (*Cum nimis absurdum*) confining the Jews of Rome to an enclosure along the Tiber river and the eventual adoption of the name *Ghetto* in both official and popular discourse to refer to this enclave. Starting at this point, it became possible to live not merely in "*the* Ghetto" but "*a* ghetto," and in the aftermath of the Vatican's decision to concentrate Jewish populations throughout the Papal States, both the institution of the compulsory Jewish quarter—and the labeling of such quarters as ghettos—spread throughout Italy (Ravid 1992).

If the age of the term "ghetto," at least in its meaning of a walled-off, all-Jewish district, can be pinpointed with near certainty, the origin of the ghetto as an idea is less easily fixed. The concept of the compulsory ghetto, if still somewhat inchoate and hazy in its contours, clearly predated the birth of the word "ghetto," even if it is also fair to say that ghettoization only truly became institutionalized in the sixteenth century. The first known legal document, ecclesiastical or otherwise, to call for residential segregation of Jews in a mandatory enclosure dates to a regional church synod held in the Polish city of Wrocław (Breslau) in 1267. Over the course of the fourteenth and in particular fifteenth centuries, city ordinances calling for the creation and walling off of separate Jewish quarters began to proliferate in France, Spain, Germany, and Italy, though they rarely achieved total segregation and generally proved abortive, whether because of a lack of follow-through or because sterner measures—most notably, expulsion—were eventually adopted.

How pivotal, then, was Christian antisemitism to the institution of the late medieval and early modern ghetto? In what follows, I begin by laying out the main arguments for viewing antisemitism as the principal factor in the rise of ghettos. I then discuss alternative explanations of ghettoization which chip away at the claim for antisemitism's centrality.

The view of Christian antisemitism as the driving force behind the creation of the ghetto system has a long pedigree in Jewish historical consciousness. During the debate over Jewish emancipation in the nineteenth century, the ghetto emerged as a freighted symbol for both sides. Its proponents, who included nearly all Jews in states where the argument raged, were mainly in agreement in seeing the ghetto as a malevolent Christian invention imposed on Jews against their will and to their detriment. Any alleged defects in contemporary Jewish society, they claimed, could be attributed either to the residual effects of centuries of spatial segregation, or, in places, like papal Rome, where the ghetto endured until 1870, to its continued toxic influence. This perception of the ghetto as, in the main, a manifestation of the Catholic Church's Jewish problem permeated most historical accounts of the ghetto and the Jewish "Middle Ages" in nineteenth-century Jewish historiography. "Every possible method to degrade and harass the Jews, and mark them off from the remainder of the population was invented and employed in the dark, medieval days," wrote the American Reform Rabbi David Philipson in his *Old European Jewries*, one of the first attempts to write a book-length survey of the institution of the ghetto (1894, p. 19).

As we will see, in the late twentieth-century Jewish historians would begin to challenge the argument for the overriding significance of antisemitism in the emergence of the ghetto. Yet, shorn of much of its lachrymosity, this argument still has its advocates. Their ranks include Kenneth Stow, one of the premier experts on the history of the Roman Ghetto and on the evolution of Catholic theology vis-à-vis the Jews. With respect to the nexus between the ghetto and antisemitism, two of Stow's most central claims merit elaboration here. The first involves what Stow considers the unifying theme of Christian antisemitism, the concern for purity and the fear of pollution; the second, his reading of *Cum nimis absurdum* and his interpretation of the sixteenth-century Catholic Reformation papacy's reasons for embracing ghettoization.

Stow (2006) approaches the issue with a wide-angle lens, believing that, to be properly understood, the ghetto must be grasped within the *longue durée* of Catholic thought concerning the Jew. The ghetto, per Stow, was one, albeit critical, component of the medieval church's larger campaign aimed at separating Jews from Christians, reflected in prescriptions such as the Jewish badge and in prohibitions on cohabitation of any kind, the frequenting of the same bathhouses, and the sharing of food (especially food that a Jew had touched). And this segregationist policy was driven in turn by a bedrock conviction, one rooted in the theology of Paul and the Church Fathers and reflected in both elite discourse and popular mentalities, that contact with—even excessive proximity to—a Jew pollutes. More than a means of displaying the supremacy of the church over the synagogue by spatializing Jewish inferiority (though it was certainly that as well), the ghetto was, at bottom, a protective measure aimed at safeguarding the Christian body politic (the *Corpus Christianorum*) against a corrosive, if theologically necessary, Jewish presence by marking, enclosing, and stigmatizing it. Secular rulers, later church officials, and even the Jews themselves might embrace the ghetto for their own reasons and invest it with other meanings and applications, but its conception as a tool to preserve the moral and physical purity of Christian space and society was, according to Stow, foundational. Indeed, the rhetoric used to justify pre-Venetian efforts to segregate Jews spatially often centered on the need for protection from contamination. While the mandatory and enclosed Jewish quarter was rarely justified by recourse to unambiguous language of sickness and pollution, there were exceptions, especially when non-clerics offered the rationale. "Our Holy Mother the Church," King Martin of Aragon explained in 1398, justifying his decision to isolate the Jews of Catalayud in their own quarter, "has ruled that the infidel and fetid Jews must live apart from the Christians, so that these unclean people will not infect the purity of the Christians by their proximity, so that these putrid people will not corrupt the health of a pure soul by their horrific wounds and crimes" (quoted in Kriegel 1979, pp. 42–43).

Already before the emergence of the first ghetto by name in 1516 Venice, the incipient spatial segregation of Jews was associated with purity and purgation. This was a critical concern in Venice as well. In 1509, an alliance of armies, led by France, the Holy Roman Empire, and the Papal States, attacked Venice and overran its mainland territories. Many refugees from these areas fled to Venice, and Jews—who had no continuous history of residence in Venice proper—were among them. The question emerged of what was to be done with these Jews. Some argued for the economic advantage in permitting the Jews to stay and serve as moneylenders in the city itself. Others, especially friars and preachers, strenuously opposed any relaxation of the government's policy forbidding Jews' residence in Venice, objecting in particular to their diffusion all over the city. Elizabeth Crouzet-Pavan has written insightfully about how this Jewish presence violated medieval Venice's image of itself as a "city of God" and "New Jerusalem" whose emergence and survival in the face of so many obstacles, from the lack of city walls to the "briny waters" that threatened to engulf it, was due solely to divine Providence—an image already shaken by the faltering war effort that had brought so many Jews to Venice in the first place. "By creating the ghetto," Crouzet-Pavan writes, "by locking up those considered in the collective concept as a stain on society, the political powers of Venice took charge of achieving the mythical Christian city, while at the same time imposing the braking force of rationality on a pathologically anti-Semitic culture" (1991, p. 164). The ghetto's establishment on the margins of the city, in Cannaregio, was in line, moreover, with the view of the outlying areas as "places of danger and pollution" and the "trend in urban politics…to exile to the extremes of Venice any activities which could threaten the city" (p. 179).

For Stow, then, the "establishment of ghettos falls along the trajectory of a centuries-long process of purification, which, by the sixteenth century, had become generalized" (2016, p. 4). This emphasis on the fear of pollution is echoed, on a wider scale, in Nicholas Terpstra's recent revisionist history of the Reformation. There, the ghetto is presented as one manifestation of a much broader western and central European social and religious obsession, starting in the fifteenth century, with ideas of purity and purgation. The growing disunity within Christendom magnified the perceived threat posed by heretics, witches, dissenters, and other marginal groups—including Jews—and inspired a wave of efforts to preserve the health and integrity of the mystical body of Christ by either expelling or enclosing the source of contagion. The Jewish ghetto functioned in the early modern period much like other institutions from the hospital to the workhouse, all of which meant to discipline and quarantine (and potentially rehabilitate) those branded as deviants (Terpstra 2015, pp. 74–132).

With Pope Paul IV's embrace of ghettoization for Jews in 1555, the fear of pollution that had underlain previous experiments with spatial segregation was effectively radicalized. Stow interprets *Cum nimis absurdum* as a significant change of course in official Church policy toward the Jews, wherein its previous efforts to maintain a balance between subjugation and toleration yielded to an avalanche of restrictions aimed at accelerating the large-scale conversion of the Jews (Stow 1977, 1992, pp. 304–7). The papal ghetto was the linchpin of this campaign. If to date, the motivation for the ghetto had been mostly prophylactic, being primarily intended to contain, if not cure, the threat Jews posed to the *Corpus Christianorum*, the papal ghetto was "an entirely new institution whose purpose was to integrate the Jews into society by way of their conversion" (Stow 1992, p. 305). While not wholly unprecedented—the short-lived clerical and civic drive in Spain, in the wake of the 1391 massacres, to confine the Jews in compulsory closed quarters also seems to have been infused with conversionary fantasies and hopes—this was the first time segregation was clearly tied to the goal of conversion. Instead of settling for keeping Jews out, the papal ghetto, as part of a battery of social and economic prohibitions designed to reduce Jews to penury and misery, would ultimately bring them in. At root, though, the fear of pollution remained operative. It was simply that the threat had grown so intolerable that it seemed necessary to remove it once and for all through the only route that seemed open to a Church persuaded of the illegitimacy of a total expulsion of the Jews—namely, conversion.

Thus far, I have tried to represent the argument for viewing Christian anxieties as the determining factor in the rise of ghettos. A few recurring elements characterize this approach: a focus on repressive programs generated from the top and a granting of, at most, a limited agency to the Jews themselves; a preference for *longue-durée* analysis sensitive to the lingering influence of venerable and potent social and religious imaginaries and cultural mentalities; and a belief that rhetoric and ideology are reliable gauges of motivation and guides to action. I now turn to thinkers who provide a more qualified assessment of the significance of antisemitism for understanding the ghetto.

One of the oldest challenges to the predominance of antisemitism in the genesis of the ghetto dates to the early decades of the twentieth century. At that time, scholars like Louis Wirth and Salo Baron began to argue that the ghetto was not simply a coercive measure imposed on Jews from without. Rather, they claimed, the ghetto was originally a product of Jews' own desire for spatial separation and communal autonomy. In other words, the mandatory ghetto of the sixteenth century was ultimately descended, conceptually, from the institution of the voluntary Jewish quarter, whose lineage extended much further back into the Diaspora past. There were several contexts for this revisionism. One was linguistic: the fact that, by the end of the nineteenth century, the word "ghetto" had come to be used to refer to densely populated Jewish immigrant enclaves in European and American cities (e.g., "the New York Ghetto," as the Lower East Side was known for a time) that were legally voluntary made it appear natural (if anachronistic) to apply the term to earlier examples of non-statutory Jewish concentration as well. Another was ideological, as the emergence of Zionism and other forms of Jewish nationalism conditioned scholars to see in premodern Jewish separatism not simply a hemming in by others, but a genuine and defiant expression of a distinct Jewish nationality. Still another was methodological: Wirth, author of *The Ghetto* (1928), was identified with the so-called Chicago school of sociology of the early twentieth century, which regarded the spontaneous clustering of diverse groups in different areas in the city as a veritable law of urban development. The scholars within this camp thus tended to view the conversion of Jewish quarters ("voluntary ghettos") into obligatory ghettos in the late Middle Ages and early modern period mainly as formalizing a separation of the Jewish minority from the Christian majority that had already come about naturally, or would have if given the chance. As Salo Baron wrote in his landmark 1928 essay, "Ghetto and Emancipation," "it must not be forgotten that the Ghetto grew up voluntarily as a result of Jewish self-government, and it was only in a later development that public law interfered and made it a legal compulsion for *all* Jews to live in a secluded district in which no Christian was permitted to dwell." For Baron, Jewish autonomy—not antisemitism per se—was the central characteristic of the ghetto, and those, like David Philipson, who portrayed the institution as unremittingly bleak and wholly involuntary, were guilty of subscribing to the "lachrymose theory of pre-Revolutionary Jewish woe."

Baron criticized the identification of the ghetto with antisemitism by proposing, in effect, a different long-distance ancestor for the institution, namely, the voluntary Jewish quarter. Yet some of the more recent challenges to this linkage spurn sweeping accounts in favor of more local and contextual analyses of the ghetto's motivations and meanings (Siegmund 2006). Applied to a case like Venice, a close-up lens of this kind might focus on the fact that the edict establishing a ghetto was, in effect, a concession that provided official (albeit temporary) backing for the creation of a Jewish community in a city that, throughout its history, had generally prohibited Jews from settling within its limits and restricted them to its mainland empire. Alternatively, it might treat Venice's growing practice of requiring foreign merchants operating in the city to live in closed compounds (*fondaci*) segregated by religion and ethnicity as a more important context for understanding the motivations behind the ghetto than the prior history of the medieval enclosure of Jews (Calabi 2016). With respect to Florence, Siegmund argues that the Medici state, in creating a ghetto in the city in 1571, sought neither to imitate the Roman and Venetian ghettos that preceded it nor to embrace a papal policy that linked ghettoization to the promotion of conversion. Rather, the Florentine ghetto was principally the result of an early modern state's efforts to enhance its power via tighter bureaucratic control and the consolidation of the confessional communities that lived within its borders. Here too, Christian antisemitism may have provided a language for justifying the establishment of a ghetto, but it did not provide a motive.

Perhaps the most forceful rebuttal to the ascription of the ghetto system to antisemitism can be found in a recent essay of counterfactual history by Bernard Cooperman, entitled "What if the 'Ghetto' Had Never Been

Constructed?" (2016). Cooperman provides an economic interpretation of ghettos, explaining their emergence as the result of demographic pressures, commercial competition, and diminishing real estate stemming from Jewish migration and urbanization in the early modern period. "Ghettoization," he writes, "was a zoning policy aimed at legally marking out a space for a substantial Jewish presence within an urban area." It was "everywhere a response to the pressure that the Jewish community placed on the stock of urban real estate" and "also a response to an expanding Jewish economic role, a shift from simple moneylending to wider forms of commercial activity." For Cooperman, "[g]hettos were justified in religious terms, but they belong primarily to the legal and commercial realm" (2016, p. 100). Cooperman thus completely rejects the construction of the ghetto into the symbol par excellence of "religious intolerance and pathological xenophobia" in nineteenth-century Jewish historiography (2016, p. 102). Yet while concerned to distinguish the ghetto from its later reinvention as a metaphor for premodern Jewish residential space, he is not as minimalist as those, like Ravid, who seek to limit the application of the term to urban neighborhoods that were legally obligatory, exclusively Jewish, and physically segregated or enclosed. In a sense, Cooperman endorses a functionalist definition of the ghetto based on what ghettoization was presumably designed to achieve in society (i.e., municipal zoning to accommodate a Jewish presence), rather than isolating the necessary features of a ghetto. On this basis, Cooperman suggests that the differences between "the Jewish town of Krakow [Kazimierz], the ghettos of Venice and Rome, and the unwalled free port in Livorno" were not materially significant, notwithstanding that Kazimierz lay outside the city limits of Krakow and Livorno lacked mandatory segregation altogether. All three represented alternatives to expulsion or non-admission of Jews; all three followed from state interventions in urban planning to achieve the "legal separation of space." Livorno did not need a physical ghetto because the Tuscan free port was "already jurisdictionally cordoned off" to permit trade and commercial activity beyond the reach of "Florence's guilds and established economic interest groups." The city itself was a "virtual 'ghetto'" (Cooperman 2016, p. 100). Cooperman's answer to his title's question is that, without the "ghetto" that made their settlement possible, some of the most important and illustrious Jewish communities of the early modern period would not have come into existence and flourished. The story of the ghetto is not, ultimately, one of antisemitic exclusion. Paradoxically, the ghetto paved the way for the civic inclusion and mass urbanization that would characterize the modern Jewish experience. With this argument, Cooperman echoes other scholars, like Ruderman (1997), Bonfil (1994), and Weinstein (2000), who have portrayed the ghetto not as the antithesis of Jewish modernity, but as one of its unwitting agents.

While it may be true that the ghetto worked to embed the Jews within the city by granting them a place of their own, however circumscribed, one wonders if the relatively benign interpretation of the early modern ghetto offered by Cooperman and others, who drain the institution of much of its segregatory and exclusionary thrust, is not a step too far. If the aim of the ghetto was simply to furnish the Jews with their own gated community, it is hard to explain why, for example, there would have been such concern with sealing off outward-facing ghetto windows, quays, and balconies so as to limit the ability of Jews to look out and Christians to see in. As Dana Katz has shown in regard to Venice in particular, the closure of ghetto windows (even if often observed only in the breach) served not only to preserve Jewish "objecthood" but to protect Christian holy space from a Jewish gaze that alone had the potential to pollute (2010). By reducing the establishment of ghettos to an economic "zoning policy," a form of urban planning, Cooperman mistakes what was undoubtedly a feature of ghettoization for its crux and purpose.

The Ghettos of the Holocaust

Whatever debate there may be about the role of antisemitism in the creation of the pre-emancipation Jewish ghettos, one would expect to find much less controversy on this issue in the case of the ghettos of Nazi-occupied Eastern Europe. These sites of mass starvation, disease, and overcrowding, which in many cases came to function as antechambers to the concentration and death camps, clearly were not part of a conceptual lineage originating in the premodern Jewish quarter. Nor were they a limbo between acceptance and exclusion intended to expedite Jewish conversion to Christianity. On the contrary, in line with Nazi antisemitism's understanding of Jewishness as a racial category, some of the largest Holocaust-era ghettos housed communities of Jewish converts to Christianity. The more than one thousand ghettos formed by the Nazis varied considerably in their degree of physical separation and enclosure (Megargee and Dean 2012). Still, the Jewish ghettos under the Nazis were designed to curtail Jewish mobility more substantially and to separate Jews and non-Jews more strictly than the ghettos of the early modern period.

In keeping with the "intentionalist" interpretation of the Holocaust, historians in the 1940s through the 1970s assumed that the ghettos were a calculated step in the direction of the "ultimate goal" (*Endziel*) of annihilating European Jewry. Through 1942, however, as Christopher Browning (2004) shows, Nazi officials were split over the purpose of ghettoization between "attritionists" (who believed the objective was to steadily decimate the Jews through impoverishment, starvation, and disease) and "productionists" (who sought to exploit ghettoized Jews as slave labor for the benefit of the Nazi war economy). The debate today over the role of antisemitism has more to do, however, with how all-embracing a factor it was in the creation of ghettos. Dan Michman (2011) traces the ghetto to Nazi "scholarship" on the danger of East European Jewry (*Ostjudentum*). Michman focuses on the work of Jewish "expert" Peter-Heinz Seraphim, and in particular on his interpretation of urban "ghettos" (by which Seraphim meant the voluntary Jewish quarters of cities like Warsaw and Lodz) as the natural habitat and breeding ground of an Eastern European Jewry that, in the Nazi imagination, was an expansionist force. The purpose of the mandatory and exclusive Nazi ghetto was to stop cold Jewish colonization by tightly hemming in the Jews who already lived in these "ghettos" and driving back into them Jews who had left. Michman regards the influence of antisemitic ideology and discourse on ghettoization as decisive.

Others, without denying that antisemitism played a central part in motivating the creation of ghettos, question whether it provides a sufficient explanation of the phenomenon. Increasingly, ghettoization is located and understood within the context of the larger German colonial project for "Germanification" of Eastern Europe, which prioritized the clearing of real estate for ethnic Germans (*Volksdeutsche*) and displaced Poles as well as Jews (Horwitz 2008). Again, though, one wonders whether the attempt of scholars to situate the ghettos of the Holocaust in the context of Nazi colonialism and "urban planning" does not fall into the same trap as does Cooperman with respect to early modern ghettos—namely, neutralizing the fear of sexual mingling and pollution that underpinned a whole arsenal of segregatory legislation in addition to ghettoization.

Conclusion

The sharp contrast between the ghettos of the early modern period and the Nazi ghettos raises the question of whether they are truly variations on an idea or are similar only in name. Ravid's definition of the ghetto as a legally compulsory, physically separated, and exclusive minority district would conceivably include them both, even allowing for the major differences between them. More recently, however, the urban sociologist Mitchell Duneier, in his book *Ghetto: The Invention of a Place, the History of an Idea* (2016), has questioned the applicability of the ghetto concept to the Nazi case. "The Nazi ghetto," he writes, "was something entirely new," for "[h]owever harsh and strictly regulated no previous Jewish quarter, ghetto or otherwise, had ever been established with the express purpose of destroying its inhabitants through violence and brutality" (2016, p. 18). That we use the same term for both the early modern Jewish and the Holocaust ghettos, Duneier argues, is a result of both the Nazis' own attempts to frame their concentration of Jews as a restoration of pre-emancipatory conditions (the chapter on Nazi ghettos is titled "A Nazi Deception") as well as the uncritical acceptance of the ghetto label (albeit often with caveats) by later journalists, sociologists, and historians in their writing about the Holocaust. This speaks to the incompleteness of definitions, like Ravid's, that incorporate specific alleged characteristics (e.g., legal coercion, homogeneity, etc.) of ghettos yet omit the crucial issue of *function*. Even before the Nazi ghettos turned deliberately genocidal, they were intended to segregate, marginalize, control, and exploit Jews well in excess of anything the founders of the early modern ghetto could have envisioned. Functionally, the early modern ghetto and Nazi ghetto were clearly divergent institutions, whatever superficial similarities they may have shared. What remains to be more fully understood is the semantic and conceptual history of the "ghetto" between the demise of the original ghettos and the "return" of the ghetto under the Nazis. What role did the idea of the ghetto and the term itself play in various national and regional antisemitic movements? Was the ghetto a "key concept" in the ideological and rhetorical toolkit of modern antisemitism? Or was it, in fact, far more influential in discourse by Jews about distinctly Jewish spaces, which they often viewed positively, e.g., *di yidishe gas* (the Yiddish term meaning "Jewish street"), as a metonym for Jewish society as a whole even when Jews were not confined to a specific street or quarter? I suspect the latter, though further research is necessary.

References

Baron, Salo W. 1928. "Ghetto and Emancipation: Shall We Revise the Traditional View?" *Menorah Journal* 14 (6) (June): 515–26.

Bonfil, Robert. 1994. *Jewish Life in Renaissance Italy*. Berkeley: University of California Press.

Browning, Christopher. 2004. *The Origins of the Final Solution: The Evolution of Nazi Jewish Policy*. Lincoln: Nebraska University Press.

Calabi, Donatella. 2016. *Venice, the Jews, and Europe, 1516–2016*. New York: Rizzoli.

Cooperman, Bernard Dov. 2016. "What If the 'Ghetto' Had Never Been Constructed?" In *What Ifs of Jewish History*, edited by Gavriel. D. Rosenfeld, 81–102. Cambridge: Cambridge University Press.

Crouzet-Pavan, Elisabeth. 1991. "Venice Between Jerusalem, Byzantium, and Divine Retribution: The Origins of the Ghetto." *Mediterranean Historical Review* 6 (2): 163–79.

Duneier, Mitchell. 2016. *Ghetto: The Invention of a Place, the History of an Idea*. New York: Farrar, Straus and Giroux.

Horwitz, Gordon J. 2008. *Ghettostadt: Lodz and the Making of a Nazi City*. Cambridge, MA: Harvard University Press.

Katz, Dana. 2010. "'Clamber Not You Up to the Casements': On Ghetto Views and Viewing." *Jewish History* 24 (2): 127–53.

Kriegel, Maurice. 1979. *Les Juifs à la fin du Moyen Age dans l'Europe méditerranéene*. Paris: Hachette.

Megargee, Geoffrey. P., and Martin Dean, eds. 2012. *Encyclopedia of Camps and Ghettos 1933–1945*. Vol. 2. Indianapolis: Indiana University Press.

Michman, Dan. 2011. *The Emergence of Jewish Ghettos During the Holocaust*. Cambridge: Cambridge University Press.

Philipson, David. 1894. *Old European Jewries*. Philadelphia: Jewish Publication Society.

Ravid, Benjamin. 1992. "From Geographical Realia to Historiographical Symbol: The Odyssey of the Word 'Ghetto.'" In *Essential Papers on Jewish Culture in Renaissance and Baroque Italy*, edited by David B. Ruderman, 373–85. New York: New York University Press.

Ruderman, David. 1997. "The Cultural Significance of the Ghetto in Jewish History." In *From Ghetto to Emancipation: Historical and Contemporary Reconsiderations of the Jewish Community of Scranton*, edited by David N. Myers and William V. Rowe. Scranton: Scranton University Press.

Siegmund, Stefanie. 2006. *The Medici State and the Ghetto of Florence*. Palo Alto: Stanford University Press.

Stow, Kenneth. 1977. *Catholic Thought and Papal Policy, 1555–1593*. New York: Jewish Theological Seminary Press.

Stow, Kenneth. 1992. *Alienated Minority: The Jews of Medieval Latin Europe*. Cambridge, MA: Harvard University Press.

Stow, Kenneth. 2006. *Jewish Dogs: An Image and Its Interpreters*. Palo Alto: Stanford University Press.

Stow, Kenneth. 2016. "The Roman Ghetto and Its Significance." Unpublished paper.

Terpstra, Nicholas. 2015. *Religious Refugees in the Early Modern World: An Alternative History of the Reformation*. Cambridge: Cambridge University Press.

Weinstein, Roni. 2000. "'Mevudadim akh lo dehuyim': Ha-yehudim ba-hevra ha-italkit be-tekufat ha-reformatzya ha-katolit." In *Mi'utim, zarim ve-shonim: Kevutzot shulayim ba-historya*, edited by Shulamit Volkov. Jerusalem: Zalman Shazar Center.

CHAPTER 11

The Holocaust

Richard S. Levy

This essay seeks to explain how the Holocaust of European Jewry has altered the understanding of those presently engaged in studying the meaning of antisemitism. It will trace the changes in the conceptualization of antisemitism since its inception in the late nineteenth century and attempt to show how the mass-murder of Jews during World War II rendered older ways of grappling with the problem obsolete, while posing new challenges to the ways men and women seek to come to terms with its persistence.

* * *

At the age of eight, I—accidentally and simultaneously—discovered the existence of antisemitism and of the Holocaust. Hanging out with my friends Bobby, Stevie, Douglas, and Douglas, we were approached by Bobby's mother, a formidable woman of the working class, who announced to the group that there would be a picnic tomorrow afternoon in her backyard. Out of the corner of my eye, I saw her gesturing to her son and mouthing the words: "Not the Jew." Although my Jewish identity was at only a rudimentary stage of development, there was no doubt in my mind that I was being excluded, not for anything I had done, but for what I was. This was both hurtful and confusing. My discovery of the Holocaust was less immediately personal but more shocking. I was a precocious reader in the third grade and my teacher let me explore in the school library during reading lessons. There I came upon a picture book on World War II. I paged through it, arriving at the end-phase of the war which included photographs, well-known to all

---

R. S. Levy (✉)
Department of History, The University of Illinois at Chicago, Chicago, IL, USA
e-mail: rslevy@uic.edu

of us now but completely new to me in 1948, of the liberation of Bergen-Belsen—piles of corpses, hollow-eyed, living skeletons in filthy striped clothing. The captions identified the victims, living and dead, as Jews.

These two experiences, coming within weeks of each other, were formative for the rest of my life. I wanted to understand the relationship between antisemitism (Bobby's mom) and the atrocities performed on the bodies of Jews like me. In the intervening seventy years, I have come to recognize how ambiguous such experiences can be. It seemed obvious then, even to an eight-year old, that one must have inevitably led to the other. But, after many decades devoted to the study of antisemitism, I would no longer classify Bobby's mother as an antisemite or what she did as antisemitism. Further, the photographs I saw in the school library were certainly ghastly evidence of horrible deeds, but, in all likelihood, the victims were not only Jews but POWs, political prisoners, Roma, "asocials," Jehovah's Witnesses, and homosexuals.

The self-referential nature of these introductory remarks is not mere self-indulgence. In the rest of this essay, I will attempt to show how this "life lesson" exemplifies the common confusion between the study of antisemitism and the Holocaust, not only for me but for generations of scholars. I will argue that the notion that antisemitism led inexorably to the Holocaust and might one day produce similar catastrophic results is not a fruitful way to understand either phenomenon. Not fruitful because of the clear teleological thrust in this sort of thinking. If we conceive of antisemitism as an eternal, inescapable part of the history of the Jews, dating back at least to the biblical Amalekites, we will be tempted to explain the Holocaust as that history's logical end—perhaps its only possible culmination. My conception of antisemitism rejects the "long view" and distinguishes anti-Jewish animosities of all kinds and degrees from the nineteenth-century action-based ideology that needed the new word "antisemitism" to describe itself. Taking this shorter view, however, does not settle the issue of how even a more circumscribed definition of antisemitism relates to the Holocaust and more specifically how the Holocaust has impacted the study of antisemitism. My conclusion is that the Holocaust has radically altered—for better *and* for worse—the study of antisemitism.

* * *

One way to start the discussion of this subject is to examine the evolving conceptions of antisemitism before the genocide of the Jews took place. First, the coining of the term: I have not been able to find a usage earlier than 1860, when the word was employed in a cultural rather than a political context (by the German Jewish Orientalist, Moritz Steinschneider). By late 1879, the German journalist, Wilhelm Marr, seized upon the word "antisemitism" as a way of distinguishing his political agenda from traditional Christian Judeophobia and from the prejudices of the day in order to give his views the aura of a scientific ideology, which is the product of historical research and has nothing to do with medieval bigotry—or so he insisted. Important to note about the early history of antisemitism is how rapidly what was essentially a neologism achieved the broadest currency. There must have existed a felt need for a new word to describe the resurgence of conflicts, long thought to have been largely overcome, but in fact becoming ever more openly expressed, between Jews and the peoples among whom they lived. This need affected not just self-identified antisemites but Jews, non-Jewish critics, and neutral bystanders throughout Europe and wherever Europeans settled in the world. The word appeared in titles of books and pamphlets and on the mastheads of newspapers in English, French, Italian, Hungarian, Dutch, and Russian—all by 1894, and in places where no organized antisemitism existed, as well as where it was developing into full-fledged political movements. Even to outsiders, something new seemed to be agitating the vexed relations between Jews and others. I take this to be the starting point for the conceptualization of antisemitism as a new phenomenon, one with clear roots in the past but also with quite novel and unique characteristics of its own. Certainly, Jewish history was full of periods of oppression and violence before the 1880s. What was markedly different, however, was the swift institutionalization of antisemitism in political parties, newspapers, learned journals, lobbying agencies, and voluntary associations. In the past, persecution had been episodic; outbursts of violence alternated with long periods of quiet relations between Jews and their neighbors. Now, the action programs aimed at Jews, buttressed by modern mass media and new technologies, were being played out in the political life of nations. The announced intention of the movement was to continue the struggle as long as it took to solve the "Jewish Question."

It is difficult, if not impossible, then or now, to find entirely objective studies of the new phenomenon. This is a subject that called forth the impulse to attack or defend, and it continues to do so. Few observers of the emergence of antisemitism were inclined to see two sides to the issues raised, much less debate them calmly. Scholarly, semi-scholarly, and pseudo-scholarly attention to this new phenomenon emerged first in Germany, where antisemitism gained a firm foothold in the country's political culture during the 1880s. Under "scholarly" and "semi-scholarly," I mean to examine the recognition of antisemitism as a new development among reasonably impartial observers, including those without academic credentials. That is to say, I do not propose to analyze the notions of self-described antisemites concerning the nature of their beliefs or what they thought they were doing. Nor do I intend to discuss the motives and methods of the Jewish or non-Jewish defense organizations that came into existence in the 1890s. Both topics are important elements in a highly charged political dialectic, but they are also remote from my subject. Both almost always stand in conflict with more dispassionate attempts to understand antisemitism.

The popular encyclopedia genre [*Konversations-Lexikon*] in Germany, aiming at the broadest possible middle-class readership, offers some insight into the growing awareness of antisemitism in its German and European context. Normally, these works steered away from partisan politics, hewing to what their publishers hoped would be least off-putting to the largest possible audience. However, this principle of neutrality was not always observed. One of the earliest encyclopedia entries devoted specifically to "Antisemitism" dates from 1901, and comes from the Herder-Verlag. Its anonymous author appears quite certain as to the cause of the antisemitic movements present in German politics. "Antisemitism: the movement called forth by special circumstances [*RSL:* the reference is to fraudulent bankruptcies related to the crash of 1873, Jewish business ethics in general, prominence in liberal politics, and disturbingly rapid upward social mobility, among other real and alleged faults and flaws] which seeks to push back against the influence of Jews in political as well as economic areas....Antisemite: an enemy of the Jews, opponent of Judaism, fighter against the peculiarities, the intrusiveness, and pushy ambitiousness of Semitism." The *Meyers Grosses Konversations-Lexikon* of 1902 (1:588–89) gave a detailed account of the history of organized antisemitism, locating it in the areas of eastern and central Europe where the largest concentration of Jews lived. Once again, the stimulus for the political movement was seen to be the economic and political strivings of the Jews. Driving them out of public life and back within the traditional limits of their pre-emancipation existence—"even their complete expulsion"—were movement goals that seemed self-evidently justifiable to the author of the article. The ulterior motives and questionable methods of the antisemites were passed over in silence (see Haase 1975, pp. 174–76).

Although jaundiced in their interpretation, these and similar treatments of antisemitism at least looked for contemporary—not just ancient historical or theological—causes of the emergence of antisemitic organizations and political movements. One might object to the superficial, prejudiced rationalizations given to readers regarding the rise of antisemitism, but it is hard not to notice the contrast between the lexicon explanations and those offered by almost all the Jewish sources of the era. The latter typically refrained from the serious search for proximate causes. With some notable exceptions, the most common response of German Jews was to shrug off the problem as the last vestige of ignorance (see Blome et al. 2010).

Before World War I, this sort of optimism was general in central and western Europe, not just in Germany. The surfacing of antisemitism was regrettable but its future prospects were dismal. This firm conviction characterized two remarkably searching analyses of the period. The earliest was by the Jewish literary critic and journalist Bernard Lazare in his systematic study, *Antisemitism: Its History and Causes*, written in 1894 on the eve of the Dreyfus Affair but at a time when antisemitism in the public sphere was already highly visible in France. Lazare was fully aware that contemporary antisemitism was something new—an ideology transcending the traditional material or religious sources of conflict (1995, pp. 8–9, 175). His forthright exploration of causes and refusal to dismiss them as mere pretexts for prejudice have made Lazare much more popular with antisemites than with Jews. Antisemites misread his willingness to criticize Jews of past and present, particularly East European Jews, as a confession that Jews were "the cause of their own ills." However, he never conceded that Jews alone were responsible for antisemitism or that their oppressors always had or have justice on their side. In fact, and especially in his contemporary France, they were usually just plain wrong in their thinking about Israelites (assimilated and acculturated Jews like Lazare himself).[1]

A second noteworthy analysis of antisemitism before World War I is a sixteen-thousand word essay composed by Lucien Wolf (1857–1930) for the classic eleventh edition of the *Encyclopaedia Britannica* in 1910–1911. A journalist, historian, and activist in Anglo-Jewish affairs, Wolf was a dedicated defender of assimilation and emancipation (Levene 2004), as well as one of the earliest debunkers of the *Protocols of the Elders of Zion* (Wolf 1921). His well-documented, extremely thorough survey of antisemitism covered the movement's genesis in Germany, and then treated developments in Russia, Austria-Hungary, France, and Romania, with a brief coda on its less menacing presence in Britain. A more congenial person than Lazare, Wolf nonetheless also conceded a Jewish role in fostering antisemitism, but rather briefly and obliquely; he, too, attributed it to incomplete assimilation and social-economic "disruptions." He recognized the development as a recent response to a misperceived Jewish emancipation, distinct from historical myths and old grudges. Having just witnessed the successful conclusion of the Dreyfus Affair and the world's condemnation of the Russian pogroms, Wolf, like Lazare, was utterly certain that a movement based on ignorance, injustice, and the appeal to the basest of human motives could not long survive:

> It…has spent itself in political intrigues of transparent dishonesty. Its racial doctrine is at best a crude hypothesis. Its political activity has revealed the vulgarity and ignorance which constitute its main sources of strength.

Antisemitism might live on a bit longer in backward Russia and Romania, but even there its days were numbered.

The optimism of Lazare and Wolf rings a bit hollow. Why would either have bothered writing about an antisemitism that was scheduled to soon disappear? What bothered them most was not the agitation of scoundrels and

---

[1] Much of what Lazare has to say about Jews in 1894 would classify him as a Jewish antisemite, particularly his distinction between Israelites and the unassimilated eastern European Jews, whose "spirit of Talmudism" he held generally responsible for Jew-hatred. His experience of the Dreyfus Affair, however, led to a significant change of heart. Eventually, he embraced a social revolutionary Zionism as the only solution of the Jewish Question.

lunatics but rather the possibility that large numbers of the ignorant masses could be mobilized by falsehoods. The violence-prone mob had always been easy prey for demagogues, especially when Jews were being targeted. The difference in 1894 and in 1910–1911 was that the mob already had or would soon have the vote and, with it, the power to do harm to Jews. In response to the looming danger, both men, confident in the power of reason, used it to educate and persuade the gullible and to inoculate "the thinking part of the public" against a destructive folly. Here an obvious point should be made. The history of the twentieth century, reaching a climax in the Holocaust, destroyed the basis for such a humanistic belief in mankind's perfectibility and the inevitable triumph of reason. Such optimism vanished during World War I and the years that followed, never to reappear.

* * *

The interwar years produced some significant changes in the study of antisemitism. Most notably, it attracted much greater attention from a wide array of thinkers and writers, many of them with academic posts, who freed themselves from the fond hope that it must soon disappear. The triumph of reason seemed much less certain after four years of savage warfare, the rise of fascism, and the crumbling of democracies. Antisemitism as a mobilizing political force may still have been understood as appealing mainly to desperate social strata, and it may still have offered opportunities to despicable, cynical, and irresponsible would-be leaders of the masses. But what sapped the optimistic worldview of postwar observers was the clear evidence of antisemitism's growing influence on the political stage and its concrete impact on the policies of sovereign states. Before the war, with the exception of Vienna, the small antisemitic parties did not wield state power in Europe. The potential damage that these usually feckless organizations could do was easy to dismiss. Even in Vienna, where Hitler lived and Mayor Lueger's Christian Social Party ruled, Jews were insulted and threatened, but their rights remained intact, and they visibly continued to prosper. During the 1920s and into the 1930s, the situation changed substantially. Hungary, Lithuania, Poland, Romania, Germany, and Italy passed legislation that was overtly or covertly antisemitic. The United States established immigration quotas that aimed at keeping out East European Jews and other undesirables. The resources of state power had been brought to bear on the rights of Jews and, at least potentially, on their economic and physical well-being. Antisemitism clearly had staying power and was something to be taken seriously.

Even before the Holocaust, the Jews' worsening situation in many parts of the world resulted in a surge of attention to the subject of antisemitism. Between 1880 and 1945, approximately 1200 books were published with the word "antisemitism" in their titles or which gave a great deal of attention to this subject; registering the mounting sense of danger, works from the 1930s and early 1940s accounted for nearly 800 of them. Certainly, not all should be considered scholarly in nature. A good many can be classified as apologetic literature or as ephemeral commentary on current events. Nevertheless, these numbers were dwarfed by the Holocaust and its aftermath. After the immediate shock of events subsided, there began an enormous outpouring of writing of all kinds and from a very large number of perspectives; this shows no sign of ending soon. For the period from 1945 to 2015, the keyword search "antisemitism" in WorldCat produces nearly 7700 hits. This more than sixfold increase constitutes perhaps the most obvious impact of the Holocaust on the study of antisemitism. Jews, and for the first time, significant numbers of non-Jews, discovered a compelling field of study.

But quantity ought not be the only measurement of the Holocaust's influence on the study of antisemitism. As knowledge of the destruction of European Jewry gradually became available in the West during World War II, two traditional responses came to the fore. Among Orthodox and Zionist thinkers, normally at odds with one another, the news about the mass-murder of Jews was not completely unforeseen. Its dimensions were no doubt horrifying, but its essential meaning was comprehensible. The enmity of the Gentile world since biblical times was part of a religiously conditioned outlook; this latest eruption was the heart-breaking confirmation of Orthodox understanding of Jewish history and destiny. Equally for Zionists as for the Orthodox, genocide sanctioned the most widely held view among them: in the Diaspora the deadly threat of antisemitism could not be overcome by education, reason, or liberal good will; assimilation was demonstrably helpless against it (see Bartov 1998, p. 76). Surely, neither group rejoiced in having its expectations fulfilled.

However, for a large number of thinkers and writers, whose worldviews offered very little in the way of explanatory comfort, the Holocaust defied their previous ways of understanding antisemitism. The palpable effects of antisemitic ideology on the physical existence of Jews gave unprecedented urgency to the search for antisemitism's causes, forms, functions, and future. Theories that had been worked out since the 1880s needed to be reconsidered, revised, or renounced.

* * *

The Holocaust was distinctly German in its inspiration; Germany was the place where organized antisemitism first appeared and from which it spread. Moreover, antisemitic ideology played such an active part in its public life before World War II that many who sought the causes of the Holocaust and the role of antisemitism in it looked to German history for answers.

There were those who found Germany the "classic land of antisemitism" (Arendt [1951] 1973) and others who agreed with Nietzsche's characterization of the Germans as particularly inclined to an "obscurantist, enthusiastic, and atavistic" spirit. Several Jewish refugees from the German cultural sphere of Central Europe attempted to explain the catastrophe, both personal and collective, as the result of an antisemitism deeply rooted in German history and culture. In the works of George Mosse, Fritz Stern, Saul Friedländer, among many others, antisemitism was not just Nazi but thoroughly German. Less understandable, and less rewarding, are the *à thèse* histories by more contemporary historians, who searched for and, eventually, found a specific German pathology. Their reductionist premise is that we need to only trace the history of German Jew-hatred, from the medieval to the modern era, in order to understand the Holocaust and the essential nature of the antisemitism that caused it (see Goldhagen 1996; Weiss 1996). Two things are wrong with this tendency: the pursuit after continuities swallows up the history of other antisemitisms; the second consequence of this teleological approach is to ignore other possible outcomes of German history and to disregard German antisemitism's discontinuities. This still popular exercise has yielded highly dubious results, much in the way of assumption, assertion, and rigidly selective examination of the evidence, and little in the way of convincing explanation for Germany's peculiarities. Others took a more cautious approach to the Holocaust's German prehistory, searching for threads of continuity and finding them in greater or lesser degree. Almost all who follow this path find continuity in the content of antisemitic ideology, arguing that little new was invented by Hitler or other Nazi ideologues. But Paul Massing (1949) and Peter Pulzer (1964) go further, asserting or implying that imperial antisemitism exerted a strong influence on post-1914 antisemitic politics, strategy, and ultimately on the decision for genocide. Among several others, Richard S. Levy (1975) and Shulamit Volkov (1989) see a distinct break between imperial and Weimar antisemitism.

This line of inquiry into the history of antisemitism has also produced mixed, often contradictory, results regarding the Holocaust. For example, the role of nineteenth- and twentieth-century antisemitic ideology in the decision-making and implementation of the Final Solution has been variously perceived as absolutely central and also as peripheral or largely inconsequential (see Aly and Heim 2002; Aly 1999). Some see ideology as crucial to the decision-makers but less significant for those who carried out their decisions; some see it as incidental to both; others see it as fundamental to both.

It is unlikely that the future study of antisemitism will ever be divorced from the history of the Holocaust or from the special place of German antisemitism in its genesis. Nor should it be. On the other hand, there is much to be said for the efforts to disentangle antisemitism from its specific German origins and development and to consider it outside the framework of individual national histories. The Holocaust, in my opinion, has hindered rather than helped us to understand antisemitism as something distinct from its German incarnation. However, an attempt to do just this, to indicate a new direction for the study of antisemitism, was outlined even as the Holocaust was reaching its peak. Shlomo Bergman (1943), a psychoanalyst and educator, manifestly stirred by evidence of an unfolding catastrophe, wrote an essay that demanded a new approach to the study of antisemitism, one informed by the social sciences. He insisted that there had to be better explanations for what was happening to the Jews of Europe than those that relied on the repetition of ritual formulas or well-worn historical narratives. There was no single cause, but rather a great variety of causes for and characteristics of antisemitic actions and attitudes; organized antisemitism served a multiplicity of purposes. Context was all important, and so were comparisons. What others commonly cited as key causes for antisemitism, such as a conflict between religions, economic rivalries, the resurgence of pagan instincts, or xenophobia, he accepted only as the occasions for physical violence or Jew-hatred. They did not sufficiently explain the special animosity visited upon Jews.

Bergman placed his hopes for a better understanding of the problem in the social sciences' innovative study of group prejudice. Jew-hatred and antisemitism, he argued, are entirely different problems and should be studied differently. Insightfully, he also advocated a shift in focus:

> In dealing with political antisemitism we have to distinguish between the agents or manipulators and the patients, or believers. The former present no psychological problem, but when we study the reaction of the latter, we want to know what it is in antisemitism that proves fascinating, compensating or alluring.... [W]e want to know what particular social strata and what particular types of personality prove most susceptible to it. (1943, p. 58)

This last observation merits serious attention. Historians have generally focused on the producers—antisemitism's theoreticians, leaders of the various movements, and their respectable allies in the larger society. The consumers of antisemitism, the mass of followers, have been treated as essentially a monolith, mere pawns of their manipulators, whose motives, even if knowable, have little explanatory power. Bergman had no patience for this approach. To plumb the meaning of antisemitism, he was, whether he realized it or not, advocating the displacement of history by the social sciences. He is emblematic of one of the pronounced effects of the Holocaust on the investigation of the root causes of antisemitism: the opening of the subject to new disciplines and new methods of inquiry.

After the Holocaust, those who took up Bergman's challenge to find new ways of understanding antisemitism, both historians and social scientists, produced work of uneven quality and in the process motivated a thought-provoking negative response to their experiments. In a trenchant essay, the historian Jacob Katz (1983), still wrestling with the post-Holocaust meaning of antisemitism, took issue with the capacity of social scientists to explain it. He divided their theories into three general categories: "the socio-political; the psychological, or psychoanalytical; and the ideological." The first ascribed the outbreak of antisemitism to socio-economic crises and the resulting political upheavals prevailing within Gentile society. The displacement of social protest, an explanatory trope that runs right through the history of antisemitism before, during, and after the Holocaust, discounted the very real conflicts between Jews and non-Jews, according to Katz. "But the mere fact of social tension is not sufficient to explain anti-Semitism.

Tensions may provide an occasion without providing a cause. The question that still has to be answered is why crises within the larger society should be particularly harmful to *Jews*."

Katz was equally dismissive of the psychoanalytical approach; here he specifically mentions the Frankfurt School and others who disdained the data provided by historical research. Their alternative strategy was a mistake, however. "Anti-Semitism, inexplicable in rational terms, is [therefore] seen as an external reflection of concealed unconscious processes within the human species." Katz objects not only that the psychoanalytical approach is ahistorical, but also that it does not seek to bring empirical data to bear on the wide variety of expressions of antisemitism or its development over time. It sidesteps the question of agency, taking antisemitism altogether out of the realm of human choice.

Finally, Katz objects to the uncritical acceptance of racial ideology as a sufficient explanation of antisemitism and, in particular, the murderousness of the Holocaust. He argues that "the notion of race per se did not automatically imply a derogatory judgment," and cites as evidence that Jewish thinkers and scholars did not hesitate to employ the concept, at least before the rise of the Nazis (see Hart 2011). The destructive tendency within German antisemitism was not simply the result of racial theory. There were certainly non-racists in Germany and all over the world who harbored deadly hatreds of Jews.

Katz's most strenuous objection to the use of social science techniques in the study of antisemitism, whether by historians or others, specified a collective failing: they in effect "de-Judaize antisemitism":

> But historians who focus exclusively on the personal traits of particular anti-Semites, or on the anti-Semitic personality in general, or on the social processes at work in a given situation, or on the psychoanalytic roots of anti-Jewish animosity, are not engaged in the proper work of their trade. What is more their ahistoricism effectively severs anti-Semitism from its connection with the Jewish people. In the interpretations of anti-Semitism produced from this standpoint, the fact that *Jews* were its victims becomes almost accidental. (1983, p. 44)

In reaffirming the primacy of the historical approach for the study of antisemitism, Katz was at the same time making the case for understanding that Jews were at the center of that history, not a convenient foil for more powerful targets, bigger cultural grievances, or economic protests. No, the Jews were not "collateral damage"; they were the intended victims of antisemitism. What generates the special hatred that they have been subject to is their refusal to stop being Jews, rather than what they were said to have done or what they actually did. It was the perception of them—note that he does not say "misperception"— that ties together anti-Jewish hostility throughout the ages.

* * *

Taken together, Bergman and Katz represent two important consequences of the Holocaust and the rethinking of antisemitism it forced upon us. Both scholars, like many others, felt compelled by the scale of the tragedy to reevaluate the way antisemitism was understood. Both expressed their dissatisfactions with the state of the field. Both made acute observations concerning the way the study of antisemitism ought to move forward. However, neither Bergman's shift of scholarly attention from leaders to led, nor Katz's determination to see Jews as the critical link in the history of antisemitism have been fully acted upon. Two great obstacles—one perhaps surmountable, the other likely insuperable—lie in the way of the better understanding called for by these two men.

First, their differences express a deep and basic disagreement about how best to grasp the meaning of antisemitism. The social scientist's search for commonalities results in generalizations that apply to the moment and cannot accommodate the ever-changing forms and functions of antisemitism. Generalizations are too often accomplished at the expense of the complexities underlying individual cases and their historical origins. Meanwhile, the historian's insistence on the uniqueness of each and every outbreak of antisemitism past and present results in a great reluctance to compare cases. In-depth studies of the development of political antisemitism in their national incarnations do not automatically contribute insights into the general phenomenon of antisemitism.

A few of the many notable attempts to bridge the methodological gap between disciplines are worth mentioning here. The historically informed work by the sociologist, Helen Fein (1979), seeks to get beyond narrative and anecdote in order to explain varying Jewish mortality rates during the Holocaust; she first presents a macroscopic view and follows it with brief case studies of the era that illustrate and support her interpretation. The political scientist Robert Melson (1992) gives historical context its due in his comparison of the Armenian and Jewish genocides, locating their similarities in the turbulent aftermath of war and revolution. As with these two works, William Brustein (2003) rejects the solitary focus on Germany, and instead subjects to statistical analysis "four varieties of racial prejudice, in five European countries." His desire to provide an empirical basis for the literature's favored generalizations—and to question these when that basis cannot be established—brings a rare rigor to the discussion. Recent anthologies treating antisemitism, the Holocaust, and related questions recognize the need to take an interdisciplinary approach to this history. An excellent example (Weiss-Wendt and Yeomans 2013) brings together several historians with political scientists, authorities on bio-medicine, the experiences of religious minorities, and legal history to explore the variations in race science in the Nazi era; the book surveys countries and ideologies that often receive slight or no attention in the literature, showing how they affected and were in turn affected by the dominant German practitioners. Although this representative sampling of attempts to integrate the disciplines is an encouraging sign, none has wholly succeeded in resolving basic conflicts among them. Nevertheless, a useful start has been made in that direction.

Also encouraging in this respect is another direct consequence of the Holocaust, the appearance of institutionalized scholarly efforts to study antisemitism. Among the most important of these are the Vidal Sassoon International Center for the Study of Antisemitism (SICSA) at the Hebrew University in Jerusalem, the Center for Antisemitism Research (Zentrum für Antisemitismusforschung) at the Technical University of Berlin, and the United States Holocaust Memorial Museum in Washington, D.C. These institutions have helped sustain and expand the field of antisemitism studies, funding and publishing research, building archives, and facilitating the exchange of ideas at conferences and in journals. In recent years Holocaust Studies has become a part of many university curricula and degree programs. Interdisciplinary by definition, they integrate demography, sociology, psychology, history and oral history, anthropology, and numerous other methodologies in their treatment of antisemitism and its relationship to the Holocaust. These collective developments certainly strengthened the field.

Although the efforts to understand antisemitism have advanced on several fronts since the end of the Holocaust, they face a second, less tractable obstacle—not a matter of approach but rather of content. What Walter Laqueur (2006) called the "changing face of antisemitism" has immensely complicated its study, rendering the subject matter harder to define, track, or understand. Antisemitism itself has become a moving target, changing its shapes and purposes, finding new and potent means of communication in the Internet, and becoming more global than ever before. Once distinct national parties formed around programs designed to disempower the all-powerful Jews; they presented specific remedies and attempted to mobilize supporters around the life or death need to solve the Jewish Question. There are no such parties in evidence today, none overtly calling for disenfranchisement or even lesser limitations on the economic or civil rights of Jews. Antisemitism today has dispensed with practical agendas and has become an explanation, more often a shrill accusation, about whatever it is in the modern world that one hates or fears. Antisemitism is nevertheless still a menace, still a tool of mobilization, even if the message is more obscure, more imprecise, more enveloped in bigger battles against globalization, Western imperialism, Wall Street, or climate change. Moreover, antisemitism no longer occupies a relatively fixed place on the political spectrum; it is just as likely to figure in the rhetoric of the left as of the right. The existence of the state of Israel has further problematized the subject. Where does anti-Zionism cross over into antisemitism?

The questions far outnumber the answers. The tools we have developed to seek those answers must keep pace with ever new developments. Disheartening though it may be, the struggle to understand antisemitism must continue. The Holocaust is over. Antisemitism is not.

References

Aly, Götz. 1999. *Final Solution: Nazi Population Policy and the Murder of the European Jews.* Translated by Belinda Cooper and Allison Brown. London: Arnold.
Aly, Götz, and Susanne Heim. 2002. *Architects of Annihilation: Auschwitz and the Logic of Destruction.* Translated by A. G. Blunden. Princeton: Princeton University Press.
Arendt, Hannah. (1951) 1973. *The Origins of Totalitarianism.* San Diego: Harcourt Brace Jovanovich.
Bartov, Omer. 1998. "Antisemitism, the Holocaust, and Reinterpretations of National Socialism." In *The Holocaust and History: The Known, the Unknown, the Disputed, and the Reexamined*, edited by Michael Berenbaum and Abraham Peck, 75–98. Bloomington: Indiana University Press.
Bergman, Shlomo. 1943. "Some Methodological Errors in the Study of AntiSemitism." *Jewish Social Studies* 5 (1) (January): 43–60.
Blome, Astrid, Holger Böning, and Michael Nagel, eds. 2010. *Die Lösung der Judenfrage: Eine Rundfrage von Julius Moses im Jahre 1907.* Bremen: Edition Lumiere.
Brustein, William I. 2003. *Roots of Hate: Anti-Semitism in Europe Before the Holocaust.* Cambridge: Cambridge University Press.
Fein, Helen. 1979. *Accounting for Genocide: National Responses and Jewish Victimization During the Holocaust.* New York: Free Press.
Goldhagen, Daniel J. 1996. *Hitler's Willing Executioners: Ordinary Germans and the Holocaust.* New York: Alfred A. Knopf.
Haase, Amine. 1975. *Katholische Presse und die Judenfrage. Inhaltsanalyse katholischer Periodika am Ende des 19. Jahrhunderts.* Verlag Dokumentation: Pullach bei München.
Hart, Mitchell Bryan, ed. 2011. *Jews and Race. Writings on Identity and Difference 1880–1940.* Waltham: Brandeis University Press.
Katz, Jacob. 1983. "Misreadings of Anti-Semitism." *Commentary* 76 (1) (July): 39–44.
Laqueur, Walter. 2006. *The Changing Face of Antisemitism: From Ancient Times to the Present Day.* Oxford: Oxford University Press.
Lazare, Bernard. 1995. *Antisemitism: Its History and Causes.* Lincoln: University of Nebraska Press.
Levene, Mark. 2004. "*Wolf, Lucien (1857–1930).*" In *Oxford Dictionary of National Biography.* Oxford: Oxford University Press. http://www.oxforddnb.com/view/article/38145.
Levy, Richard S. 1975. *The Downfall of the Anti-Semitic Political Parties in Imperial Germany.* New Haven: Yale University Press.
Massing, Paul. 1949. *Rehearsal for Destruction: A Study of Political Anti-Semitism in Imperial Germany.* New York: Harper.
Melson, Robert. 1992. *Revolution and Genocide: On the Origins of the Armenian Genocide and the Holocaust.* Chicago: University of Chicago Press.
Pulzer, Peter. 1964. *The Rise of Political Anti-Semitism in Germany and Austria.* New York: Wiley.
Volkov, Shulamit. 1989. "The Written Matter and the Spoken Word. On the Gap Between Pre-1914 and Nazi Anti-Semitism." In *Unanswered Questions: Nazi*

Germany and the Genocide of the Jews, edited by François Furet, 33–53. Schocken: New York.

Weiss, John. 1996. *Ideology of Death: Why the Holocaust Happened in Germany*. Chicago: I.R. Dee.

Weiss-Wendt, Anton, and Rory Yeomans, eds. 2013. *Racial Science in Hitler's Europe, 1938–1945*. Lincoln: University of Nebraska Press.

Wolf, Lucien. 1910–1911. "Anti-Semitism." In *Encyclopaedia Britannica*, vol. 2, 11th ed., 134–46. Cambridge: Cambridge University Press.

Wolf, Lucien. 1921. *The Myth of the Jewish Menace in World Affairs: The Truth About the Forged* Protocols of the Elders of Zion. New York: MacMillan.

CHAPTER 12

Jewish Self-Hatred

Sol Goldberg

Introduction

Jewish self-hatred is complex and contentious. Used precisely, the term refers to a subset of Jews who, besides their dissociation from Jewry and Judaism, express extremely critical or negative attitudes toward Judaism, other Jews, or themselves qua Jewish—or, at least, criticism or negativity perceived as extreme by some other Jews.[1] Such observable, albeit ambiguous, behavior is explained by Jewish self-hatred, an emotional complex[2] that, *ex hypothesi*, underlies extreme anti-Jewishness among Jews. Jewish self-hatred, in turn, is explained by social conditions in which some Jews feel pressured or motivated to conform, either sincerely or strategically, to "antisemitic" norms within a wider, non-Jewish culture. This account has explanatory power. It also, however, permits rhetorical abuses. Other Jews exploit "Jewish self-hatred" as an accusation to silence and discredit (justifiably or not) those Jews whose overly unfavorable attitudes toward their Jewish heritage or overly favorable

---

[1] My qualifications about communal or individual perceptions should be taken for granted throughout the essay. In other words, for the purposes of this essay, "Judaism" is whatever a community says it is or whatever an individual understands her community to expect of its accepted members (e.g., support for Israel). I assume no normative essence of Judaism, only an agent-relative description.

[2] Hatred, though in the name, is one of several possible, non-exclusive emotional states covered by the term "self-hatred." Others are shame, guilt, anger, and resentment.

S. Goldberg (✉)
Associate Professor (Teaching Stream), University of Toronto,
Toronto, ON, Canada
e-mail: sol.goldberg@utoronto.ca

attitudes toward non-Jewish culture allegedly threaten the survival or well-being of Judaism or Jewry. Due to the frequency of such abuses, the scholarly merits of the topic as well as the term are widely doubted (Finlay 2005; Glenn 2006; Lerman 2008).

This essay respects this skepticism about Jewish self-hatred, but also tries to redirect it toward productive ends. Doing so requires clarifying the term, the topic, and their importance for the study of antisemitism. However much rhetorical abuses undermine the academic reputability of Jewish self-hatred, discarding it would have far worse consequences. Jewish identity has long been shaped by the fact of antisemitism. Historical misperceptions and exclusions of Jews have actually engendered both (exaggeratedly) proud reaffirmations and (exaggeratedly) ashamed denunciations (Meyer 1989). The study of Jewish self-hatred, we should appreciate, thus concerns primarily one way Jews respond to antisemitic misperceptions and exclusions, but also secondarily the reactions of other Jews to certain Jewish responses to antisemitism. Ignoring these dimensions of antisemitism would impoverish the field.

The Discursive Turn in the Literature

Since the mid-1980s, the scholarship on Jewish self-hatred has witnessed a major shift. The focus has turned from the social–psychological phenomenon to the discursive constructions and polemical deployments of "Jewish self-hatred." My survey highlights this discursive turn and its skepticism about the concept's epistemic validity.

Jewish self-hatred's place in a wider conceptual history must first be noted. That history begins no later than general philosophical reflections like G. W. F. Hegel's famous portrayal of the failures of mutual recognition in the master–slave dialectic, and it continues through Friedrich Nietzsche's account of resentment and guilty conscience in Christianity's slave morality; Thorstein Veblen's notion of pecuniary emulation of higher classes by lower ones; and Sigmund Freud's psychoanalytical description of the self-denigration characteristic of melancholy. Their theorizing has suggested frameworks in which subsequent scholars explain a person's damaged relationship to himself as a function of his membership in a disfavored or non-normative racial, ethnic, religious, sexual, economic, or gendered identity group. Space precludes any elaboration of these conceptual roots and ramifications of self-hatred; but this wider history must not be forgotten once our sights are set on Jewish self-hatred.

In its primary (but not initial!) sense, the concept of Jewish self-hatred originated with social scientists like Freud (1964) and Kurt Lewin (1948) and with cultural analysts like Theodor Lessing (1930), Jean-Paul Sartre (1948), and Hannah Arendt (1944), though not all of them use the term. Despite the differences among them, their writings basically agree that self-hating Jews regard negatively all or some aspect of Jewish identity, including their own, in terms acquired from a dominant, non-Jewish culture in which mistaken and malicious perceptions of Jews and Judaism prevail. Intellectual historians picked up this understanding of Jewish self-hatred. Paul Mendes-Flohr (1978) and Peter Gay (1978), for instance, use it to illuminate the particularly intense trials and tribulations of modern European thinkers, writers, and artists estranged both from the Jewish world that they tried to leave behind and from the non-Jewish world that they tried to join.

Sander Gilman's *Jewish Self-hatred: Antisemitism and the Hidden Language of the Jews* (1986) redirected scholars' attention. Although Gilman, like his predecessors, defines Jewish self-hatred as the internalization of another group's racism, his book features the discourse about "Jewish self-hatred" rather than its purported social–psychological referent. Subsequent research mostly accepts Gilman's discursive focus. Even scholars who resist it cannot ignore its upshot. Take Todd Endelman (1991), who criticizes Gilman's cultural-studies approach. He faults Gilman for an insufficient treatment of Jewish self-hatred's real social dimensions and psychological consequences. Yet to defend its analytic viability, Endelman (2001) still addresses the term's problematic origins and constant abuses.

Endelman's criticism notwithstanding, attention to Jewish self-hatred as a discourse has undoubtedly advanced our understanding of the term's history. Two especially noteworthy contributions are Paul Reitter's *On the Origins of Jewish Self-Hatred* (2012) and Susan Glenn's "The Vogue of Jewish Self-Hatred in Post-World War II America" (2006). Reitter offers an alternative genealogy of Jewish self-hatred that uncovers the term's original sense and actual provenance. Scholars like Gilman, Reitter shows, mistakenly trace Jewish self-hatred back to disputes among representatives of Orthodoxy, Reform, Zionism, and Assimilationism in *fin-de-siècle* Germany and Austria, disputes in which seemingly synonymous terms like Jewish antisemitism, Jewish Jew-hatred, and Jewish anti-Zionism emerged. Jewish self-hatred arrives on the scene, however, not only *after* but also *in response to* this discursive context. Coined by the journalist Anton Kuh after World War I, the term originally connoted a redemptive opportunity as well as an existential affliction: the messianic promise of a redeemed humanity awaits not those who try to repudiate antisemitism, but, paradoxically, those who embrace it constructively in their self-abnegation (Reitter 2012, pp. 40–41). This redemptive sense of Jewish self-hatred migrated to America where Clement Greenberg (1950) responded to the "chauvinistic" campaign for "positive Jewishness." This ideal, he argues, results from self-hatred no less than its "negative" counterpart, but fares far worse than the latter in understanding its own psychological roots: the sense of inferiority behind the propensity to "polemical violence and name-calling" when confronted with alternative conceptions of Jewishness.

Greenberg belongs to a mid-twentieth-century American context that Glenn discusses not to achieve "an objective understanding of the idea of Jewish self-hatred," but rather to "analyze the historicity of the concept itself" (2006, p. 97). Whereas Reitter recovers the concept's redemptive origins, Glenn describes its popularization. Lewin's theorizing about inferiority complexes among Jews as well as other minorities due to antisemitism or racism lent the social–psychological conception of Jewish self-hatred a new degree of authority and prestige—and, therewith, of popularity, too. With American Jews' concerns about the Holocaust and assimilation, "self-hatred" became a useful and central term. During this period, the term provided an explanation for communal dissociation and a reproach to curtail it.

The various meanings and suspicious uses of Jewish self-hatred exposed in the discursive turn raise serious doubts about the concept's application. In its most extreme form, this skepticism rejects the concept as an "ideological myth" that belongs in history's dustbin. This radical skepticism is often expressed by those accused of being self-hating Jews—e.g., Anthony Lerman (2008), Judith Butler (2003, 2012), and Jacqueline Rose (2007). Some might be tempted to dismiss their defensive position as an ideological counter-myth. But, even if their motivations are no less partisan than those of their accusers, their skepticism agrees for all intents and purposes with the doubts widespread among scholars. Academic treatments of Jewish self-hatred regularly suffer from tendentious rhetoric, clandestine value-judgments, careless misattributions, and epistemic circularity. These intellectual vices, many insist, have irreparably tainted the analytic viability of the term and the topic (Reitter 2009).

But this skepticism has its limits, as Allan Janik and Mick Finlay acknowledge. Janik, a cultural historian who highlights "the dubious facility with which even distinguished writers about the Jewish case have ideologically conjured with this notion," accepts that "there is such a phenomenon as a rejection of one's heritage and…that this is fundamentally a problem of identity" (1987, pp. 87, 84). Likewise Finlay, a social psychologist who argues "that the term is often used rhetorically to discount Jews who differ in their life-styles, interests or political positions from their accusers, and that such misapplications of the concept result from essentialized and normative definitions of Jewish identity," concedes that "dominant discourses can affect minority identities and group behavior…and examples of Jews repeating anti-Semitic attitudes and rejecting Jewish identity are easy to find" (2005, pp. 202, 217). Janik and Finlay thus concede that the justified doubts about the evidence of self-hatred in alleged cases do not warrant a wholesale denial of the phenomenon.

Even if we reject completely Jewish self-hatred as a social–psychological concept, the rhetorical phenomenon of Jewish self-hatred as invective still deserves serious attention for the normative issues it raises. Efforts to demonstrate the lack of analytical precision in most uses of Jewish self-hatred treat too seriously the term's semantics and not seriously enough its pragmatics. Although Jewish self-hatred might have become a technical term defined strictly and impartially in social scientific discourses, its meaning in intra-communal polemics approximates the betrayal (i.e., Israel's dalliances with other gods) that the Hebrew Bible characterizes as idolatry (Halbertal and Margalit 1998) much more than anything in the *Diagnostic and Statistical Manual of Mental Disorders*. The accusation provides, in other words, a means of policing group boundaries and preserving group integrity that "deviants within" allegedly undermine. Whatever their explanatory component, attributions of Jewish self-hatred undoubtedly have a basic moral or moralizing intent (Finlay 2007, pp. 332–33; 2014, p. 703). Moralizing, of course, does not conduce to good scholarship. But the moral issues raised in this emotionally-charged language still have a reputable pedigree in the scholarship. Questions like whether, when, and to what extent an identity group has a rightful claim to the loyalty of its members, and whether, when, and to what extent members of an identity group may reasonably invoke their autonomy against such claims appear in recent works by Marilyn Friedman (2014, 2015) as well as in the earliest theorizing about self-hatred, both Jewish and general. Moral issues such as the consequences of inequality, failures of authenticity, the limits of legitimate moral criticism, and the fairness of cross-cultural normative evaluations may comprise only a small fraction of the latest scholarship. But don't infer therefore that these issues are not vital to the topic of Jewish self-hatred or that they could not be tackled in an academically rigorous manner.

What Signals Jewish Self-Hatred?

My literature review noted the widespread equation of Jewish self-hatred with Jewish antisemitism. Their conflation results in a confusion about Jewish self-hatred's symptoms and diagnosis. Yet, surprisingly, this confusion has escaped censure. Skeptics could object, however, that scholars who turn to Jewish self-hatred to account for the observable behavior of certain Jews typically fail to establish the reliability of such behavior as an indicator of the underlying psychological phenomenon. Just as a runny nose might suggest a common cold, seasonal allegeries, or no ailment whatsoever, so too a Jew's negative attitude towards Jews or Judaism could point to different underlying phenomena. Whenever a Jew is nominated as a self-hater, the case should be probed with due methodological suspicion to prevent any quick leap to a mistaken diagnosis of so-called "Jew-flu." So, rather than dismiss the concept altogether, we should seize the opportunity to make our doubts about its application more precise and productive.

Jewish antisemitism is, I suggest, not only the most commonly presumed, but also the most propitious indicator of Jewish self-hatred. If nothing else, Jews' repetition of antisemitic beliefs or behaviors is counter-intuitive enough to call for some explanation. Jewish antisemitism therefore seems better suited to predict the presence of Jewish self-hatred than such other overt signs of dissociation as conversion, intermarriage, or assimilation. As Endelman (2015, p. 331) stresses, modern Jews who left the fold mostly did not forsake relations with other Jews and pursue the company of Christians exclusively; conversion and assimilation were often simply a means of expanding their professional and social options. Dissociation can result from sheer indifference or even be compatible with continued affection, as in the case of Oswald Rufeisen ("Brother Daniel"). Israel's Supreme Court permitted him, a convert to Catholicism who continued to identify as ethnically Jewish, to settle in Israel under the Law of Return, i.e., as a Jew.

In contrast with the full range of attitudes compatible with mere dissociation, a negative attitude toward Jews or Judaism is a *sine qua non* of Jewish antisemitism. Hence an important counterfactual conditional: *if there's no evidence of Jewish antisemitism, then there's no possibility of Jewish self-hatred.*

JEWISH VERSUS OTHER KINDS OF ANTISEMITISM

The concept of Jewish antisemitism demands precision. To be sure, one might reason that, if a Jew says something which would be described as antisemitic when said by a non-Jew, then its utterance by a Jew should be deemed antisemitic, too. As Mark Gelber claims: "The Jewish or non-Jewish identity of a writer would have nothing to do with the [text's] possible 'antisemitic' aspect" (1985, p. 7). Such reasoning accords with the fact that different species of hatred—Sinophobia, Islamophobia, misogyny, homophobia, antisemitism, etc.—are differentiated by the identity of their respective victims without any restrictions on the possible identities of the victimizers. But obscured here is the crucial difference in the Jew's and non-Jew's respective relationships to the source of antisemitic prejudice: Jews derive antisemitic prejudices from sources within their *adopted* culture, antisemites from within their *native* culture. It is this very difference that theories of Jewish self-hatred promise to explain.

Jewish antisemitism and other kinds of antisemitism can be differentiated in another way. The previous paragraph regarded Jewish and non-Jewish antisemites alike as perpetrators of antisemitism. But Jews are its victims as well as its culprits, and not only in the sense that some Jews are its victims while others are its culprits. A Jewish antisemite inflicts harm *qua* antisemite, but also endures harm *qua* (probably) self-hating. Jewish self-hatred might be a harm of a less visible and material sort than those done to Jews in violent pogroms, economic sanctions, social restrictions, political exclusion, or legalized discrimination; but its "merely" psychological nature makes it no less a harm as a result, even if some Jews are likely to disregard it or regard it derisively.

The term Jewish antisemitism might therefore be a misnomer. It looks analogous to Christian antisemitism, Left-wing antisemitism, Nazi antisemitism, etc., with the adjective Jewish modifying the noun antisemitism apparently just as Christian, Left-wing, and Nazi do. But Jewish antisemitism could not be simply one of many species of antisemitism. The noun stands to the adjective not as genus to species, but rather as cause to effect: Jewish antisemitism depends explanatorily on antisemitism since internalization assumes an antisemitic group—or, at least, one perceived as such—that a Jew has or wants the opportunity to join. Precision thus recommends differentiating individual kinds of Jewish antisemitism from each other according to the distinct kind of antisemitism internalized. We should speak accordingly of Jewish Christian antisemitism, Jewish Left-wing antisemitism, and even Jewish Nazi antisemitism (Lewin 1948, p. 187) as species of the genus Jewish non-Jewish-antisemitism. Common usage and convenience, however, favor the linguistic status quo.

Now, my claim that the source of Jewish antisemitism must be a non-Jewish milieu should not be taken as a denial of the resources *within Judaism* for Jews to criticize the norms of their community—as if I believed that Judaism's prophetic tradition really did end, as Rabbinic accounts insist, with the close of the Biblical canon. Neither do I imagine a clear-cut distinction between internal and external criticism. Jewish self-hatred, whether used to explain the psychologically-fraught phenomenon of distancing from one's group identity or used to vilify and thus inhibit dissociation and deviance, attests to the permeable boundaries and the worries generated by permeable boundaries between Jewish and non-Jewish communities. Homogenous groups whose members uniformly embrace their norms and hermetically-sealed cultural traditions preserved within an impenetrable and inescapable society are fictions.

"Jewish" in the Relevant Sense

These considerations suggest the need to restrict appropriately the concept of Jewish antisemitism. A first restriction concerns the definition of "Jew" or "Jewish." Not all Jews should be eligible for consideration as Jewish antisemites, and so *a fortiori* as self-hating Jews. Imagine someone Jewish according to Jewish law but who does not identify as Jewish religiously, culturally, or ethnically. If he were also an antisemite, that fact would be irrelevant to his Jewishness. He would have internalized the antisemitism not of *another* culture, but of *his own* culture. This hypothetical fits the real case of Csanád Szegedi, a leading figure in Hungary's nationalist and largely-antisemitic Jobbik political party until he discovered his Jewish roots. Hence the following rule about the range of Jewish antisemitism's applicability: the less evidence that we find of an antisemite's having previously internalized a Jewish identity, the less reason we have to characterize the person as a Jewish—as opposed to some variant of non-Jewish—antisemite.

In his consideration of Jewish anti-Zionism, Philip Mendes similarly restricts the extension of "Jewish," albeit to identify individuals different from those of interest here. He locates contemporary Jewish anti-Zionism within "a long-term political tradition whereby some left-wing groups persuade Jewish members to exploit their own religious and cultural origins in order to vilify their own people," e.g., "Jews who defended the 1929 pogrom in Palestine, and…Jews who endorsed Stalin's anti-Jewish campaigns in the early 1950s." These Jews should not be "classified as 'self-hating,'" claims Mendes (2008, p. 97), since they attest to "a political not a psychological phenomenon": they "do not positively identify as Jews in terms of any collective cultural, religious, or ethnic/national connection with other Jews," but rather "their Jewish identity appears to be solely negative." Mendes here distinguishes political from psychological modes of identification to classify a subset of Jews who lack an emotional connection to Judaism or Jewry and invoke their Jewishness merely as a legitimation device to speak critically of Jews on behalf of Jews. His subset of Jews is thus precisely the kind that I would exclude with my eligibility criterion for Jewish antisemitism. But notice that our opposed interests lead Mendes and me to a common need to separate "Jews" whose Jewish identity has significant psychological roots from those whose Jewish identity doesn't. To study those critical or negative Jews whom the other disregards, each of us delineates the same conceptual boundary.

This boundary marker has nothing to do with who should be counted normatively or nominally as a Jew. The curious case of Krusty the Clown illustrates the point from the opposite angle. In an episode of *The Simpsons* titled "Today I am a Clown," Krusty is informed by his local Jewish community that he isn't a Jew. Dejected, he leaves the community building ("Where the Chosen Get Chosen") and immediately runs into Lisa and Bart, to whom he explains the implication of the news: "I thought I was a self-hating Jew; but it turns out I'm just a plain old antisemite." Krusty, however, is mistaken: no one who first comes to know Jewish life from the inside could ever be a plain old antisemite, even if it turns out that he never was technically Jewish. Social and cultural origins, not biological ones, determine whether Jewish antisemitism and Jewish self-hatred are applicable, since the concepts relate only to the cases of Jews who repeat antisemitic canards out of some real or perceived social–psychological need to confirm their new, true loyalties by proving their distance from their origins.

ANTISEMITISM AND JEWISH ANTISEMITISM CIRCUMSCRIBED

The second restriction on Jewish antisemitism as a sign of Jewish self-hatred concerns the definition of antisemitism. No consensus exists on the essential features of the phenomenon. Most scholars at least agree, however, that not every historically unfavorable, critical, or hostile attitude toward Jews ought to count as antisemitism. An old witticism defines antisemitism as hating Jews more than is reasonable, implying both that some hatred of Jews is reasonable and that reasonable Jew-hatred does not count as antisemitism proper. The scholar who argues most rigorously for separating unreasonable hatred of Jews from its reasonable variant is Gavin Langmuir (1990a, b). He uses "anti-Judaism" to refer to a historically-typical kind of xenophobia with a basis in real social interactions and "antisemitism" to refer, by contrast, exclusively to a historically-atypical kind of chimerical or fantastical prejudice based in a disturbed psyche. Langmuir's distinction guides my discussion of Jewish antisemitism, except that I will replace "anti-Judaism" with "anti-Jewishness" to avoid any impression that the negative attitude is toward Judaism rather than Jews. Whether the antipathy toward Jews is religiously or racially oriented does not matter; only the distinction between reasonable and unreasonable forms of antipathy does.

This distinction between anti-Jewish and antisemitic antipathy wisely recommends demarcating within all cases of Jewish antipathy toward Jews and Judaism only a particular subset as unreasonable and therefore antisemitic. But applying the general distinction to Jewish cases requires special care, as a widespread intuition about racial slurs shows. Members of an identity group commonly—even if not prudently—permit themselves to speak about traits associated with their group in ways not permitted to outsiders. A sardonic observation differentiates Jews' and antisemites' typical dislike of Jews by suggesting that, whereas antisemites hate Jews generally but occasionally make exceptions for individual Jews whom they like despite their Jewishness, Jews like Jews generally but occasionally make exceptions for individual Jews whom they hate despite their Jewishness. An insult like "that greedy Jew" thus might have rather different connotations depending on the speaker's identity. At a minimum, we cannot insist without further ado that every witting utterance of an antisemitic canard, especially if by a Jew, confirms antisemitism.

Consider possible misinterpretations of self-deprecating or "politically-incorrect" Jewish humor like that of Lenny Bruce, Woody Allen, Rodney Dangerfield, or Joan Rivers. Reitter (2009, p. 361) warns similarly about misinterpretations of Karl Kraus that occur because scholars pay insufficient attention to this Austrian-Jewish writer's use of irony, paradox, hyperbole, or similar devices of indirect communication. These subversions of language's straightforward meaning alter the significance of his invocation of antisemitic motifs. Kraus accordingly figures prominently in Reitter's recovery of Jewish self-hatred's original, redemptive sense: Reitter's ironically self-hating Jews provide a dose of much-needed antisemitic "hatred" to correct the excessive "self-love" of Jews who believe their own press. A more recent case of a redemptive, but perhaps excessive, critic of Jews and Judaism might be Yeshayahu Leibowitz, the controversial and outspoken Israeli intellectual, who coined the term "Judeo-Nazis" to liken the State's policies toward Palestinians to the Nazis' genocidal policies toward the Jews.

Should Kraus' and Leibowitz's rhetorical kind of Jewish antisemitism be lumped together with the kind that signals the social–psychological phenomenon of Jewish self-hatred? Almost certainly not. I say "almost" because we cannot rule out the possibility that some sort of social–psychological inferiority complex plays a part in motivating the corrective impulse. But, even if we must admit that the two kinds of antisemitic speech might coincide, we may still separate them analytically.

Prophetic Versus Jewish Antisemitism

Let me propose that, in contrast to Jewish antisemitism, we call the kind of antisemitism instantiated by Kraus and Leibowitz *prophetic antisemitism*. The term prophetic antisemitism adapts to our needs John Gager's description of "prophetic anti-Judaism," which is "the sort of intra-Jewish critique characteristic of the biblical prophets and of later sectarian and reformist movements within Judaism" (1983, p. 8). By "later...within Judaism," he means the period of the first centuries of the Common Era in which Judaism and Christianity had not yet completely parted ways. We may fairly extend his use of the term, though, to any and all later cases in which the prophets inspire Jewish self-assessment, some of which will be self-derogation. A case in point is again Reitter's self-hating Jews, at least some of whom understand the biblical prophets to provide the deep, historical precedent for their fierce rhetoric of redemptive criticism (Reitter 2012, pp. 24–25, 116). Finally, to adjust Gager's description to Langmuir's distinction, we must limit our interest in intra-Jewish critique to the kind whose style or manner of expression sounds unreasonably or excessively vicious and therefore antisemitic rather than merely anti-Jewish.

For this reason, prophetic and Jewish antisemitism's excessively negative locutions are still likely to resemble one another. But these phenomena differ from each other much as apostasy and heresy do: Jewish antisemites try to express their distance from the Jewish community that they (wish to) exit actually or symbolically, while prophetic antisemites try to refashion the Jewish community within which they (wish to) remain. Richard Landes makes a similar point in a comparison of the most extreme Jewish anti-Zionists today to the biblical "prophets who mingled their millennial promises with a violent rhetoric of rebuke—the first scourges of their people," observing that, unlike Israel's ancient prophets who "addressed their critique only to their own people," its contemporary ones "instead engage in self-recriminations before enemies who use the admission of faults to justify their violence and hatred" (2015, abstract).

At least in theory, therefore, prophetic antisemitism distinguishes itself from Jewish antisemitism by its target audience and its rhetorical intent: we'd expect prophetic antisemites to address their antisemitic language to other Jews whose beliefs and behaviors they hope to reform, whereas we'd expect Jewish antisemites to address their antisemitic language to the non-Jewish group to whose perspective they hope to (appear to) conform. In practice, however, the difference between prophetic and Jewish antisemitism might be nearly impossible to establish.

Three interrelated reasons explain the epistemic challenge. First, as mentioned above, the prophetic and Jewish antisemite's vicious criticisms of this or that Jewish doctrine or practice could be essentially identical in substance and tone. Second, there is nothing other than these locutions and the wider context of their occurrence through which to determine someone's authorial intentions, which, again, might be disguised by meaning-altering modes of communication like hyperbole or irony. Finally, a prophetic antisemite might opt to achieve internal reform by recruiting external pressure to bear on the Jewish community. Imagine, for instance, a contemporary Jewish columnist who writes op-eds in *The New York Times* in support of BDS with the goal of influencing some Israeli policies or an Enlightenment Jewish philosopher who echoes some Christian prejudices against Jews to facilitate Judaism's reform and Jews' inclusion in a (no longer (exclusively)) Christian society.

If our uncertainty about the distinction between prophetic and Jewish antisemitism in individual cases cannot be overcome, then think how much more uncertain would be any inference we might make from observable Jewish antisemitism to Jewish self-hatred as its underlying psychological cause. I concede the difficulty and its problem for the study of Jewish self-hatred, and reply: so what? Certainty is virtually never afforded to us in almost any area of the human sciences, and least of all when inquiring into the inscrutable mental states of others. But we are not about to abandon every investigation of human behavior and belief just because its result is less than certain.

Illustrating the Issues

Let me illustrate key issues raised here by reference to a recent affair that played out during this essay's composition. The episode is ambiguous. Although a case of (self-)critical dissociation, it might not be a case of Jewish self-hatred according to the criteria set out above. Regardless, it provides a sense of why the topic remains vital to understanding antisemitism, its possible effect on some Jews, and other Jews' worries about disaffected or critical members of their community and its potential decline.

On August 1, 2016 the Israeli daily newspaper *Haaretz* published "We're American Jewish Historians. This Is Why We've Left Zionism Behind" by two notable scholars of American Jewry, Hasia Diner ("The Israel I Once Loved Was a Naïve Delusion") and Marjorie Feld ("The Moment I began My Re-education"). Each describes her moral opposition to the Zionism on which she was raised, as well as her growing ostracism within and antagonism toward her local Jewish community as a result of her vocal opposition to some key policies and specific actions of the Israeli government. Especially relevant is Feld's confession that "non-Jews…in liberal and left organizations in college" who articulated "strong critiques of Zionism as Western colonialism, as a militarist project, as racism" made her "terrifically uncomfortable."

Their public declarations provoked critical responses by Jewish journalists, lay-leaders, and other academics. Alan Jay Gerber, a columnist for *The Jewish Star* (a weekly, Orthodox newspaper based in Long Island), accused them of Jewish self-hatred. His "At Tisha B'Av: On Self-Hating Jews and Mesira" cites approvingly Jonathan Sarna's criticism of Diner and Feld in *Haaretz*.

Now, Sarna, a preeminent historian of American Jewry, never uses "Jewish self-hatred" or "Jewish antisemitism." But his piece's title, "The American Jews Who've Exchanged Their Utopian Myths about Israel for Demonic Ones," implies that Diner and Feld echo antisemitic canards in their rejection of Zionism, i.e., implies their antisemitism.

This episode raises many questions underscoring the difficulty and value of gaining clarity about "Jewish self-hatred." What evidence of demonic imagery does Sarna find in Diner's and Feld's declarations? Does he accept the widely-accepted equation of demonization with antisemitism? If so, then why doesn't he charge them with Jewish antisemitism or self-hatred? Does he simply not like these often sensationalistic and abused terms? Or does he think the charge misplaced despite the demonization? What does Gerber's charge of "Jewish self-hatred" amount to? Why does he link it to *mesira* (the Rabbinic law covering cases in which one Jew turns another over to non-Jewish authorities)? Why does he interpret their statements within the ritual framework of *Tisha B'Av*, the Jewish fast day commemorating the destructions of the First and Second Temples and therewith providing a template for memorializing all future Jewish tragedies? Do Diner's or Feld's sharp moral criticisms suffice to count as instances of Jewish antisemitism? Would their antisemitism (if such it is) together with their declared dissociation from their communities confirm an inference of their Jewish self-hatred? Or might their alleged antisemitism have another character and cause, e.g., prophetic antisemitism? Indeed, if they had the term, might they have used it to label their criticisms like the original self-hating Jews did? Finally, and generally, to which audience—Jewish and/or non-Jewish; these (non-)Jews, but not those (non-)Jews; etc.—is each article primarily addressed? In short, how might these speech-acts be interpreted reliably or responsibly?

These questions don't permit straightforward or conclusive answers. But they are nonetheless worth asking, and hopefully the distinctions drawn here help ask them more fruitfully.

A Skeptical and Hopeful Conclusion

This essay raises several doubts about Jewish antisemitism and Jewish self-hatred as concepts. These doubts differ, however, from the prevalent skepticism about their use. That skepticism overreacts to the all-too-frequent occurrence of careless applications or ideologically-motivated accusations. Unlike it, my skepticism is methodologically driven. It promotes more, not less, care in attributing or denying Jewish self-hatred to anyone. But beyond my hope for greater precision in approaching the topic is my hope for a greater appreciation of its importance and interest. Deployed responsibly, Jewish self-hatred (i) explains plausibly the curious phenomenon of Jewish antisemitism; (ii) identifies a psychologically damaging effect of antisemitism; and (iii) names a peculiar reaction of some Jews to both antisemitism and excessive Jewish pride. Moreover, its use, even when irresponsible, provides a window into (i) the anxieties of some Jews in the face of antisemitism; (ii) their perception of internal threats to their community's welfare; and (iii) a linguistic resource among others—e.g., idolater and "Jewish Amalekites" (Horowitz 2006, p. 4)—that they have for ostracizing or vilifying those who "betray" Jews or Judaism. Without due consideration of all these facets of Jewish self-hatred, we'd have an impoverished understanding of antisemitism's real and perceived impact upon the social and psychological lives both of Jews uncertain about their place between different milieus and of Jews anxious about communal solidarity.

REFERENCES

Arendt, Hannah. 1944. "The Jew as Pariah: A Hidden Tradition." *Jewish Social Studies* 6 (2): 99–122.

Butler, Judith. 2003. "No, It's Not Anti-Semitic." *London Review of Books* 25 (16) (August 21): 19–21.

Butler, Judith. 2012. "Judith Butler Responds to Attack." *Mondoweiss*, August 27. http://mondoweiss.net/2012/08/judith-butler-responds-to-attack-i-affirm-a-judaism-that-is-not-associated-with-state-violence/.

Endelman, Todd. 1991. "Jewish Self-Hatred in Britain and Germany." In *Two Nations: British and German Jews in Comparative Perspective*, edited by Michael Brenner, Rainer Liedtke, and David Rechter, 331–36. Tubinden: J.C.B. Mohr.

Endelman, Todd. 2001. "In Defense of Jewish Social History." *Jewish Social Studies* 7 (3): 52–57.

Endelman, Todd. 2015. *Leaving the Jewish Fold*. Princeton: Princeton University Press.

Finlay, W. M. L. 2005. "Pathologizing Dissent: Identity Politics, Zionism and the Self-Hating Jew." *British Journal of Social Psychology* 44 (2): 201–22.

Finlay, W. M. L. 2007. "The Propaganda of Extreme Hostility: Denunciation and the Regulation of the Group." *British Journal of Social Psychology* 46 (2): 323–41.

Finlay, W. M. L. 2014. "Denunciation and the Construction of Norms in Group Conflict: Examples from an Al-Qaeda-Supporting Group." *British Journal of Social Psychology* 53 (4): 691–710.

Freud, Sigmund. 1964. "If Moses Were an Egyptian." In *Moses and Monotheism: An Outline of Psycho-Analysis and Other Works*. London: The Hogarth Press and the Institute of Psychoanalysis.

Friedman, Marilyn. 2014. "Jewish Self-Hatred, Moral Criticism, and Autonomy." In *Personal Autonomy and Social Oppression: Philosophical Perspectives*, edited by Marina Oshana. New York: Routledge.

Friedman, Marilyn. 2015. "Authenticity and Jewish Self-Hatred." In *Authenticity, Autonomy and Multiculturalism*, edited by Geoffrey Brahm Levey, 184–202. New York: Routledge.

Gager, John. 1983. *The Origins of Anti-Semitism: Attitudes Toward Judaism in Pagan and Christian Antiquity*. New York: Oxford University Press.

Gay, Peter. 1978. "Hermann Levi: A Study in Service and Self-Hatred." In *Freud, Jews, and Other Germans: Masters and Victims in Modernist Culture*. New York: Oxford University Press.

Gelber, Mark. 1985. "What is Literary Antisemitism?" *Jewish Social Studies* 47 (1): 1–20.
Gilman, Sander. 1986. *Jewish Self-Hatred: Anti-Semitism and the Hidden Language of the Jews*. Baltimore: Johns Hopkins University Press.
Glenn, Susan. 2006. "The Vogue of Jewish Self-Hatred in Post-World War II America." *Jewish Social Studies: History, Culture, and Society* 12 (3): 95–136.
Greenberg, Clement. 1950. "Self-Hatred and Jewish Chauvinism: Some Reflections on 'Positive Jewishness.'" *Commentary* 10 (January): 426–33.
Halbertal, Moshe, and Avishai Margalit. 1998. "Idolatry and Betrayal." In *Idolatry*, 9–36. Cambridge, MA: Harvard University Press.
Horowitz, Elliott. 2006. *Reckless Rites: Purim and the Legacy of Jewish Violence*. Princeton: Princeton University Press.
Janik, A. 1987. "The Jewish Self-Hatred Hypothesis: A Critique." In *Jews, Anti-Semitism, and Culture in Vienna*, edited by Ivar Oxaal, Michael Pollack, and Gerhard Botz. New York: Routledge.
Landes, Richard. 2015. "Proud to be Ashamed to be a Jew: On Jewish Self-Criticism and Its Pathologies." *ISGAP Working Paper Series*, no. 9, April. New York: Institute for the Study of Global Antisemitism and Policy. https://isgap.org/wp-content/uploads/2015/05/Landes_Proud_to_be_Ashamed_Working_Paper.pdf.
Langmuir, Gavin. 1990a. "Anti-Judaism as the Necessary Preparation for Antisemitism." In *Toward a Definition of Antisemitism*, 57–62. Berkeley: University of California Press.
Langmuir, Gavin. 1990b. "Toward a Definition of Antisemitism." In *Toward a Definition of Antisemitism*, 311–52. Berkeley: University of California Press.
Lerman, Antony. 2008. "Jewish Self-Hatred: Myth or Reality?" *Jewish Quarterly* 55 (2): 46–51.
Lessing, Theodor. 1930. *Der jüdische Selbsthaß*. Berlin: Jüdischer Verlag.
Lewin, Kurt. 1948. "Self-Hatred among Jews." In *Resolving Social Conflicts: Selected Papers on Group Dynamics*, 186–200. New York: Harper.
Mendes, Philip. 2008. "The Strange Phenomenon of Jewish Anti-Zionism: Self-hating Jews or Protectors of Universalistic Principles?" *Australian Journal of Jewish Studies* 23: 96–132.
Mendes-Flohr, Paul. 1978. "The Throes of Assimilation: Self-Hatred and the Jewish Revolutionary." *European Judaism: A Journal for the New Europe* 12 (1): 34–39.
Meyer, Michael A. 1989. "Antisemitism and Jewish Identity." *Commentary* 88 (5) (November): 35–40.
Reitter, Paul. 2009. "The Jewish Self-Hatred Octopus." *The German Quarterly* 82 (3): 356–72.
Reitter, Paul. 2012. *On the Origins of Jewish Self-Hatred*. Princeton: Princeton University Press.
Rose, Jacqueline. 2007. "The Myth of Self-Hatred." *The Guardian*, February 7. https://www.theguardian.com/commentisfree/2007/feb/08/holdjewishvoices6.
Sartre, Jean-Paul. 1948. *Anti-Semite and Jew: An Exploration of the Etiology of Hate*. New York: Schocken Books.

CHAPTER 13

Nationalism

Brian Porter-Szűcs

Antisemitism and nationalism have frequently marched together, but is this connection necessary or contingent? Did antisemitism penetrate modern nationalism because of specific circumstances and conditions, or was there something fundamental to the nature of the former that helped constitute the latter (or vice versa)? We cannot entirely disentangle the threads of cause and effect between these two ideological strands because they were developed and propagated by many of the same people. But the two are not entirely conjoined: as paradoxical as it sounds, there have been both cosmopolitan antisemites and multicultural nationalists. There are not many of either nowadays, to be sure, but any such exceptions help us see that nationalism does not lead to antisemitism in any simple or direct way.

The main reason it is impossible to map out a clear relationship between these phenomena is that neither of them has a fixed meaning. In fact, neither antisemitism nor nationalism is a *thing* with an independent existence or independent causal vectors; rather, each is a cluster of terms and concepts that people have assembled in a variety of ways to help them make sense of the modern world. Insofar as both Gandhi and Hitler have been labeled "nationalists," any definition of the term would have to be so capacious and vague as to have limited utility. Like most terms in our political and social vocabulary, "nationalism" can only have a historically dynamic *description*, not a static *definition*. Perhaps we could say that nationalism is a political ideology that prioritizes the nation, but this would only push the question one level deeper. Many words change meaning over time, but unlike terms

B. Porter-Szűcs (✉)
Department of History, University of Michigan, Ann Arbor, MI, USA
e-mail: baporter@umich.edu

that have pre-linguistic referents (tree, sky, water, run, eat, etc.), words like "nation" (or class, state, country, etc.) constitute the very phenomena that they purport to describe. Nations are called into existence by nationalists, who mobilize disparate and ill-defined sentiments and social bonds for varied political purposes.

The etymological history of the word "nation" extends back to the ancient Mediterranean, and the concept as we know it today has tributaries that spread to every corner of the globe, and even deeper into the past. But the enmeshment of nationalism and antisemitism happened in a specific time and place: Europe from the late eighteenth century to the present. Intellectual historians searching for the origins of nationalism typically point to European Enlightenment writers like Johann Gottfried Herder, who argued that humanity was divided into distinct national communities, delineated by culture, geography, language, and history. These nations, in Herder's view, possessed singular interests, needs, and goals. As he put it: "Time, place, and national character alone…govern all the events that happen among mankind" (1803, p. 107). Political historians, meanwhile, focus on a cluster of proximate political events (the French and American Revolutions, the Partitions of Poland, the Napoleonic Wars), which involved claims that sovereignty belonged in the hands of "the people." Already in the early nineteenth century it was quite common in Europe and North America to hear calls for the transformation of "artificial" dynastic polities into unified nation-states. At the time, nationalist texts were invariably sprinkled with references to "liberty," "freedom," "democracy," and "revolution." Whether calling for unification (like the German or Italian movements) or liberation (like the Polish or Irish movements), these early nationalists were on the left edge of the political spectrum.

That position was inverted by the end of the nineteenth century. As mass mobilization transformed political life, nationalists had to contend with the actual linguistic and cultural practices and preferences of all the people who had previously been idealized as "the people." Earlier it had been possible to extrapolate from a blend of high culture and homogenized, sanitized ethnography, so that (for example) "Germanness" was understood to be a combination of Goethe, Bach, and Beethoven on the one hand, and the Brothers Grimm on the other. By the late nineteenth century this fabric was harder to weave, because "the people" (*Volk, lud, populo*, etc.) were now protesting in the streets and making concrete demands that were unsettling to an older generation of intelligentsia nationalists. Social and economic grievances came to the forefront, as did demagogues peddling various forms of collective hatred.

Meanwhile, unprecedented accomplishments in the natural sciences made it rhetorically powerful to use the terminology of biology or physics when talking about society and history. In particular, slogans like "the struggle for survival" or "the survival of the fittest" became common parlance, transforming the vague utopian socialism of the early nineteenth century into Karl Marx's focus on class struggle, and corroding the optimistic liberalism of the early nationalists into Herbert Spencer's dystopian claim that progress comes through the destruction of the weak and inferior. Spencer was particularly explicit in grounding the social and political spheres in the physical sciences. "We commonly enough compare a nation to a living organism," he wrote, "but we usually employ these expressions as metaphors, little suspecting how close is the analogy, and how far it will bear carrying out. So completely, however, is a society organized upon the same system as an individual being, that we may almost say there is something more than analogy between them" (1851, p. 448). And like organisms, Spencer argued, human collectives evolve through a "struggle for survival."

> The forces which are working out the great scheme of perfect happiness, taking no account of incidental suffering, exterminate such sections of mankind as stand in their way, with the same sternness that they exterminate beasts of prey and herds of useless ruminants…What are the pre-requisites to a conquering race? Numerical strength, or an improved system of warfare, both of which are indications of advancement….Evidently, therefore, from the very beginning, the conquest of one people over another has been, in the main, the conquest of the social man over the anti-social man; or, strictly speaking, of the more adapted over the less adapted. (1851, p. 416)

Earlier talk about a "brotherhood of nations" that would unite in order to overthrow tyranny and injustice had morphed into a zero-sum game in which each nation was locked in an unrelenting conflict with its neighbors.

In this new atmosphere, which was dominant almost everywhere in Europe by 1900, nationalists grew increasingly preoccupied with the means needed to survive and conquer. If the nation was constantly in a state of actual or implied war, it was argued, then ideological and cultural disunity were unaffordable luxuries at best, and signs of subversive machinations at worst. Ethnographers moved away from the fuzzy idealization of the first half of the nineteenth century, and instead tried to specify clear taxonomies separating one national community from another. Historians spun tales about national victories and defeats in which the deciding factors were social unity, determination, and discipline. Most ominously, political activists embraced the paired ideals that (1) every state should be nationally homogeneous, and (2) no one could be "free" until they were inside the boundaries of "their" state. Given the ethno-linguistic patchwork throughout much of Europe, achieving those ideals was impossible. Pursuing the impossible led, by definition, to failure, which in turn stoked frustration and anger, which fed resentments and hatreds, which strengthened the original Sisyphean goals.

It would be an exaggeration to say that the protracted catastrophe of 1914–1945 was simply the pit at the bottom of a nationalist slippery slope. Nationalism *as such* did not cause those wars: instead, Europe plunged into an orgy of suicidal violence because of the specific combination of nationalism, mass politics, and "struggle-for-survival" ideologies. More than any of the proximate diplomatic disputes of 1914, the war broke out because nearly every politician, diplomat, and military commander of the time believed that war between nations was inevitable—not because of any specific disputes or unreconciled interests, but because conquest and expansion was just what nations did. The options on the table were perceived to be not peace vs. war, but conquest vs. extermination. The First World War served as an antidote to this way of thinking for many Europeans, though clearly not enough to prevent the Second World War.

After 1945, nationalism in Europe was pushed to the background for several decades (but never buried, despite the optimistic claims of the early proponents of European unification). Meanwhile, nationalism took on a new, radically reconfigured form throughout the colonial world. The independence movements throughout Asia, Africa, and Latin America in the second half of the twentieth century drew upon nationalist rhetoric that harkened back to the early nineteenth-century revolutionaries of Europe, updated with socialist infusions. Gandhi, for example, deployed nationalist terminology even while decisively repudiating the struggle-for-survival mentality of the early twentieth-century European right. The malleability of the term "nation" was more evident than ever.

* * *

It was during the post-WWII era, when the European empires were being torn apart by nationalist independence movements, that the academic study of nationalism blossomed. A handful of early twentieth-century historians and social scientists had tackled the subject, but the field really took off in the 1960s. The first wave of scholars focused on categorizing and defining the different forms of nationalism, most (in)famously with Hans Kohn's dichotomy between "Western" (liberal, civic) and "Eastern" (ethnic, authoritarian, xenophobic, racist) versions of the phenomenon (1956). Later scholars, like John Breuilly and Miroslav Hroch, saw stages of development progressing over time in a predictable manner (Breuilly 1982; Hroch 1985). Taxonomies like these, whether mapped onto space or narrated over time, brought clarity to a messy field of study, but (for precisely this reason) they have not held up well against further study. The civic/ethnic dichotomy sat atop an explicit orientalism, with Western reason, democracy, and inclusivity set against Eastern irrationality, tribalism, and backwardness. This ignored the racial foundations of the United States, as well as de facto exclusions that were always just below the surface of *de jure* inclusivity in France. Conversely, it erased the long tradition of civic inclusion in the Polish–Lithuanian Republic, and the imperial pluralism of the Habsburg and Ottoman Empires, Persia, India, China, and more. Meanwhile, the chronological typology offered by scholars like Hroch proved to have limited utility outside East-Central Europe. Like most predictive models, that scheme had to confront the non-linear nature of history itself.

A breakthrough in the study of nationalism came in 1983, with the publication of the most frequently cited book ever written about this topic: Benedict Anderson's *Imagined Communities*. As the title suggests, Anderson's central argument was that identity was grounded not in an actual pre-existing collectivity, but in one that was ideologically constructed as part of the process of modernization. Anderson, along with a few other seminal authors from that period (particularly Eric Hobsbawm and Ernest Gellner) demonstrated that national identity, as we use that concept today, is of relatively recent vintage. In Anderson's rendition, nationalism replaced both older ideologies of identity (religious or imperial) and the local micro-communities of people who actually knew and interacted with each other. Nationalism did not emerge organically from sociologically, ethnographically, or historically established communities. Quite the contrary: nationalism was the ideological and cultural force that *created* those forms of identity. Scholars have continued to argue about the precise dating of nationalism's emergence, and some have stressed that the rhetorical building blocks of the nationalist vocabulary originated long before the rise of large-scale nationalist movements. But the primary insight of *Imagined Communities*—that nationalists make nations, not the other way around—is accepted by the overwhelming majority of scholars nowadays.

The so-called "linguistic turn" in historical scholarship allowed us to "deconstruct" nationalism down to its core. More and more, scholars were tracing the use of the word "nation" itself in particular times and places, showing how it was used as a tool of political mobilization, as a means to draw lines of inclusion and exclusion around communities, and as the core concept in a "discourse" of power (e.g., Bhabha 1990; Chatterjee 1993; Eley and Suny 1996; Porter 2000). Scholars were increasingly inclined to see all identities as fluid, plural, and contested, as unstable objects of political struggle rather than static states of being. The very field of nationalism studies began to grow fuzzy at the edges, insofar as attention turned toward the many people who stood aside from, or even directly challenged, the insistence that everyone in the modern world was supposed to have one and only one national identity (e.g., Brubaker 2008; Judson 2007; King 2005; Zahra 2008).

* * *

Nationalists have often been antisemitic, particularly in late nineteenth- and early twentieth-century Europe. There was an undeniable structural reason for this: nationalists of the past century or so have focused above all on ethno-cultural homogeneity, and the persistent existence of the Jewish diaspora mitigated against the attainment of that sort of unity. But there has to be more to it than this, because antisemitism has inspired a unique ferocity in the nationalist imagination. Moreover, nationalist antisemitism had (at best) only a rough correspondence to the demographics of the Jewish population. In fact, insofar as we can track any correlation at all, it seems to be inverse:

the smaller and more assimilated the Jewish community, the more likely we are to find antisemitic nationalism. To understand how this could be so, we have to begin with a crucial distinction between two primary ways of expressing hostility toward Jews within a nationalist framework, one based on demands of assimilation and the other based on fears of infiltration.

The first framework was most prominent during the eighteenth and early nineteenth centuries, and has been affiliated with more liberal variants of nationalism. It begins with a set of convictions that would strike most people today as lofty and admirable: equality before the law and freedom of thought, speech, and assembly. Moreover, the argument posits the continued existence of prejudice as a significant problem that must be addressed. The *way* it was addressed, however, had unintended consequences. One of the early formulations of this argument comes from December 21, 1789, when a delegate to the French National Assembly, Count Stanislas–Marie–Adélaide de Clermont–Tonnerre, offered a framework for thinking about religious minorities in a renewed, revolutionary French state. He posited a stark dichotomy: either the new constitution must recognize a national religion and then use the law to regulate it (and other religions), or it must grant full religious liberty to everyone, and treat everyone as equal before the law. He repudiated the idea that Jews were unsuited to be equal citizens because of alleged traits or characteristics; instead, he insisted that "the worst of these reproaches is unjust; the others are only specious." Clermont-Tonnere accepted that Jewish customs separated them from their neighbors, but he considered this to be a very minor issue that would, in any case, fade away as everyone in France united around their common citizenship. With this point, he broached an issue that every liberal nationalist would eventually have to grapple with:

> But, they say to me, the Jews have their own judges and laws. I respond that is your fault and you should not allow it. We must refuse everything to the Jews as a nation and accord everything to Jews as individuals. We must withdraw recognition from their judges; they should only have our judges. We must refuse legal protection to the maintenance of the so-called laws of their Judaic organization; they should not be allowed to form in the state either a political body or an order. They must be citizens individually. But, some will say to me, they do not want to be citizens. Well then! If they do not want to be citizens, they should say so, and then, we should banish them. It is repugnant to have in the state an association of non-citizens, and a nation within the nation.... In short, Sirs, the presumed status of every man resident in a country is to be a citizen. (reprinted in Hunt 1996, pp. 86–88)

Most Enlightenment thinkers built their worldviews on the premise that humanity was linked by natural laws and a universal rationality. This made it possible to advocate equality before the law, and to assume that genuine liberty would lead to good things. After all, how could nature and reason produce evil or injustice? There was always a certain awkwardness in linking this universalistic foundation to the concept of national distinctions, but that could be finessed if cultural differences were bracketed as inconsequential to citizenship. In other words, for civic liberty and national culture to align, the latter could not interfere with the homogenization of the former. The problems emerged—and would continue to emerge from then until now—when citizenship came to imply assimilation to a particular cultural norm. Perhaps in theory this need not have been an issue, but in practice it always was. It was not merely that many Jews wanted to sustain their cultural distinctions, but that they wanted those distinctions to *matter*. For people like Clermont-Tonnere, however, Judaism had to be reduced to a set of relatively inconsequential private rituals and beliefs, which in turn would always give way when they conflicted with any aspect of "universal" French civic law. Ever since then, we find repeated examples of liberals who begin their careers very sympathetic to the Jews (and other minorities), only to slide toward hostility when confronted with a persistence of *meaningful* diversity and a resistance to assimilation. Old religious complaints about Jewish "stubbornness" (the refusal to accept Christianity) were translated into liberal nationalist complaints about the Jewish refusal to re-categorize their religious identity as a mere folk practice with no consequences for public life (see Weir 2014).

A fundamental divide separated this sort of national antisemitism from more virulent forms that emerged toward the end of the nineteenth century. Liberal nationalists were all-purpose homogenizers: they complained as much (perhaps more) about the refusal of Catholics to acknowledge that religious faith in the world of civic nation-states could only exist within a carefully patrolled private sphere. And they (usually) meant it when they said that assimilated Jews should be treated as equal citizens. In other words, whatever they thought about Judaism (understood as both a religion and a distinctive way of life), they didn't really have a problem with Jews as such. When some of the assimilated, Polish-speaking Jews of Warsaw expressed their allegiance to the struggle for national independence from Russia, the response from liberal Polish nationalists was enthusiastic. The leaders of the independence movement proclaimed that "a visible grace of Providence for Poland, which is only now being redeemed from the sins of captivity, is the union, sealed by the joint martyrdom of Poland's Christian and Israelite sons: these arks of a funeral covenant were borne on the shoulders of both Levites and Christians to the fraternal cemetery and thus to a joint resurrection. Since this day there have no longer been two population groups on the common soil of oppression, but one nation" (cited in Eisenbach 1991, p. 437). We must not overlook that these affirmations of kinship were highly conditional, and could turn quickly toward hostility at any sign of resistance by Jews who didn't really want to become "one nation." But nonetheless, liberal nationalist antisemitism always offered a carrot as well as a stick.

The second framework for nationalist antisemitism, however, precluded that sort of harmonious redemption. As mentioned above, the scientism of the late nineteenth century penetrated the rhetoric of nationalism, transforming the project of civic unity and liberal emancipation into a movement for social discipline and ethnic homogeneity, justified by an inevitable and unending "struggle for survival." Most immediately, this intensified the pressure for assimilation in the face of the new nationalist equation between diversity and weakness. But that wasn't the main reason for the altered shape of nationalist antisemitism. Pressure for cultural assimilation and unity was a general force that struck every minority population in Europe. In Hungary, for example, Slovaks, Romanians, and Croats felt this much more acutely than the Jews, many of whom lived in Budapest and were already nearly indistinguishable from their Christian neighbors. But this turned out to be precisely the issue for late nineteenth- and early twentieth-century nationalists: instead of casting assimilation within the framework of civic inclusion, they reframed it as a matter of pollution and infiltration. The Jews had once been depicted as the enemies of a universal, liberal worldview; in this new context, they became the *representation* of cosmopolitanism and the greatest danger to national distinction and purity.

The new nationalist antisemitism began in Western Europe, particularly France and Germany—precisely where the Jewish community was the most fully incorporated into "mainstream" society. In fact, it's unclear whether the phrase "Jewish community" is even appropriate in that context, because so many West European Jews thought of themselves first as French, German, English, Italian, etc., with their Judaism turned into an adjective to modify their national noun. Yet it was in France that antisemitism first became a major political issue (with the so-called "Dreyfus affair" in the 1890s), and it was in Germany that the very word "antisemitism" was invented. The ideology represented by that neologism was not aimed at assimilation, but at purification. Whereas earlier Jews had been attacked for the refusal to assimilate, by the end of the nineteenth century they were attacked even if they wanted to do so, on the grounds that their very presence was a form of corruption.

It was hard for nationalists at the end of the nineteenth century to make sense of the Jews. In their imagined world of unending conflict between nations, the basic vehicle for struggle was the nation-state, and the measures of victory were (1) the unification of all co-nationals into one state; (2) the elimination, subordination, or cultural absorption of all "minorities;" and (3) the expansion of the nation-state to new lands. For example, after Germany took Alsace-Lorraine from France in 1870, Heinrich von Treitschke rejected the idea that the national self-identity of the local population should be considered. "These territories are ours by the right of the sword," he wrote "and we shall dispose of them by virtue of a higher right, the right of the German nation, which will not permit its lost children to remain strangers to the German Empire...Against their will we shall restore them to their true selves" (1870, p. 20). One upshot of this worldview was that people like Treitschke could entirely understand why France, in turn, would want to resist German expansion. Paradoxically, nationalists in the late nineteenth century often recognized a moral equivalence between nations (within Europe, at least), arguing that efforts to depict the enemy as uniquely evil (or oneself as uniquely good) distracted people from the need for "rational" and "scientific" policies. What did *not* make sense within this worldview was the existence of a distinct ethnic community that didn't even possess its own state, much less an explicit or even evident plan for national expansion. The Jews, for a late nineteenth-century nationalist, were a conundrum.

The only possible answer was that the Jews had some other—secret—plan to maintain their existence and domination. Thus emerged the conspiratorial mindset of the twentieth-century nationalist antisemite. Those trying to understand nationalist conspiracy theories about the Jews often focus on the specific content of the legends, but that approach doesn't get us very far. On the one hand, there is a history going back (at least) to the medieval period of Christians accusing Jews of plots and machinations, but nearly every detail varies from context to context. On the other hand, most of the key components of the "international Jewish conspiracy" myths were lifted from earlier paranoid musings about another group altogether: the Freemasons. The foundational text was a five-volume work from 1797 by Abbé Augustin Barruel entitled *Mémoires pour servir à l'Histoire du Jacobinisme*, which set forth an understanding of modern history that would become enormously popular on the right. Barruel explained the French Revolution as the culmination of a massive plot by the Illuminati and the Freemasons, aimed ultimately at the enslavement of all humanity under the rule of a secret cabal. Historians have given this strain of conservative thought little attention because it is so patently absurd, but it was in fact hugely influential. The existence of such a plot was conventional wisdom, for example, among nineteenth-century Catholic thinkers. The Church repeatedly banned members from joining the Masons, and as late as 1884 Pope Leo XIII issued the encyclical *Humanum genus*, in which he painted a horrifying image of an incarnate enemy:

> The partisans of evil seem to be combining together, and to be struggling with united vehemence, led on or assisted by that strongly organized and widespread association called the Freemasons. No longer making any secret of their purposes, they are now boldly rising up against God Himself. They are planning the destruction of the holy Church publicly and openly, and this with the set purpose of utterly despoiling the nations of Christendom, if it were possible, of the blessings obtained for us through Jesus Christ our Savior.

Leo wrote that the Masons planned to seize absolute power by undermining all morality, "since generally no one is accustomed to obey crafty and clever men so submissively as those whose soul is weakened and broken down by the domination of the passions." He itemized the many evils that could be attributed to this plot: the legalization of divorce, the spread of secular education, the "satiation of the multitude with a boundless license of vice," the promotion of the idea "that all men have the same rights, and are in every respect of equal and like condition; that each one is naturally free...that, when the popular will changes, rulers may lawfully be deposed" (1884, paragraphs 2, 20, 22).

This entire line of thought developed independently (at first) from any antisemitic ideologies. Barruel's book only mentioned in passing that a few minor characters in his story were Jewish, and the papal texts condemning the Masons did not mention the Jews at all. Moreover, the Masonic conspiracy myth was linked to the conservative right, and for much of the nineteenth century, nationalism was considered revolutionary and liberal. But toward the end of the century, the conceptual dilemma of the new, right-wing, struggle-for-survival nationalism dovetailed with this old historical legend. The role of the Masons was usually retained, though they were re-characterized as the vehicle through which the Jews carried out their nefarious plans. This allowed the insertion of the Jews into an understanding of modern history that fit within the broader imagery of nations locked in a never-ending battle for existence and domination. Indeed, it positioned the Jews as a distinctly dangerous foe, because they did not fight openly as other nations did. The notorious *Protocols of the Elders of Zion* imagined the leaders of the Jews defending their plans of conquest in words that could have come directly from nationalists like Treitschke:

> The political has nothing in common with the moral. The ruler who is governed by the moral is not a skilled politician, and is therefore unstable on his throne. He who wishes to rule must have resource both to cunning and to make-believe. Great national qualities, like frankness and honesty, are vices in politics, for they bring down rulers from their thrones more effectively and more certainly than the most powerful enemy. Such qualities must be the attributes of the kingdoms of the goyim, but we must in no wise be guided by them. Our right lies in force. The word "right" is an abstract thought and proved by nothing. The word means no more than: Give me what I want in order that thereby I may have a proof that I am stronger than you. (1923, p. 145)

The myth of the international Jewish conspiracy, then, can be seen as a means of reconciling the existence of the Jews with the broader framework of nationalism, as it existed in Europe from the late nineteenth to the mid-twentieth century. It ascribed to the Jews a form of national existence, even as debates continued among nationalists about whether the Jews could in fact be counted as a true nation. One way or the other, by WWI it was widely assumed by nationalist politicians across the continent that the Jews were carrying out their own struggle for survival and conquest, through the mechanism of infiltration and subversion. Significantly, this sort of nationalist antisemitism became most popular where there were fewer actual Jews, or where Jews tended to be more assimilated. In the eastern parts of the continent, where Yiddish-speaking Jews constituted a large percentage of the population, the ideology did indeed penetrate, but only later and after a great deal of political agitation and propaganda. A contributor to a Polish nationalist, antisemitic magazine repeated a familiar complaint in 1908.

> As far as the villages in our region are concerned, we are all backward, without education, and if someone the least bit reasonable could be found, it would mean as much as a little piece of sugar thrown into a pot of bitter or sour water. In almost every village one can find Jewish tenants; the villagers say that it would be impossible to get along without them, because it is more convenient to go for various little errands to the Jew than to town; here you can even send a child, but it is necessary to go to town yourself, and moreover it is also best to sell something from home to the Jew. No one can persuade the villagers that it is a great evil that the Jew can be found in the countryside. (Tyzik 1908)

Hostility toward Jews certainly existed in rural Eastern Europe, but modern *nationalist* antisemitism, with its grounding in conspiracy theories and a struggle-for-survival worldview, arrived only in the first half of the twentieth century, as the product of a concerted campaign of political agitation. This returns us to the question with which I began this essay: were nationalism and antisemitism necessarily connected, or did they merely overlap because of a concatenation of events in a specific context? It seems clear that nationalism *as such* was not preconfigured as antisemitic, mostly because nationalism *as such* is a rhetorical framework for talking about politics, not a single coherent ideology with a linear history. Moreover, nationalism did not become antisemitic simply because of the social or demographic context from which it emerged. To be more precise, the liberal assimilationist approach to the Jews by the early nationalists was indeed a response to observed social conditions, but the more familiar (and more virulent) versions of racialized nationalist antisemitism came to fruition in the absence of significant communities of easily identifiable Jews. After all, it was hard to imagine an international Jewish conspiracy of infiltration and corruption, if one saw poor, powerless, Yiddish-speaking Hasidim on a daily basis. Hard, but sadly, not impossible.

References

Bhabha, Homi, ed. 1990. *Nation and Narration*. New York: Routledge.
Breuilly, John. 1982. *Nationalism and the State*. New York: St. Martin's Press.
Brubaker, Rogers. 2008. *Nationalist Politics and Everyday Ethnicity in a Transylvanian Town*. Princeton: Princeton University Press.
Chatterjee, Partha. 1993. *The Nation and Its Fragments: Colonial and Postcolonial Histories*. Princeton: Princeton University Press.
Eisenbach, Artur. 1991. *The Emancipation of the Jews in Poland, 1780–1870*. Edited by Antony Polonsky. Translated by Janina Dorosz. Oxford: Blackwell.
Eley, Geoff, and Ronald Suny, eds. 1996. *Becoming National: A Reader*. New York: Oxford University Press.

Herder, Johann Gottfried. 1803. *Outlines of a Philosophy of the History of Man*. Vol. 2. Translated by T. Churchill. London: J. Johnson.

Hroch, Miroslav. 1985. *Social Preconditions of National Revival in Europe: A Comparative Analysis of the Social Composition of Patriotic Groups Among the Smaller European Nations*. Translated by Ben Fowkes. Cambridge: Cambridge University Press.

Hunt, Lynn, ed. and trans. 1996. *The French Revolution and Human Rights: A Brief Documentary History*. Boston: Bedford/St. Martin's.

Judson, Pieter. 2007. *Guardians of the Nation: Activists on the Language Frontiers of Imperial Austria*. Cambridge, MA: Harvard University Press.

King, Jeremy. 2005. *Budweisers into Czechs and Germans*. Princeton: Princeton University Press.

Kohn, Hans. 1956. *The Idea of Nationalism: A Study in Its Origins and Background*. New York: The Macmillan Company.

Leo XIII, Pope. 1884. *Humanum genus*. http://www.vatican.va/content/leo-xiii/en/encyclicals/documents/hf_l-xiii_enc_18840420_humanum-genus.html.

Porter, Brian. 2000. *When Nationalism Began to Hate: Imagining Modern Politics in 19th Century Poland*. New York: Oxford University Press.

Protocols of the Elders of Zion. 1923. Translated by Victor Marsden. London: The Britons Publishing Society.

Spencer, Herbert. 1851. *Social Statics, or The Conditions Essential to Human Happiness Specified and the First of Them Developed*. London: John Chapman.

Tyzik, T. 1908. "Listów do 'Posiewu.'" *Posiew* 3/4 (January 23): 61.

von Treitschke, Heinrich. 1870. *What We Demand from France*. London: Macmillan.

Weir, Tood H. 2014. "The Specter of 'Godless Jewry': Secularism and the 'Jewish Question' in Late 19th Century Germany." *Central European History* 46: 815–49.

Zahra, Tara. 2008. *Kidnapped Souls: National Indifference and the Battle for Children in the Bohemian Lands, 1900–1948*. Ithaca: Cornell University Press.

CHAPTER 14

Nazism

Doris L. Bergen

The only Nazi state that ever existed has been gone for more than seventy years. Still Nazism persists, as a symbol and synonym for antisemitism, and not just any antisemitism but a strand of antisemitism that is inseparable from genocidal violence against Jews. The swastika scrawled across a wall or scratched onto a door is universally understood as an attack on Jews and Judaism. At the same time, the Nazi symbol conveys an open-ended threat against all who are cast as enemies by a fantasized, white, Christian order endlessly battling to defend its purity. Based on a polymorphous, multifaceted definition of "the Jew" as simultaneously a racial, religious, political, sexualized, ideological, and symbolic entity, Nazi antisemitism blurs readily into other assaults. Antisemitism as the destructive core of Nazism is what remains of the Nazi system, yet the reduction of Nazism to antisemitism is not a narrowing of either concept but rather a broadening and intensification of both.

"Nazism" is a key concept in the study of antisemitism because it marks the merging of possibility and power. The Nazi state's implementation and systematization of anti-Jewish ideas transformed what antisemitism was and could be. With this claim I take a different tack from the linear equation often assumed (extreme antisemitism => Nazism => Holocaust) to consider instead how antisemitism functioned within the Nazi system of power and was changed by it. Here antisemitism must be understood not only as a set of convictions and rituals but as policies and practices that targeted Judaism and Jews, individually and collectively. Under Hitler's leadership, anti-Jewish

D. L. Bergen (✉)
Department of History, University of Toronto, Toronto, ON, Canada
e-mail: doris.bergen@utoronto.ca

attitudes became concrete actions against Jews, sanctioned and mandated by the state and enforced by its bureaucrats, courts, and police. This transformation—from antisemitism as an idea to antisemitism as policy and practice—occurred as a process that is best explained by describing its concrete impacts.

This essay accordingly explores the linkages between antisemitism and Nazism, two concepts that are also processes. By "processes" I mean that antisemitism and Nazism are not static labels but dynamic developments that emerged out of particular contexts and have persisted, changed, and changed the world around them. Viewed historically, antisemitism and Nazism have influenced and shaped one another. Long and shorter lines of continuity connect them to shared roots in Christian triumphalism, European racisms (anti-Black and anti-Asian), colonialism, and anti-Communism. But Nazism was not only a culmination of earlier tendencies; it revolutionized what was possible and transformed familiar anti-Jewish fantasies into pragmatic strategies of exclusion and annihilation (Confino 2014). State power and the implementation of antisemitic notions produced a new type of antisemitism. It drew and draws its force from individual and group hatred of Jews but even more from impersonal structures, systemic violence, and the irreversible knowledge that "unimaginable" destruction is not only possible, it is a historical reality.

During World War II, led by Hitler and the National Socialist (Nazi) state, Germans and their accomplices around Europe murdered six million Jews.[1] They destroyed Jewish communities that dated back to ancient Rome and almost completely annihilated the Jewish presence, from the Rhine to the Volga, from Estonia to the island of Rhodes. The Nazis had other victims—people deemed disabled (who were the first targets of mass murder), homosexuals, Polish elites, Roma, Black French soldiers, Soviet prisoners of war—but they unleashed their fullest fury against Jews, whom they hunted across every border, into every hiding place, in a drive for annihilation.

Antisemitism was essential to Nazism but it was not the only factor in Nazi destruction. Some historians have argued that Nazism was fundamentally about power and that antisemitism, indeed ideology in general, was of minor importance. Others emphasize greed, careerism, and opportunism as motives or subsume antisemitism into broader forms of racism and imperial conquest. The ubiquity of antisemitism in the Nazi system, combined with its explosive, annihilatory force, seems to defy analysis, and scholars who do address it sometimes present it as a given. Raul Hilberg's foundational work, *The Destruction of the European Jews*, opens with reflections on the continuities of anti-Jewish stereotypes from the medieval period to World War II but returns to that theme only rarely in the hundreds of pages that follow. Daniel Goldhagen offered "eliminationist antisemitism" as a corrective, and

---

[1] Parts of this chapter are revised from Bergen (2010).

although he was criticized as simplistic, his work sparked renewed attention to Nazi antisemitism. Susannah Heschel's analysis of *The Aryan Jesus* situates Christianity in the center of the discussion.

The combination of familiar prejudices with the unprecedented scope and ruthlessness of the Nazi assault on Jews was disorienting even for contemporaries. Victor Klemperer, a professor of French literature in Dresden, is a case in point. Klemperer, the son of a rabbi, converted to Protestant Christianity, married a gentile, served in the German army in World War I, and identified fully with German culture. Under Nazi law, however, he counted as a Jew. In his detailed and insightful diary, one of the issues that preoccupied him was what he referred to as the *vox populi*. What did "ordinary Germans"—that is, the non-Jewish Germans around him—think of Jews? What did they make of Nazi anti-Jewish measures? Between 1933 and 1945, Klemperer went back and forth on these questions, often within the same diary entry. Yet he understood one thing from the outset: the Nazi rise to power spelled disaster for all people defined as Jews in Germany, regardless of how they identified or perceived themselves.

We can identify three stages of Nazism, each anchored in a chronological period yet building on and subsuming earlier developments, and each playing a particular role in the persecution and murder of Jews. These stages are discussed in sequence below. The first part deals with antisemitism as ideology, that is, antisemitism as a motivating force and an input into processes of persecution. Here the focus is on the period before Adolf Hitler became Chancellor of Germany in 1933.

The second stage can be called "antisemitism in power." Once Hitler came to power, antisemitism was shaped through processes of institutionalization, legalization, implementation, and destruction that occurred from 1933 to 1945. In this period, antisemitism spread rapidly, through propaganda and education but also through official measures and actions that implicated ever more individuals and groups in attacks on Jews and gave them vested interests in upholding a system that sought to eliminate Jews, whether or not the non-Jews involved shared that goal.

The third segment, antisemitism as a product of the Holocaust, follows from the second. Violence against Jews produced and promoted particular forms of hatred, resentment, and destruction (including erasure and denial) that began during the Holocaust and continued to exist and mutate after it ended with the defeat and collapse of Nazi Germany in 1945. Nazism before and during the war comprised more than antisemitism, but what remained of Nazism after was practically nothing but hatred of Jews. This reduction of Nazism to antisemitism can be seen, decades after the collapse of Hitler's empire, in the proclivity of white supremacists to display swastikas and chant slogans that merge anti-immigrant, anti-Black, and anti-Jewish themes, like the 2017 rallying cry of the "alt-right" in Charlottesville, Virginia: "Jews will not replace us."

Antisemitism and Nazi Ideology

Antisemitism constituted the core of Hitler's worldview and the center of National Socialist ideology. For Hitler the two notions of "race" and "space"—racial purification and spatial expansion—were intertwined (Weinberg 1995). To achieve the world dominance it supposedly deserved, the "Aryan" race, Hitler reasoned in Social Darwinist fashion, had to be in a constant state of increase. Such reproduction required land, and conquest of territory meant war. In Hitler's eyes, because the Jewish "race" was the mortal enemy of the "Aryans," any war would be a war against "the Jews." Indeed, by Nazi logic, other enemies were either puppets or dupes of "international Jewry." For Hitler and others who shared his views, the notion that Germany had lost the previous World War because of a "stab in the back" from a treacherous home front led by cowardly Jews meant that driving Jews out was necessary in order to win the wars to come.

Saul Friedländer's term "redemptive antisemitism" is useful to understand Hitler's radical antisemitism (Friedländer [1997] 2007). According to Hitler, defeating something called "the Jew" was the only way to save Germany from disaster. Characteristic of "redemptive antisemitism" was a religious zeal that linked fighting "Jewish influence" to the struggle against evil. In *Mein Kampf*, Hitler claimed that when he attacked "the Jew" he was doing God's work. At the same time, redemptive antisemitism built on racialist notions: "Jewishness," it assumed, was "in the blood" and could not be removed or undone through religious conversion, legal emancipation, or cultural assimilation. Indeed, proponents of racial antisemitism reviled those processes as masks the "Jewish threat" used to catch its victims off guard. Redemptive antisemitism also sounded a note of urgency. The clock was ticking, Hitler and others intoned, and it was almost too late for the "Aryan race" to save itself from the corrupting forces that had already defiled its collective bloodstream.

An amalgamation and accumulation of many varieties of Jew-hatred, redemptive antisemitism offered countless strands onto which people with their own agendas could grab hold. It was not necessary to buy into the entire package to find common ground with Nazism. The legacies of older kinds of antisemitism provided points of contact to Nazism's redemptive brand which both borrowed from and fed on them. Christian anti-Judaism was one such pre-existing form. The notion that Jews were children of the devil who had betrayed and crucified Jesus prepared the way for the accusation that Jews were traitors to the fatherland. The image of Jews as enemies of Christianity merged with charges of Jews as the masterminds behind atheist Communism.

Political, economic, and social stereotypes about Jews that predated the emergence of Nazism meshed with Nazi antisemitism as did sexual anxieties.

Starting in the 1920s, Julius Streicher's newspaper, *Der Stürmer*, and other propaganda instruments played on images of the Jew as the racially inferior male predator, the ugly yet fantastically fertile female, and the devious temptress who led unsuspecting "Aryans" to their doom. These sexualized figures echoed racist and imperialist thinking at the same time as they connected different sets of target populations in mutually reinforcing stereotypes. Homophobes blamed Jews for spreading homosexuality and profiting from a gay subculture that purportedly undermined German strength. People suspicious of Roma pointed out that, like Jews, "Gypsies" had no homeland, perhaps the result of a divine curse that somehow revealed their innate criminality. Germans uneasy with the restoration of an independent Poland sometimes merged anti-Slavic and antisemitic notions in the stereotype of "eastern barbarism."

The antisemitism preached in Nazi speeches and tracts was rife with contradictions. Jews, it insinuated, had invented Christianity to make their enemies meek and weak, yet it was Jews, antisemites charged, who killed Jesus and assaulted true Christians everywhere. Nazi antisemitism depicted Jews as at once oversexed (sexual predators, seductresses) and weak and androgynous (effeminate men, masculine women). To Nazi antisemites, Jews were both capitalists and Communists; congenitally inferior yet capable of mounting a diabolically clever conspiracy to rule the world; never able to conceal their true essence yet hiding everywhere.

Instead of weakening the power of Nazism's particular variety of antisemitism, such contradictions strengthened it. They provided an infinite number of places to connect with suspicion and fear of Jews, according to an individual's own fears and desires. They rendered Nazi antisemitism simultaneously amorphous yet absolutely vivid and specific. All these conflicting images came together in representations of Jews as germs and bacteria (small, invisible things that are nevertheless deadly) and rats (ubiquitous, dirty, ugly, contemptible, clever, and menacing).

Antisemitism provided an organizing principle for Nazism, an adhesive that connected various components of the Party's platform. How would Nazis end Germany's "encirclement" by international enemies? By exposing the Jews who plotted to keep Germany from its proper place in the world. How would Nazism address domestic challenges including unemployment, poverty, and public indecency? By removing Jews from public life. What was the "positive Christianity" that Nazism officially espoused? A Christianity purged of all Jewish elements. Hitler was a true believer in the antisemitism he espoused, not merely a charismatic manipulator of popular sentiment. Indeed, he and his associates had to work to "educate" the German public about the purported danger that Jews and Judaism posed to the "Aryan race." As they learned after 1933, their strongest ally in this task was power itself.

Antisemitism in Power

Power institutionalized Nazi antisemitism and diffused it throughout society in ways that merged its extraordinary force and vehemence with the ordinary, even banal, manifestations of everyday life. In the first six years of Nazi rule, a series of laws and regulations isolated German Jews and produced what historian Marion Kaplan (1998), borrowing from the sociologist Orlando Patterson, has called their "social death." With the invasion of Poland in 1939, antisemitism fused with the national cause to become a German wartime duty. The pressures of war reinforced notions of a Jewish conspiracy that Nazi propaganda mobilized to present German aggression as self-defense. By 1941, when killing Jews emerged as the top Nazi German priority, antisemitism had developed a new function as a justification for violence and new force as the point where ambition, greed, self-interest, and the desire to please the Führer all converged.

On 30 January 1933, Hitler became Chancellor of Germany. Initially his position was weak: he did not command a majority in the Reichstag, and his cabinet included only two other members of the Nazi Party. Nevertheless, Hitler still found ways to target Jews. Nazism provided opportunities for its adherents to express antisemitism, even as its concrete implementation also raised practical challenges.

The number of Jews in Germany was small: in 1933, approximately 500,000 Jews constituted less than one percent of the population. Disproportionately present in some highly visible areas of the economy—publishing, medicine, performing arts—German Jews were under-represented elsewhere: in the higher ranks of the military, judiciary, and bureaucracy; among the police; in agriculture. In April 1933, in an effort to highlight the Jewish presence in the economy and ostracize German Jews, the Nazi leadership proclaimed a boycott of Jewish businesses.

This first public act of organized antisemitism had mixed results for Hitler and his Minister of Propaganda, Joseph Goebbels. Old-fashioned antisemitism alone was not strong enough to counter non-Jewish Germans' habits of consumption and sense of comfort. Even some Stormtroopers and Nazi Party members violated the boycott to frequent shops convenient for them. In any case, what constituted a Jewish business? If the issue was Jewish ownership, what about "Aryan" employees? What about enterprises owned jointly by Jews and non-Jews? To Nazi leaders, the boycott revealed how tightly Jews were woven into the fabric of German economic life and proved the need to isolate Jews before mounting a direct attack.

Also in April 1933, Nazi authorities introduced a law to remove Jews from the German civil service. This measure met with more obvious success. Non-Jews, the regime learned, preferred anti-Jewish measures that they perceived as improving their lives over those that cost them effort. Firing Jewish civil servants, from lowly clerks to high-profile professionals, opened up positions for non-Jewish Germans, or at least held out the promise of doing so, and provided opportunities for self-serving initiatives that sometimes went beyond the law. The civil service law was a crucial step in transforming antisemitism from an attitude that required members of the public to share Nazi ideals into a wide range of actions that did not.

The subsequent five years brought countless measures that built up the pressure on German Jews and cut them off from the non-Jews around them. The Nuremberg Laws of 1935 defined as "Jews" those Germans who had three or four grandparents of the Jewish religion. With a definition in place, the Nuremberg Laws went on to forbid marriage and criminalize relations between "Jews" and so-called Aryans, to ban people who counted as Jews from flying the national flag or hiring "Aryan" women under the age of forty-five to work in their homes, and to strip Jews of most of the rights and protections of German citizenship.

These stipulations in turn sparked a wave of investigations and prosecutions (Wünschmann 2015). Non-Jews who may have harbored no particular ill will toward Jews discovered it was dangerous to associate with them. Displays of affection or friendship could result in charges of *Rassenschande*— crimes against the race—or in public humiliation. Policemen, lawyers, and judges solicited detailed testimonies from men and women accused of violating laws against sexual contact between people who found themselves deemed members of different races. Convictions meant long sentences in prison or concentration camps, and even acquittals left reputations damaged and careers shattered (Szobar 2005). Stormtroopers and other thugs harassed Jews and non-Jews suspected of violating the race laws, by beating them up or forcing them to stand in the street with insulting signs.

This combination of official measures and public bullying proved poisonous for Jews and uncomfortable for their gentile relatives and friends. An endless stream of restrictions and prohibitions heaped indignities and hardships one on top of the other and separated Jews from their neighbors. Jews were forbidden from using public swimming pools; owning radios, telephones, and typewriters; attending school; practicing medicine; wearing dirndls and lederhosen; shopping other than at specified times; and giving the "German greeting," *Heil Hitler!* Hundreds of such prohibitions tormented and stigmatized Jews by translating antisemitic ideas into everyday routines that required no effort from non-Jewish Germans.

The Christian churches played a significant role in furthering and legitimating the isolation of Jews. Nazi law required Germans in a wide range of professional and even volunteer positions to prove their "Aryan blood" by establishing the religion of their forebears, and records of baptism into the Roman Catholic or Protestant churches were the only way to do so. Overwhelmed with requests for documentation, many church offices hired extra staff to handle the job (Bergen 1996). There is no evidence that the workers who combed through dusty tomes and copied out dates of births and baptisms were hardcore antisemites. Probably most were just doing a job. But their work was essential to identify and marginalize Jews. Meanwhile, the eagerness of Christian leaders to maintain good relations with the state and capitalize on Hitler's popularity added to the churches' normalization of Nazi antisemitism.

By early 1939, Nazi aggression had pushed almost half of Germany's Jews out of the country. Instead of waning as Jews departed, antisemitism intensified. Many "Aryan" Germans who acquired homes, businesses, jobs, or promotions, thanks to the expropriation or emigration of Jewish Germans, discovered compelling reasons to hate Jews or at least support policies against them. The widespread perception of Jews as fabulously wealthy meant even gentiles who had not yet profited expected to do so and worried that criticism of the regime could cost them their share of the spoils. Given these circumstances, debates about whether or not "ordinary Germans" held antisemitic beliefs miss the point. Nazism in power offered powerful incentives for people to behave like antisemites even if they did not share that worldview.

In late 1938, as Hitler and his inner circle planned the demolition of Czechoslovakia and the invasion of Poland, both of which followed in 1939, they also engineered a massive assault on the Jews of Germany, newly enlarged by the annexation of Austria. This offensive culminated in the *Kristallnacht* pogrom of 9–10 November 1938. Hitler's regime benefited in numerous ways from this putatively spontaneous but actually coordinated attack on Jews, Jewish property, and sites of Jewish worship and communal life (Steinweis 2009). Impatient Nazis satisfied their thirst for violent action. German gentiles, initially uncomfortable with their government's brutal tactics, found that paying rock-bottom prices for property from Jews eager to get out of the country fostered a new loyalty to the Nazi system (Bajohr 2002). Still, many Germans grumbled about public disorder, and international observers decried the violence. Why were Hitler and Goebbels, generally so keen to maintain a positive image at home and abroad, willing to take this public relations risk? A key reason was their desire to force Jews out of Germany before launching into war. By Nazi logic, every Jew gone meant one traitor fewer who would betray Germany.

This line of reasoning exposes the self-fulfilling logic of Nazi antisemitism. The more than 200,000 Jews who fled Germany between 1933 and 1939 settled where they could: elsewhere on the European continent, in Britain and its dominions, the United States, Palestine, China, the Caribbean, India, or Africa. From those new homes, Nazi conspiracy theorists claimed, Jews would plot against Germany. By making it impossible for Jews to live in Germany but simultaneously increasing their numbers abroad, Nazi Germans fed their own paranoia about international enemies and hardened the conviction that what was needed was total destruction of the Jewish threat.

From the outset Nazi ideology and practice linked attacks on Jews with preparation for war. In March 1935, Hitler announced German rearmament, including the draft. Within weeks, German Jews were banned from military service. This exclusion implied that Jews were dishonorable, unfit to be soldiers, and in league with Germany's enemies. In 1936, a wave of propaganda prepared Germans for involvement in the Spanish Civil War by painting defenders of the Spanish Republic as bloodthirsty anarchists, Communists, and Jews. This reversal of roles—presenting Jews as if they were vicious aggressors rather than victims of Hitler's Germany—became a hallmark of Nazi antisemitism at war.

Even before Hitler's war began, it was an assault on the Jews. "Europe cannot find peace until the Jewish question has been solved," Hitler told the Reichstag on 30 January 1939, less than three months after *Kristallnacht*. War, Hitler had already decided, would start that year. "In the course of my life I have very often been a prophet," he proclaimed, "and have usually been ridiculed for it." Now, he concluded, things were different:

> Today I will once more be a prophet: if the international Jewish financiers in and outside Europe should succeed in plunging the nations once more into a world war, then the result will not be the bolshevizing of the earth, and thus the victory of Jewry, but the annihilation of the Jewish race in Europe! (quoted in Noakes and Pridham 2001, p. 441)

War raised the stakes of Nazi antisemitism in every possible way. Most obvious, it multiplied tenfold the number of Jews under German rule. The invasion and conquest of Poland in September 1939 put several million Polish Jews in German hands and made those Jews targets against whom anything and everything was permitted. To the Germans in Poland, Jews embodied both the racial threat to "Aryan" blood and a major obstacle to German order.

German practices in conquered Poland reinforced notions of Jews as dangerous and created "proof" of Jewish inferiority. Ghettoization of Jews began in late 1939. According to the official line, Jews had to be confined to preserve German safety and prevent the spread of disease. In fact, ghettoization facilitated stealing Jewish property and drove a wedge between Polish Jews and non-Jews. Like other Nazi antisemitic measures, ghettoization functioned as a self-fulfilling prophecy. Locked up under conditions of terrible shortage, of food, housing, sanitation, and everything else, Jews in the ghettos of occupied Poland were desperate (Engelking and Leociak 2009). Starving, dressed in rags, and dying in the street, they embodied the opposite of the Aryan ideal. No wonder Germans shot movies in the ghettos, most famously, *The Eternal Jew*, which juxtaposed hordes of rats with crowds of emaciated Jews.

During wartime as before, antisemitism gave lethal coherence to Nazi prejudices and policies. After the German and Soviet Foreign Ministers signed a Non-Aggression Pact between their countries in August 1939, antisemitism remained the only constant in Nazi ideology. Hitler's deal with Stalin blocked anti-Communist statements and actions (for the time being), but the notion of a Jewish conspiracy persisted. Meanwhile, violence against Jews became the accepted way to solve problems. When Himmler's Race and Settlement authorities began bringing ethnic Germans from Eastern Europe "home into the Reich," that is, resettling them in occupied Poland, they ran into difficulties. Where could they house the hundreds of thousands, eventually to be millions, of people they had lured from Soviet territories with promises of prosperity? Their answers invariably targeted Jews. In Łódź, SS men went door-to-door through Jewish neighborhoods, demanding people leave their homes within hours. Back home, when municipalities ran short of money, they cut Jews off from public assistance, even before the central government in Berlin requested they do so. Antisemitism enabled ambitious Germans to "work toward the Führer" while serving their own schemes.

As Hannah Arendt pointed out in *Eichmann in Jerusalem*, the perpetrators of Nazi crimes were not abnormal. Under the Nazi system as elsewhere, it was normal to obey the laws, support the national war effort, and protect one's self-interest. Yet doing those "normal" things made people part of the machinery of destruction (Fulbrook 2013). A German soldier did not have to be a fanatical antisemite to help herd Jews into a ghetto. A woman's enjoyment of the silver candlesticks she acquired did not require any particular hatred of Jews (Harvey 2003). Nazi antisemitism was pervasive but it was neither inevitable nor imposed on innocent non-Jews. Still, to oppose it required awareness and courage.

Antisemitism as Annihilation: Causes and Effects

By the middle of 1941, Nazi Germans were systematically murdering Jews. Special killing squads followed the Wehrmacht into Soviet territory where they rounded up Jews of all ages and killed them, usually by shooting them into mass graves. These actions, carried out by the so-called Einsatzgruppen, the German Order Police, and non-German auxiliary groups, also targeted non-Jews—Roma and high-ranking Communists—but most of the one million victims they amassed by the end of 1941 were Jews.

After the invasion of the Soviet Union in June 1941, antisemitic themes became ubiquitous in German propaganda as Goebbels and his underlings found endless grist for their mills in the notion of a Jewish-Bolshevik conspiracy (Herf 2006). When the war was going well for Germany, propaganda trumpeted the impending defeat of the diabolical foe. Military setbacks, for their part, served to "prove" how fearsome the Jewish enemy was and therefore to justify the most extreme measures against a menace that allied itself with the hammer and sickle and pulled the strings of Churchill and Roosevelt. In this view of the world, no Jew was innocent, and any appearance of harmlessness was just another cunning ploy.

Nazi antisemitism was not only pervasive, it was contagious. As the Germans advanced into territories occupied by the Soviet Union and further into Soviet lands, they sparked pogroms against local Jews, instrumentalizing local resentments for their own purposes. Some non-Jews needed little goading. In the summer of 1941, in Lithuania and parts of eastern

Poland, persecution of Jews exploded into massacres that destroyed entire communities (Kopstein and Wittenberg 2018). In July 1941, Polish gentiles in Jedwabne killed hundreds of their Jewish neighbors. Almost seventy-five percent of the 200,000 Jews of Lithuania were murdered in the first three months of German occupation, many of them under the rule of the Lithuanian Provisional Government (Ginaite-Rubinson 2005). Inside Romania, Germany's ally, authorities forced Jews across the border into Ukraine, where they were slaughtered in the killing fields of Transnistria (Dumitru 2015). For Poles, Lithuanians, Ukrainians, and others who had endured Soviet rule, attacking Jews provided a way to take revenge for their suffering, even though Jews had shared all the terrors of Stalinism. At the same time, assaulting Jews gained German approval and distracted attention from non-Jews who themselves had collaborated with the Soviets. For Germany's allies, attacks on Jews became a way to win German favor and position themselves for present and future rewards. Annihilatory antisemitism acted like a magnet, pulling initiatives of all kinds in the same direction and binding them together in a deadly consensus.

In 1943, although German power began slowly to wane, killing of Jews did not ease up. To Nazi killers, increasing evidence of Jewish resistance only confirmed their fears of Jewish "bandits" in cahoots with Germany's enemies. At the same time, practices of humiliating their victims fed the killers' contempt of Jews as disgusting beings who deserved to die. The monstrous scope of killing itself meant many perpetrators and onlookers grew accustomed to seeing Jews as corpses who, if they were not yet dead, would be soon. That image bled into a stereotype of the passive Jew who almost asked for death (Sereny 1983). All such notions facilitated killing of Jews and gained strength from the ongoing destruction. Perhaps even twinges of discomfort added to the killers' desire to see the Jews eradicated. Who wants a reminder of their own bad conscience?

Himmler's infamous 1943 speech to SS leaders points to another component of Nazi antisemitism in the stage of annihilation: guilt, and related to it, shame. For all their brutality, most of the killers and their accomplices remained "normal" people who longed for the comforts of family life and thought of themselves, to use Himmler's word, as "decent." How could they cover over the guilt of killing old people, women, children, and men who had done nothing to them? Here the antisemitic inversion came into play, with its accusations of Jews as evil personified, conspirators against everything German and good (Koonz 2003).

By the last stage of the war, killing Jews had become normal for people from many parts of Europe. As German forces retreated westward after Stalingrad and eastward after D-Day, administrators and guards at camps and killing centers began to evacuate the remaining prisoners and march them toward territories still in German hands. Daniel Blatman (2011) shows how these death marches spiraled into another form of mass killing of Jews and non-Jews. For the perpetrators, self-interest also played a role. By the end of 1944, the safest place any German could be, Allied bombs notwithstanding, was inside the admittedly rapidly shrinking area under German control. Columns of starving, half-dead Jews and other prisoners represented tickets toward home. Without them, a German man would be sent to the front. To refuse that perilous duty meant to desert, and German military authorities shot some 30,000 German men accused of desertion and defeatism, most of them in the last months of the war. By the time of the death marches, antisemitism pervaded every aspects of life in Nazi Germany: the war effort, cowardice, careerism, even common sense.

Defeat and collapse of Nazi Germany, it is often said, discredited antisemitism. Yet aspects of Nazi antisemitism survived the Holocaust and even thrived in postwar conditions. For individuals and communities who had benefited from the disappearance of Jews by taking their property and positions, antisemitism offered a way to justify and normalize those acts. The Jews had asked for it, the reasoning went: they were too rich, they failed to assimilate, they had not resisted. Hatred of Jews and postwar violence against Jewish survivors served to drive them out and remove painful reminders of the complicity of non-Jews (Feinstein 2010). Politicians used postwar antisemitism, too: Communists eager to consolidate power in Eastern Europe refused to acknowledge Jewish suffering in order to highlight their own martyrs and curry favor with local populations. Opponents of Zionism accused Jews of profiting from victimization in order to grab restitution payments and support creation of a Jewish state.

In his book *Fear*, Jan Gross (2006) examines postwar antisemitism in Poland. Three million Polish Jews were murdered in the Holocaust, and only a few hundred thousand remained on Polish soil in May 1945, when the Allies declared "Victory in Europe." Less than two years later, most of that remnant was gone too, hounded out by violent neighbors, hostile local administrators, and indifferent authorities. The July 1946 pogrom in Kielce was the most dramatic postwar attack on Jews but it was not unique. Gross' analysis reveals a combination of material incentives, exacerbated by Poland's forced shift westward; political exigencies—the unpopular Communist Party chose to side with "the people" against "the Jews"; and opportunistic neglect: the Roman Catholic Church let attacks on Jews continue so as not to alienate its population or Communist officials. It was simply easier for everyone—everyone but Polish Jews—if the Jews would disappear (Auerbach 2013). The situation in Poland stands out because of the size of the prewar Jewish population, but comparable phenomena occurred in Czechoslovakia, Hungary, and elsewhere.

The massive violence of the Nazi Holocaust left a stigma on Judaism and Jews. In the face of radical evil and unbearable loss, observers, including some Jews, found comfort in the sense that anyone who suffered such catastrophe must somehow be to blame. One of the cruel legacies of Nazism is an image of Jews as eternal victims, who not only attract suffering but profit from it. Though sometimes mixed with philosemitic declarations of fascination, this notion constitutes another expression of antisemitism.

References

Auerbach, Karen. 2013. *The House at Ujazdowskie 16: Jewish Families in Warsaw After the Holocaust.* Bloomington: Indiana University Press.

Bajohr, Frank. 2002. *'Aryanisation' in Hamburg: The Economic Exclusion of Jews and the Confiscation of Their Property in Nazi Germany.* New York: Berghahn.

Bergen, Doris L. 1996. *Twisted Cross: The German Christian Movement in the Third Reich.* Chapel Hill: University of North Carolina Press.

Bergen, Doris L. 2010. "Antisemitism in the Nazi Era." In *Antisemitism: A History*, edited by Albert S. Lindemann and Richard S. Levy, 196–210. Oxford: Oxford University Press.

Blatman, Daniel. 2011. *The Death Marches: The Final Phase of Nazi Genocide.* Cambridge, MA: Belknap of Harvard University Press.

Confino, Alon. 2014. *A World Without Jews: The Nazi Imagination from Persecution to Genocide.* New Haven: Yale University Press.

Dumitru, Diana. 2015. *The State, Anti-Semitism, and the Holocaust: Romania and the Soviet Union.* New York: Cambridge University Press.

Engelking, Barbara, and Jacek Leociak. 2009. *The Warsaw Ghetto: A Guide to the Perished City.* New Haven: Yale University Press.

Feinstein, Margarete Meyers. 2010. *Holocaust Survivors in Post-War Germany, 1945–1957.* New York: Cambridge University Press.

Friedländer, Saul. (1997) 2007. *Nazi Germany and the Jews.* 2 vols. New York: HarperCollins.

Fulbrook, Mary. 2013. *A Small Town Near Auschwitz: Ordinary Nazis and the Holocaust.* Oxford: Oxford University Press.

Ginaite-Rubinson, Sara. 2005. *Resistance and Survival: The Jewish Community in Kaunas, 1941–1944.* Oakville: Mosaic.

Gross, Jan. 2006. *Fear: Anti-Semitism in Poland after Auschwitz.* New York: Random House.

Harvey, Elizabeth. 2003. *Women in the Nazi East: Agents and Witnesses of Germanization.* New Haven: Yale University Press.

Herf, Jeffrey. 2006. *The Jewish Enemy: Nazi Propaganda During World War II and the Holocaust.* Cambridge, MA: Belknap of Harvard University Press.

Kaplan, Marion. 1998. *Between Dignity and Despair: Jewish Life in Nazi Germany.* New York: Oxford University Press.

Koonz, Claudia. 2003. *The Nazi Conscience.* Cambridge, MA: Harvard University Press.

Kopstein, Jeffrey S., and Jason Wittenberg. 2018. *Intimate Violence: Anti-Jewish Pogroms on the Eve of the Holocaust.* Ithaca: Cornell University Press.

Noakes, Jeremy, and Geoffrey Pridham, eds. 2001. *Nazism, 1919–1945: A Documentary Reader.* Vol. 3. Exeter: University of Exeter Press.

Sereny, Gitta. 1983. *Into that Darkness: An Examination of Conscience.* New York: Vintage.

Steinweis, Alan. 2009. *Kristallnacht 1938*. Cambridge, MA: Harvard University Press.
Szobar, Patricia. 2005. "Telling Sexual Stories in the Nazi Courts of Law: Race Defilement in Germany, 1933 to 1945." In *Sexuality and German Fascism*, edited by Dagmar Herzog, 131–63. New York: Berghahn.
Weinberg, Gerhard L. 1995. *Germany, Hitler, and World War II*. New York: Cambridge University Press.
Wünschmann, Kim. 2015. *Before Auschwitz: Jewish Prisoners in the Prewar Concentration Camps*. Cambridge, MA: Harvard University Press.

CHAPTER 15

Orientalism

Ivan Kalmar

An opinion piece by a contributor to the Israeli newspaper *Haaretz* concluded that "Israel within the Green Line belongs naturally to the West; the territories are not Israel, but rather a colony that heaps shame on Zionism and on Jewish history" (Sternhell 2016). A statement like this one would astonish those who imagined a future Jewish state a hundred and fifty years ago. To such visionaries who lived in the age of colonialism, the current division of Israel—then Palestine—into a Jewish State and its Arab colony might not seem all that surprising. But they would be shocked by the assertion that Israel—the Jewish State—belonged to the West, and "naturally" at that.

Until the middle of the twentieth century, people in the North Atlantic world commonly thought of the Jews as "Asiatic refugees" in Europe, to quote one of the Enlightenment supporters of equal rights for Jews (Dohm 1957, p. 1). No one who examines the historical record can miss that all Jews, including those living in Europe, were universally considered people from the East, "orientals." Edward Said (1978, p. 28) even suggested that orientalism was the "Islamic branch" of antisemitism (the other branch being the Jewish branch). Antisemitism was not only *related* to orientalism; it *was* one of its central aspects.

Orientalism, which in its most basic definition is a way to talk about and to imagine a region called "Orient," long included as its target the Jews, imagined as an oriental people. The establishment of the State of Israel, along with the development of the notion of a "Judeo-Christian tradition" to which

I. Kalmar (✉)
Department of Anthropology, University of Toronto, Toronto, ON, Canada
e-mail: i.kalmar@utoronto.ca

it was related, was the main event that led to the abandonment of the identification of Jews with Arabs (and, by extension, Muslims) as fellow orientals. As before, antisemitism continued to be connected in many ways to prejudice against Muslims, which we now call "Islamophobia." However, the "Orient" no longer served as an active trope for characterizing Muslims and Jews together as the West's threatening Other.

The purpose of this essay is to outline the history of orientalism and to explain reasons why it once included both Jews and Muslims and then ceased to do so. The notion of orientalism is an indispensable tool for understanding the history of antisemitism, but it is less useful for understanding its present.

The Term "Orientalism"

Among the original meanings of "Orientalism," now obsolete, was the style or character of anything typically associated with the Orient. Orientalists were scholars and artists who were preoccupied with the Orient, often professing an admiration for it (Schwab 1984). With the critique of academic and literary orientalism by Edward Said (1978), the term "orientalism" took on pejorative connotations. Implicitly, orientalism as "discourse"—which is how Said discussed it—came to be used also, and perhaps primarily, to label an affect. It is now mostly used to refer to a derisive valuation of the Orient, a prejudiced view associated with the history of western imperialism in and toward the Orient, and its legacy. It is often used in an even broader sense to label all western prejudice against the non-West, including Africa and Latin America (Kalmar 2016).

In this last, greatly expanded sense, the relationship between orientalism and antisemitism may get obscured. However, in the more traditional sense, where "Orient" means firstly the predominantly Muslim areas of North Africa, the Levant, and Arabia, and secondly South Asia, orientalism is inextricably connected to the representation, in the western world, of the Jews. This is because of the aforementioned association of the Jews with the Orient. The association was based on the perception that the Orient was the homeland of the Bible and its people.

There are various ways to periodize orientalism (Kalmar and Penslar 2005; Renton and Gidley 2017). For the purposes of this chapter, we can distinguish at least two phases. In each of these phases, there was an implicit political concern and a specific population that was the main object of the orientalist imagination. There was what I would like to call (a) the *precolonial/Turkish* phase, and (b) the *colonial/Arab* phase. Today, we may perhaps speak of a third one, (c) the *postcolonial/Muslim* phase. This, however, is where we approach the question of the continued relevance of the connection between representing Muslims and representing Jews today. It may be best, partly for the very reason that in this last phase the trope of the "Jew" becomes uncoupled from that of "Muslim," to consider phase c) no longer a part of orientalism, but the beginning of something else. The current period may be not only *postcolonial* but also *post-orientalist*.

THE PRECOLONIAL/TURKISH PHASE

Said seemed at times to think that orientalism existed as far back as ancient Greece (1978). That is probably anachronistic, but what is of great relevance is that the obligatory reading of the Greek and Latin classics predisposed educated western observers, from the Renaissance on, to assimilate what they had read about the Greek image of Persia to their own imperial rival to the East: the Ottoman Empire. This Muslim power incorporated Constantinople, the classic capital of Christendom, in 1452 and its expansion into Europe was not stopped until it was defeated at the gates of Vienna in 1672. The Ottomans and their Muslim subjects were described as "Turks." Well into the eighteenth century "Turk" was often used as a synonym of "Muslim." Accordingly, we can refer to the first period of orientalism as the "Turkish period." It lasted from the late fifteenth to the late eighteenth century.

Just as Ottoman power rose in the Orient, western political arrangements came under intense scrutiny in Europe. European accounts of the Orient focused on burning political issues in Europe itself: sovereignty and autocracy. In an important sense, absolutist government was caricatured *in extremis* in the imagined form of the Ottoman (known as "Turkish") or, somewhat less frequently, Persian court. The sultan's realm was imagined as his private pleasure grounds. Men followed the despot's orders unquestioningly, even if it meant someone else's or their own death. Women offered themselves cheerfully for his infinite sexual appetite, considering it an honor to enter his harem.

European art of the period shows that biblical Jews were visualized, at least from the late fifteenth century when Constantinople fell to the Ottomans, on the pattern of what European Christians knew of the "Turks." The iconography of biblical personages in Ottoman costume and especially Ottoman turbans was established as early as the late thirteen hundreds (Kalmar 2005). As earlier in the Middle Ages, Islam continued to be seen as a throwback to Judaism (Akbari 2005). But now the European imagination, preoccupied with the notion and practice of absolutist government, projected not only Ottoman costume, but much more importantly the alleged extreme authoritarianism of the Ottoman government, onto the religion of not only Muslims but also Jews.

"Allah" was imagined as a heavenly despot in whose name and image the earthly oriental despot ruled (Kalmar 2012). Conjointly, the modern notion developed of the "God of the Old Testament" or "Jehovah." With deep roots in Pauline theology, this modern way of looking at Christianity's biblical heritage contrasted a pitiless, legalistic Old Testament view of God with the merciful, loving Trinity and especially Jesus. Allah came to be seen as the expression of Old Testament-like, arbitrary discipline, uninformed by the "good news" of a loving Christ (see Bloom 2005).

The Colonial/Arab Phase

An even more explicit connection between Jews and Muslims was, however, articulated later, in the nineteenth century, when the "Turk" was replaced by the "Arab" as the principal metonymic trope for "Muslim."

The connection between Jews and Arabs, and certainly between Hebrew and Arabic, had been made during the "Turkish" period already. In the Renaissance, the Hebrew Bible had been studied by many Christian scholars such as Pico della Mirandola (1463–1494) in connection with Arabic language texts. In the eighteenth century, the Arabists who founded orientalism as a scholarly discipline were, as a rule, also Hebraists. Albert Schultens (1686–1750), the leading Arabist of his time, argued in print that studying Arabic was a necessary preparation for understanding the Hebrew Scriptures (1729).

Indeed, the very term "orientalism" appears to have been first mentioned in English in connection with the Hebrew Bible. In his *Essay on Pope's Odyssey*, Joseph Spence referred admiringly to a turn of phrase in Homer's epic as an "orientalism," that is, as influenced by the Orient (1727, pp. 214–15). This probably reflected the then popular belief that Homer knew and was influenced by the Bible. In the work of an early philologist, Robert Lowth (1710–1787), the linguistic link had clearly become also a cultural one. Lowth observed that "difficulties must occur in the perusal of almost every work of literature," and particularly with "Orientals above all foreigners, they being the farthest removed from our customs and manners; and of all the Orientals, more especially in the Hebrews, theirs being confessedly the most ancient compositions extant. (…) Not only the antiquity of these writings forms a principal obstruction in many respects; but the manner of living, of speaking, of thinking, which prevailed in those times, will be found altogether different from our customs and habits" ([1787] 1847, p. 65).

The very conception of the "Arab" as a people and a culture or civilization, and not just the name of a language originating in Arabia, appears datable to this philological effort. Previously, "Arab" was seldom if ever heard as an ethnic label. To invent an "Arab nation" was consistent with the philological spirit of the long nineteenth century, a time when the notion of the linguistically defined nation crystalized in the western consciousness. Czech, Slovene, Finnish, and Turkish speakers followed the example of German and Italian speakers and enthusiastically embraced the idea that their language defined them as ancient peoples whose national spirit would be reawakened as they strove to revive their languages and found their own states. Arab nationalism and Zionism both have strong roots in this movement of "national self-determination." It is within this broader context of philologically based ethnic "reawakenings" that it is best to see the kind of biblical revivalism that, by associating the Jewish and Arab "races," sought a "return" of the Jews to their oriental roots, either through the radical solution of Zionism or through philo-oriental cultural expression such as Moorish style synagogues, on which more will be said below.

The foundations of the philological imagination owe much to the German idealist philosopher, G. F. W. Hegel. Hegel turned to the Orient with the same goal as the poets Hölderlin and Coleridge. Both poets' objective was to reinvent Protestant Christianity in the face of the challenge posed to it by the discovery of oriental scriptures such as the Persian Zend Avesta and the Sanskrit Holy Books (Schwab 1984), and the related relativization of Bible scholarship. Theirs was, as Emily Shaffer wrote, "a new apologetics of free-thinking theism which was to salvage Christianity until very nearly the end of the Victorian era" (1980, p. 63).

In such apologetics, the Orient and not only its Jewish version served as the Mother of true religiosity. Hegel's picture of "Arab" religion was echoed by Benjamin Disraeli, the Jewish- born future Prime Minister under Queen Victoria, who put in the mouth of a sympathetic character in his novel *Tancred* the astonishing declaration that "God never spoke except to an Arab" ([1847] 1904, p. 319). Obviously, he thought that not only Muhammad, but also Abraham, Isaac, Jacob, Moses, and Jesus were "Arabs."

Hegel described the oriental, and more specifically the Near Eastern, imagination as the last stepping stone of the world spirit before it entered the pinnacle of Germanic Protestant culture. Islam, according to Hegel, was a belated and anachronistic throwback to the same Jewish-and-Arab spirit that had earlier produced Judaism and was then superseded by Christianity.

Hegel's incipient racialization of religion—in the form of *Volksgeist* or ethnically determined spirit—received a more biologizing form post Darwin, in the late nineteenth century. Only now did the modern notion of race mature, as the combined cultural, linguistic, and physical heritage of a group of people imagined to be of common descent. And Jews and Arabs were universally imagined as racial relatives.

Eventually, in the mid-nineteenth century, the term "Semite" would replace the ambiguous term "Arab" as the joint label for Jews and Arabs (and imprecisely, Muslims). "Semite" like "Arab" was a newly conceived extension of a linguistic term to a national/ethnic/racial one. We may speak of the "Arab period" of orientalism, from the early nineteenth to the mid-twentieth century.

The most important influence on this change was Ernest Renan's *Histoire générale et système comparé des langues sémitiques* ([1855] 1863). Renan (1823–1892) did have some praise for the Semites in a later work. "It is the Semitic race," he would write, "which has the glory of having made the religion of humanity. Far beyond the confines of history, resting under his tent free from the taint of a corrupted world, the Bedouin patriarch prepared the faith of mankind" ([1860] 1894, p. 70). But the *Histoire* abounds with apparent insults: "The Semitic people lack curiosity almost completely" ([1855] 1863, p. 10); "In general, the perception of nuances is deeply absent among the Semitic peoples... polygamy, a consequence of an original nomadic way of life, has blocked among the Semites the development of all that we call society, and has formed a race that is exclusively virile, without flexibility or *finesse*" (p. 11); "The military inferiority of the Semites is due to this total lack of ability for discipline or subordination" (p. 14); and, "Morality has always been understood by this race in a manner very different from ours" (p. 15). Obviously, the admirable qualities of the Semites do not compare with "ours."

Shlomo Sand (Renan and Sand 2010) suggests that the young Renan who wrote the *Histoire*, with its negative judgments of the Semites, later had a change of heart. This would account for his apparently contradictory, positive assessment of the Semites later. But Renan never renounced the opinions in his early tome. Rather than considering admiration and condemnation as a contradiction here, it is more useful—as it is in the case of orientalism in general—to think of consistent supersessionism. One can admire the contribution of a relatively primitive race to a civilization that would then be superseded by that of a more advanced race. But from the vantage point of the more advanced, the achievement of the less advanced, though valuable and praiseworthy, ultimately fails to arrive at the goals to which history has tended.

Renan was no more a biological racist than was Hegel: both posited a cultural/civilizational ladder of how the human spirit developed, and not necessarily a physiological one. That said, Renan's Aryan racism goes well beyond Hegel's. Monotheism is Renan's nemesis. He is able to write, for example, that "the intolerance of the Semitic peoples is a necessary consequence of their monotheism" ([1855] 1863, p. 7). Renan's real goal was to devalue the Semitic monotheism that underlies Christianity, and to identify instead with the Indo-European mind, which is based in a polytheist tradition but which, Renan thinks, is better suited than Judaism to evolve into a rational religion:

> Research that is reflexive, independent, rigorous, courageous, philosophical – in a word, the search for truth – seems to have been the heritage of that Indo-European race that has, from deep India to the northern extremities of the West and of the North, from the remotest centuries to modern times, sought to explain God, man and the world by a rational system, and left behind, like rungs to different levels (*echelonnées aux divers degrés*) of its history, philosophical creations that have always and everywhere been submitted to the laws of logical development. But to the Semitic race belong those firm and certain intuitions that have been first to free the divinity of its veils and, without reflection or reasoning, attained the most purified religious form that antiquity has known. ([1855] 1863, p. 3)

Later, in his famous *Life of Jesus*, Renan made an effort to rescue Christianity from its Hebraic roots and to show whatever is left as the product of the non-Semitic, Aryan genius. To collect data for this book (and obviously, to increase its credibility among his readers), Renan traveled to the Holy Land. He used his field work as the basis for describing Jesus as completely human, but also a human who rises radically above his oriental environment. Renan insisted that Jesus, a native resident of the ethnically mixed Galilee, was hardly a Semite ([1860] 1894, p. 83). Here, arguably, Jesus supersedes Christianity, which supersedes Judaism but remains marked by Semitism. More radical developments of this theme would later include the hugely popular *Foundations of the Nineteenth Century* (1899) by Houston Chamberlain, and in the following century the search for an "Aryan" Jesus would be a preoccupation of Nazi theologians (Heschel 2008). Those Europeans who were against the Jews began to use the term "anti-Semite." They were seldom interested in Arabs. Their reference to the Jews as Semites was meant mainly to underscore what they saw as the alien, oriental origin and character of the Jews in Europe.

Although among the traditionalist Ashkenazi Jewish majority, somewhat carelessly described as "East European" today, the issue of oriental origins was not particularly prominent, it did receive passionate discussion among the modernizing, "assimilated," largely German-speaking Jewry of Central and Western Europe and later of North America. Some thought of their oriental heritage as a burden to overcome. Personalities like the prewar German government minister, Walter Rathenau (1965, p. 90) and the philosopher Hannah Arendt (1992, p. 435), are known to have despised the "oriental" character of Europe's traditionalist "Eastern Jews" or *Ostjuden,* whose westward migration from the Russian Empire and Austrian Galicia (a province now straddling Poland and Ukraine) had brought their own progenitors to "the West" (which was then imagined as including today's Kaliningrad, Poznań, Wrocław, Prague, and Budapest).

But these anti-eastern sentiments often coexisted, within the same "western" communities, with proud self-identification as Semitic orientals, cousins of Arabs. Visible proof is still found in the hugely popular architectural device of decorating synagogues with Islamic elements such as horseshoe windows. The tallest minarets in the United States today are still those of the Plum Street Temple in Cincinnati, built in 1862 (Kalmar 2001).

One of the Jewish architects who adorned synagogues with Islamic features was Wilhelm Stiassny (1842–1910), who also played an active role as a politician in Vienna. Stiassny published his vision of an ideal city in a booklet called *The Construction of a Colony in the Holy Land or in One of Its Neighboring Countries* (Stiassny 1909). A "neighboring country" would do just as well as the Holy Land (where at the time the Ottoman government was of two minds about allowing Jewish settlement). That to Stiassny the Jewish home could also be somewhere else in the Orient is symptomatic of the Jewish identification with the Orient that was common (though far from universal) at the time. Some went as far as an important Prague rabbi, who saw the Zionist movement as leading a sort of anti-colonial revenge of the East on the West. As Aladar Deutsch wrote: "The Orient as the old sight of spiritually infused Semitism (*Semitentum*) will – recognizing the spiritual emptiness and cowardice of the Aryan so-called culture – force back the Aryan where he belongs" (n.d., p. 144).

This axiomatic equation of the Jews and the Orient was bolstered not only by orientalist scholarship and non-fiction, but also by all sorts of elite and popular art. From the early nineteenth century, orientalist painting was particularly fascinated by the *odalisque*, a classic reclining nude pictured wearing scant "oriental" attire. The young woman was often surrounded by lush draperies and ornate pipes and utensils for serving the oriental intoxicants, tobacco and coffee. Although the accouterments of the women and their rooms are unmistakably "Turkish" or Arab, the alluring harem inmate was often associated in the western imagination with the Jewish woman, seen as an oriental beauty (Ockman 1995, pp. 67–83). It was a fairly common cliché to refer to the Jewish woman's "oriental eyes," as did, with particular enthusiasm, Honoré de Balzac when describing his famous courtesan character, Esther (2006, p. 35).

Outside the harem genre, throughout the nineteenth century and beyond, among the most popular works of orientalist art were what was considered, often correctly, as true-to-life sketches of life in the Arab world, especially among the Bedouin nomads of the deserts. For the Bedouin, because of their lack of contact with westernized urban centers, were thought of as the purest Arabs—and the purest of Semites.

A romantic preoccupation with virile, horseback-riding, desert-dwelling, harem-owning chieftains eventually found its popular cinematic cliché in one of the first blockbusters of all time, *The Sheik*, starring Rudolph Valentino (1921). The hero, a tent-dwelling desert autocrat on cozy terms with the French colonizers in Northwest Africa, kidnaps and rapes an American woman, Lady Diana Mayo. She eventually falls in love with him. Once it is discovered that the sheik is actually of French stock, the couple marry without fear of miscegenation.

This imperialist kitsch-epic coincided with the establishment of Arab kingdoms in the Levant, freed of Ottoman suzerainty and ruled by Bedouin chieftains under British "protection." Saudi Arabia, Iraq, and Jordan were largely the result of a British plan to replace the Ottoman Empire with ethnically defined nations: Arab, Kurdish, and Armenian (the last two did not happen) as well as Jewish (Renton 2007).

The Postcolonial/Muslim Phase

The British encouragement of the Zionist project was codified in the Balfour Declaration of 1917, which committed the United Kingdom to the notion of a Jewish homeland in Palestine. In 1922, the promise was kept when the League of Nations entrusted Britain with a "Mandate" as a charter for ruling Palestine (including today's Israel, Palestinian Territories, and Jordan) in part as a way to organize the support of Jewish migrants and their institutions.

If we ask how the identification of the Jews with the Orient, which was for such a long time universal and unquestioned, became what Said called a "secret," then the success of the Zionist project is the answer.

By the middle of the twentieth century (but not before!), it was easy to think of the Jews as a western and not an eastern people. The notion of the "Judeo-Christian tradition" was invented. The genealogy of this representation of the Jews as a western and not (as was previously imagined) an eastern people plainly lies in the continuing struggle between Jews and Arabs over the land of the Bible. Contrary to what some early Zionists expected, the Arabs almost overwhelmingly rejected their project, including the discourse of racial kinship between them and the Jews. The Arabs understood (as did, to be fair, many Zionists as well) the Jewish settlers as Europeans exploiting the opportunity offered by western colonialism. In reality, and ironically, as Amnon Raz-Krakotzkin (2015) points out, the Zionists, many of whom saw themselves as exiles returning to the Orient, managed instead to make it possible to relocate the Jews, in the imagination of many, from an oriental to an occidental people.

As a result of the de-judaization of the imagined Orient, Said suggests that the Palestinians and the Arabs found themselves the last of the orientals (Said 1976). But was that really so? Or is it more that Said was observing part of a larger change within orientalism itself or perhaps, its very end? Could it be that, unbeknownst to Said, the West's image of the Muslim East was on the cusp of becoming something else, something other than the old orientalism? Is it possible that the Arabs, no more than the Jews, were becoming disassociated from the *old* tropes of the Orient, though in far less liberating ways than the Jews?

In hindsight, it appears that a new form of discourse about the Muslim world was already in an intensive course of development while Said was writing, though the rupture with the earlier orientalist episteme was not yet clear to him and his contemporaries. The range of the classic orientalist imagination may be summed up in three words as "bible, harem, empire." In the 1960s, the first two were already disappearing, leaving "empire" *the* burning issue.

Religious mythology had more or less lost its importance to generations no longer brought up on compulsory readings of Scripture. That connection between Jesus and his people to their place of origin mattered less, partly because Jesus and his people mattered less. But the increasing separation between the image of the Jew and of the Orient also had its effects on Christian representations of the Bible themselves. In the twentieth century, the convention of representing the Jews of the Bible as wearing Turkish turbans or Arab *kafiyyeh* all but disappeared (Kalmar 2005). Among the Ashkenazi Jews, too, orientalist self-identification ended. In the second half of the twentieth century, horseshoe windows or minarets on synagogues became almost unthinkable.

"Harem" disappeared almost entirely from the contemporary image of the Arab and Muslim world as well, with the feminine orientalist trope changing from the semi-clad harem girl to the fully veiled personage, often viewed as made to repress or repressing her sexual desire. The harem inmate of orientalist art was a visual relative of the Beautiful Jewess, mentioned earlier. It is unusual, however, and this in spite of ultra-Orthodox women also covering and even shaving their hair, to hear Arab women discussed today as belonging to the same "type" as female Jews. This disappearance of the Jew was matched by the *appearance* of the Muslim.

In Said's *Orientalism*, the nemesis of the West is much more an Arab than an Islamic Orient. The orientalist "knowledge" that, in Said's critique, produced the "Orient" was, as he detailed it, knowledge more about Arab psychology and ethnology than about the religion of Islam. He seemed to be just as insensitive to the Islamic undercurrent of Arab anti-colonialism as were most of the Cold War analysts, who were obsessed with Arab nationalism and its difficult alliance with the Soviet Union. (Perhaps he realized this when three years later he named religion and not nation as the target of western prejudice in *Covering Islam* [Said 1981].)

At first sight the statement that the "Muslim" appears only in the current postcolonial period may seem surprising. After all, even if Jews were also targeted by orientalism, it is undeniable that its main target for centuries has been adherents of Islam. However, just like the so-called "Mahometans" of orientalist literature, metonymically described as "Turks," were different from the "Mohammedans" who were in the colonial period discussed as "Arabs," the present-day figure of the "Muslim" is, in spite of formal and genealogical continuity with the earlier figures, new, and sometimes radically so.

The present-day image of the Muslim, as drawn by Islamophobes (who unfortunately provide the most dynamic source for new representations of Muslims today), is best characterized not by "bible, harem, empire," but by two other words, "terrorism" and "migration." Both are connected to older stereotypes of Muslim cruelty and the Muslim desire to invade, destroy, and rule the Christian West, but the connection is rather subterranean; on the surface at least, and in the consciousness of most Islamophobes, Muslim terrorism and migration are a purely contemporary condition and do not recall the obscurities of deep history.

If it was the movement to settle Jews in Palestine that first led to the disconnection between the western world's predominant representations of Jews and of Muslims, it was the September, 2001 terrorist destruction of the World Trade Center in New York that sealed it. During the "migrant crisis" of Europe that began in 2015, it is true, it became almost obligatory among critics of anti-Muslim and anti-migrant measures to compare what was happening now to Muslims to what had been happening to Jews just before Hitler and under the Nazis. On the other side of the issue, the Jewish topic did not disappear either. Among the many conspiratorial canards was one that saw the Hungarian-American-Jewish investor, George Soros, as financing the Muslim "intrusion" (Žižek 2017). The tropes used in such discussions were certainly related to those of the past: Soros seems to have taken the place of Rothschild in the notorious forgery from 1903, the *Protocols of the Elders of Zion* (Ben-Itto 2005). But they were denuded of any content that we might call orientalist, unless we were willing to lose completely the geographic and racial hues of the orientalist notion of the Semite, which saw Jews and Arabs as relatives from the East.

Antisemitism in the contemporary world has much more to do with hostility to Israel, including "anti-Zionism," and whatever one may say about it, such hostility does not normally stress the oriental provenance of the Jews. On the contrary, it is often denied.

Conclusion

The explosion of Islamophobia in Europe and America has often brought Muslims and Jews together, mindful not of orientalism's past, but of the history of the Jews as a people persecuted in the western world before it included many Arabs or Muslims, and often persecuted in similar ways (including obstacles to migration). Yet disagreement about Israel means that, at the same time, some Muslims can be counted among the most violent antisemites, and some Jews among the worst Islamophobes.

This deplorable situation may hopefully be combatted, at least to some extent, by scholars pointing out that many of the tropes of Islamophobic language and imagery resemble earlier antisemitic tropes. That the hatred of Jews and the hatred of Muslims stem from the same orientalist source may serve as a warning to Jews and Muslims alike not to be seduced by intolerance. It may help them to recognize their common vulnerability and therefore their common humanity. To understand the connection between antisemitism and orientalism is therefore both a scholarly and a moral imperative. Nevertheless, orientalism, for reasons I have discussed, seems to have lost much of its utility for understanding antisemitism in the purely contemporary context.

References

Akbari, Suzanne Conklin. 2005. "Placing the Jews in Late Medieval English Literature." In Kalmar and Penslar 2005, 32–50.
Arendt, Hannah. 1992. *Hannah Arendt/Karl Jaspers Correspondence, 1926–1969.* New York: Harcourt Brace Jovanovich.
Balzac, Honoré de. 2006. *Scenes from a Courtesan's Life.* Gloucester: Dodo Press.
Ben-Itto, Hadassa. 2005. *The Lie That Wouldn't Die: The Protocols of the Elders of Zion.* London: Vallentine Mitchell.
Bloom, Harold. 2005. *Jesus and Yahweh: The Names Divine.* New York: Riverhead Books.

Deutsch, Aladar. n.d. Untitled Manuscript. Jewish Museum of Prague. Archives. File no. 60295.
Dohm, Christian Wilhelm. 1957. *Concerning the Amelioration of the Civil Status of the Jews*. Cincinnati: Hebrew Union College-Jewish Institute of Religion.
Disraeli, Benjamin. (1847) 1904. *Tancred*. London: R. Brimley.
Heschel, Susannah. 2008. *The Aryan Jesus: Christian Theologians and the Bible in Nazi Germany*. Princeton: Princeton University Press.
Kalmar, Ivan. 2001. "Moorish Style: Orientalism, the Jews, and Synagogue Architecture." *Jewish Social Studies: History, Culture and Society* 7 (3): 68–100.
Kalmar, Ivan. 2005. "Jesus Did Not Wear a Turban: Orientalism, the Jews, and Christian Art." In Kalmar and Penslar 2005, 3–31.
Kalmar, Ivan. 2012. *Early Orientalism: Imagined Islam and the Notion of Sublime Power*. London: Routledge.
Kalmar, Ivan. 2016. "Orientalism." In *Encyclopedia of Islam and the Muslim World*, edited by Richard Martin. New York: Macmillan Reference USA.
Kalmar, Ivan, and Derek Penslar, eds. 2005. *Orientalism and the Jews*. Lebanon: University Press of New England.
Lowth, Robert. (1787) 1847. *Lectures on the Sacred Poetry of the Hebrews*. 3rd ed. London: S. Chadwick.
Ockman, Carol. 1995. *Ingres's Eroticized Bodies: Retracing the Serpentine Line*. New Haven: Yale University Press.
Rathenau, Walter. 1965. *Schriften*. Edited by Arnold Harttung et al. Berlin: Berlin Verlag.
Raz-Krakotzkin, Amnon. 2015. "Secularism, The Christian Ambivalence Toward the Jews, and the Notion of Exile." In *Secularism in Question: Jews and Judaism in Modern Times*, edited by A. Joskowitz and E. B Katz, 276–98. Philadelphia: University of Pennsylvania Press.
Renan, Ernest. (1855) 1863. *Histoire générale et système comparé des langues sémitiques: 1. ptie. Histoire générale des langues sémitiques*. 4th ed. Paris: Lévy.
Renan, Ernest. (1860) 1894. *The Life of Jesus*. London: K. Paul.
Renan, Ernest, and Shlomo Sand. 2010. *On the Nation and the "Jewish People."* London: Verso.
Renton, James. 2007. "Changing Languages of Empire and the Orient: Britain and the Invention of the Middle East, 1917–1918." *The Historical Journal* 50 (3): 645–67.
Renton, James, and Ben Gidley. 2017. "Introduction: The Shared Story of Europe's Ideas of the Muslim and the Jew--A Diachronic Framework." In Renton and Gidley, 1–21.
Said, Edward. 1976. "Arabs, Islam and the Dogmas of the West." *New York Times*. October 31. https://www.nytimes.com/1976/10/31/archives/arabs-islam-and-the-dogmas-of-the-west-arabs.html.
Said, Edward. 1978. *Orientalism*. New York: Vintage Books.
Said, Edward. 1981. *Covering Islam: How the Media and the Experts Determine How We See the Rest of the World*. New York: Pantheon Books.
Schultens, Albert. 1729. *Oratio de linguæ Arabicæ antiquissima origine, intima ac sororia cum lingua Hebræa affinitate, nullisque seculis præflorata puritate: habita quum fasces academicos iterum deponeret*. Frankfurt a/M: Willem Coulon.

Schwab, Raymond. 1984. *The Oriental Renaissance: Europe's Rediscovery of India and the East, 1680–1880*. New York: Columbia University Press.

Shaffer, Emily S. 1980. *"Kubla Khan" and "The Fall of Jerusalem:" The Mythological School in Biblical Criticism and Secular Literature, 1770–1880*. Cambridge: Cambridge University Press.

Spence, Joseph. 1727. *An Essay on Pope's Odyssey, in Which Some Particular Beauties and Blemishes of That Work Are Considered*. London: Wilmot.

Sternhell, Zeev. 2016. "The Americans Simply Don't Care About Israel and the Palestinians." *Haaretz online*, August 22. http://www.haaretz.com/opinion/. premium-1.738045.

Stiassny, Wilhelm. 1909. *Anlage einer Kolonie in Heiligen Lande oder in einem seiner Nebenländer*. Vienna: Verlag des Jüdischen Kolonisations-Vereines.

Žižek, S. 2017. Interview on *Channel 4 News* (UK), May 16. https://www.facebook.com/Channel4News/videos/10154845916691939/.

CHAPTER 16

Philosemitism

Maurice Samuels

INTRODUCTION

In an oft-cited article, Salo Baron (1928) argued against what he termed the "lachrymose" conception of Jewish history, the deeply implanted notion that the European Jewish experience prior to emancipation consisted of unremitting persecution and suffering. According to Baron, while European Jews were occasionally the victims of horrific violence, they also enjoyed special privileges that enabled their communities to thrive and their populations to increase at many times the rate of non-Jews or of Jews in other parts of the world. For Baron, an accurate view of the Jewish experience must reckon with not only the negative but also the positive. It must account for the many ways in which non-Jews welcomed Jews and treated them well.

Antisemitism has been extensively analyzed. Yet, Baron's influence notwithstanding, philosemitism—commonly understood as the defense, love, or admiration of Jews and Judaism—has received only minimal scholarly attention. This is true not only for the pre-emancipation period, as Baron noted, but also for the modern period, when Jews gained rights and entered the cultural mainstream. Even scholars who have praised emancipation have very seldom analyzed what made it possible: until recently, they have paid comparatively scant attention to the ideologies that led to the granting of citizenship to the Jews or that promoted Jewish welfare. The primary reason for this lacuna is not hard to see. Shortly after the publication of Baron's article, the great calamity that befell European Jewry made antisemitism a far more urgent topic than its seeming opposite.

M. Samuels (✉)
Yale University, New Haven, CT, USA
e-mail: maurice.samuels@yale.edu

And yet, the study of philosemitism is essential not just for gaining a more balanced view of Jewish history, but also for understanding antisemitism itself. This is true for at least four reasons. First, philosemitism and antisemitism are linked dialectically. In the eighteenth century, architects of emancipation based their arguments for granting Jews rights, at least in part, on the perceived injustice of anti-Jewish persecution. The recognition of the unfair way that Jews had been treated historically contributed to calls for equality. In the late nineteenth century, the pendulum swung back in the other direction: the new political antisemites based their case against the Jews on what they perceived as the excessive philosemitism of the modern liberal state (e.g., Drumont ([1886] 1994, p. v), who attacked the way philosemitism of the French revolutionary tradition supposedly led to a Jewish "takeover" of France). Likewise, racist antisemitism, which sought to define Jewishness as a biological trait, arguably developed in response to efforts by reformers to liberate Jews from the multiple restrictions that kept them physically apart in the early modern period: it was only once Jews began to resemble non-Jews in their manner of living and dress that it became necessary to locate Jewish difference as a series of bodily signs. In other words, animus and openness to the Jews each provoke the other. To attempt to understand the development of antisemitism without understanding philosemitism is like listening to only one side of a conversation.

Second, as most scholars now acknowledge, antisemitism and philosemitism are not opposites, but rather partake of a similar process of generalization and stereotyping. As the old joke goes: "What is a philosemite? An antisemite who likes Jews." This does not mean that philosemites are always just antisemites in disguise, but rather that antisemites and philosemites both treat the Jews as "other." Both see the Jews as a distinct people with a set of identifiable traits that are either coded positively or negatively. Both project fantasies of "the Jew," which they then use as a kind of mirror to form their own sense of identity (Judaken 2006, p. 20). Studying philosemitism alongside antisemitism provides us with a different angle to view how stereotyping works.

Sometimes, however, philosemitism really does conceal antisemitism, and this represents a third reason to study the two together. Praise for Jewish intelligence, for example, frequently accompanies animosity or envy. Sometimes certain groups of Jews will be praised in order to castigate others. One clear example of this dynamic is the gender dichotomy that runs through so much nineteenth-century European literature: male Jews are denounced as ugly and greedy while female Jews are praised for their beauty and generosity (Valman 2007; Samuels 2006). The philosemitism that consists of an idealization of the Jewish woman goes hand-in-hand with an antisemitic demonization of the Jewish man. They are two sides of the same coin and ultimately spring from the same complex of disturbing fantasms, which benefit from being analyzed together as a single entity.

Fourth, any study of antisemitism should ideally point to ways of moving beyond it. And although philosemitism may share certain philosophical assumptions and psychic processes with antisemitism, it can also offer a real alternative to hatred. Philosemitism, it must be emphasized, has often led to open and welcoming attitudes toward Jews. And these moments of openness are certainly worth our attention. But can we ever come to terms with hatred, if we fail to consider the mechanism of its refusal? Rather than ignore philosemitism as a marginal phenomenon, or denounce it because it can sometimes be problematic, we should instead attempt to understand what makes some people come to love or admire the Jews, and probe the historical, political, sociological, and psychological basis for such attitudes.

VICISSITUDES OF A CONCEPT

The term "philosemitism" (*Philosemitismus*) is a neologism coined in 1880 in Germany by the new group of political "antisemites"—another neologism popularized in 1879 by Wilhelm Marr—in order to mock and demonize their opponents (Karp and Sutcliffe 2011, p. 1).[1] It contains the Greek word "philo," meaning "love," linked to "semite," a term derived from the then-new field of historical linguistics to refer to people who spoke one of the ancient languages of the Middle East, mainly Jews. As Jonathan Karp and Adam Sutcliffe point out, those accused of being philosemites in the late nineteenth century almost always strove to disassociate themselves from the label, insisting that their view of the Jews was in fact neutral and untainted by positive bias (2011, p. 1).

But while the term philosemitism has been in circulation since the end of the nineteenth century, scholars have begun to theorize it only in recent years. As we have seen, studies of antisemitism tended to overshadow studies of philosemitism in the decades following World War II. The increasing interest in philosemitism as a concept beginning in the 1980s can perhaps be traced to the decline of antisemitism at that time and to the entry of Jews into the cultural mainstream in many Western contexts (especially the United States, the United Kingdom, and France).[2] Still, the number of theoretical studies devoted to philosemitism is miniscule compared to the attention that continues to be devoted to antisemitism. By "theoretical studies," I am referring to efforts to define and explain the concept of philosemitism, rather than to descriptions of what might be called "philosemitism in action," such as accounts of efforts to rescue Jews during the Holocaust. To my knowledge, there are only a handful of book-length theoretical studies of philosemitism in English—all of which I mention here—and very few that examine it outside a single national context.

---

[1] They cite Kinzig (1994), L. Fischer (2007), and Zimmermann (1987, pp. 118–32).

[2] According to the Commission nationale consultative des droits de l'homme, between 1995 and 1999 there were fewer than 100 antisemitic acts committed in France, the country with the highest level of antisemitic violence. In 2000 alone there were 743 acts and the number has stayed high since.

Philosemitism poses a number of questions for scholars. These include questions of categorization: what should be considered philosemitism? Are all acts of generosity toward Jews philosemitic? What if someone does not harbor positive feelings toward Jews but acts out of a general spirit of justice? Must philosemitism always involve some form of idealization of the Jew? In a related manner, some scholars have questioned whether simply opposing antisemitism constitutes philosemitism. Jonathan Judaken, for instance, prefers the label "anti-antisemitism" to describe intellectuals who intervene on behalf of Jews in contexts where they are under threat but who do not necessarily "love" the Jews (2006, pp. 19–20). As Judaken recognizes, however, anti-antisemitism is itself not free of biases and often involves its own "imaginary and symbolic idealization of 'the Jew'" similar to that found in philosemitism. Alan Edelstein's approach is helpful in this regard: he views different forms of philosemitism on a spectrum ranging from "strong" to "weak." At the "strong" end, he places philosemites who express an intense devotion to, or historical identification with, Jews and Judaism. On the "weak" end, he places those who are merely sympathetic to Jews and includes anti-antisemites in this category (1982, p. 12). Edelstein also notes that philosemitism must be directed against the Jews as a group rather than toward individual Jews.

Most theorists of philosemitism confront the basic question: is it good or bad for the Jews? Is philosemitism the opposite of antisemitism or is it somehow equivalent to it? Edelstein, for example, seeks to defend philosemitism against charges that it participates in harmful ethnic stereotyping by maintaining that some stereotyping can have beneficial consequences. He goes so far as to argue that it was philosemitic attitudes, particularly within Church teachings, that enabled the Jews to survive during the Middle Ages (1982, p. 5). In a similar manner, Gertrude Himmelfarb heaps praise on the philosemitic strain within English religious and political thought, which she argues reflects "the principles and policies that have made modern England a model of liberality and civility" (2011, p. 4). Himmelfarb explicitly conceives her book as a response to Baron's call to counter the lachrymose view of Jewish history, and argues that it is important to underline the long tradition of positive discourse on Jews in England in order to resist the resurgence of antisemitism that began around 2000. While both of these works are interesting and erudite, they betray a defensive/apologetic posture in their treatment of philosemitism that at times veers from analysis into celebration of the philosemitic thinkers they study.

On the flip side, Frank Stern's study of West German philosemitism in the post-War era betrays a deep suspicion of positive discourse on Jews, which he sees as imbued with, if not camouflage for, a deep, underlying antisemitism (1991; cf. Karp and Sutcliffe 2011, p. 5). Likewise, in their edited volume of essays, *Antisemitism and Philosemitism in the Twentieth and Twenty-First Centuries*, Phyllis Lassner and Lara Trubowitz set out to emphasize the "intersections between philosemitism and antisemitism in twentieth and twenty-first-century literature and culture." Their introduction calls attention specifically to "new, often disturbing meanings and uses of philosemitism" and emphasizes the ways in which "antisemitism disguises itself as philosemitism," constituting a danger "more insidious than a transparent antisemitism dependent on and recognizable as age-old stereotypes" (2008, pp. 7–8; see Karp and Sutcliffe 2011, p. 5). Philosemitism emerges from their account as a greater threat than antisemitism, which seems to me to be an overly pessimistic view of the phenomenon. While the essays in their volume offer highly valuable and for the most part highly nuanced reflections on the phenomenon in question, their introduction is typical of the deep suspicion that surrounds philosemitism in most academic discourse.

It should be noted that certain scholars have questioned whether philosemitism should be studied as a distinct phenomenon at all. Bryan Cheyette, for example, rejects the opposition between anti- and philosemitism, preferring instead to use the term "allosemitism," a term he borrows from Polish-Jewish writer Artur Sandauer (1985), to refer to a racializing typology that is neither wholly positive nor negative (Cheyette 1993, p. 8). For Cheyette, it is more useful to speak of a "semitic discourse" that contains within it a fundamental ambivalence toward Jews. Recognizing this ambivalence allows us to see that admiration and love for Jews very often tap into the same unconscious fantasies as hate. The sociologist Zygmunt Bauman also adopts Sandauer's term "allosemitism," derived from the Greek word meaning "other," to denote the setting of the Jews apart as a people. According to Bauman: "'Allosemitism' is essentially non-committal [...] it does not unambiguously determine either hatred or love of Jews, but contains the seeds of both, and assures that whichever of the two appears, is intense and extreme" (1998, p. 143). The problem with such an approach, in my view, is that it fails to explain the very real differences between positive and negative discourse on Jews. It does not allow us to account for the specific reasons that philosemitism develops—often quite different from those that lead to antisemitism—or to comprehend the vastly different effects that philosemitism and antisemitism generate.

Jonathan Karp and Adam Sutcliffe (2011) attempt to move beyond these debates. Rather than praising or faulting individual instances of philosemitism, or seeing positive and negative discourse as essentially the same, Karp and Sutcliffe call for an approach that analyzes the larger significance of philosemitic attitudes in different historical contexts: "Our aim should not be to expose 'false' or self-interested philosemites, or to identify 'true' ones, but rather to comprehend the significance and function of positive perceptions of Jews and Judaism within their broader intellectual frameworks" (p. 5). Their introduction and the essays in their volume offer a detailed historical account of the vicissitudes of philosemitism from Greek and Roman antiquity to the present day, revealing the many ways that philosemitic attitudes are "broad, complex, and worthy of attention" (p. 6).

While I would argue that individual instances of disturbing or even antisemitic philosemitism do certainly exist and deserve to be exposed, I generally agree with the call by Karp and Sutcliffe to focus on the "significance and function" of philosemitism both for philosemites and for the Jews themselves. In other words, we need to pay attention to the "cultural work" that expressions of philosemitism perform at different points in history and in different national environments (see Tompkins 1985, p. xi). We need to investigate how defense, love, and admiration of Jews and Judaism take shape within specific discursive contexts, are determined by a range of social factors, and serve as vehicles for specific political agendas. We also need to see Jews less as passive objects of benevolence than as active agents who frequently court defenders in order to advance their own agendas.

Utility of the Concept

As we have seen, the concept of philosemitism is very often useful for understanding the nature and development of antisemitism. Following David Nirenberg's *Anti-Judaism: The Western Tradition*, however, we may also see it as useful for understanding the development of key political ideologies and major philosophical systems. For if, as Nirenberg maintains, antisemitism (or anti-Judaism) has been central to the evolution of critical thought in the West, so too has philosemitism (2013, p. 5). To begin with the ancient world, attention to positive as well as negative discourse on Jews provides a more nuanced understanding of early Christianity. Scholars have recently corrected the overly simplistic view that traces the source of Christian hatred of Jews to the writing of Saint Paul (Boyarin 1994; see Nirenberg 2013, p. 60). On the one hand, Paul is responsible for the supersessionist teaching that sees Christianity as a replacement of Judaism, and that attempts to overcome the supposed literalism and tribalism of Judaism by instituting a spiritual and universalist creed that no longer ties salvation to the law or to a particular group. On the other hand, Paul always saw himself as a Jew and thought that salvation would come through the Jews. Paul said there is "neither Jew nor Greek," often taken to imply that Jewish ethnic distinctions must be overcome, but also said: "And if you are Christ's, then you are Abraham's offspring, heirs according to promise" (Gal. 3:29). Moreover, despite his vaunted universalism, Paul did not renounce his belonging to a particular people (Marty 2003, p. 74): "I myself am an Israelite, a descendant of Abraham, a member of the tribe of Benjamin," he wrote in the Epistle to the Romans (2:1). Exploring the implications of this philosemitic strain within Pauline theology reveals a new level of complexity not only in the Christian view of Jews and Judaism, but also in the nature of key Christian concepts, such as universalism.

Philosemitism also allows us to understand the development of economic history in a new way. As Robert Chazan and others have noted, Jews filled a special niche in the medieval economy by lending money at interest, which the Church forbid Christians to do. Although this economic role opened Jews to expressions of violent resentment, it also caused them to be viewed as beneficial for economic growth (Chazan 2011, p. 30). Scholars like Jonathan Karp (2008, p. 4) have shown that philosemites in the early modern period often cast their defenses of the Jews in utilitarian terms: the Jews should be welcomed—or welcomed back to the communities that had formerly expelled them—because they could promote trade and stimulate industry (Israel 1989). Jews became a symbol for a certain way of thinking about commerce, and philosemitism played a key role in the way that economic life was understood and theorized during the early modern period (Karp 2008, p. 2; Trivellato 2019).

In the modern period, philosemitism became central to the development of political as well as economic ideologies. While it has long been recognized that the French Revolution's emancipation of the Jews represents a watershed moment in Jewish history, mainstream scholars have mostly treated this event as a relatively minor episode in the tumultuous history of the Revolution. Actually, most histories of the Revolution don't even mention Jewish emancipation at all. Given the exceedingly small number of people affected by it (there were only about 30-40,000 Jews out of a total French population of 25 million at the time of the Revolution), it is not hard to see why. And yet, as Ronald Schechter (2003) has shown, the Revolution's Constituent Assembly took up the question of whether or not the Jews deserved citizenship on something like thirty separate occasions—and this at a time when they faced seemingly more pressing concerns, including famine, war, and the complete reorganization of the state—because they felt that something momentous was at stake.

For Schechter, the Jews were "good to think" with. In the years leading up to the Revolution, they provided Enlightenment philosophers with a perfect test-case for the powers of what they termed "regeneration," the transformation of the individual through reason. If even this most "backward" of Europe's peoples could be improved by treating them fairly, then anybody could. During the Revolution, according to Schechter, the meaning embodied by the Jews expanded: Jews became "good to think" about "what a citizen was, what a nation was, and under what conditions such entities might come into existence" (2003, p. 67; Sutcliffe 2003). In other words, debates over philosemitism—the desire to help the Jews—became one of the primary ways that the revolutionaries wrestled with the implications of the new political model they were in the process of creating. As I have argued elsewhere, the decision to treat the Jews fairly and include them within the new nation allowed the revolutionaries to define the contours of a new notion of political universalism: if even a group as different as the Jews could become citizens without restrictions, then French universalism was truly universal. It was the difference of the Jews, their position on the literal and figurative margins of the nation, that made them so central to the French revolutionary project (Samuels 2016). And philosemitism continued to play this function throughout the nineteenth century in other national contexts, allowing modern liberal states to define their difference from the repressive regimes they replaced and to express new notions of liberty, equality, and fraternity.

In the twentieth century, and particularly after WWII, philosemitism enabled a different set of identities and affiliations. In countries that saw some or all of their Jewish population destroyed by the Holocaust, expressions of defense, love, and admiration of Jews often became a way of signaling an opposition to fascism. This was certainly the case in West Germany, although, as Frank Stern (1991) illustrates, the situation was a complex one. For decades following the War, knowledge about the Jewish genocide was repressed. Many Germans managed to sweep their Nazi past under the rug and Jewish survivors did not always find a responsive audience when they were able to discuss their suffering. The situation in East Germany, the USSR, Poland, and other Soviet-Bloc countries was still more extreme, as official propaganda minimized or ignored Jewish victimhood for decades.

The late 1960s represent a turning point in thinking about Jews for the countries of Western Europe. This is especially true for France, the only European country with a larger Jewish population today than before the War thanks to the massive influx of Jews from North Africa following decolonization in the 1950s and 60s. According to Jean-Paul Sartre and other contemporary observers, the French public did not want to hear about the Holocaust in the immediate post-War years, as Charles De Gaulle and other leaders attempted to forge national cohesion around a narrative of shared suffering and resistance under Nazi Occupation (Sartre 1965, p. 71). Although scholars have recently begun to question this "myth of silence," there is no denying that there was far more discussion of the Holocaust in France after the 1960s than before (Azouvi 2012). Indeed, the historian Henry Rousso (1987) has coined a term—the "Vichy Syndrome"—to refer to the sympathetic French obsession with the War, and especially with Jewish suffering, that began in the last decades of the twentieth century and continues to this day.

During the counter-cultural revolts in 1968, philosemitism—particularly identification with the suffering of the Holocaust—took on a distinctly political cast. The slogan "We are all German Jews!" became a rallying cry for a young French generation wishing to express solidarity with the marginalized and oppressed. But as some scholars would later claim, the slogan generalized and banalized Jewish suffering. To the philosopher Alain Finkielkraut (2003, p. 21), "We are all German Jews!" turned the Holocaust into a fashionable symbol that could be appropriated by any group claiming victim status (Hammerschlag 2010, p. 5). In the last several decades, the French government has enshrined the notion of Jewish victimhood in French law not only by criminalizing Holocaust denial but also by making Holocaust education mandatory in public schools. Despite the good intentions of French authorities, the end results of such actions have not been all positive for the Jews. According to many observers, the efforts at Holocaust sacralization have often backfired, leading to a destructive competition among victims, as French citizens of North African descent struggle to get equal recognition for the crimes of colonization and people of African heritage militate to commemorate slavery (on "competition among victims," see Dean 2010). In some cases, Holocaust instruction has also inspired a backlash against Jews, who are frequently perceived as receiving special—philosemitic—treatment from the state. The popularity of the antisemitic comedian Dieudonné, whose most outrageous routines are based on a perverse mockery of the Holocaust, testifies to the resentment created by the government's well-meaning policies.

Studying philosemitism also provides an interesting perspective on Eastern European cultural politics after the fall of Communism in 1989. Poland now boasts a thriving tourist industry based on Holocaust commemoration. Tour companies advertise bus trips to Auschwitz and other sites of mass murder. Some Poles have also begun to romanticize the Jewish life that was destroyed by the War. The Kazimierz neighborhood of Krakow has become a kind of Jewish theme-park, with old sites of Jewish life, such as synagogues and *mikvas*, converted into trendy restaurants and boutiques (Lehrer 2013). Small towns that were once majority Jewish have begun to commemorate their former residents. Philosemitism serves as a vehicle for the expression of political and cultural ideologies tied both to nostalgia for a multi-ethnic past and a vision of a more cosmopolitan, Europe-oriented future. Of course, one could certainly argue that such expressions of philosemitism became possible in Poland only once there were very few actual, living Jews. It should be pointed out, however, that Polish intellectuals have reacted to this new philosemitism in complex and interesting ways, and that it has also produced well-regarded, large-scale projects like the POLIN Museum of the History of Polish Jews in Warsaw.

It should also be pointed out that the United States has seen its share of controversial forms of philosemitism. Foremost among these is the fervent Zionism of many American evangelical Christians (Hummel 2019), which the Israeli government has actively fostered since the 1950s. Evangelical Zionism has provided a boost to the Israeli tourism industry and is often seen as having more of an impact on American foreign policy than Jewish advocacy groups such as AIPAC. But as Yaakov Ariel (2011) has illustrated, evangelical Zionism often stems from apocalyptic visions involving Jewish conversion at the end of days. Evangelical support for Jews and Israel often accompanies an eschatological vision that many find deeply antisemitic. As Jonathan Freedman writes of the enormously popular evangelical Zionist *Left Behind* series of books, which combines apocalyptic theology and science fiction, "this is a philosemitism of which Jews might wish to be wary" (2008, p. 156).

Directions for Future Research

More work needs to be done to explore the place of philosemitism outside "the West." Not a single author in either of the two major recent collections of essays about philosemitism (Lassner and Trubowitz; Karp and Sutcliffe) treats a subject that is not European or American. We know that philosemitism, like antisemitism, can exist in countries with no or very few Jews, such as Japan (Golub 1992, p. 3, cited in Judaken 2008, p. 29). But, aside from a handful of studies (e.g., Menocal 2002) glorifying the openness to Jews in Al-Andalus, i.e., medieval Muslim Spain, only very recently have scholars begun to probe the significance of philosemitism in the Muslim world, especially the contemporary Muslim world (e.g., Katz 2015). This lacuna is especially significant given that the focus of antisemitism studies has shifted in the past decade to the Middle East (e.g., Taguieff 2002; Wistrich 2010; Rosenfeld 2019).

We have seen how the peculiar place occupied by Jews in Christian theology has led to expressions of both antisemitism and philosemitism through the ages. Has the place of Jews within Islamic theology produced an analogous type of ambivalence? What specific features of Islam enabled co-existence between Muslims and Jews for centuries? Some scholars of antisemitism in the Muslim world have focused on the second-class "dhimmi" status accorded to Jews (and Christians), but this does not exhaust or explain the complexity of Muslim-Jewish relations.

More work needs to be done to compare philosemitism to analogous forms of love or admiration for other minority groups. How does the fascination with Jews in contemporary Poland, for example, compare to the romanticization of Native American culture in the United States? Or to the admiring appropriation of aspects of African American culture? Is love for Jews a special case because of the unique place of Jews in Christian and Muslim theology? Or is the process of idealizing the other the same in these different cases?

More work also needs to be done to explore the relation of philosemitism to what scholars have labeled the "new antisemitism," which is mainly anti-Zionist in focus. One avenue of research might interrogate the popular form of anti-Zionism often referred to as "diasporism," the celebration of Jewish life and accomplishments outside of Israel, which is then held up as a moral alternative to existence within the Jewish state. Diasporism glorifies the contributions of Jewish thinkers like Marx, Freud, and Kafka and seeks to explain their extraordinary intellectual ferment as a function of their diasporic culture, praising the same aspects of Jewish identity that the old type of antisemites long reviled, such as rootlessness, cosmopolitanism, and a resistance to nationalism (Boyarin and Boyarin 2002; Butler 2012; Traverso 2016). While there is nothing wrong with the idealization of qualities that made diaspora Jews—especially European Jews in the nineteenth and twentieth centuries—so intellectually productive, this discourse can become problematic when it is used to denigrate a different set of Jews who supposedly fail to embody these qualities. By praising positive forms of Jewishness in order to castigate their opposite, diasporism risks engaging in what we have identified as a classic gesture of philosemitic discourse that Bruno Chaouat has labeled "Jew-splitting" (2016, p. xix, and, on Judith Butler especially, pp. 206–22). Like those nineteenth-century philosemites who fetishized the Jewish woman the better to demonize the Jewish man, this "new philosemitism" can serve as a cover for attitudes that are arguably antisemitic.

At least some forms of diasporism seem to me to constitute what I would call a "new philosemitism" analogous to the "new antisemitism." One example of what I take to be a problematic "new philosemitism" can be found in the writing of the French philosopher Alain Badiou (2011, p. 230), who praises Jews throughout history who have denied or critiqued their Jewish identity (according to him, Spinoza, Marx, and Freud), and especially those contemporary Jews who explicitly disavow their affiliation not just with Zionism, but with the trilogy of values he derisively lumps under the acronym SIT for Shoah-Israel-Tradition (cf. Hammerschlag 2010, pp. 261–67). Badiou considers Jews who cling to these values—which, it should be pointed out, form the basis of most forms of modern Jewish identity—traitors to the universalist values that he defines as the true essence of Jewishness. The State of Israel thus becomes, as Badiou puts it, "the country in which there are the fewest Jews" (2011, p. 167).[3] Note that Badiou explicitly casts himself as a philosemite who wants to save the Jews from themselves (2011, p. 170). To be clear, I am not suggesting that all diasporists are guilty of demonizing Israeli Jews—indeed, some of those who most idealized diasporic Judaism like Maurice Blanchot ([1969] 1993), who was perhaps the originator of this philosemitic strain of thought in contemporary critical theory, were not anti-Zionist at all.[4] Nor am I suggesting that all thinkers who oppose Zionism are antisemitic. Rather, I am arguing that just as more research is necessary to understand the relationship of anti-Zionism to antisemitism, so too should we probe instances when the "new philosemitism" might contain the seeds of something more sinister.

Scholars like Karp and Sutcliffe have argued that we should put aside value judgments when studying philosemitism, focusing instead on its "significance and function" in different contexts. But while I am sympathetic to their call for examining philosemitism objectively and with historical precision, I want to suggest by way of conclusion that perhaps a bit of judgment may in fact be beneficial for understanding philosemitism's "significance and function." Even if our goal as scholars should be to understand rather than praise or condemn, evaluating both the positive and negative effects of philosemitism can only further our efforts to shed light on this very complex phenomenon.

---

[3] This is the title of the first chapter of Alain Badiou's "Uses of the Word 'Jew.'"
[4] Blanchot describes the "vocation" of the Jews as exile, but he was not an anti-Zionist.

References

Ariel, Yaakov. 2011. "'It's All in the Bible:' Evangelical Christians, Biblical Literalism, and Philosemitism in Our Times." In Karp and Sutcliffe 2011, 257–85.

Azouvi, François. 2012. *Le Mythe du grand silence*. Paris: Fayard.

Badiou, Alain. 2011. "Uses of the Word 'Jew.'" In *Polemics*, translated by Steve Corcoran, 157–256. London: Verso.

Baron, Salo W. 1928. "Ghetto and Emancipation: Shall We Revise the Traditional View?" *Menorah Journal* 14 (6) (June): 515–26.

Bauman, Zygmunt. 1998. "Allosemitism: Premodern, Modern, Postmodern." In *Modernity, Culture and the Jew*, edited by Bryan Cheyette and Laura Marcus. Stanford: Stanford University Press.

Blanchot, Maurice. (1969) 1993. *The Infinite Conversation*. Translated by Susan Hanson. Minneapolis: University of Minnesota Press.

Boyarin, Daniel. 1994. *A Radical Jew: Paul and the Politics of Identity*. Berkeley: University of California Press.

Boyarin, Jonathan, and Daniel Boyarin. 2002. *Powers of Diaspora: Two Essays on the Relevance of Jewish Culture*. Minneapolis: University of Minnesota Press.

Butler, Judith. 2012. *Parting Ways: Jewishness and the Critique of Zionism*. New York: Columbia University Press.

Chaouat, Bruno. 2016. *Is Theory Good for the Jews?* Liverpool: Liverpool University Press.

Chazan, Robert. 2011. "Philosemitic Tendencies in Medieval Western Christendom." In Karp and Sutcliffe 2011, 29–48.

Cheyette, Brian. 1993. *Constructions of "the Jew" in English Literature and Society: Racial Representations 1875–1945*. Cambridge: Cambridge University Press.

Dean, Carolyn J. 2010. *Aversion and Erasure: The Fate of the Victim After the Holocaust*. Ithaca: Cornell University Press.

Drumont, Édouard. (1886) 1994. *La France juive: Essai d'histoire contemporaine*. Vol. 1. Beyrouth: Edition Charlemagne.

Edelstein, Alan. 1982. *An Unacknowledged Harmony: Philo-Semitism and the Survival of European Jewry*. Westport: Greenwood Press.

Finkielkraut, Alain. 2003. *Au nom de l'autre: Réflexions sur l'antisémitisme qui vient*. Paris: Gallimard.

Fischer, Lars. 2007. *The Socialist Response to Antisemitism in Imperial Germany*. Cambridge: Cambridge University Press.

Freedman, Jonathan. 2008. "Antisemitism Without Jews: *Left Behind* in the American Heartland." In Lassner and Trubowitz 2008.

Golub, Jennifer. 1992. *Japanese Attitudes Towards Jews*. New York: Pacific Rim Institute of the American Jewish Committee.

Hammerschlag, Sarah. 2010. *The Figural Jew: Politics and Identity in Postwar French Thought*. Chicago: University of Chicago Press.

Himmelfarb, Gertrude. 2011. *The People of the Book: Philosemitism in England, From Cromwell to Churchill*. New York: Encounter Books.

Hummel, Daniel. 2019. *Covenant Brothers: Evangelicals, Jews, and US-Israeli Relations*. Philadelphia: University of Pennsylvania Press.

Israel, Jonathan. 1989. *European Jewry in the Age of Mercantilism 1550–1750*. Oxford: Clarendon Press.

Judaken, Jonathan. 2006. *Jean-Paul Sartre and the Jewish Question: Anti-Antisemitism and the Politics of the French Intellectual.* Lincoln: University of Nebraska Press.

Judaken, Jonathan. 2008. "Between Philosemitism and Antisemitism: The Frankfurt School's Anti-Antisemitism." In Lassner and Trubowitz 2008.

Karp, Jonathan. 2008. *The Politics of Jewish Commerce: Economic Thought and Emancipation in Europe, 1638–1848.* Cambridge: Cambridge University Press.

Karp, Jonathan, and Adam Sutcliffe, eds. 2011. *Philosemitism in History.* Cambridge: Cambridge University Press.

Katz, Ethan. 2015. *The Burdens of Brotherhood: Jews and Muslims from North Africa to France.* Cambridge, MA: Harvard University Press.

Kinzig, Wolfram. 1994. "Philosemitismus Teil I: Zur Geschichte des Begriffs." *Zeitschrift für Kirchengeschichte* 105: 208–28.

Lassner, Phyllis, and Lara Trubowitz, eds. 2008. *Antisemitism and Philosemitism in the Twentieth and Twenty-First Centuries: Representing Jews, Jewishness, and Modern Culture.* Newark: University of Delaware Press.

Lehrer, Erica. 2013. *Jewish Poland Revisited: Heritage Tourism in Unquiet Places.* Bloomington: Indiana University Press.

Marty, Eric. 2003. *Bref séjour à Jérusalem.* Paris: Gallimard.

Menocal, Maria Rosa. 2002. *The Ornament of the World: How Muslims, Christians, and Jews Created a Culture of Tolerance in Medieval Spain.* New York: Little, Brown.

Nirenberg, David. 2013. *Anti-Judaism: The Western Tradition.* New York: W. W. Norton.

Rosenfeld, Alvin H., ed. 2019. *Anti-Zionism and Antisemitism: The Dynamics of Delegitimization.* Bloomington: Indiana University Press.

Rousso, Henry. 1987. *Le syndrome de Vichy, 1944–198--.* Paris: Seuil.

Samuels, Maurice. 2006. "Metaphors of Modernity: Prostitutes, Bankers, and Other Jews in Balzac's *Splendeurs et misères des courtisanes.*" *Romanic Review* 97 (2): 169–84.

Samuels, Maurice. 2016. *The Right to Difference: French Universalism and the Jews.* Chicago: University of Chicago Press.

Sandauer, Artur. 1985. "On the Plight of the Polish Writer of Jewish Origin in the Twentieth-Century: An Essay which I should not have Written" [In Polish]. In *Pisma Zebrane.* Vol 3. Warsaw: Czytelnik.

Sartre, Jean-Paul. 1965. *Anti-Semite and Jew.* Translated by George J. Becker. New York: Schocken Books.

Schechter, Ronald. 2003. *Obstinate Hebrews: Representations of Jews in France, 1715–1815.* Berkeley: University of California Press.

Stern, Frank. 1991. *The Whitewashing of the Yellow Badge: Antisemitism and Philosemitism in Postwar Germany.* London: Heinemann.

Sutcliffe, Adam. 2003. *Judaism and Enlightenment.* Cambridge: Cambridge University Press.

Taguieff, Pierre-André. 2002. *La nouvelle judéophobie.* Paris: Mille et une nuits.

Tompkins, Jane. 1985. *Sensational Designs: The Cultural Work of American Fiction, 1790–1860.* New York: Oxford University Press.

Traverso, Enzo. 2016. *The End of Jewish Modernity.* Translated by David Fernbach. London: Pluto Press.

Trivellato, Francesca. 2019. *The Promise and Peril of Credit: What a Forgotten Legend about Jews and Finance Tells Us About the Making of European Commercial Society.* Princeton: Princeton University Press.

Valman, Nadia. 2007. *The Jewess in Nineteenth-Century Literary Culture.* Cambridge: Cambridge University Press.

Wistrich, Robert. 2010. *A Lethal Obsession: Anti-Semitism from Antiquity to Global Jihad.* New York: Random House.

Zimmermann, Moshe. 1987. *Wilhelm Marr: The Patriarch of Anti-Semitism.* New York: Oxford University Press.

CHAPTER 17

Pogroms

Jeffrey S. Kopstein

What causes pogroms? The outbreaks of deadly violence against Jewish civilians that punctuate recorded history suggest a straightforward answer: antisemitism. What else could possibly explain the rituals of humiliation, including torture, rape, looting, and the forced violation of sacred norms if not antisemitism?

This intuitive explanation has, however, at least two problems, one definitional and another causal. Although "pogrom," having passed into common parlance to describe violence not only against Jewish but also other civilians, now refers to interethnic violence generally, scholars disagree about the necessary and sufficient criteria for the term's proper application. And, if we cannot agree on what pogroms are, then trying to figure out why they happen can seem pointless.

The causal problem is even more vexing. If antisemitism causes pogroms, then the manifestation of the former should predict the occurrence of the latter. But most scholarship on the subject either implicitly or explicitly identifies manifestations of antisemitism by the occurrence of pogroms: antisemitism, which causes pogroms, is inferred from them. This circularity is awkward, but not a completely disqualifying feature of social explanation. Rather, it should spur us to put antisemitism in its proper causal place.

Of course, we would never see a pogrom if everyone loved Jews. But even if nobody ever loved Jews and they were universally despised, which seems empirically unlikely, this lack of affection or outright distaste would not automatically translate into intergroup violence. In the argot of sociology, we

---

J. S. Kopstein (✉)
University of California, Irvine, CA, USA
e-mail: kopstein@uci.edu

need to establish the relationship between an orientation (hatred of Jews) and an action (acts of violence against them). The latter follows not only from the former, and the former does not always result in the latter.

Below I first discuss what pogroms are before turning to historical cases to identify plausible causes. Even if a consensual definition of "pogrom" existed, the conditions of their occurrence still aren't easily identified. My first main point here will be that, since antisemitism is more of a constant than a variable, it should be considered a necessary rather than a sufficient condition for pogroms. Were it sufficient, then pogroms should have been ubiquitous over the past two millennia. Since pogroms are not omnipresent, they must be situational rather than inherent. On the other hand, anti-Jewish violence recurs. Scholars thus have the task of trying to determine which situational factors make pogroms much more likely to occur. My second main point here will accordingly be to identify especially important political and social situational factors.

What Is a Pogrom?

"Pogrom," which derives from the Russian verb *gromit'* (to thunder, smash, or break), seems to have been used first in 1871 to describe anti-Jewish riots in Odessa during Holy Week, while its diffusion began with the waves of locally based violence against Jewish civilians that swept through dozens of cities and towns in the Russian empire in 1881–1884, 1903–1906, and 1917–1920. Each wave became more violent than the previous one. The violence spread from larger cities to smaller towns and villages (Klier and Lambroza 1992). Less deadly pogroms also broke out sporadically in the interwar period in the multiethnic borderlands of independent Poland (Żyndul 1994). In the weeks following the German attack on Soviet occupied Eastern Europe in June 1941, local non-Jews attacked and murdered their Jewish neighbors in approximately 300 cities and towns, claiming approximately 25,000 lives. Jewish victims and German military units frequently referred to these atrocities as pogroms.

Can these concrete instances tell us what a pogrom is? What features do they share? Common among these otherwise different events is the violence against civilians targeted for their religion and/or ethnicity. But the pogromists' identities, the level of violence, and the victims' characteristics vary from case to case.

Historians of the first Russian pogroms have identified transient workers and the unemployed in some pogroms, but peasants in others. The 1917–1920 pogroms were carried out primarily by marauding White Army units seeking restoration of the monarchy after the Russian Revolution and Ukrainian soldiers subordinated to Symon Petliura or regional Ukrainian warlords during the civil war (Abramson 1999; Gergel 1951; Klier and Lambroza 1992). By contrast, victims' civilian neighbors committed the pogroms in formerly Soviet occupied territory in Eastern Europe immediately following the June 1941 German attack. Perpetrators in 1941 included lumpen elements but also doctors, lawyers, and even priests (Kopstein and Wittenberg 2018; Struve 2015). Pogroms were frequently initiated by forces outside of the community, but almost always involved local non-Jewish participation. This element distinguishes a pogrom from a military massacre, though the line distinguishing the two types of events is sometimes blurry.

Although pogroms always involve violence, the level of violence varies greatly, running from plunder to assault to murder. The 1881–1882 pogroms claimed approximately 25 lives, while 47 died in the 1903 Kishinev pogrom (Judge 1995). The sporadic pogroms in interwar Poland created mayhem, but were not especially deadly. The 1941 pogrom wave, by contrast, claimed approximately 25,000 lives (Pohl 2007), while approximately 50,000 Jews died in the Ukrainian and Polish violence following World War I (Gergel 1951).

Many scholars cite as another regular feature of these pogroms rituals of humiliation, rape, torture, and the forced violation of victims' sacred norms and spaces. Other authors point to the carnivalesque atmospheres surrounding pogroms—the mood of the perpetrators and bystanders is often less grim than celebratory (Himka 2011). These rituals and celebrations indicate the purpose of pogroms: to put Jews back in their (subordinate) place within the community or, more rarely, to push them out completely. But even characterizing pogroms as ethnically encoded, ritualized violence designed to return Jews to some sort of inferior status does not genuinely distinguish the era of violence normally associated with pogroms in Eastern Europe from other instances of anti-Jewish violence in other times and places. In fact, contemporary scholars use "pogrom" to describe anti-Jewish riots and "exclusionary violence" in virtually every era of Jewish history from antiquity to the present (Hoffmann et al. 2002).

Causes

The causes for such varied events are, not surprisingly, multiple. Contemporary historians view the pogroms of the late nineteenth and early twentieth century as resulting from the general weakness of the state in many outlying areas of the Russian empire; the small and generally poorly trained internal police forces; large variations in the willingness of local authorities to use force to preserve public order; and important economic, social, and political tensions simmering throughout the empire (Aronson 1990; Judge 1995). If state weakness was a frequent source of pogrom violence in the nineteenth and twentieth centuries, it was all but universally true in the pre-modern era when "states" as we understand them today did not exist and the distinction between public and private authority was hazy at best.

State complicity or action, instead of weak or defunct state authority, is also highlighted in many accounts of pogroms. Contemporary observers of the first waves of pogroms in the Russian empire (1881–1884 and 1903–1906) often maintained the violence was organized, inspired, or otherwise tolerated by central authorities (Klier and Lambroza 1992). Although modern historians of Russia doubt the state's hidden hand in organizing the pogroms, failure to restrict the antisemitic press and especially the dissemination of ritual murder accusations during the Easter/Passover holidays stoked the impression of official complicity.

Deeper sociological factors are highlighted by turning from states to perpetrators and victims. By the 1870s economic competition between non-Jewish and Jewish workers and merchants within the Pale of Settlement could not be attenuated by further restrictions on Jewish residency and employment. The Jewish enlightenment and government policy increased participation in secular educational institutions, which in turn created demands for citizenship rights and expectations for increased social status and mobility. Non-Jews often understood these demands as a challenge to the ethnic power structure. Official Russian explanations of the early pogroms thus cited as the primary causes of violence Jewish "exploitation" of the population, Jews' self-imposed separatism, and a Jewish monopoly over the rural liquor trade. Non-Jewish liberal intellectuals blamed the low cultural level of the non-Jewish masses (Klier and Lambroza 1992, p. 34). Kopstein and Wittenberg (2011, 2018) explain the 1941 pogroms in Poland as an attempt to relegate Jews to their inferior position in the social and political hierarchy by those threatened by the prospect of Jewish equality.

Does this quick tour through the history of modern pogroms help identify the relationship of antisemitism to anti-Jewish violence? Yes, but it does not fully clarify the matter. A satisfactory treatment requires a definition not only of "pogrom," but also of "antisemitism." We must minimally distinguish between dislike of people—e.g., small scale merchants or money lenders—*who happen to be Jewish* and dislike of people *because they are Jewish*. Only the latter type of case should count as antisemitism.

A great deal of Jewish historiography has been bent on connecting anti-Jewish violence to antisemitism, a task roundly attacked in recent years for its problematic characterization of antisemitism. David Nirenberg notes that so much of Jewish history writing trace genealogies of hatred that result in cases of "irrational" violence that are then strung together to show that antisemitism causes violence. "In Jewish historiography, for example, scholars have drawn a line of mounting intolerance from the Rhineland massacres of the First Crusade, through the expulsions and massacres of the thirteenth, fourteenth, and fifteenth centuries, through German ritual murder trials and Russian pogroms, to *Kristallnacht* and the concentration camps" (Nirenberg 1996, p. 7). His corrective is to place the violence that interests him (fourteenth-century France and the Crown of Aragon) into the social, political, and cultural contexts of the time. Only then may one begin teasing out the specific role of anti-Jewish sentiments in producing the violence at hand.

Hatred of Jews as Jews per se, i.e., antisemitism, frequently matters less than the "particularities" of the circumstances, i.e., than the place of Jews within the politics and society of the age. Most anti-Jewish violence turns out not to have been "irrational" and consequently not entirely or even primarily antisemitic in its origins. Largely instrumental, pogroms need to be understood not only in cultural terms, but also and mainly as politically driven violence.

Does this observation hold for the "pogroms" of different eras? I explain below the concern about "ownership" of the polity as causally central to the 1941 Lviv pogrom in order then to illuminate a similar concern in the pogroms in 38CE Alexandria and 1391 Valencia. Despite huge contextual differences, these cases display significant commonalities regarding neighbor-on-neighbor violence in the context of weakened public authority. All these pogroms, my comparison shows, resulted not primarily from a ubiquitous dislike of Jews (which could be likened more to a slow burn than a hot fire), but from particular social and political circumstances in which the Jews as a minority people found themselves. Politics rather than antisemitism, we shall see, explains the outbreaks of violence.

Lviv 1941

On June 30, 1941, on the eighth day of operation Barbarossa, the German invasion of the Soviet Union, a pogrom broke out in Lviv, the capital city of Eastern Galicia. Ukrainians, and to a lesser extent Poles, massacred their Jewish neighbors and fellow citizens. With the Soviet officials having fled only a day before under heavy German bombardment, the city's Polish population, approximately half its inhabitants, awaited the German arrival with a mixture of fear and hope. They had been the political owners from 1918 to 1939 when, under the terms of the Molotov Ribbentrop pact, control passed to the Soviet Union, which quickly incorporated them into Soviet Ukraine.

The Ukrainians, although only 15% of the city's population, viewed Lviv as their cultural Piedmont. Under the Soviets they were the nominal owners. But the Ukrainian nationalist intelligentsia of this deeply divided city found Soviet rule a huge disappointment, an insult to their hopes for a truly independent Ukraine. They hoped for German liberation and German help in recapturing the city as the capital of their own nation-building project (Amar 2015; Himka 2011; Struve 2015).

The city's Jews, the remaining 35% of local inhabitants, were terrified. The few who could, left with the retreating Soviets; the vast majority who could not, remained. When the Germans arrived, on June 30 and July 1, they discovered three NKVD prisons stuffed with the rotting corpses of massacred prisoners, mostly (though not only) Ukrainian nationalists, whom the Soviets did not succeed in deporting eastward before the arrival of the Germans. Ukrainian militiamen were brought to the prisons, and with their help word quickly spread that "the Jewish Bolsheviks" had carried out this atrocity and should be made to pay.

For the next two days Lviv witnessed terrible anti-Jewish violence at the hands of the local Ukrainian population and the Ukrainian militia, and under the Nazis' approving eyes (Struve 2015, pp. 247–370). The prisons became the primary scene of the pogroms, as Jews were forced to bury the corpses. But the scenes of violence, humiliation, and brutality spread throughout the city and quickly took on an almost carnival-like atmosphere (Himka 2011). Several blocks away from one of the main pogrom sites, as the pogrom gathered steam, Ukrainian nationalists declared independence and national rebirth in a solemn ceremony. Over the next few days thousands of Jews were killed at close range.

The pogrom in Lviv was but one in a much larger set of pogroms in June and July 1941, before the organized Nazi extermination effort really got underway (Kopstein and Wittenberg 2013; Struve 2015). Jews were robbed, beaten, tortured, and mutilated by their non-Jewish neighbors throughout the strip of land from the Baltic to the Black Sea that the Soviets occupied between 1939 and 1941.

What accounts for these pogroms? Three factors figure prominently in most accounts: (1) the role of the Germans, especially the *Einsatzgruppen*; (2) the impact of 21 months of Soviet rule, especially the massacres in the NKVD prisons before the Soviet departure; and (3) the role of Ukrainian nationalists in organizing and carrying out the pogroms.

At this stage of the war, the Germans preferred others to do their dirty work for them, as the documentary record makes clear. They encouraged "self-cleansing" of "communists and Jews" by locals. Internal German communications make explicit reference to pogroms, e.g., a telegram sent on June 29, 1941, by SS-Gruppenführer Reinhard Heydrich who reminded the *Einsatzgruppen* heads that "nothing should stand in the way" of the local "self-cleansing actions" against Jews and Bolsheviks (quoted in Struve 2015, p. 130). Yet, the Germans also frequently failed to set off pogroms and expressed frustration where they couldn't. A further fact casts doubt on the pogroms as an essentially German affair: in many localities, pogroms occurred in the chaos before the Germans arrived, after they had left, or without much German help.

The similarities in pogrom rituals across cities and towns–Jews being forced to play the Jewish Bolshevik fools, to carry torahs while singing *hatikva* and *moskva maya*, and to bury Lenin statues in mock funerals before themselves being shot, beaten, or burned alive—may suggest a centralized, German script; but the Germans did not force anyone to follow this script. Above all, the presence or absence of the Germans does not help us distinguish between pogrom and non-pogrom locations within Ukraine. Their presence in Lviv may have facilitated a pogrom and may have made it more brutal. The invasion certainly contributed to the temporary elimination of public authority that could have stopped the pogroms. But Nazi presence was neither a sufficient nor, in many cases, even a necessary condition for neighbor-on-neighbor violence.

What about the Soviet occupation? Did it stoke antisemitism? These pogroms did occur within a specific territory occupied by the Soviets from 1939 to 1941, east of which no significant pogrom activity took place. Most scholars agree that the median Jews probably welcomed the Soviets in 1939 as they entered Western Ukraine as the lesser of two evils. But were Jews the distributional beneficiaries of Soviet rule? Some were, but the vast majority weren't. For every Jew who could not serve in the police force or the civil service, several in small-time trade went out of business or fell under suspicion. Moreover, no evidence suggests that Soviet rule was any worse, or Jews' positions and visibility any different, in villages and cities where pogroms occurred than in those where they didn't. If Soviet rule were enough to cause a pogrom, many more pogroms should have been documented. It is also noteworthy that Ukrainians, but not Jews, who collaborated with Soviet authorities were largely spared retribution by their fellow Ukrainians, a fact suggesting that the pogroms were less the product of anti-Soviet than anti-Jewish sentiments.

This observation points to the third factor: antisemitic nationalism. Ukrainian Nationalist networks (the most prominent being the Organization of Ukrainian Nationalists or OUN) figure prominently in both eyewitness and scholarly accounts of the Lviv pogroms. Germans armed and trained them. Their own leaders made statements of solidarity with the German aims of ridding Ukraine of Jews and creating a Ukraine for Ukrainians. Jewish testimony speaks frequently of the blue and yellow armbands being worn. NKVD interrogations of Ukrainians after the war speak of the same story over and over, and evidence exists of an attempted cover-up with a decree issued to Ukrainian insurgents to destroy all records speaking of a pogrom (Carynnyk 2011).

And yet, any account of the pogroms in Western Ukraine as primarily an OUN operation misses something important. The OUN was a small organization spread thinly on the ground. They tried to recruit locals, but adherence was spotty and opportunistic. As compelling as the case against the Ukrainian nationalists might be, therefore, excessive focus on their role risks overlooking an essential feature of these pogroms: the participation of broad segments of the Ukrainian population in the pogrom's mass, carnival character. German and Jewish accounts indicate that these chaotic events encompassed many more perpetrators, bystanders, and rescuers than could possibly have been members or even sympathizers of the OUN. Accounts that feature the OUN thus risk letting off the hook large segments of the population that stood by without lifting a finger, looked on approvingly, or actively participated in the violence. Antisemitic Ukrainian nationalism certainly played a role in June and July 1941; but just how important the presence of nationalist networks and even antisemitism were remains an open question.

In fact—and now we come to the crux of the matter—antisemitism alone cannot account for why pogroms occurred in some communities and not in others. No doubt antisemitism in Lviv was widespread. But no less antisemitism is evident in many locations where pogroms did *not* occur within Western Ukraine. What, then, was the meaning and cause of the pogroms of 1941? Let me restate this question in terms of the decisive facts: pogroms occurred in only 126 of 1600 towns and villages in Western Ukraine where Jews lived; in the 1474 others, pogroms were either stopped, many by local heroes, or never got off the ground. What distinguished these two very different kinds of localities?

One crucial difference is political affiliation. Pogrom locations tended to have Jewish populations far more mobilized proportionately into Zionist politics in the 1920s and 1930s than communities where pogroms did not occur. The most glaring pieces of data are twofold. First, where pogroms occurred the median percentage of Jewish vote for the Zionists back into the 1920s in this Ukrainian area of Poland was 86%. In Lviv, 70% of Jews voted for Zionist parties in the 1920s. Where no pogroms occurred, the median was approximately half this value, 40% (Kopstein and Wittenberg 2018).

What was Zionism at the time? It was much less a desire to make *aliyah* (indeed, emigration to Palestine was a difficult, expensive, and not very desirable proposition) than a full-chested refusal to join another people's nation-building project, even if the site of a Jewish national home was uncertain. Jews would be Jews, and assertive ones at that. Competing nationalisms, not antisemitism, were therefore decisive in Lviv, and this competition was experienced as a political threat by both Ukrainians and Poles, who saw in the pogroms an opportunity to dispose of their political rivals. This rivalry was itself, however, a function of Jews' own sense of belonging.

Further evidence for a political interpretation of the pogroms is that, wherever the local Ukrainian support for communism had historically been high, as in many towns throughout the province of Volhynia, pogroms were much less likely to occur. The logic here is that communism constituted a non-liberal form of universalism that either helped inoculate the local non-Jewish population against calls to attack their Jewish neighbors or induced them to offer Jews protection. The story, therefore, may be less about the Germans, the chaos, the Soviets, and antisemitism—as necessary as all were for anti-Jewish violence—than about competing nationalism and the ownership of the polity. The explanation proposed here is directly political and instrumental rather than cultural or ideological. The circumstances surrounding the outbreak of intercommunal violence that directly preceded the Holocaust prove not too different from other instances of anti-Jewish riots that punctuate Jewish history, as I will now demonstrate via two pre-modern pogroms.

ALEXANDRIA 38CE

One may question whether it is proper to use the term pogrom to talk about the anti-Jewish riots that broke out in Alexandria in 38CE under the rule of governor Flaccus while Gaius Caligula sat in Rome. But the term has been used by specialists at least since the 1930s to characterize the riot, and the latest edition of the only first-hand account of the events, the Greco-Jewish philosopher Philo's *In Flaccum*, carries the subtitle "The First Pogrom" (van der Horst 2003).

The context for the pogrom is clear enough. With the weakening of Alexandrian governor Flaccus after Gaius' ascent to power, the local Greek elite used the visit of the new Judean tetrarch Agrippa, himself a Jew on his way to Judea, to press for Flaccus' permission to use force against the Jewish population in ousting it from neighborhoods where Jews had not traditionally resided. The pogrom lasted several days and entailed beatings, murder, and other ritualized humiliations such as desecrating Jewish places of worship, forcing the city's Jewish women to eat pork, and public punishment by scourging.

Philo himself does not offer a theory for why the pogrom occurred. But scholars have long identified the main reasons. Three groups lived in the city: Greeks, Jews, and Egyptian peasants. Although only the Greeks possessed full rights of citizenship, the Jews had certain communal privileges and rights as well, including the right to free worship: they prayed for, but not to, the emperor. They nonetheless had to pay the head-tax, like the Egyptian peasantry. Greeks and Egyptians had long resented the Jews for having sided with the conquering Romans and for continued Jewish attempts to upgrade their citizenship status, both communally and as individuals (Mondesert 1999, pp. 899–900). Potential Jewish citizenship is what really drove the intercommunal conflict in Alexandria (Tcherikover 1959, pp. 312–13).

What about anti-Jewish sentiments? Scholars have documented the multiple sources of anti-Jewish prejudices in the Hellenistic world: Jews' all powerful yet invisible god coupled with their refusal to worship the emperor or his likeness; their refusal to dine with others which sparked charges of misanthropy; their practice of circumcision; and their supposed clannishness (Schäfer 1997; Gruen 2002). But these scholars are quick to tell us that these prejudices on their own could not have caused the pogrom because they had long been around and such outbreaks of intercommunal violence were exceedingly rare. In short, the violence seems to have been much more situational, instrumental, and political than cultural, religious, or inherent. When the opportunity presented itself with the weakening of public authority, Alexandria's Greeks and Egyptians were less interested in wiping out the Jews than asserting their own preeminence by putting the Jews back in their place (quite literally, since one of the main results of the violence was residential re-segregation). The onset of Roman rule sparked a competition over communal ownership and citizenship, and this competition, rather than cultural difference or antisemitism, drove the conflict. The conflict, in short, was about politics.

Several pieces of evidence support this assertion. First, the immediate trigger for the pogrom was the Jewish King Agrippa's visit. His stopover on his way to Judea occasioned public expressions of pride among the city's Jews who still had more than a touch of residual patriotism for their homeland. Alexandria's Greeks organized a parody of this visit in theatrical fashion with a local fool, Carrabas, dressed up as Agrippa just before the onset of anti-Jewish violence. Second, Philo's account references the local Greek interest in restricting Jewish citizenship and "ownership." Greek "nationalist" organizations had long been present and active in stoking resentment against the city's Jews; but the Governor's weakened position and the mobilization around Agrippa's visit provided the opportunity for organization (Bergmann and Hoffmann 1987). Third, in a letter addressed both to the Greek and Jewish communities written in 41CE, Claudius, Gaius' successor, first admonishes the Alexandrians "to behave gently and kindly toward the Jews." He then advises the Jews "not to aim at more than they have previously had...and not to intrude themselves into the games presided over by the *gymnasiarchoi* and the *kosmetai*, since they enjoy what is their own, and in a city which is not their own they possess all good things" (quoted in Schäfer 1997, p. 187). This letter, one of the only documents directly dealing with the Alexandrian disturbances apart from Philo's account, strongly indicates that the essence of the conflict, as well as of the pogrom itself, was about "ownership" of the local polity (Smallwood 1970, p. 14) and concern with demographic balance (Gruen 2002, p. 81). Thus, even in this ancient polity where intercommunal relations were not subject to democratic electoral competition, the case anticipates the core of the "ethnic political threat" hypothesis that informs so much of the literature on racial violence in the United States and ethnic violence in other contexts (Blalock 1967).

The violence in Alexandria, while carnivalesque and escaping the control of those instigating it, was less irrational than instrumental. Of course, hatred of Jews mattered and could only be a phenomenon because their distinctive customs, practices, and ties to fellow Jews outside of Alexandria marked them as a group apart. Perhaps anti-Judaism constitutes a necessary condition for the pogrom; but the crowd moved from hatred to violence for political reasons (Bergmann and Hoffmann 1987).

Valencia 1391

The context for Valencia's anti-Jewish riot of 1391—also referred to as a "pogrom" in the secondary literature–would seem to be a straightforward, if more extreme, version of the Christian antisemitic mob exacting revenge for the passion of Christ that Jewish communities had periodically confronted for centuries (MacKay 1972). But both the timing and the scale of violence set this pogrom apart. For one thing it occurred not during holy week but in the summer, indicating causes separate from or beyond run-of-the-mill Christian anti-Judaism. Even more telling is the differences in scale. The riot amounted to an ethnic cleansing, as after 1391 hardly any Jews remained in Valencia. The pogrom itself occasioned a forced mass conversion of Jews to Christianity, creating a huge class of *conversos*, which ultimately led to the momentous expulsions of 1492.

The violence began in Seville in June 1391 and spread throughout Castile and the Crown of Aragon, reaching Valencia on July 6. The script remained similar in most cases (Wolff 1971). Youths milled about outside of the Jewish ghettos calling for the Jews to convert or die. From there it escalated when the ghettos themselves were infiltrated. In Valencia, attackers used drain pipes and openings in walls to enter the Jewish quarter, raping, looting, and killing its inhabitants once inside. 300 Jews died and the remaining mostly converted to Christianity (Baer 1966, p. 100). The story, upon first reading, seems one of Christianity confronting Jews and violating its own prohibition against forced conversion.

Does it make sense to characterize what occurred in Valencia (and in many other locations in Iberia in the summer of 1391) as motivated by anything other than dislike or hatred of Jews? Modern historians, as it turns out, do not primarily tell a religious or cultural story about 1391; instead they relate it in much more political terms. The particulars and the language may have been Christian, but the main factors involved the social and political role of Spain's Jews in the late Middle Ages. As Mark Meyerson (2004), David Nirenberg, and others have noted, the Jews were considered the King's "treasure," his patrimony, existing outside of the law regulating the relationship between Kings and people (Nirenberg 2014, p. 75). The Jews performed "work" for the King, in Nirenberg's terms, not only as a source of taxation and service, but also as defining the King as being outside of the law. Their position as the King's patrimony induced opponents of royal absolutism to define the Crown, and to characterize royal overreach, as Judaizing and such Kings as Judaizers. Precisely because Jews represented royal power at its most absolute, they could be used to signal that power and even exercise it.

Temporal royal power itself could be defined in these terms, a reality that left Jews in a precarious position should the actual power of the King ever be brought into question, or if the position of the Crown were weakened—as happened in 1391 in Seville first with the death of Juan I of Castile, leaving a minor as heir. Sensing royal weakness, both bourgeois and noble enemies throughout both Castile and the Crown of Aragon sought to redefine the relationship between Kings and people through an attack on the Jews. The Jews were caught up in a constitutional battle.

Throughout the thirteenth and fourteenth centuries Christians questioned Jewish "power" as the King's servants in society and in the economy. Churches never ceased calling for conversion. But popular distaste and religious anti-Jewish instigation remain a constant rather than a variable and therefore cannot account for why the violence moved from ritualized and sporadic to widespread and devastating in the summer of 1391. This required royal sovereignty and the Jews' position within it being brought into question. Where sovereign authority remained resolute, such as in Morvedre, Jews could be and were protected in 1391 (Meyerson 2004). These pogroms were less about Christianity than about royal absolutism and resistance to its assertion.

Although the case of 1391 does not easily fit the more "political," as opposed to cultural or religious, model of pogrom violence that I am proposing here, we can easily redirect our attention to the competing sovereign claims of would-be absolutist Kings versus people, and the Jews' position within this relationship as a strategic partner or enemy. Putting the matter this way does not eliminate Christian antisemitism as a factor in the anti-Jewish pogroms of 1391—as Meyerson notes (2004, p. 279), such a move would-be "folly"—but it does place it in its proper perspective as a language, a vocabulary for understanding Jews' place within a situation of dangerous dual sovereignty rather than the master account of anti-Jewish violence in the Middle Ages.

Conclusion

The "politics" of Alexandria 38CE or Valencia 1391 are not identical with the "politics" that, I have argued, are causally important in the 1941 Lviv pogrom. The age of mass democracy, of parties competing for power in relatively free and fair elections, translated ethnic and religious demography into political power far more directly and efficiently than politics in the pre-modern world. But the existence of parties and free elections, the above analysis indicates, does not in itself constitute a confining scope condition for a political theory of pogroms. Even in Alexandria 38CE and Valencia 1391, that is, even in eras far before the advent of mass democracy, competing ethnic and religious communities keenly experienced the politics of political ownership. Under conditions of perceived threat to their political dominance, non-Jews could lash out with restorative violence.

Thus, although antisemitism potentially provides the permissive environment for violence, the history of pogroms indicates that, absent other factors, it does not suffice to move collectivities to the kind of violence characteristic of pogroms. Otherwise, many more pogroms would occur than actually do. I have argued here that a crucial supplement to hatred is real conflict over collective goals, over membership in, and ownership of the polity. Other factors may also be at work. The main point, however, bears repeating: pogroms are not inherent to Jewish life nor are they driven only by intractable and permanent cultural conflict; rather they are also situational and politically inspired. And that on its own should be enough to bring the unmediated relationship between antisemitism and pogroms into question.

References

Abramson, Henry. 1999. *A Prayer for the Government: Ukrainians and Jews in Revolutionary Times, 1917–1920.* Cambridge, MA: Harvard University Press.
Amar, Tarik Cyril. 2015. *The Paradox of Lviv: A Borderland City Between Nazis, Stalinists, and Nationalists.* Ithaca: Cornell University Press.
Aronson, Michael I. 1990. *Troubled Waters: Origins of the 1881 Anti-Jewish Pogroms in Russia.* Pittsburgh: University of Pittsburg Press.
Baer, Yitzhak. 1966. *A History of the Jews in Christian Spain.* Vol. 2. Philadelphia: The Jewish Publication Society.
Bergmann, Werner, and Christhard Hoffmann. 1987. "Kalkül oder Massenwahn: Eine soziologische Interpretation der antijüdischen Unruhen in Alexandria 38 n. Chr." In *Antisemitismus und Jüdische Geschichte: Studien zu Ehren von Herbert A. Strauss*, edited by Rainer Erb and Michael Schmidt. Berlin: Wissenschaftlicher Autorenverlag.
Blalock, Hubert M. 1967. *Toward a Theory of Minority-Group Relations.* New York: Wiley.
Carynnyk, Marco. 2011. "Foes of Our Rebirth: Ukrainian Nationalist Discussions About Jews 1929–1947." *Nationalities Papers* 39 (3): 315–52.
Gergel, N. 1951. "The Pogroms in Ukraine 1918–1920." *YIVO Annual of Jewish Social Science* 6: 237–52.
Gruen, Erich S. 2002. *Diaspora: Jews Amidst Greeks and Romans.* Cambridge, MA: Harvard University Press.
Himka, John Paul. 2011. "The Lviv Pogrom of 1941: The Germans, Ukrainian Nationalists, and the Carnival Crowd." *Canadian Slavonic Papers* 53 (2–4): 209–43.
Hoffmann, Christhard, Werner Bergmann, and Helmut Walser Smith, eds. 2002. *Exclusionary Violence: Antisemitic Riots in Modern German History.* Ann Arbor: University of Michigan Press.
Judge, Edward H. 1995. *Easter in Kishinev: Anatomy of a Pogrom.* New York: New York University Press.
Klier, John D., and Shlomo Lambroza. 1992. *Pogroms: Anti-Jewish Violence in Modern Russian History.* New York: Cambridge University Press.
Kopstein, Jeffrey S., and Jason Wittenberg. 2011. "Deadly Communities: Local Political Milieus and the Persecution of Jews in Occupied Poland." *Comparative Political Studies* 44 (3): 259–83.
Kopstein, Jeffrey S., and Jason Wittenberg. 2013. "Pogrom." In *Enzyklopädie jüdischer Geschichte und Kultur*, Band 4, 572–75.
Kopstein, Jeffrey S., and Jason Wittenberg. 2018. *Intimate Violence: Anti-Jewish Pogroms on the Eve of the Holocaust.* Ithaca: Cornell University Press.
MacKay, Angus. 1972. "Popular Movements and Pogroms in Fifteenth-Century Castile." *Past and Present* 55: 33–67.
Meyerson, Mark D. 2004. *Jews in an Iberian Frontier Kingdom: Society, Economy, and Politics in Morvedre, 1248–1391.* Leiden: Brill.
Mondesert, C. 1999. "Philo of Alexandria". In *The Cambridge History of Judaism*, volume three, edited by William Horbury, W.D. Davies, John Sturdy, 877–900. Cambridge: Cambridge University Press.
Nirenberg, David. 1996. *Communities of Violence: Persecution of Minorities in the Middle Ages.* Princeton: Princeton University Press.

Nirenberg, David. 2014. *Neighboring Faiths: Christianity, Islam, and Judaism in the Middle Ages and Today*. Chicago: University of Chicago Press.
Pohl, Dieter. 2007. "Anti-Jewish Pogroms in Western Ukraine: A Research Agenda." In *Shared History, Divided Memory: Jews and Others in Soviet-Occupied Poland, 1939–1941*, edited by Elazar Barkan, Elizabeth Cole, and Kai Struve, 305–14. Leipzig: Leipziger Universitätsverlag.
Schäfer, Peter. 1997. *Judeophobia: Attitudes Toward the Jews in the Ancient World*. Cambridge, MA: Harvard University Press.
Smallwood, Mary. 1970. *Philo Legatio ad Gaium*. Leiden: Brill.
Struve, Kai. 2015. *Deutsche Herrschaft, ukrainischer Nationalismus, antijüdische Gewalt: Der Sommer 1941 in Westukraine*. Oldenbourg: De Gruyter.
Tcherikover, Victor. 1959. *Hellenistic Civilization and the Jews*. New York: Atheneum.
van der Horst, Pieter W. 2003. *Philo's Flaccus: The First Pogrom: Introduction, Translation, and Commentary*. Leiden: Brill.
Wolff, Philippe. 1971. "The 1391 Pogrom in Spain: Social Crisis or Not?" *Past and Present* 50 (1): 4–18.
Żyndul, Jolanta. 1994. *Zajścia antyżydowskie w Polsce w latach 1935–1937*. Warsaw: Fundacja Im. K. Kelles-Krauza.

CHAPTER 18

Postcolonialism

Bryan Cheyette

INTRODUCTION

When I was the youngest member of the Department of English Literature, at the University of Leeds, I was asked to choose the texts for the summer reading group. At the time, I was completing *Constructions of "the Jew" in English Literature and Society* and was attending conferences which inaugurated postcolonial studies. I chose to introduce to my colleagues the so-called "Holy Trinity" (Young 1994, p. 163) of postcolonial theorists—Homi Bhabha, Edward Said, and Gayatri Chakravorty Spivak—who founded contemporary postcolonial studies in the West. All of these figures articulate racial and colonial discourse in ways which speak either explicitly or implicitly to the history of antisemitism. Said was most explicit when he described Orientalist discourse, in a well-known although under-explored formulation, as a "strange secret sharer of Western antisemitism" (1978, p. 27). Bhabha complicated Said's work by introducing the question of ambivalence into theories of racial and colonial discourse (1994, pp. 85–92). Spivak (1988, pp. 197–221) raised the issue—familiar within Holocaust Studies—of the limits of representation (Friedländer 1992). In general, the founding figures of Westernized postcolonial studies influenced a range of new thinking on antisemitism. The discursive nature of colonial racism meant that antisemitism, in the light of postcolonial theory, could also be seen to be at the heart of European liberal culture rather than an exceptional "evil" that only applies to totalitarian regimes (Cheyette and Valman 2004, pp. 1–26).

Postcolonial theory certainly informed my own work on racial representations in English and American (and later continental European) culture. My

B. Cheyette (✉)
Department of English, University of Reading, Reading, UK
e-mail: b.h.cheyette@reading.ac.uk

early books (1993, 1996) followed the "Holy Trinity" and foregrounded the ambivalence of racial discourse ("good" and "bad" Jews); the gulf between discourse and representation (Jews' behavior does not account for antisemitism); and the notion of Semitic discourse (rather than reducing complex cultural forms to "anti-" or "philo-" semitism). But while postcolonial theory began to influence mainly Jewish cultural studies (Boyarin and Boyarin 1997) and Jewish literary studies (Cheyette and Marcus 1998), there was a good deal of resistance from mainstream Jewish Studies. This resistance was not, however, a one-way street. Henry Louis Gates' influential collection on racial difference, for instance, which introduced postcolonial studies to the United States in the 1980s, includes little or no discussion of antisemitism among its essays. Commenting on the volume in its epilogue, Tzvetan Todorov is "shocked" by the "lack of reference to one of the most odious forms of racism: anti-Semitism" which, he argues, has been "actively ignored" by its authors (Gates 1986, pp. 370–80). This omission was due in large part to the routine use of "Western Judeo-Christian" to signify a dominant and dominating white colonial culture (Grossman 1989). The history of antisemitism, and Jews as a minority community, fits uneasily within this formulation. This uneasy fit is highlighted when we see that the only discussion of Jews and "race" in Gates' volume concerns discrimination by Jews in the State of Israel (1986, pp. 38–55).

Postcolonial studies was (and still is) a form of area studies which focuses mainly on Africa and the Indian sub-continent. At first, it discounted the Middle East, China, and most other Asian countries. It was also rooted in anti-colonial nationalist movements in these various regions and emphasized, understandably, the victims of colonialism. In contrast, mainstream Jewish Studies, until recently, has tended to focus on European, chiefly Ashkenazic history and to marginalize Sephardic and Mizrahi history in North Africa, as well as other smaller Jewish communities scattered throughout Asia and the Caribbean. Conventional Jewish historiography (especially in Israel and the United States) also played down Jewish victimhood, following Salo W. Baron, as "lachrymose" (Baron 1928). One reason for postcolonialism being relegated to a strand of Jewish cultural and literary studies is that mainstream Jewish Studies was better established, compared to postcolonial studies, and did not wish to be associated with its younger, postcolonial counterpart. Whereas postcolonial studies avoided being Eurocentric, Jewish Studies highlighted the European context of much of Jewish history. The long tradition of Judeo-Christianity was valued within Jewish studies but, as we have seen, rejected as a form of Western dominance in postcolonial studies. Even the post-Holocaust association of acculturating Jews with whiteness was validated as a form of progress within Western Europe and the United States. But it was exactly this form of Westernized "progress" that, from a postcolonial and Jewish cultural studies perspective, was complicit with colonialism and slavery as well as the Holocaust (Bauman 1989).

One clear divide between Jewish and postcolonial studies is the question of Israel/Palestine as illustrated in the Henry Louis Gates volume. The reason for the lack of scholarly insight on all sides, as the editors of a recent collection, *Colonialism and the Jews,* contend, is the "place of colonialism in the history of Zionism and the State of Israel" (Katz et al. 2017, p. 2). From the perspective of postcolonial studies, "Jews and colonialism frequently became reduced to polemics over Zionism, flattening the issue rather than taking account of its nuances" (p. 2). Other reasons for the troubled stance of many postcolonial theorists toward Jewish victimhood include the history of individual Jews who were part of the colonial project; the European history of Zionism; and the contemporary cultural conflicts between "whitened" American Jews and African Americans (Craps 2013, pp. 80–88). But such politics does not explain the resistance to the history of antisemitism within postcolonial studies, especially given the extent to which canonical anti-colonial thinkers, as I will explore in this essay, understood the implications of Western antisemitism for their own colonial history.

Despite such mutual resistance, scholars within postcolonial studies have become among the most important interlocutors, over the past two decades, with those working on new theoretically informed accounts of antisemitism. A recent special issue of *The Cambridge Journal of Postcolonial Literary Inquiry,* for instance, argues that the "Jewish experience of modernity can be said to provide fertile templates for understanding questions as varied as minoritarianism, diaspora, nostalgia, racialization, ethnicity, cultural difference, creolization, hybridity and colonialism, all of which are central concerns in postcolonial studies" (Goetschel and Quayson 2015, p. 6). What brings together postcolonial and Jewish studies in this formulation is the stress on "minoritarian" Jews as an ethnic minority in the diaspora who are the objects of "racialization" or antisemitism. This contrasts with the "majoritarian" formulation of Jewish history which focuses on the Jewish nation-state of Israel and its maltreatment of indigenous Palestinians. Here the "Jewish experience of modernity" can be mapped onto a Western colonial tradition (Hesse 2016). The ambivalence between "minoritarian" and "majoritarian" versions of Jewish history shows the extent to which the postcolonial understanding of antisemitism is still open to dispute. Equally, accounts of antisemitism which regard it as a unique form of prejudice, wholly different from other forms of "racialization," reject any comparative or intersectional approach.

My essay will distinguish different strands within postcolonialism since the immediate postwar. I will account for the varying disciplinary formations of postcolonial studies in relation to antisemitism which were equally accommodating and unaccommodating. Such tensions were resolved in the flowering of interdisciplinary studies, which do not confine colonial racism and antisemitism to separate spheres. I will explore these different aspects of postcolonialism separately to highlight the resistances and responses to the intersecting histories of colonial racism and antisemitism.

Antisemitism and Colonialism After the Second World War

The study of colonialism was deeply imbricated in the experience of contemporary antisemitism in the 1940s and 1950s. Many anti-colonial theorists and camp survivors at the end of the Second World War—most prominently, Jean Améry, Hannah Arendt, Aimé Césaire, Primo Levi, Albert Memmi, and Jean-Paul Sartre—made connections between the history of genocidal antisemitism in Europe and European colonialism. Améry, for instance, drew on the anti-colonial writings of Frantz Fanon to help him overcome his sense of Jewish victimhood after his time in Auschwitz-Birkenau (Améry [1971] 2005). The anti-colonial Césaire, on the other hand, thought of Nazism as colonialism brought home to Europe ([1955] 2000). Fanon, Memmi, Levi, and Sartre made lasting linkages and analogies between French colonialism and antisemitism throughout their writings (Cheyette 2014, pp. 43–113). But the extent to which the historically intertwined work of these postwar activists and memoirists shaped the later discipline of postcolonial studies is particularly fraught. The progression from this earlier to the later work is not straightforward.

The shifting identification and dis-identification between postcolonialism and the history and experience of antisemitism is best illustrated with reference to Hannah Arendt, the influential philosopher and political theorist who fled Nazi Germany for the United States. After her death in 1975, Arendt's *The Origins of Totalitarianism* ([1951] 1973) was primarily interpreted as an account of "totalitarianism" rather than a book where the histories of "Anti-Semitism," "Imperialism," and "Totalitarianism" (the titles of its three sections) intersect. In fact, the section on "Totalitarianism" was added late in the day, in response to the Cold War, and the original title of Arendt's book was *The Elements of Shame: Anti-Semitism, Imperialism, Racism*. The mixed fortunes of Arendt's *Origins*—marginalized in the second half of the twentieth century as Cold War propaganda only to be foregrounded in the twenty-first—indicates just how troubling the conjunction of antisemitism and colonialism has been until quite recently. One reason for the marginalization of Arendt's foundational work within postcolonial studies is that it was mistakenly perceived to construct colonial racism and genocide in Africa as a precursor to genocidal antisemitism rather than as an autonomous history. Today, however, we could describe *Origins* as an intersectional analysis of colonial racism and antisemitism *avant la lettre*.

It is a paradox of Arendt's reception that while her work is both central to the formation of postcolonial studies and Holocaust Studies—the former following *Origins*, the latter following the fierce debate sparked by Arendt's *Eichmann in Jerusalem* (1963)—it is only in the twenty-first century that she has been a catalyst for bringing these two disciplines together. One reason for this mixed reception is that the contextualized history of antisemitism exposes the tensions and contradictions within and between early anti-colonial activism (which drew on the experience of European antisemitism) and later postcolonial studies (which largely ignored it). Arendt's account of Adolf Eichmann has proved contentious to this day which has meant that she has had little influence within Holocaust Studies.

But the extent to which Arendt is a catalyst for new thinking with regard to the history of antisemitism should not be underestimated. Shortly after the end of the Second World War, Arendt in *Origins* refuted the belief in an "eternal antisemitism" (p. 16) as a means of explaining the rise of Nazism. According to Arendt, this timeless conceptualization of "Jew-hatred" turned antisemitism into a "normal and natural reaction to which history gives only more or less opportunity. Outbursts need no special explanation because they are natural consequences of an eternal problem" (p. 16). By restoring the history of antisemitism to time, place, and context (by rejecting an eternalist approach), Arendt was able to compare the "imperialist and totalitarian versions of antisemitism" (p. 9) at the heart of Nazi ideology. A contextualized history of antisemitism takes up the first part of *Origins*, the question of genocidal racism in African colonial culture the second, and Nazi and Soviet totalitarianism the third. In other words, Arendt's comparative perspective is not possible without her rethinking an "eternal antisemitism" and returning it to history. That is why in recent years *Origins* has become a common point of reference for those within postcolonial studies who wish to explore the historical inter-connections between racism, fascism, colonialism, and antisemitism.

A Jewish refugee from Nazi-occupied Germany and France (having escaped from Gurs internment camp in 1940), Arendt was a stateless person for more than a decade. After the failure of European humanism, she struggled to find a language to articulate what she called in her preface to *Origins*, "homelessness on an unprecedented scale, rootlessness to an unprecedented depth" ([1951] 1973, p. vii). Likewise, Arendt's contemporary, the anti-colonial activist Frantz Fanon, searched for a new global humanism, insisting at the start of *The Wretched of the Earth* on "the kind of tabula rasa which from the outset defines any decolonization" (1961, p. 1). Both Arendt and Fanon engaged with the "common enslavement" (Fanon 1967, p. 33) of the oppressed, both on the continent of Europe and within its colonies, and spoke of a "new beginning" (Arendt [1951] 1973, p. 478) for humanity after decolonization and the defeat of fascism.

But these thinkers did not speak with a uniform voice with regard to the value of European humanism after the Holocaust and decolonization, another point of friction with later postcolonial studies that tended to reject European humanism *tout court*. One of the lasting strengths of this early work was its varied attempts to find a language to recuperate the humanist values of Europe that had so recently descended into barbarity. Whereas Fanon, Césaire, and Sartre thought that humanism was mired in the colonialist history of Europe and was beyond salvation, Levi, Memmi, Améry, and Arendt all attempted to reclaim humanist values. With the breakdown of the grand narratives of the first half of the twentieth century, however, these debates concerning European humanism seemed increasingly irrelevant until the recent focus on global humanism. The rise of ethnic identity politics since the 1970s has meant that these early intersecting histories, written mainly in the 1940s and 1950s, have been largely confined to separate spheres. What is more, it was difficult to locate these entwined histories across Europe and its colonies, given the growth of distinct scholarly disciplines, such as Holocaust Studies and postcolonial studies, which focus on particular racialized victims of the camps and of colonialism.

POSTCOLONIAL STUDIES

When it comes to the history of antisemitism, the early anti-colonial work stands in stark contrast to the resistances in later postcolonial studies. In *White Mythologies*, for example, Robert Young, in an early summary of Said's *Orientalism*, speaks of the history of antisemitism as a form of Western "internal Orientalism" (1990, pp. 125–39) thereby acknowledging it, but only in a degraded form different from the main focus of the field of inquiry. This equivocal gesture fails to link the history of antisemitism to a main variant of Western Orientalism—German Orientalism—that focused attention on the Jewish body and was missing from Said's book (Kalmar and Penslar 2005, pp. 51–67).

To be sure, Said does rightly describe Orientalism as a "strange secret sharer of Western antisemitism" (Said 1978, p. 27) in his formative work. But he also speaks of the "Jew of pre-Nazi Europe" as being eventually "bifurcated": "one Semite went the way of Orientalism, the other, the Arab, was forced to go the way of the Oriental" (pp. 286–307). That *Orientalism* draws from two writers of Jewish origin, Benjamin Disraeli and Karl Marx, in its epigraphs foreshadows this bifurcation. Disraeli's legacy goes the way of Empire, "race," and myth-making; Marx goes the way of internationalism, anti-imperialism, and intellectual critique. In recent years, Aamir Mufti, in his *Enlightenment in the Colony: The Jewish Question and the Crisis of Postcolonial Culture*, has complicated this binary divide. His book shows that the politics of the so-called "Jewish Question" in modern Europe was globalized in South Asia with the partition of the sub-continent along religious grounds (2007, pp. 2–3). The result of this globalized "Jewish Question" is a crisis-ridden Muslim minority in India whose enforced minority status was, Mufti contends, comparable with modern European Jewry before the Holocaust. Such unacknowledged doublings (on both sides of the debate) were part of the formation of postcolonial studies. But the similarity in subject area and approach between the history of colonialism and antisemitism meant that postcolonial and Holocaust studies were to strictly differentiate themselves. In that way, they could be separate academic disciplines.

Such disciplinary distinctions were reinforced by the supposed historical transformation of Jews from minority to majority, victim to persecutor, after the Holocaust. The colonized condition of the Palestinians within the post-1967 occupied territories of Israel made the incorporation of European antisemitism into a postcolonial perspective problematic as Jewish suffering in Europe led to Palestinian displacement. Ethnic studies in the United States, from which much postcolonial scholarship grew, emerged, for instance, at a moment of Third World solidarity with the Palestinians. This, in turn, resulted in sharp academic, political, and cultural divisions between ethnic and Jewish studies, and postcolonial and Holocaust studies. After 1967, the State of Israel, from a Third World perspective, was no longer a bastion of anti-colonial resistance to British rule and was, moreover, increasingly perceived as a colonial-settler state in its own right. The national struggle, at the heart of the Marxian strand of postcolonialism, excluded Jewish nationalism in these terms. But the Zionist school of historiography also thought that suffering peoples could only determine history via a national movement.

Given these uncomfortable similarities, it is hard not to conclude that an intersecting anti-colonial history was repressed so that the new discipline of postcolonial studies could retain a misguided political clarity. Postcolonial studies stressed the plight of the Palestinians; Jewish studies the plight of the Jews in pre-war Europe. Above all, the longevity and supposed hegemony of the Jewish experience within Western culture (hence "Judeo-Christian") made it difficult for those in postcolonial studies to engage with the history of antisemitism without a feeling of being overwhelmed by a more influential and well-established narrative. The history of the Holocaust and antisemitism was mistakenly perceived to undermine the nascent discipline of postcolonial studies in the 1980s, especially in the Euro-American academy. That is why self-designated "new" disciplines—such as diaspora studies, postcolonial studies, and ethnic and racial studies—have defined themselves as superseding a history of antisemitism or diaspora, often constructed as age-old or "classic" (Cohen 1997, pp. 1–29), despite the recent vintage of this history in the twentieth century (Cheyette 2017).

THE COSMOPOLITAN INTELLECTUAL

There is also a less obvious reason for the resistance of postcolonial studies to the history of antisemitism: the twentieth-century figure of the rootless cosmopolitan who was particularly prominent within Nazism and Stalinism and personified as the stateless refugee after the Second World War. In stark contrast to the phenomenon of mass national uprisings against colonialism, which characterizes nationalist anti-colonialism, the figure of the rootless cosmopolitan was perceived as elitist, detached from the fray, and unable to engage with Marxian politics. This figure was part of the history of anti-colonialism, as can be seen in Fanon's *The Wretched of the Earth* (1961).

Fanon was haunted by the image of the deracinated cosmopolitan who contrasted, starkly, with the reborn intellectuals, not unlike himself, who were to lead the anti-colonial revolution. The cosmopolitan has to tear itself away from "the white man's culture":

> ...painful and difficult though it may be.... If it is not accomplished there will be serious psycho-affective injuries and the result will be individuals without anchor, without horizon, colorless, stateless, rootless– a race of angels. (p. 175)

The deracinated intellectual—"colorless, stateless, rootless"—is contrasted starkly with the organic intellectual who was "a living part of Africa and her thought" (p. 167). In this reading, the figure of the rootless cosmopolitan (one of a "race of angels") needs to be transformed completely. These concerns were first highlighted by Fanon's friend and comrade, the Tunisian-Jewish Albert Memmi, who notes the long-standing anxieties about supposed cosmopolitan Jews in French colonial culture. In an influential essay on Fanon's "Impossible Life" (taken up by Henry Louis Gates), Memmi argues that it was the disavowal of his origins in Martinique and its people in particular that characterizes a diasporic, cosmopolitan Fanon who "broke with France, the French people and Europe" (Memmi 1973, p. 19). In this reading, Fanon's life becomes something of a family romance with the surrogate fatherland of Algeria taking the "place of Martinique" (p. 24). Memmi thinks of his subject as akin to a déraciné "Jewish intellectual," which accounts for a series of conversion narratives culminating in Fanon's rejection of Algerian nationalism and his turn to pan-Africanism:

> I suspect that Fanon's sudden and intransigent Africanism roused new hostility against him. He might have shared the fate of those Jewish intellectuals who declare themselves universalists and are suspected of cosmopolitanism and even treason; they are not considered sufficiently legitimate members of the community to be permitted such aloofness. For an Algerian so late in the making it was imprudent, to say the least, to put so recent a bond to the test. (p. 32)

Memmi's account of Fanon, it is important to recognize, was based on lived experience. Fanon was denounced by Memmi's acquaintance, Dr. Ben Soltan, as a "Zionist," as well as a "Black Doctor" (p. 26), after a conflict of interest at the Clinique Manouba in Tunis, where Fanon worked for three years following his exile from Algeria in 1956. After working at the clinic for years, Ben Soltan, its director, argued that Fanon was maltreating Algerian and Tunisian patients "on Israeli orders" (Memmi 1973, p. 26) and, according to David Macey, as a "spy and ally of the Jews" (2000, p. 313). The accusation of being an Israeli spy (three years after France's involvement with Israel and Britain in the Suez adventure to neutralize Egyptian influence in North Africa) meant that Fanon had to remove his family from the hospital grounds. Fanon's status as a cosmopolitan outsider or, in Gates' telling phrase, a "European interloper" (1991, p. 468) reinforced these allegations. No wonder Fanon, in his last book, stresses the role of the organic intellectual, part of the masses who were opposing colonialism, rather than the isolated and rootless intellectual who, from the 1930s onwards, was part of the lethal antisemitic discourse of both Stalinism and Nazism.

As Bruce Robbins has argued, the routine dismissal of the (often Judaized) rootless cosmopolitan within a mainly Marxian strand of postcolonial studies (on the side of the "organic intellectual") continued long after the Second World War. The cosmopolitan is said to have disavowed nationalist anti-colonialism and, in doing so, is assumed to have disempowered and disregarded the wretched of the earth (Robbins 1997, p. 72). Aijaz Ahmad, for instance, uses the Orwellian distinction (in all senses) between the principled "exile"—at one with the subjugated masses—and the depthless "vagrant"—a rootless cosmopolitan above the fray—to portray Salman Rushdie and Edward Said as "vagrants" (Ahmad 1992, pp. 157–58). Only Said's public pronouncements on behalf of the Palestinian people and the death threat looming over Rushdie are said to redeem them from their self-indulgent "political vagrancy" (1992, p. 198). This line of argument was given prominence by Kwame Anthony Appiah who argued, in a much quoted passage, that "postcoloniality is the condition of what we might ungenerously call a comprador intelligentsia: of a relatively small, Western-style, Western-trained, group of writers and thinkers who mediate the trade in cultural commodities of western capitalism at the periphery" (Appiah 1992, p. 149). Arif Dirlik wrote that "postcoloniality is the condition of the intelligentsia of global capitalism" (1994, pp. 329, 356) in a notorious simplification of this passage (which nonetheless is much cited within postcolonial studies). In this Marxian line of argumentation, the rootless cosmopolitan—and by extension the focus on diaspora, minority histories, and mixed or hybrid expressions of intellectual dissidence—are reduced to an expression of global capitalism, itself a reflection of cultural dominance.

But Said, identified by Ahmad as a cosmopolitan "vagrant," explicitly rejected this strand of postcolonial studies and, like Bhabha and Spivak, distanced himself increasingly from institutionalized postcolonial studies *tout court*. In a similar act of distancing in his later years, Said (2003, 2004, 2006) embraced a supposed humanist cosmopolitanism—including Jewish exilic figures and the history of antisemitism—in an intellectual and political return to those whom he regarded as "last Jews" (Cheyette 2012) such as Theodor Adorno, Eric Auerbach, and Sigmund Freud, all refugees from Nazi Germany. In foregrounding these Jewish intellectuals, all in the name of exilic singularity and dissidence, Said highlighted those aspects of postcolonial studies, especially the histories of fascism and antisemitism (and by implication their impact on the Palestinian people), which had been hitherto missing. But he preferred "exile" over "diaspora" in his work and refused the designation "new Jews" for Palestinians when it came to their suffering, so as to articulate a narrative that was not merely an appropriation of the better-known history of the Jews. What is more, his late work remade all of these Jewish figures in his own image as exiled and isolated intellectuals. The incorporation and distancing of this history by Said was summed up by his self-image, in one of his final interviews, as a "last Jew" or "Jewish-Palestinian" (Viswanathan 2001, p. 458).

Whereas Said incorporated the cosmopolitan Jew within his purview, in stark contrast to the Marxian strand of postcolonial studies, Bhabha took the opposite route. In his early work Bhabha engaged fully with the Frankfurt School, referring widely to exilic German-Jewish figures such as Walter Benjamin and Theodor Adorno, as well as Freud, and constructed Fanon (following Memmi) as a cosmopolitan figure. In these terms Bhabha, in his influential introduction to Fanon's *Black Skin, White Masks* (1952), no longer thought of Fanon as a revolutionary anti-colonialist but argued that Fanon cannot be "easily placed in a seamless narrative of liberationist history" (Bhabha 1986, p. viii). But this prominent repositioning of Fanon has proved to be short-lived with his biographer arguing, in a damning summary, that Bhabha's version of Fanon has transformed him into a free-floating and empty cosmopolitan "outside of time and space and in a purely textual dimension" (Macey 2000, pp. 27–28). Bhabha, in response to such criticisms, wrote an introduction to *The Wretched of the Earth* (1961) which restored Fanon, unconvincingly, as a revolutionary Marxist (Bhabha 2004). The revolutionary certainties of *The Wretched of the Earth*, and what it is to be a "racialized person" (Bhabha 2004, pp. xix–xx), replace the cosmopolitan uncertainties of *Black Skin, White Masks*. This quest for political certainty, in short, is why the history of antisemitism and the Judaized cosmopolitan figure have been expunged from a Marxian postcolonialism.

Old/New Areas of Research

Hannah Arendt's oeuvre—somewhere between literature, history, philosophy, and politics—responded to the horrors of the modern world "without a banister" (quoted in Bernstein 1996, p. 41), without the help of established categories. That was why she was to read novels and other narratives as a way of understanding and articulating, with fierce independence, her experience of totally unprecedented times (Gottlieb 2007). It is not a coincidence, in this regard, that imaginative literature was a key component of the anti-colonial work of the 1940s and 1950s, and also of those who recuperated this history in the twenty-first century. The most important anti-colonial thinkers and Holocaust survivors all incorporated complex and mixed narrative forms to help them comprehend the uncharted territories of mass decolonization and genocidal antisemitism in Europe. Thinking "without a banister" (or established disciplinary boundaries) is also the way in which postcolonial studies and the study of antisemitism can be brought together to enrich the historical record.

In this spirit, Paul Gilroy's work in the late 1990s was the catalyst for a return to these intersecting histories and specifically in generating the "colonial turn" (Rothberg 2009, pp. 101–7) in Holocaust Studies provoked by a new reading of Arendt's *Origins*. Gilroy, an independent-minded anti-racist, extended the reach of Arendt's work by including the black Atlantic within his purview. It was also significant that he began his work with Fanon's oft-cited belief that "an antisemite is inevitably anti-Negro" (Fanon 1952, p. 122). Such cross-cutting histories have resulted in Gilroy refusing any form of identity politics or race-thinking. His work also militated against conventional disciplinary thinking that made it "so difficult for so many people to accept the knotted intersection of histories" (Gilroy 2000, p. 78) which, in an early example, brought together black American soldiers as witnesses to the horrors of the Nazi death camps (Gilroy 1998, pp. 282–97). Such examples were multiplied in his later work, which collected a wide range of popular and cultural histories across national and racial divides and which enabled him to "connect the presence of colonial peoples in Europe" with the "history of Europe's Jews and other vulnerable minorities" (Gilroy 2000, p. 77). Following Gilroy, various comparative histories have been written to understand the inter-connections between fascism, antisemitism, colonialism, and racism that either drew directly from Arendt or from a critical relationship to Holocaust Studies. The main approaches of this new work can be found in two important books: one by Aamer Mufti (2007), who globalizes the "Jewish Question" in South Asia, and a second by Michael Rothberg, who reconceives the politics of memory following the Nazi occupation and French decolonization as forms of "multidirectional memory" (Rothberg 2009, pp. 1–12).

Mufti, following Arendt's historicist approach, begins with the "paradigmatic narratives" of Jewish existence within the liberal nation-state: "assimilation, emancipation, separatism, conversion, the language of state protection and minority rights, uprooting, exile and homelessness" (2007, pp. 2–3), which constituted the so-called Jewish Question in Western Europe. Rothberg, on the other hand, distances himself from Arendt's historicism by drawing on memory and trauma studies, which were developed mainly within Holocaust studies, so as to define multidirectional memory as a "counter tradition in which remembrance of the Holocaust intersects with the legacies of colonialism and slavery and ongoing processes of decolonization" (2009, p. xiii). His work is focused on postwar France which is described as a "laboratory" (p. 107) where the differing histories of colonialism and Nazism overlap. For Rothberg, the emergence of Holocaust memory on a global scale has enabled other, more marginalized, histories to be articulated, such as the Algerian War of Independence (1954–1962). But the main difference between Mufti and Rothberg is Rothberg's dismissal of a "historicist perspective" (Rothberg 2009, pp. 25, 137) in the name of validating a self-consciously "anachronistic" (pp. 135–72) multidirectionality.

What the study of antisemitism can learn from the history of colonialism and decolonization is the sheer quotidian nature of colonial racism, which is best exemplified in Said's discursive and all-encompassing *Orientalism*. Rather than thinking of antisemitism as a unique "evil," postcolonial theory rightly understands colonial racism as part of the everyday, and of a widely disseminated knowledge economy, even though this racism ranged from the assimilatory to the genocidal. Too much of the historiography of antisemitism has been shaped by the extremities of the Holocaust, especially industrialized mass murder in the death camps, as if all antisemitism leads inevitably to Auschwitz. The unique extremity of this teleological version of antisemitism has made any comparative perspective particularly difficult and has marginalized the study of antisemitism outside of a genocidal context. In recent years, the "colonial turn" (Rothberg 2009, pp. 101–7) in Holocaust studies has been a particularly welcome means of decoupling the study of antisemitism from teleology so as to return it to place, context, and history. Once the history of antisemitism is seen to be part of race-thinking in general (and vice versa), then a much richer understanding of the intertwined histories of colonial racism and antisemitism is made possible.

Conclusion

The great strength of the intersecting work by and about anti-colonial leaders and intellectuals is that it understands the history of Nazism as a form of imperialism and has shown that the history of genocide is part of the history of colonialism (Mazower 2008). From this perspective, different victims of racism and antisemitism are not confined to separate "communities of suffering," in Edward Said's resonant phrase (2000, p. 208), but are able to discover common experiences with other victims. New studies of antisemitism, with the work of postcolonialism in mind, understand the racial representations of Jews as a microcosm of broader historical concerns. This now established approach follows Arendt in refusing a free-floating, "eternal" antisemitism (outside of time and space) in order to locate discourses about Jews in a particular context. Such a critical approach to the study of antisemitism may help postcolonial studies to be more self-critical not only about its subject matter, which is all too clearly demarcated, but about its willingness to engage with intersecting histories which cannot be contained easily within a single "banistered" disciplinary perspective. The main advantage of thinking of antisemitism and postcolonialism together is that these related histories stay true to the history of the pioneering anti-colonial work of the 1940s and 1950s. Such mutual affinities, at their most accommodating, enable both the study of antisemitism and of colonial racism to move beyond exceptionalist histories of victimization and to adopt a more open-minded sense of historical connectedness.

References

Ahmad, Aijaz. 1992. *In Theory: Classes, Nations, Literatures.* London: Verso Books.
Améry, Jean. (1971) 2005. "The Birth of Man from the Spirit of Violence: Frantz Fanon the Revolutionary." *Wasafiri* 44 (Spring 2005): 13–18.
Appiah, Kwame Anthony. 1992. *In My Father's House: Africa in the Philosophy of Culture.* New York: Oxford University Press.
Arendt, Hannah. 1963. *Eichmann in Jerusalem: A Report on the Banality of Evil.* New York: Viking.
Arendt, Hannah. (1951) 1973. *The Origins of Totalitarianism.* San Diego: Harcourt Brace Jovanovich.
Baron, Salo W. 1928. "Ghetto and Emancipation: Shall We Revise the Traditional View?" *Menorah Journal* 14 (6) (June): 515–26.
Bauman, Zygmunt. 1989. *Modernity and the Holocaust.* New York: Polity Press.
Bernstein, Richard J. 1996. *Hannah Arendt and the Jewish Question.* New York: Polity Press.
Bhabha, Homi. 1986. "Remembering Fanon: Self, Psyche and the Colonial Tradition." Introduction to *Black Skin White Masks*, by Frantz Fanon, vii–xxvi. New York: Grove Press.
Bhabha, Homi. 1994. *The Location of Culture.* London: Routledge.
Bhabha, Homi. 2004. "Framing Fanon." Introduction to *The Wretched of the Earth*, by Frantz Fanon, vii–xli. New York: Grove Press.
Boyarin, Jonathan, and Daniel Boyarin, eds. 1997. *Jews and Other Differences: The New Jewish Cultural Studies.* Minneapolis: University of Minnesota Press.
Césaire, Aimé. (1955) 2000. *Discourse on Colonialism.* New York: Monthly Review Press.
Cheyette, Bryan. 2012. "A Glorious Achievement: Edward Said and the Last Jewish Intellectual." In *Edward Said's Translocations: Essays in Secular Criticism*, edited by Tobias Döring and Mark Stein, 74–97. New York: Routledge.
Cheyette, Bryan. 2014. *Diasporas of the Mind: Jewish and Postcolonial Writing and the Nightmare of History.* New Haven: Yale University Press.
Cheyette, Bryan. 2017. "Against Supersessionist Thinking: Old and New, Jews and Postcolonialism, the Ghetto and Diaspora." *Cambridge Journal of Postcolonial Literary Inquiry* 4 (3): 424–39.
Cheyette, Bryan, and Laura Marcus, eds. 1998. *Modernity, Culture and "the Jew."* Stanford: Stanford University Press.
Cheyette, Bryan, and Nadia Valman, eds. 2004. *The Image of the Jew in European Liberal Culture, 1789–1914.* London: Vallentine Mitchell.
Cohen, Robin. 1997. *Global Diasporas: An Introduction.* New York and London: Routledge.
Craps, Stef. 2013. *Postcolonial Witnessing: Trauma Out of Bounds.* New York: Palgrave Macmillan.
Dirlik, Arik. 1994. "The Postcolonial Aura: Third World Criticism in the Age of Global Capitalism." *Critical Inquiry* 20: 328–56.
Fanon, Frantz. 1952. *Black Skin, White Masks.* Translated by Charles Lam Markmann. New York: Grove Press.
Fanon, Frantz. 1961. *The Wretched of the Earth.* Translated by Constance Farrington. New York: Penguin Books.

Fanon, Frantz. 1967. *Toward the African Revolution: Political Essays*. Translated by Haakon Chevalier. New York: Grove Press.
Friedländer, Saul, ed. 1992. *Probing the Limits of Representation*. Boston: Harvard University Press.
Gates, Henry Louis, ed. 1986. *"Race," Writing, and Difference*. Chicago: University of Chicago Press.
Gates, Henry Louis. 1991. "Critical Fanonism." *Critical Inquiry* 17: 457–70.
Gilroy, Paul. 1998. "Not Being Inhuman." In *Modernity, Culture and "the Jew,"* edited by Bryan Cheyette and Laura Marcus, 282–97. Stanford: Stanford University Press.
Gilroy, Paul. 2000. *Against Race: Imagining Political Culture Beyond the Color Line*. Cambridge, MA: Belknap of Harvard University Press.
Goetschel, Willi, and Ato Quayson. 2015. "Jewish Studies and Postcolonialism." *The Cambridge Journal of Postcolonial Literary Inquiry* 3 (1): 1–9.
Gottlieb, Susannah Young-ah, ed. 2007. *Hannah Arendt: Reflections on Literature and Culture*. Stanford: Stanford University Press.
Grossman, Marshall. 1989. "The Violence of the Hyphen in Judeo-Christian." *Social Text* 22 (Spring): 115–22.
Hesse, Isabelle. 2016. *The Politics of Jewishness: The Holocaust, Zionism, and Colonialism in Contemporary World Literature*. London: Bloomsbury Academic.
Kalmar, Ivan, and Derek Penslar, eds. 2005. *Orientalism and the Jews*. Lebanon: University Press of New England.
Katz, Ethan, Lisa Leff, and Maud Mandel, eds. 2017. *Colonialism and the Jews*. Bloomington: Indiana University Press.
Macey, David. 2000. *Frantz Fanon: A Life*. London: Granta Books.
Mazower, Mark. 2008. *Hitler's Empire: Nazi Rule in Occupied Europe*. New York: Penguin Books.
Memmi, Albert. 1973. "The Impossible Life of Frantz Fanon." *Massachusetts Review* 14: 9–39.
Mufti, Aamir. 2007. *Enlightenment in the Colony: The Jewish Question and the Crisis of Postcolonial Culture*. Princeton: Princeton University Press.
Robbins, Bruce. 1997. "Secularism, Elitism, Progress and Other Transgressions." In *Cultural Readings of Imperialism: Edward Said and the Gravity of History*, edited by Keith Ansell Pearson, Benita Parry, and Judith Squires, 67–87. London: Lawrence and Wishart.
Rothberg, Michael. 2009. *Multidirectional Memory: Remembering the Holocaust in the Age of Decolonization*. Stanford: Stanford University Press.
Said, Edward. 1978. *Orientalism*. New York: Vintage Books.
Said, Edward. 2000. *The End of the Peace Process: Oslo and After*. London: Granta Books.
Said, Edward. 2003. *Freud and the Non-European*. London: Verso Books.
Said, Edward. 2004. *Humanism and Democratic Criticism*. New York: Palgrave Macmillan.
Said, Edward. 2006. *On Late Style: Music and Literature Against the Grain*. New York: Bloomsbury.
Spivak, Gayatri Chakravorty. 1988. *In Other Words: Essays in Cultural Politics*. New York: Routledge.

Viswanathan, Gauri, ed. 2001. *Power, Politics and Culture: Interviews with Edward W. Said*. New York: Pantheon Books.

Young, Robert. 1990. *White Mythologies: Writing History and the West*. New York: Routledge.

Young, Robert. 1994. *Colonial Desire: Hybridity, Culture and Race*. New York: Routledge.

CHAPTER 19

Racism

Robert Bernasconi

The precise relation of racism to antisemitism is highly contested not least because of the moral force that has come to be attached to both of these words. This is reflected in the controversy that arises whenever someone either asserts or denies that antisemitism is a racism. In this article I attempt to investigate some of the widely held intuitions about the relation of these two terms by taking a genealogical perspective on the complex history of the word *racism* and by focusing especially on some of the moments when it intersects with the word *antisemitism*. I begin with the fact that the word *racism* to all intents and purposes entered the English language in the late 1930s as one of the preferred ways to refer to the biologically based antisemitism promoted by National Socialism and friends of National Socialism. It was thus initially understood as a much narrower term than either *racialism* or *race prejudice,* both of which had been current for some time. During the 1950s racism was primarily understood as a set of ideas, a doctrine, rather than an emotional attitude, and one of the tendencies that was most pronounced among those who chose to use this word at that time was a belief that it could be opposed on a scientific basis. Racism was not so much evil as it was an epistemological error that arose from a false inference from the physical to the mental or from an ignorance of biology. At the same time as an understanding of the extent of the horrors of the Holocaust developed the moral force of the word grew. The paradox was that in consequence antisemitism and racism generally were soon treated both as evil and as an easily refutable and simple mistake.

R. Bernasconi (✉)
Penn State University, University Park, PA, USA
e-mail: rlb43@psu.edu

Racial antisemitism was the initial paradigm around which the understanding of racism was formed and in many ways it continues to shape how we think about racism even down to today, even though the dominant paradigm of racism is no longer antisemitism but an anti-Black racism that was shaped less by biological theories than by slavery, segregation, and colonialism. This is why a number of prominent Black intellectuals, most notably Stokely Carmichael and Charles V. Hamilton, promoted the idea of institutional racism (1967, p. 4).

To be sure, to the extent that specifically racist forms of antisemitism still exist today they rarely conform to the model of Nazi antisemitism that was targeted by intellectuals in the late 1930s. Around 1940, when English speakers heard the word *racism* they would most likely not have understood by it first and foremost the systems of oppression that had been directed against people of African descent since long before there was anything that could remotely be called a racialized biology. They would have thought of the use of a racial biology against the Jews among Nazis and their supporters. Today the term *racism* may not have lost any of its moral force, but it has lost some of its diagnostic usefulness, because the context in which it now tends to be applied is very different from the one in which it was originally formulated and to which it was supposed to be applied.

In the first section I will take up the concepts of racism and antisemitism in more detail, focusing especially on their intersection. I will develop my argument that antisemitism, insofar as it is understood as the doctrine that the Jews constituted a separate and dangerous race or people, helped to shape a relatively narrow idea of racism as a set of ideas which legitimates discrimination against some person or persons on account of their race biologically conceived. In the second section I will focus on the history of the late nineteenth- and early twentieth-century debate concerning whether the Jews were better understood as constituting a race or a religion. I will show how that debate helped to shape the dominant strategy about how best to combat racism. Because the nineteenth-century debate in Germany over whether a Jew who had assimilated was still a Jew resembles in some respects the fifteenth-century debate in Spain over whether a Jew who had converted to Christianity was still a Jew, I will in the third section turn to the ongoing debate over whether the Purity of Blood Statutes can be seen as one of the origins of modern racism. Finally, in the fourth section I will turn briefly to the broader understanding of a "racism without races" as a context in which to consider briefly some current issues.

I

Both *racism* and *antisemitism* were originally proposed as positive terms used to describe ideas that needed to be cultivated, and not, as in later usage, to refer to something to be condemned. Wilhelm Marr is often wrongly credited with having introduced the neologism *Antisemitismus* because the term quickly gained popularity in the context of the *Antisemitenliga* (The League of Antisemites) that was formed in 1879 by Marr as a consequence of the success of the early editions of his pamphlet *Der Sieg des Judenthums über das Germanenthum* (*The Victory of Jewry over Germandom*) (Bruns 2011, pp. 125, 135–36). Although Marr often took the somewhat pessimistic tone of a person who thought it was too late to try to do anything to undo what had already happened, antisemitism was in his eyes the proper reaction of Germans to the fact that they had succumbed to Jewish influence, which is what he thought had happened. Similarly, in France the term *racisme* originally referred to attempts to promote a reshaping of France's national identity (Taguieff 2001, pp. 82–96). Nevertheless, before long both terms had assumed negative connotations. The term *antisemitism* was so negative that in the early 1920s even *The Dearborn Independent*, one of the most antisemitic organs in the United States at the time, presented itself as an opponent of antisemitism (Anonymous 1920). At roughly the same time in France *racisme* was increasingly being associated with the German *völkisch* movement and so was widely condemned from the standpoint of French universalism. The word *Rassismus* slowly found its way into German in the works of critics of National Socialism, such as the biologist Hugo Iltis, who specifically linked it with "the 'scientific' antisemitism" of such figures as Hans F. K. Günther (Iltis 1935, p. 7). When the word finally entered the English language it had the same narrow usage. The first book in the English language which included it in the title, Magnus Hirschfeld's *Racism* (1938), was mainly a translation of some articles that had appeared separately in the German language much earlier. The book is wide-ranging but it is clear that the ultimate focus was Germany under the Nazis and the argument was that racism was a temporary and largely local problem.

The main proponents of the concept of racism when the word was introduced into the English language were Jewish anthropologists, in particular Franz Boas and his students, Ruth Benedict and Ashley Montagu. They used the word *racism* primarily to describe a form of racial antisemitism, prominent especially among Nazi anthropologists, that they believed themselves able to refute by arguing that one cannot legitimately infer cultural or moral characteristics from someone's physical appearance or their lineage. That is to say, they applied their signature distinction between nature and culture to isolate biological claims about the races in the conviction that these were at the root of many of the negative judgments against Jews and by extension against other populations too (Bernasconi 2011). Jews, they could simply argue, did not constitute a race in the technical biological sense; they wanted to restrict the notion of race to three to five main races (Bernasconi 2014). In other cases, they could suggest that inferences from physical characteristics to intellectual or cultural characteristics were illegitimate. On their account racism rested on false scientific claims. If we take into account the fact that racial science was only one source of Nazi antisemitism, it becomes clear that this approach was far too narrow and poorly designed to address even the cases it was supposed to address (Hutton 2005, p. 15).

In 1938, in an effort to intervene in the debate around immigration that had become more intense as Jews sought to leave Germany for the United States, Boas, on behalf of the New York Section of the American Anthropologist Association, published *Science Condemns Racism* (Boas et al. 1938). Science could be an effective tool against racism because racism was understood to be bad science. This was the approach that was continued in the 1950s following the impact of the UNESCO Statement on Race of 1950, which was formulated under the chairmanship of Ashley Montagu, a student of Boas (1952, p. 5). UNESCO argued that it was the international institution best equipped to lead the campaign against race prejudice because race hatred thrived on scientifically false ideas and was "nourished by ignorance" (1952, p. 5). So, for example, although Boas and some of his students had from early in the century rejected the idea that the Jews constituted a race in the biological sense of the word, the UNESCO Statements of 1950 and 1951 still acknowledged the existence of the four main biological races. They focused only on dismantling the idea of biological races as they existed in the popular mind, but they put very little effort into examining how racism actually operated (Bernasconi 2019).

One should not diminish the importance of what Boas and his students accomplished. Nevertheless, at a time when there had been little attempt to understand how systems of racial oppression operated, it meant that the focus of the attack on racism long remained, not on dismantling the way institutions operated to favor individuals of one race over others, or even on attacking laws designed to maintain the alleged racial integrity of highly diverse populations, but on outlawing illicit uses of the word *race*. The Nazi racial scientist Fritz Lenz was among the experts UNESCO consulted, somewhat surprisingly given that he had been head of the Kaiser Wilhelm Institute for Anthropology under the Nazis and had supported the legislation of the Natural Socialist state and insisted in that context that Jews should not be defined by external race characteristics but by descent (1941, p. 397). Lenz complained that the 1951 statement, like its predecessor, was designed to counteract antisemitism, that this was only one aspect of racism, and that UNESCO made "no distinction between the different forms of it" (UNESCO 1952, pp. 30–31). That is to say, the UNESCO strategy, which has been widely adopted, was fundamentally directed against antisemitism rather than anti-Black racism. To refute racism, Boas and his followers had defined it so narrowly that it failed to target those forms of Nazi antisemitism that in their own terms were best defined as cultural, a point Frantz Fanon made when attacking the UNESCO approach to racism that had been formulated by Montagu (Fanon 1967, p. 32).

II

I will now turn to examine the history of how the Jews came to be thought of as a race as a prelude to an examination of how Nazi racial scientists thought of the Jews. It should not be forgotten that in the nineteenth century the term *race* was in many discourses more of a historical category than it was either a linguistic or a biological one. Even so the reference to Semites in the term *antisemitism* was primarily drawn neither from history nor biology, but from the study of languages. In any event, the term was introduced at the same time as attempts to define Jews in terms of their biological race, rather than their religion, were gaining ground. This is relevant to the question of trying to determine to what extent a racial view of the Jews can already be attributed to Wilhelm Marr. His denial that he was writing from the point of view of religious, national, or racial hatred was highly disingenuous (1879, pp. 38, 48). Furthermore, his argument was not that the Jews presented a biological threat to the Germans, as later ideologues would maintain, but that they had imposed their culture on Germany, just like any other "conquerors" would: "Our German people are too judaicized to have any enthusiasm for their self-preservation. ... World domination belongs to Semitism" (1879, pp. 45–46). However, there is no ambiguity at all in the writings of Eugen Dühring. He was a much stronger exponent of the view that Jews should be seen through the lens of biological race than Marr ever was. Dühring described the change from seeing Jews not in terms of religion but as a race ([1881] 1997, p. 56). He drew the clear implication: "A Jewish question will exist even if all Jews turn their back on their religion and were converted to one of the ruling churches among us" ([1881] 1997, p. 57).

The idea that Jews constituted a biological race was late but did not await the introduction of the term *antisemitism*. Already in the 1780s, Johann David Michaelis can be found applying the newly minted scientific concept of race to the Jews in the context of insisting that even after ten generations Jews would not have the bodily strength to be able to serve militarily in Germany (Michaelis 1783, p. 51; Hess 2000). At this time racial characteristics were increasingly being understood as permanent (Kant [1775] 2013, p. 46), so the idea that Jewish characteristics were supposedly more permanent and less susceptible to environmental change than the characteristics of other groups became an important component of the way in which the Jews came to be seen racially. In this spirit Johann Blumenbach in 1795 claimed that Jews were not only suited to every climate, but, unlike other races, changes in climate left them unchanged (1865, p. 234). Bruno Bauer took this idea further when, albeit without explicit reference to race, he formulated the Jewish question as the question about whether the Jews could change their essence or nature (*Wesen*) (1843, p. 3). His answer was that a tenacious unsteadiness and a consistent inconsistency, which makes that nature contradictory, even a wrong (*Unrecht*), belonged to Jews by nature (1843, p. 34). This view readily lent itself to the vicious racial essentialism that came to see the Jews as a biological danger.

Even so, the tendency in the middle of the nineteenth century was still to consider the Jews not as a separate race but as a subrace within the Caucasian race. In 1844 Disraeli had Sidonia, one of the characters in his novel *Coningsby*, describe Jews as "a pure race of the Caucasian organization" (p. 200). However, by 1862 Moses Hess presented the Jewish race as one of the primary races of mankind. Furthermore, he issued the warning that "the German hates the Jewish religion less than the race," thereby already recognizing the shift that is often thought to have come later. Hess did not wait for Dühring. Already in 1869 he wrote: "Even conversion itself does not relieve the Jew from the enormous pressure of German *Judenhass*" (1918, p. 58).

To be sure, at the end of the nineteenth century and the beginning of the twentieth century there was a sustained debate— even among Jews themselves— about whether or not the Jews constituted a race (Hart 2011). In 1894 Bernard Lazare was instrumental in establishing the distinction between a theoretical antisemitism and an instinctive antijudaism (1995, p. 173), when he argued against the antisemites that there are no races, but only peoples and nations: "What is improperly called a race is not an ethnological unity, but is an historic, intellectual and moral unit. The Jews are not an *ethnos*, but they are a nationality, they are diversified types, it is true, but what nation is not diversified?" (p. 128). It was an argument that mirrored the one proposed by Ernest Renan in 1883 in his "Judaism as Religion and Race" (Renan and Sand 2010, pp. 96–97). Indeed, Arthur Ruppin described the question of whether the Jews were defined by their racial disposition (*Rassenveranlagung*) or their economic and political situation over two thousand years as the fundamental research problem concerning the Jews (1906, p. 129). We should not be surprised that Jewish writers were fully engaged with scientific studies about the Jews as a race. As late as 1934 Max Brod described the process of negotiating the racist books that characterized them negatively as follows: "Zionism faces a double task: to learn from race theorists and at the same time to refuse critically important elements of their conclusions" (1934, p. 16).

However, the focus of the anti-racists on questioning the idea of the Jews as a race, while significant in attacking popular beliefs, did not get to the heart of the biological theories promoted by Nazi scientists. Eugen Fischer, director of the Kaiser Wilhelm Institute of Anthropology, Human Heredity, and Eugenics acknowledged that the Jews were a racial mixture, but insisted that they nevertheless constituted a *Volk* with a strong mental-psychological unity (1938, p. 135). Otmar Freiherr von Verschuer, director of the Institute for Genetic Biology and Racial Hygiene, agreed that the Jews were not a race in the strict sense, but he believed that they had a different racial origin from the Germans and indeed that they had "bred" their race (in a less technical sense) themselves (von Verschuer 1938, p. 142). Hans Günther, the most widely read author on racial issues in Nazi Germany, also denied that there was a Jewish race: "The Jews are a nation (*Volk*), and like other nations, may belong to several religions; like other nations, too, they are made up of several races" (1927, p. 74). This means that the American and other scientists who opposed Nazi antisemitism by denying that the Jews could be considered a race did not meet their targets as successfully as they imagined that they did. They were attacking an idea of race that many Nazi racial theorists did not actually hold with the result that one can say that the template of a biological racism that the Boasians constructed around 1940 did not even fit the case it was designed to address. If one examines closely Nazi anti-Jewish scholarship one finds that it is located as much in the historical conception of the Jewish race as on biological conceptions and that one major source of anxiety was the difficulty of separating German identity from Jewish identity (Rupnow 2008). One can perhaps see here a remarkable affinity with Marr's conception of the problem facing the Germans in respect of the influence Jews had had over them.

Even though there was a widespread agreement among race-scientists that the Jews did not constitute a race in the biological sense of the word, this did not inhibit Nazi officials from applying racial laws to them. When they did so they quickly found that they had a problem determining who was and who was not a Jew. It was especially difficult in the case of a so-called Jewish *Mischling*. For example, in 1935 the Reich Interior Ministry insisted that who was a Jew was to be determined not by a person's religion but by their race. However, that only pushed the displacement of religion by race back a couple of generations. To determine whether a grandparent was of the Jewish race the Ministry took as sufficient that one was considered to have been of the Jewish religion (Noakes 1989, p. 315). In other words, even the most cold-hearted attempts to see the Jews as a race found themselves drawn back to seeing Jews in terms of their religion.

This problem is not altogether surprising when viewed genealogically. The assumption that there is a clear distinction between racial categories and religious categories is the product of the eighteenth century and has much to do with the need to establish that converting African slaves did not compromise their status as slaves. In the sixteenth and seventeenth centuries, terms that we would think of as either distinctively racial (such as *White*) or distinctively religious (such as *Christian*) were often used interchangeably. Scholars working on the history of the concept of race, like those working on the history of the concept of religion, are familiar with the way that the project of classifying everybody into races or religions was a product of modernity. But, to the extent that we tend to see these two concepts as fundamentally different, largely because of the way we tend to think of conversion, scholars have yet to give sufficient attention to the complex history which problematizes the anachronistic application of our concepts of religions and races to pre-modernity.

III

In attacking biological racism in 1940, Boas and his students did not want to appear to be attacking segregation in the United States because they wanted to form a consensus among their colleagues and gain the backing of politicians. There was in consequence a concerted effort at that time to write the history of racism in such a way as to make a belief in the existence of biological races indispensable to it, while identifying North American, colonial, and even South African systems of oppression that we today would not hesitate to think of as racist in other terms. Ruth Benedict wrote a history of racism that illustrates this tendency perfectly (1940, pp. 151–219).

The place of Judaism in the construction of the very idea of a biological racism has meant that the Jews are frequently seen as occupying a unique place in the history of racism understood specifically as a history of biological racism. Insofar as the possibility of conversion serves now as a major criterion distinguishing a religion from a race, it is inevitable that the focus would fall on the Purity of Blood Statutes (*estatutos de limpieza de sangre*) that were first formulated in fifteenth-century Spain. These held that the descendants of Jews and Muslims should be barred from certain secular offices, guilds, monasteries, and other religious organizations, as well as from marriage with old Christians (*Cristianos viejos*) or Christians by nature (*Cristianos de natura*), even if they had converted to Christianity, as indeed by the end of the century they had been obliged to do in order to avoid expulsion from Spain. So already in this case the possibility of conversion was discounted, as it was later in the case of African slaves in North America who had converted. For this reason it has sometimes been argued that the Purity of Blood Statutes mark the beginning of modern racism (Popkin 1980, pp. 79–81).

It is perhaps no coincidence that the question of whether the purity of blood statutes already marked a shift from a form of religious intolerance to a form of racism was already being raised at the start of the Second World War (Roth 1940). If biological racism had a clear, identifiable beginning, then this gives some cause for hope that it might have a definite end. It is apparent that the suspicion directed against the *conversos* went much further than suspicion as to whether their conversion was genuine, because the suspicion extended to the descendants of the *conversos*. The issue was not the purity of the faith of the *conversos*, but something defined by lineage or ancestry to which the metaphor of blood could be applied: "purity of blood came to overshadow purity of faith" (Yerushalmi 1982, p. 12). To this extent, as Yosef Hayim Yerushalmi explains, forced conversion solved nothing: "The traditional mistrust of the Jew as outsider now gave way to an even more alarming fear of the Converso as insider" (1982, p. 10). Nevertheless, if the claim is that concern with an individual's "purity of blood" constituted a biological racism, then it is hard to reconcile with what the promoters of these measures against the Jews were actually saying: they were not drawing on the kind of religious and social complaints later compiled in that compendium of calumnies, Johann Andreas Eisenmenger's *Judaism Revealed* [*Entdecktes Judentum*] (1711), but they were also not deploying biology as we understand it. Commentators searching for evidence for a specifically biological form of antisemitism in Spain are forced to find it in the belief that people "of the purest lineage (*de limpiissima generacion*)" develop "perverse inclinations" because they had been fed the milk of Jewish wet-nurses (Soyer 2014, pp. 34–38, 269–70). However, this example, drawn from Francisco de Torrejoncillo's *Centinela contra Judios* (1674), shows how distant fifteenth-century ideas of heredity and race are from twentieth-century ideas or even from the kinds of ideas found in eighteenth-century *Naturgeschichte*. This seems to suggest that Jewishness was not inherited biologically but transmitted like a disease or a form of pollution that can be passed on through bodily fluids. To apply to the fifteenth century the distinction between nature and culture in the way it was formed by Boas' students in the twentieth century is anachronistic (e.g., Bartlett 1993, p. 197). Albert Sicroff's phrase, "religious racism" (2000), seems to capture best the idea that Spanish hostility to Jews was still fundamentally directed against their religion rather than their ancestry, while confirming that the two cannot be entirely separated. In the light of our current understanding of the novelty of the scientific idea of heredity in the eighteenth century (Müller-Wille and Reinberger 2012, pp. 71–74), one is forced to conclude that the fifteenth-century concern with lineage was not yet biological, especially if the use of the term *biological* is intended to establish a continuity in the history of biological racism that supports the narrow use of the term *racism* associated with the Boasian school.

IV

There is a further reason to think of the distinction between racial discrimination and discrimination based on religion and belief as less secure than it seems to be at first sight. Just as the purity of blood statutes and racialized slavery can be understood with appropriate qualifications as racisms or proto-racisms before the second half of the eighteenth century when the term *race* was adopted as the preferred term to describe human varieties, so there is racism after the biological account of race has been dismissed: another racism without *races*.

Although no single narrative can capture all of the current shifts in the way the terms *racism* and *antisemitism* are thought in relation to each other, certain pointers can be given. First, while there are clear differences both in tone and content between the old antisemitism and the new antisemitism, sometimes called the new Judeophobia, the latter is not as new as is sometimes thought. The fact that the racialized language of an earlier time is not so pronounced in these new forms is not decisive. To put it another way, there are often, but by no means always, remnants of a racial antisemitism concealed within an aggressive critique of Israeli policies and especially Israel's position in global politics. This has exacerbated the already existing split between those who would return to the privileging of antisemitism as the paradigmatic form of racism and those who find a racism within forms of Zionism. Cousin and Fine have documented a number of ways in which antisemitism and racism have come to be increasingly separated in the post-'68 era, including intellectual specialism and the privileging of victim experience (2015, p. 23). Navigating this terrain is not easy because focusing on the racism that is addressed against one group invariably leads to charges that other groups are being unjustly neglected. In this way the division between racism and antiracism has led to a breakdown in the antiracist coalition, the so-called "common cause."

Secondly, one reason for the breakdown of the connection between racism and antisemitism that needs further explanation takes us back to the issue of the way in which the term *race* is still widely used in the context of the four or five main races, even in the absence of any biological legitimation of this usage, because it is important to retain these terms in order to eradicate the effects of past injustices performed in their name. Meanwhile, to talk specifically of a Jewish race today would seem to most people to be inappropriate, even racist.

Thirdly, today the term *antisemitism* is itself under attack. It has even been suggested by Alain Badiou and Eric Hazan that "the constant use of the word" *antisemitism* has led to its devaluation to the point where it has lost all meaning apart from the power of intimidation that it still possesses (2013, pp. 31–32). But it is far from clear how that differs from the constant use of the word *racism*, which, as was said earlier, has lost much of its diagnostic power because of the vast range of instances to which it is applied. One thing that should be clear is that the question of whether the concept of racism is useful for studies of antisemitism today should be divorced from the question of whether the Jews are or are not a race, just as attempts to reject the biological idea of race is too narrow a basis on which to fight anti-Black racism.

References

Anonymous. 1920. "Anti-Semitism—Will It Appear in the U. S.?" In *The International Jew*, 55–67. Dearborn: Dearborn Publishing.

Badiou, Alain, and Eric Hazan. 2013. "'Anti-Semitism Everywhere' in France Today." In *Reflections on Anti-Semitism*, edited by Alain Badiou, Eric Hazan, and Ivan Segré, 1–42. London: Verso.

Bartlett, Robert. 1993. *The Making of Europe: Conquest, Colonization, and Cultural Change, 950–1350*. Princeton: Princeton University Press.

Bauer, Bruno. 1843. *Die Judenfrage*. Braunschweig: Friedrich Otto.

Benedict, Ruth. 1940. *Race: Science and Politics*. New York: Modern Age Books.

Bernasconi, Robert. 2011. "Nature, Culture, Race." In *The Philosophy of Race*, edited by Paul Taylor, vol. 1, 41–56. New York: Routledge.

Bernasconi, Robert. 2014. "Where Is Xenophobia in the Fight against Racism?" *Critical Philosophy of Race* 2 (1): 5–19.

Bernasconi, Robert. 2019. "A Most Dangerous Error: The Boasian Myth of a Knock-Down Argument against Racism." *Angelaki* 24 (2): 92–103.
Blumenbach, Johann. 1865. *The Anthropological Treatises of Johann Friedrich Blumenbach.* London: Longman, Green, Longman, Roberts & Green.
Boas, Franz, et al. 1938. *Science Condemns Racism.* New York: New York Section of The American Committee for Democracy and Intellectual Freedom.
Brod, Max. 1934. *Rassentheorie und Judentum.* Prague: J. A. Verb.
Bruns, Claudia. 2011. "Toward a Transnational History of Racism: Wilhelm Marr and the Interrelationships Between Colonial Racism and German Anti-Semitism." In *Racism in the Modern World*, edited by Manfred Berg and Simon Wendt, 122–39. New York: Berghahn.
Carmichael, Stokely, and Charles. V. Hamilton. 1967. *Black Power: The Politics of Liberation in America.* New York: Random House.
Cousin, Glynis, and Robert Fine. 2015. "A Common Cause. Reconnecting the Study of Racism and Antisemitism." In *Antisemitism, Racism and Islamophobia*, edited by Christine Achinger and Robert Fine, 14–33. London: Routledge.
Dühring, Eugen. (1881) 1997. *Eugen Dühring on the Jews.* Brighton: Nineteen Eighty-Four Press.
Eisenmenger, Johann. 1711. *Entdecktes Judenthum.* Königsberg: n.p.
Fanon, Frantz. 1967. *Toward the African Revolution: Political Essays.* Translated by Haakon Chevalier. New York: Grove Press.
Fischer, Eugen. 1938. "Rassenenstehung und älteste Rassengeschichte der Hebräer." *Forschungen über das Judentum* 3: 121–36.
Günther, Hans. 1927. *The Racial Elements of European History.* New York: E. P. Dutton.
Hart, Mitchell Bryan, ed. 2011. *Jews and Race: Writings on Identity and Difference 1880–1940.* Waltham: Brandeis University Press.
Hess, Moses. 1918. *Rome and Jerusalem.* New York: Bloch.
Hess, Jonathan M. 2000. "Johann David Michaelis and the Colonial Imaginary: Orientalism and the Emergence of Racial Antisemitism in Eighteenth-Century Germany." *Jewish Social Studies* 6 (2): 56–101.
Hirschfeld, Magnus. 1938. *Racism.* London: Victor Gollanz.
Hutton, Christopher. 2005. *Race and the Third Reich.* Cambridge: Polity Press.
Iltis, Hugo. 1935. "Der Rassismus im Mantel der Wissenschaft." In *Rasse in Wissenschaft und Politik*, 1–9. Prague: Wahrheit.
Kant, Immanuel. (1775) 2013. "Of the Different Human Races." In *Kant and the Concept of Race*, edited by Jon M. Mikkelsen, 41–54. New York: SUNY Press.
Lazare, Bernard. 1995. *Antisemitism: Its History and Causes.* Lincoln: University of Nebraska Press.
Lenz, F. 1941. "Über Wege und Irrwege rassenkundlicher Untersuchungen." *Zeitschrift für Morphologie und Anthropologie* 39 (3): 385–413.
Marr, Wilhelm. 1879. *Der Sieg des Judenthums über das Germanenthum: Vom nicht confessionellen Standpunkt aus betrachtet.* Bern: Rudolph Costenoble.
Michaelis, Johann. 1783. "Hr. Ritter Michaelis Beurtheilung ueber die bürgerliche Verbesserung der Juden von Christian Wilhelm Dohm." In *Ueber die bürgerliche Verbesserung der Juden*, edited by Christian Wilhelm Dohm, vol. 2. Berlin: Friedrich Nicolai.
Müller-Wille, Staffan and Hans-Jörg Rheinberger. 2012. *A Cultural History of Heredity.* Chicago: University of Chicago Press.

Noakes, Jeremy. 1989. "The Development of Nazi Policy Towards the German-Jewish 'Mischlinge' 1933–1945." *Leo Baeck Institute Yearbook* 34: 291–354.
Popkin, Richard. 1980. "The Philosophical Bases of Modern Racism." In *The High Road to Pyrrhonism*, 79–102. San Diego: Austin Hill Press.
Renan, Ernest, and Shlomo Sand. 2010. *On the Nation and the "Jewish People."* London: Verso.
Roth, Cecil. 1940. "Marranos and Racial Antisemitism: A Study in Parallels." *Jewish Social Studies* 2 (3): 239–48.
Rupnow, Dirk. 2008. "Racializing Historiography: Anti-Jewish Scholarship in the Third Reich." *Patterns of Prejudice* 42 (1): 27–59.
Ruppin, Arthur. 1906. "Begabungsunterschiede christlicher und jüdischer Kinder." *Zeitschrift für Demographie und Statistik der Juden* 2: 129–35.
Sicroff, Albert. 2000. "Spanish Anti-Judaism: A Case of Religious Racism." In *Encuentros and Desencuentros: Spanish Jewish Cultural Interaction Throughout History*, edited by C. Parrondo, M. Dascal, F. Villanueza, and A. Badillos, 589–613. Tel Aviv: University Publishing Projects.
Soyer, Francois. 2014. *Popularizing Anti-Semitism in Early Modern Spain and Its Empires.* Leiden: Brill.
Taguieff, Pierre-André. 2001. *The Force of Prejudice: On Racism and Its Doubles.* Minneapolis: University of Minnesota Press.
UNESCO. 1952. *The Race Concept: Results of an Inquiry.* Paris: UNESCO.
von Verschuer, Otmar. 1938. "Rassenbiologie der Juden." *Forschungen über das Judentum* 3: 139–54.
Yerushalmi, Yosef. 1982. *Assimilation and Racial Anti-Semitism: The Iberian and the German Models.* New York: Leo Baeck Institute.

CHAPTER 20

Secularism

Lena Salaymeh and Shai Lavi

INTRODUCTION

Recent debates in Europe about the building of mosques, Islamic education in public schools, the wearing of headscarves, and exemption from sports education for girls appear to have counterparts in nineteenth-century debates concerning the building of synagogues, Jewish education in public schools, the wearing of yarmulkes, and exemptions from schooling on the Sabbath. Both Jews and Muslims in the West have been accused of being threats to public values. Similarly, both Jews and Muslims have been caricatured and treated as threats to public safety. Jews were accused of being a fifth column and Muslims are accused of being subversive and violent. Contemporary anxieties concerning a Muslim "parallel society" bring to mind accusations against the Jewish "state within a state." These often-identified similarities are significant; however, they compare expressions of judeophobia and islamophobia rather than their shared causes. We propose that one substantial and often neglected cause of judeophobia and islamophobia is secularism. Secularism normalizes judeophobia and islamophobia by delineating a category of religion that is incongruent with Jewish and Islamic traditions, thereby systematically subjugating non-Christian minorities.

This chapter explores secularism as a link between two modern forms of prejudice: judeophobia and islamophobia. Secularism is not a neutral or

L. Salaymeh (✉)
British Academy Global Professor, University of Oxford, Oxford, England
e-mail: lena.salaymeh@area.ox.ac.uk

S. Lavi
Professor of Law, Tel Aviv University, Tel Aviv, Israel
e-mail: slavi@tauex.tau.ac.il

© The Author(s) 2021
S. Goldberg et al. (eds.), *Key Concepts in the Study of Antisemitism*, Palgrave Critical Studies of Antisemitism and Racism, https://doi.org/10.1007/978-3-030-51658-1_20

universalist ideology because its origins in the European Enlightenment molded its formulation of "religion." As a post-Christian ideology, secularism did not adopt an impartial view of Judaism or Islam (Klug 2014, p. 453; Romeyn 2014, p. 94). While we build upon the critical genealogical approach of recognizing the role of Protestant Christianity in secularism's beginnings, we also appreciate the limitations of this approach. In this piece we focus on how secularism promotes intolerance of and excludes *certain* traditions as compared to Protestant Christianity. Ultimately, we argue that secular ideology conflicts with Jewish and Islamic traditions.

Preliminaries

We recognize that there are extensive debates about the meanings of judeophobia and islamophobia and that some scholars prefer to use alternative terms (Halliday 1999; López 2011). Nevertheless, we choose these two terms in order to emphasize that our study deals with two parallel phenomena in the modern secular state. (Moreover, we use judeophobia rather than anti-Semitism because of the historical particularity and political sensitivity of the latter term.) Recent studies demonstrate striking parallels as well as noteworthy distinctions between judeophobia and islamophobia. Some scholars emphasize that many Europeans viewed Jews and Muslims similarly, as strangers in Europe and as people of the Orient. Other scholars distinguish judeophobia and islamophobia, observing that in numerous Western states, Jews *were* viewed as internal threats, whereas Muslims *are* viewed as external threats. We review the existing scholarly literature in order to propose that an underappreciated dimension of the relationship between judeophobia and islamophobia is secularism and, specifically, the secular state and secular law. We argue that the legal ideology of secularism structures "religion" and "religious practices" in ways that generate judeophobia and islamophobia. We focus on secular law because, as Calo observes: "Law is the scaffolding that gives shape and definition to the secular.... The secular, after all, is not an abstract formulation, but a form of moral order that finds expression in and through law" (2014, p. 1). By comparing judeophobia and islamophobia and analyzing them in conjunction, we can observe a secular pattern of creating prejudice that would otherwise be indiscernible.

Secularism, despite its local and historical variations, is an ideology and array of practices that promotes prejudice not against religion in general, but against particular groups, especially Jews and Muslims (Kaya 2014). Rather than removing religion from the public sphere, secularism shapes religion in ways that are incongruent with Jewish and Islamic traditions (Mahmood and Danchin 2014, p. 131; Salaymeh and Lavi, forthcoming). Indeed, secularism's very construction of "religion" as a distinct sphere of human life discriminates against groups who do not separate religion from the secular public sphere. Moreover, we maintain that secular ideology portrays Judaism and Islam as threatening in ways that do not appear to have parallels with other religions. Though not the focal point of this chapter, anti-religiosity is not interchangeable with judeophobia and islamophobia because the latter are specific, racialized forms of prejudice. Importantly, we acknowledge that secularism has no essence and that there are variations in the European, North American, and other traditions of secularism. Secular states may have an established religion, no established religion, or be overtly anti-religion (Kuru 2007, p. 570; O'Brien 2016, p. 144). Moreover, whether they promote assimilation or multiculturalism, secular states construct "religion" and regulate "religious freedom" in similar ways (Mahmood and Danchin 2014, p. 155).

Though not every limitation of Jews or Muslims should immediately be labeled as judeophobia or islamophobia, it would be an even graver mistake to ignore how states and state law create, spread, and enhance these forms of systematic prejudice. Furthermore, we recognize that secular states treat Jews and Muslims distinctly. However, we contend that these distinctions often result from demographic (Jews number approximately 15 million and Muslims number approximately 1.8 billion today) and historical differences, rather than from the particularities of secularism in specific states. In a variety of historical settings, secular states have depicted and treated Jews and Muslims as threats to the secular public sphere and the modern state's security.

Some readers may question the attribution of agency to secular states. In this piece, we use the definition of a state developed by Bevir and Rhodes, who explain that a state constitutes a "series of contingent and unstable cultural practices, which in turn consist of the political activity of specific human agents" (2010, p. 1). Thus, we recognize that modern, secular states are not fundamentally judeophobic or islamophobic. Nonetheless, while the secular state's practices are diverse and flexible, we concentrate on secular state practices that marginalize and demonize Muslims and Jews. This chapter highlights judeophobia and islamophobia in the contemporary Western world, although the dynamics we outline here may be relevant to secular prejudice beyond the Western world. While we acknowledge that there are important issues of islamophobia among Jews and judeophobia among Muslims, these topics are beyond the scope of this chapter.

Literature Review

Comparing judeophobia and islamophobia is a newly developing field of research, as well as a controversial one (Mende 2010). Some of the controversies may stem from a problematic presumption that comparing judeophobia and islamophobia constitutes an attempt "to draw Muslims and Jews closer together" as part of "a political intervention" (Feldman 2017, p. 79). We doubt the validity of this presumption. We suspect that sociopolitical implications explain why much scholarly literature focuses on debating the reasonableness or unreasonableness of the comparison. Indeed, several scholars deny from the outset any comparison, insisting that judeophobia and islamophobia are analytically distinct and incomparable (Bunzl 2007; Bangstad and Bunzl 2010). For instance, Bunzl claims: "To argue for the fundamental analogy of anti-Semitism and Islamophobia is misleading, not only historically but also in terms of their contemporary articulations" (2005, p. 502). In resisting comparisons between judeophobia and islamophobia, scholars like Bunzl often assume that judeophobia serves distinct political or social purposes, while others view it as unlike any other form of prejudice. This argument for the exceptionalism of judeophobia is problematic because it highlights the extraordinary at the price of downplaying the ordinary. For example, some scholars emphasize that whereas past judeophobia (in the specific form of anti-Semitism) motivated the Nazi genocide of Jews (and other groups), contemporary islamophobia does not appear to promote genocide. While this distinction is, in principle, historically accurate, it is important to recognize that judeophobia did not always culminate in mass atrocities and that islamophobia too has led to large-scale bloodshed. Specifically, under the auspices of the islamophobic "global war on terror," Western states have killed more than 1.3 million Muslims since the September 11, 2001 attacks (PSR 2015, pp. 11, 15). While these deaths may not meet normative definitions of genocide, they should not be discounted.

In addition, some scholars claim that the "continuity of anti-Semitism from its ancient origins to today" makes it incomparable to islamophobia (Dobkowski 2015, p. 326). This assertion is based on two problematic presumptions: that early Christian critiques of Judaism were expressions of anti-Semitism and that anti-Muslim sentiments lack a lengthy history. While there are historical precursors to judeophobia and islamophobia, we approach judeophobia and islamophobia as modern phenomena. Thus, we concur with Bunzl that: "Anti-Semitism and Islamophobia, then, need to be understood in secular perspective, and that immediately reveals them as time- and place-specific phenomena" (2005, p. 502). Following many scholars, we acknowledge certain affinities between anti-Judaism and judeophobia, but ultimately distinguish between the two as historical and modern phenomena, respectively. Of course, there are scholars who have studied connections between premodern and modern forms of prejudice against Judaism/Jews and Islam/Muslims (Nirenberg 1996). Likewise, we recognize resemblances between anti-Muslim prejudice and islamophobia, but emphasize the distinction between the premodern and modern forms of this prejudice. Because the secular state plays a significant role in the production of judeophobia and islamophobia, both of these forms of prejudice are distinct from their non-secular, predecessor corollaries.

An additional claim for the incomparability of judeophobia and islamophobia is grounded in the prevailing, but misguided, assumption that either form of prejudice is a reaction to valid threats. For example, some allege that Muslim demographics and violence are triggers for islamophobia, whereas there are fewer contemporary triggers for judeophobia (Dobkowski 2015, pp. 328–29). A corresponding allegation presumes that islamophobia is an irrational form of xenophobia that makes it distinct from judeophobia (Tibi 1993). Both of these perspectives ascribe legitimacy to islamophobia or judeophobia by suggesting that these forms of prejudice are the consequences of actual threats or problems posed by Muslims or Jews. In both cases, these arguments are prejudiced as neither islamophobia nor judeophobia has a rational or empirical basis.

Finally, some scholars deny comparison by claiming that judeophobia and islamophobia appear in different sociopolitical and temporal contexts. Bunzl, for instance, claims that:

> Whereas anti-Semitism emerged in the late 19th century and had its greatest influence in the early 20th century, Islamophobia is a phenomenon of the current age. And whereas anti-Semitism was designed to protect the purity of the ethnic nation-state, Islamophobia is marshaled to safeguard the future of European civilization. (2005, p. 506)

We concur with Bunzl's observations about differences between judeophobia and islamophobia; however, we disagree with his claim against comparison. The political (nationalism versus Europeanism) and temporal (nineteenth versus twentieth centuries) distinctions Bunzl identifies do not render these two forms of prejudice incomparable. Nineteenth-century judeophobia concerned not only nationalism, but also an emerging sense of "civilized" Europe. Similarly, contemporary islamophobia often results from interwoven Europeanism and nationalism (Bayrakli and Hafez 2018, p. 16). The conclusion that should be drawn from these distinctions is that judeophobia and islamophobia are comparable and that every comparison should include acknowledging differences. Bunzl's observations direct us to Klug's conclusion that "what judeophobia was to the project of the ethnic nation-state, Islamophobia is to the project of a postnational Europe" (2014, p. 456). In other words, judeophobia and islamophobia are not identical, but analogous.

In contrast to scholarship denying comparison, some scholarship focuses on identifying and analyzing similarities between these two forms of prejudice. Kalmar and Ramadan classify three unique similarities of judeophobic and islamophobic stereotypes: the so-called clash of civilizations, attempting world domination, and conspiracy or dual loyalty (Kalmar and Ramadan 2016, pp. 352–53). These three comparable stereotypes are why many scholars view judeophobia and islamophobia as equivalent forms of prejudice. Schiffer and Wagner concur that "the exact same metaphors and ideas are used to incite hatred against Muslims as were and are used to incite hatred against Jews" (2011, p. 80). Jewish and Muslim identities are viewed in racial or ethnic terms, without consideration for the ethnic and racial diversity among Jews and Muslims. Meer and Noorani argue that biological racism against Jews and cultural racism against Muslims together contribute to "the racialisation of religious minorities" (2008, p. 214). Meer elaborates: "racialized categories have saturated cultural portrayals of Muslims and Jews, endowing each with characteristics that offered 'reassurance that their difference could be easily identified by Christians'" (2014, p. 4). Similarly, Schiffer and Wagner criticize the "total identification" that judeophobia and islamophobia advance "as if 'being Muslim' were the sole and decisive factor explaining all of a Muslim person's actions and attitudes" (2011, p. 81). In other words, both judeophobia and islamophobia contribute to the false presumption that a Jew is nothing more than a Jew and a Muslim is nothing more than a Muslim.

It should be noted that comparative scholarship usually considers the similarities and differences between *past* judeophobia and *contemporary* islamophobia. In some exceptional cases, some scholars have comparatively measured contemporary judeophobia and islamophobia. For example, Meer estimates that "in the USA, France and Germany unfavourable views of Muslims are roughly at twice the rate of unfavourable views of Jews, while in Poland and Spain the former are only a few percentage points more" (Meer 2013, p. 506). Padovan and Alietti observe that intolerance toward Muslims is significantly higher than intolerance toward Jews in Italy (2012). In these and other cases, many scholars maintain that judeophobia is currently less prevalent than islamophobia and explore these two forms of prejudice accordingly.[1]

The comparative study of judeophobia and islamophobia is a growing and instructive field. Our literature review illustrates that bigotry against Jews in the past and against Muslims in the present are viewed as incomparable, comparable but different, or comparable and similar. As a result of these debates, the existing scholarly literature generally does not move beyond describing differences or similarities. Moreover, when scholars of judeophobia or islamophobia identify potential causes, they often point to the specifics of right-wing nationalism, tension about immigration, and "security" concerns. These micro explanations for judeophobia and islamophobia are informative, but they overlook a macro and global perspective. Put differently, the existing scholarship rarely provides a larger analytical framework for understanding how judeophobia and islamophobia are related to deeper political dynamics. One important exception is the literature on Orientalism.

---

[1] We reject the allegation that anti-Zionism, in its diverse manifestations, is a form of judeophobia. Therefore, any attempt to conflate the two and argue for a growing presence of judeophobia is highly questionable.

Orientalism, Judeophobia, and Islamophobia

Some scholars argue that the comparable prejudices against Muslims and Jews are the consequence of Orientalism. Said, and many who follow in his footsteps, critiqued Orientalism for being a discursive practice that caricatured Eastern societies in ways that justified imperialism. "The Orient"—as it appears in the writings of Western colonialists, Orientalist scholars, as well as in the popular imagination—is not simply an ambiguous geopolitical designation, but a problematic cultural and political trope that portrays the inhabitants of the region as simultaneously backward, exotic, and in need of Western "liberation." Islamophobia may be understood as a derivative of Orientalism (Gingrich 2005, p. 515; Skenderovic and Späti 2019). Although Orientalism primarily targeted Arabs and Muslims, it has implicated Jews from its very beginning. Said asserted that "hostility to Islam in the modern Christian West has historically gone hand in hand with, has stemmed from the same source, has been nourished at the same stream as anti-Semitism" (1985, p. 99). Thus, we might understand Orientalism, judeophobia, and islamophobia as interrelated forms of prejudice.

Recent scholarship expands and complicates our understanding of the relationship between Orientalism and judeophobia. Some scholars show how German Orientalists, such as the eighteenth-century Johann David Michaelis, increasingly associated Jews with the East and, accordingly, more with Muslims than with Christians (Hess 2000). Other scholars observe different implications of Orientalism for Jews and Muslims. Jews, unlike Muslims (or Arabs), were often portrayed as simultaneously Western and Oriental (Kalmar and Penslar 2005). Relatedly, some scholars note the ways in which European Jews self-consciously adopted an "Oriental identity" in order to distinguish themselves from non-Jewish Europeans (Brenner 1996). Though this literature elaborates our understanding of the relationship between European Jews and the "Orient," it does not alter the premise that Orientalism is entangled with both judeophobia and islamophobia.

Although Said emphasized that Orientalism was intertwined with judeophobia and islamophobia, he neglected secularism, for reasons we will not address here. Asad moves beyond Said's Orientalist critique to demonstrate the central role of "the secular" in the advent of Christian colonial Europe.[2] Asad distinguishes between secularism as a self-congratulatory enlightenment ideology, and "the secular" as a concrete set of practices, ideations, sensitivities, and insensitivities that shapes the relationship of colonial Europe toward Islam. The secular thus further illuminates underappreciated dimensions of islamophobia and judeophobia. Asad views the very category of "religion,"

---

[2] Throughout this piece, references to the Christian heritage of Europe is intended specifically to refer to Protestantism (see Asad 1993).

as commonly used today, as alien to non-Western traditions and only understandable within the context of a post-Christian and secular framework. Secularism's imposition of the (Protestant Christian) category of "religion" results in discrediting Muslim and Jewish practices, as we will elaborate more fully below.

Continuing Asad's line of inquiry, Anidjar demonstrates the important connection between judeophobia and islamophobia, emphasizing the role that "the secular," as a product of Europe, has in shaping relations with Jews and Muslims, as well as setting these two groups against each other (2008, 2009). Anidjar explores the Christian theological prehistory of modern secular views of Jews and Muslims; he explains that "the Jew is the theological (and internal) enemy, whereas the Muslim is the political (and external) enemy" (2003, p. 38). The overlaps between Orientalism, racism, and secularism are evident in how secular law treats religion. For instance, Jivraj and Herman expose how English judges, reflecting their secular orientation, deal with child welfare cases in Orientalist, racist, and Christian-biased ways (2009). Relatedly, some recent scholarship on the relationship between Jews and Muslims in France points to the role of French secularism in generating conflicts between these two communities (Katz 2015). As we will elaborate, a critique of secularism offers a more profound lens for analyzing judeophobia and islamophobia than the critique of Orientalism.

Indeed, there is an emerging trend of analyzing how state secularism contributes to perpetuating both judeophobia and islamophobia. Feldman observes that recent studies "have emphasized the common roots of anti-semitism and Islamophobia in a conception of Europe, and of modern national identity within Europe, which has been essentially Christian" (2017, p. 78). We propose that Feldman is describing secular ideology in Europe. Gilman points to European state secularism as a source of judeophobia and islamophobia (2017). Similarly, Renton and Gidley argue that both judeophobia and islamophobia "change over time as the state form changes" (2017, p. 6). Building on these observations, we outline how state secularism, despite its geographic and temporal variants, contributes to judeophobia and islamophobia.

The Prejudice of Secularism

Secularism's limitations on religion in the public sphere do not affect all citizens equally. Secular states use law "to restrict freedom of religion or belief and, in particular, its exercise by members of minority groups" (IDLO 2016, p. 7). Thus, the secular legal notion of "freedom of religion" does not prevent bias. When states demand secularity, they oppress particular groups disproportionately. The basic secular principle of removing religion from the public sphere inequitably disadvantages Jews and Muslims and exposes them to judeophobia and islamophobia. Özyürek observes that in Europe "the law which ostensibly aims to promote equality among citizens by eliminating religion in public space ... limits the freedom of expression among observant Muslims and Jews" (2005, p. 510). Similarly, Helly demonstrates how secularism in Québec regulates religious minorities (2012, p. 18). Such observations extend beyond the Western world; non-Western secular states also generate prejudice against religion. For instance, islamophobia is discernible in Muslim-majority states, such as Turkey, where secularism is central to the state's ideology (Yel and Nas 2014).

In some cases, secularism is a thinly veiled form of minority oppression that cuts across the political spectrum (Bangstad and Bunzl 2010, p. 226; Balibar 1991). Historically, as well as in contemporary society, prejudice against Jews and Muslims comes from both the right and the left (Bayrakli and Hafez 2018, pp. 16–18). While right-leaning groups in the West insist on the Christian basis of their societies, left-leaning groups insist on the secular, universal foundations of their states; nevertheless, both groups often view Jews and Muslims as inferior, exotic, and dangerous (Gessier 2010, p. 41). The secular accord between right and left groups is particularly evident in recent controversies concerning Muslim women and modest dress. In a wide range of secular states, the false claim of secular neutrality is used to regulate and to oppress women who choose to dress modestly, whether with headscarves or face-veils (IDLO 2016, p. 22). As Brown illustrates, the notion that secularism promotes gender equality is a fallacy (2012). Islamophobes on the right and the left use the same secular arguments to legitimate their oppression of Muslim women (Salaymeh 2019).

Some scholars distinguish how distinct types of secularism treat religious groups. For example, Kuru identifies a difference between combative secularism and pluralistic secularism. He argues that France's ideology of exceptionalism causes combative secularism, which is antagonistic toward Muslims (2008, p. 14). Despite the ideological and historical contingencies of secularism, secular states share a secular orientation toward religion that produces varying levels of judeophobia and islamophobia. While there is a spectrum of secular ideology, secularisms are highly likely to engender judeophobia and islamophobia, regardless of the particularities of the state.

Secularism as Protestant Christian Bias

State secularism is not neutral because it perpetuates a Protestant Christian bias in its separation of religion from other life-spheres, especially politics. Many scholars identify one primary kind of state bias, namely, discrimination against Judaism and Islam based on the dominance of cultural Christianity (Weiler 2007). Examples of this majority-Christian state bias (in Western states) include: recognition of Christian holidays (Sunday as a day of rest, Christmas as a state-recognized holiday, etc.); imposition of Christian symbols in the public sphere (e.g., Ten Commandments, crucifix, Christmas tree); limitations on the construction of non-Christian places of worship (mosques, minarets, synagogues); limitations on non-Christian religious clothing (e.g., headscarves, yarmulkes) (Ferrari 1988). Some recent decisions by the European Court of Human Rights reflect a Christian bias by permitting Christian symbols and limiting Muslim ones (Moyn 2014, p. 65). The Christian bias of (Western) states is often viewed as balanced by secular legal doctrines: separation of church and state, freedom of religion, and multiculturalism (Bhuta 2012). However, these secular legal principles operate by determining distinctions between what practices should be classified as religious or cultural, obligatory or optional, or inhumane or humane. That process of classification is not impartial, but rather prejudicial against Judaism and Islam. Indeed, a Christian bias operates even in states without a Protestant Christian majority.

In some secular states in the West, there is a presumption that the state's majority-Christian bias can be resolved by including other religions; that is, recognizing non-Christian holidays and including non-Christian symbols is assumed to be an antidote to the secular state's majority-Christian bias. By way of example, the U.S. Supreme Court decided in 1989 that a local government's menorah display did not constitute endorsement of religion; permitting the display of the menorah obviated any potential judicial scrutiny of the legal validity of the Christmas tree display (*County of Allegheny* 1989). This case is one of many indications that the inclusion of minority religions serves as a cover for Christian bias, particularly when that minority religion conforms to Christian practices. For example, because Hanukah celebrations in Christian-majority areas are modeled after Christmas, Hanukah is a normalized Jewish holiday that fits within a Christian-majority society. Rather than preventing a majority-Christian bias, religious pluralism in secular states often perpetuates conformity to majority-Christian practices.

There are some identifiable characteristics of the dominant, secular definition of religion; these characteristics reflect Protestant Christian assumptions (Jensen 2011; Smith 2004, pp. 92–94).[3] First, secular law defines religion as a private belief. Sullivan illuminates that U.S. judges perceive religion as a matter of private "views," rather than acts (2005, pp. 92–95). Second, secular law identifies religion as an individual matter (Marshall 1996, p. 386). Third, as many scholars observe, secular law defines religion as a choice, while most adherents do not experience it as such (Marshall 1996, p. 386). Reflecting these observations, Berger demonstrates, in his appropriately titled book *Law's Religion*, that secular law constructs religion as private, individual, and autonomous (2015). This construction is significant for a simple reason: it does not correspond to the realities of being Jewish or being Muslim.

---

[3] U.S. constitutional law applies a broadly Protestant understanding of religion.

The secular legal construction of "religion" is not merely biased, it is also fundamentally repressive. Connolly observes: "This innocent and tolerant-sounding definition [of religion] promotes Christian secularism into the center of Europe and reduces Islamic peoples [sic] into a minority unlike other minorities; they are distinctive because they alone are unwilling or unable to abide by the modern agenda" (Connolly 2006, p. 78). Secular law's three definitional axes of religion (private belief, individual right, and autonomous choice) have important opposites: public acts, communal membership, and submission (Salaymeh and Lavi, forthcoming; Mahmood 2005). Without entering into definitional complexities, we can acknowledge that Judaism and Islam are both traditions that involve public acts. Accordingly, secular law attempts to transform Jews and Muslims from public actors of communal traditions into individual believers of private choices. By forcing Jews and Muslims to become "religious," secular law prevents them from fully being Jews and Muslims. Secular law profoundly marginalizes Jews and Muslims by denouncing any non-individualized manifestation of their traditions as undermining the public order. Secular law hammers square pegs into round holes.

Some recent legal controversies exemplify these dynamics. Debates and campaigns against male circumcision and ritual animal slaughter reflect Protestant Christian ideas about bodily integrity and animal suffering (Lavi 2009; Salaymeh 2015; Salaymeh and Lavi, forthcoming). The laws of many secular states accommodate these practices only under strict limitations that are not neutral, secular legal principles, but rather adaptations of Protestant Christian polemics against (and abrogations of) Jewish traditions. In these cases, secular law demands the child's informed consent for circumcision and humane treatment of the animal during slaughter; both of these demands impose post-Christian morals about legitimate ways to inflict pain on the body that purport to be neutral limitations on religious freedom. Accordingly, legal controversies about circumcision and animal slaughter display judeophobic and islamophobic ideas. Similarly, the notion of "gender equality" that animates numerous forms of secular opposition to Islamic practices is not neutral, but rather an islamophobic misunderstanding of Islamic legal traditions (Salaymeh 2019).

Secular law's subjugation of Jews and Muslims under "religion" stigmatizes them for being incompatible with public values and for being threats to political authority and public security (Salaymeh 2014). (The stigmatizing of Muslims and Jews is seen as the first step towards what many scholars describe as their racialization or ethnicization [Meer and Modood 2012, p. 39; Meer 2014].) The International Development Law Organization (IDLO) observes: "Recent and historical experience has amply demonstrated that restrictions on religious expression, often defended by the State on grounds relating to national security, public order, or even human rights, could in fact be intended to target and marginalize particular religious minorities on a discriminatory basis" (2016, p. 23). Exploring the intricacies of—and debates concerning—premodern Muslim and Jewish political identities is beyond the scope of this chapter. It should suffice to point out that in the pre-secular world in which there was no distinction between religion and politics, Jewish and Muslim identities were inevitably political (Salaymeh 2016). By contrast, in a modern secular state, citizenship is presumed to transcend all other collective identities; thus, Jewish and Muslim collective identities pose a threat to secular state security. Secular law's repression of Jews and Muslims through the category of religion limits the political dimension of Jewish and Muslim identities that do not fit within the secular definition of religion and therefore challenge state hegemony. Indeed, the prevailing state-based discourse surrounding "moderating religion" is a state exercise in controlling religious minorities (Tareen 2014, p. 209).

Conclusion

Conventional scholarship about the relationship between judeophobia and islamophobia focuses on the legitimacy of the comparison or on differences and similarities between these two forms of prejudice. Some scholars point to Orientalism or secularism as a link between judeophobia and islamophobia, without elaborating how these prejudices are generated. In this chapter, we have set out the broad outlines for further explorations into some ways in which secularism (particularly secular law) stigmatizes both Jews and Muslims. This stigmatizing of Jews and Muslims renders them threats within the public sphere and violent threats to the secular state. As we illustrated in this chapter, secularism propagates judeophobia and islamophobia. More specifically, secular law's stigmatizing of Jews and Muslims is a key component of judeophobia and islamophobia.

Acknowledgements We thank Or Shay for his research assistance. We also thank Rhiannon Graybill, Iris Idelson-Shein, Ira Lapidus, Joshua Price, and the participants in the *Key Concepts in Antisemitism* workshop for their comments on this piece.

References

Anidjar, Gil. 2003. *The Jew, the Arab: A History of the Enemy*. Stanford: Stanford University Press.
Anidjar, Gil. 2008. *Semites: Race, Religion, Literature*. Stanford: Stanford University Press.
Anidjar, Gil. 2009. "Muslim Jews." *Qui parle: Critical Humanities and Social Sciences* 18 (1) (Fall/Winter): 1–23.
Asad, Talal. 1993. *Genealogies of Religion*. Baltimore: Johns Hopkins University.
Balibar, Etienne. 1991. "Is There a 'Neo-racism'?" In *Race, Nation, Class: Ambiguous Identities*, edited by Etienne Balibar and Immanuel Maurice Wallerstein, 17–28. London: Verso.
Bangstad, Sindre, and Matti Bunzl. 2010. "'Anthropologists Are Talking' About Islamophobia and Anti-Semitism in the New Europe." *Ethnos* 75 (2): 213–28.

Bayrakli, Enes, and Farid Hafez. 2018. "Co-optation of Islamophobia by Centrist Parties." In *European Islamophobia Report 2017*. Ankara: SETA.
Berger, Benjamin L. 2015. *Law's Religion: Religious Difference and the Claims of Constitutionalism*. Toronto: University of Toronto Press.
Bevir, Mark, and R. A. W. Rhodes. 2010. *The State as Cultural Practice*. Oxford: Oxford University Press.
Bhuta, Nehal. 2012. "Two Concepts of Religious Freedom in the European Court of Human Rights." *EUI Working Papers*, no. 33: 1–19.
Brenner, Michael. 1996. *The Renaissance of Jewish Culture in Germany*. New Haven: Yale University Press.
Brown, Wendy. 2012. "Civilizational Delusions: Secularism, Tolerance, Equality." *Theory & Event* 15 (2): 1–16.
Bunzl, Matti. 2005. "Between Anti-Semitism and Islamophobia: Some Thoughts on the New Europe." *American Ethnologist* 32 (4): 499–508.
Bunzl, Matti. 2007. *Anti-Semitism and Islamophobia: Hatreds Old and New in Europe*. Chicago: Prickly Paradigm Press.
Calo, Zachary R. 2014. "Constructing the Secular: Law and Religion Jurisprudence in Europe and the United States." In *EUI Working Papers*. European University Institute: Robert Schuman Centre for Advanced Studies.
Connolly, William E. 2006. "Europe: A Minor Tradition." In *Powers of the Secular Modern*, edited by David Scott and Charles Hirschkind, 75–92. Stanford: Stanford University Press.
County of Allegheny V. American Civil Liberties Union. 1989. 492 U.S. 573.
Dobkowski, Michael. 2015. "Islamophobia and Anti-Semitism." *CrossCurrents* 65 (3): 321–33.
Feldman, David. 2017. "Islamophobia and Antisemitism." In *Islamophobia: Still a Challenge for Us All (a 20th-Anniversary Report)*, edited by Farah Elahi and Omar Khan, 78–81. London: Runnymede.
Ferrari, Silvio. 1988. "Separation of Church and State in Contemporary European Society." *Journal of Church and State* 30 (3): 533–47.
Gessier, Vincent. 2010. "Islamophobia: A French Specificity in Europe?" *Human Architecture: Journal of the Sociology of Self-Knowledge* 8 (2): 39–46.
Gilman, Sander. 2017. "The Case of Circumcision: Diaspora Judaism as a Model for Islam?" In Renton and Gidley 2017, 143–64.
Gingrich, Andre. 2005. "Anthropological Analyses of Islamophobia and Anti-Semitism in Europe." *American Ethnologist* 32 (4): 513–15.
Halliday, Fred. 1999. "'Islamophobia' Reconsidered." *Ethnic and Racial Studies* 22 (5): 892–902.
Helly, Denise. 2012. "Islamophobia in Canada? Women's Rights, Modernity, Secularism." In *Recode Working Paper Series*, 11. http://www.recode.fi/publications: European Science Foundation.
Hess, Jonathan M. 2000. "Johann David Michaelis and the Colonial Imaginary: Orientalism and the Emergence of Racial Antisemitism in Eighteenth-Century Germany." *Jewish Social Studies* 6 (2): 56–101.
IDLO (International Development Law Organization). 2016. *Freedom of Religion or Belief and the Law: Current Dilemmas and Lessons Learned*. Rome: IDLO.
Jensen, Tim. 2011. "When Is Religion, Religion, and a Knife, a Knife—And Who Decides?: The Case of Denmark." In *After Secular Law*, edited by Mateo

Taussig-Rubbo, Robert A. Yelle, and Winnifred Fallers Sullivan, 341–64. Stanford: Stanford Law Books.

Jivraj, Suhraiya, and Didi Herman. 2009. "'It's Difficult for a White Judge to Understand': Orientalism, Racialisation, and Christianity in English Child Welfare Cases." *Child and Family Law Quarterly* 21 (3): 283–308.

Kalmar, Ivan, and Derek Penslar, eds. 2005. *Orientalism and the Jews*. Lebanon: University Press of New England.

Kalmar, Ivan, and Tariq Ramadan. 2016. "Anti-Semitism and Islamophobia: Historical and Contemporary Connections and Parallels." In *The Routledge Handbook of Muslim-Jewish Relations*, edited by Josef W. Meri, 351–72. Basingstoke: Taylor & Francis.

Katz, Ethan. 2015. *The Burdens of Brotherhood: Jews and Muslims from North Africa to France*. Cambridge, MA: Harvard University Press.

Kaya, Ayhan. 2014. "Islamophobia." In *The Oxford Handbook of European Islam*, edited by Jocelyne Cesari, 746–69. Oxford: Oxford University Press.

Klug, Brian. 2014. "The Limits of Analogy: Comparing Islamophobia and Antisemitism." *Patterns of Prejudice* 48 (5): 442–59.

Kuru, Ahmet T. 2007. "Passive and Assertive Secularism: Historical Conditions, Ideological Struggles, and State Policies Toward Religion." *World Politics* 59 (4): 568–94.

Kuru, Ahmet T. 2008. "Secularism, State Policies, and Muslims in Europe: Analyzing French Exceptionalism." *Comparative Politics* 41 (1): 1–19.

Lavi, Shai. 2009. "Unequal Rites: Jews, Muslims and the History of Ritual Slaughter in Germany." In *Juden und Muslime in Deutschland: Recht, Religion, Identität*, edited by Jose Brunner and Shai Lavi, 164–84. Göttingen: Wallstein Verlag.

López, Fernando Bravo. 2011. "Towards a Definition of Islamophobia: Approximations of the Early Twentieth Century." *Ethnic and Racial Studies* 34 (4): 556–73.

Mahmood, Saba. 2005. *The Politics of Piety: The Islamic Revival and the Feminist Subject*. Princeton: Princeton University Press.

Mahmood, Saba, and Peter G. Danchin. 2014. "Immunity or Regulation? Antinomies of Religious Freedom." *South Atlantic Quarterly* 113 (1): 129–59.

Marshall, William P. 1996. "Religion as Ideas: Religion as Identity." *Journal of Contemporary Legal Issues* 7 (2): 385–406.

Meer, Nasar. 2013. "Semantics, Scales and Solidarities in the Study of Antisemitism and Islamophobia." *Ethnic and Racial Studies* 36 (3): 500–15.

Meer, Nasar. 2014. Introduction to *Racialization and Religion: Race, Culture and Difference in the Study of Antisemitism and Islamophobia*, by Nasar Meer, 1–14. London: Routledge.

Meer, Nasar, and Tariq Modood. 2012. "For 'Jewish' Read 'Muslim'? Islamophobia as a Form of Racialisation of Ethno-Religious Groups in Britain Today." *Islamophobia Studies Journal* 1 (1): 35–53.

Meer, Nasar, and Tehseen Noorani. 2008. "A Sociological Comparison of Anti-Semitism and Anti-Muslim Sentiment in Britain." *The Sociological Review* 56 (2): 195–219.

Mende, Claudia. 2010. "Islamophobia and Anti-Semitism—Mechanisms of Exclusion and Discrimination: Interview with Wolfgang Benz, Head of the Center for Research on Anti-Semitism at Berlin's Free University." *Qantara*. https://en.qantara.de/content/islamophobia-and-anti-semitism-mechanisms-of-exclusion-and-discrimination.

Moyn, Samuel. 2014. "From Communist to Muslim: European Human Rights, the Cold War, and Religious Liberty." *South Atlantic Quarterly* 113 (1): 63–86.
Nirenberg, David. 1996. *Communities of Violence: Persecution of Minorities in the Middle Ages*. Princeton: Princeton University Press.
O'Brien, Peter. 2016. "Secularism." In *The Muslim Question in Europe: Political Controversies and Public Philosophies*, 144–98. Philadelphia: Temple University Press.
Özyürek, Esra. 2005. "The Politics of Cultural Unification, Secularism, and the Place of Islam in the New Europe." *American Ethnologist* 32 (4): 509–12.
Padovan, Dario, and Alfredo Alietti. 2012. "The Racialization of Public Discourse: Antisemitism and Islamophobia in Italian Society." *European Societies* 14 (2): 186–202.
PSR (Physicians for Social Responsibility). 2015. "Body Count: Casualty Figures After 10 Years of the 'War on Terror' (Iraq, Afghanistan, Pakistan)." https://www.psr.org/wp-content/uploads/2018/05/body-count.pdf.
Renton, James, and Ben Gidley, eds. 2017. *Antisemitism and Islamophobia in Europe: A Shared Story?* London: Palgrave Macmillan.
Romeyn, Esther. 2014. "Anti-Semitism and Islamophobia: Spectropolitics and Immigration." *Theory, Culture & Society* 31 (6): 77–101.
Said, Edward. 1985. "Orientalism Reconsidered." *Cultural Critique* 1 (Fall): 89–107.
Salaymeh, Lena. 2014. "Propaganda, Politics, and Profiteering: Islamic Law in the Contemporary U.S." *Jadaliyya*, September 29. http://www.jadaliyya.com/pages/index/19408/propaganda-politics-and-profiteering_islamic-law-i.
Salaymeh, Lena. 2015. "'Comparing' Jewish and Islamic Legal Traditions: Between Disciplinarity and Critical Historical Jurisprudence." *Critical Analysis of Law, New Historical Jurisprudence* 2 (1): 153–72.
Salaymeh, Lena. 2016. "Taxing Citizens: Socio-Legal Constructions of Late Antique Muslim Identity." *Islamic Law and Society* 23 (4): 333–67.
Salaymeh, Lena. 2019. "Imperialist Feminism and Islamic Law." *Hawwa* 17 (2–3): 97–134.
Salaymeh, Lena, and Shai Lavi. "Religion Is Secularized Tradition: Jewish and Muslim Circumcisions in Germany." *Oxford Journal of Legal Studies*, forthcoming.
Schiffer, Sabine, and Constantin Wagner. 2011. "Anti-Semitism and Islamophobia— New Enemies, Old Patterns." *Race & Class* 52 (3): 77–84.
Skenderovic, Damir, and Christina Späti. 2019. "From Orientalism to Islamophobia: Reflections, Confirmations, and Reservations." *ReOrient* 4 (2): 130–43.
Smith, Scott. 2004. "Constitutional Meanings of Religion Past and Present: Explorations in Definition and Theory." *Temple Political Civil Rights Law Review* 14 (1): 89–142.
Sullivan, Winnifred Fallers. 2005. *The Impossibility of Religious Freedom*. Princeton: Princeton University Press.
Tareen, Sherali. 2014. "Islam, Democracy, and the Limits of Secular Conceptuality." *Journal of Law and Religion* 29 (1): 206–22.
Tibi, Bassam. 1993. "Deutsche Ausländerfeindlichkeit - Ethnisch-Religiöser Rechtsradikalismus der Ausländer. Zwei Gefahren für die Demokratie." *Gewerkschaftliche Monatshefte* 44 (8): 493–502.
Weiler, Joseph H. H. 2007. "A Christian Europe? Europe and Christianity: Rules of Commitment." *European View* 6 (1): 143–50.
Yel, Ali Murat, and Alparslan Nas. 2014. "Insight Islamophobia: Governing the Public Visibility of Islamic Lifestyle in Turkey." *European Journal of Cultural Studies* 17 (5): 567–84.

CHAPTER 21

Sinat Yisrael (Hatred of Jews)

Martin Lockshin

Among contemporary religious Jews, gentile hatred of Jews is often perceived as inevitable. In 1977, responding to a question that a rabbi in England had sent him, Rabbi Moshe Feinstein (1895–1986), the leading Haredi (ultra-Orthodox) rabbi of the United States in the twentieth century, cited the old rabbinic phrase that it is "a well-known *halakhah* that Esau hates Jacob" (1980).[1] This sentiment is confirmed by the former chief rabbi of Israel, Shlomo Amar, who wrote similarly:

> … Even in those places where the hatred of Jews is [apparently] unknown and it appears that they love us, know that this is just a lie and an illusion. For it is a *halakhah* that Esau hates Jacob. (n.d.)

This essay examines the early history of this now common Jewish understanding of *sin'at yisrael* (hatred of Jews). It does not deal with the actual prevalence or inevitability of this hatred, but only with **perceptions** of the hatred of Jews found in biblical and rabbinic texts. Examining first the biblical period—approximately the first millennium BCE—and then the classical rabbinic period—approximately the first six centuries CE (the period of the

---

[1] The word *halakhah* almost always means "Jewish law." In this quotation from the old rabbinic work Sifre Numbers 69 (third or fourth century) it is difficult to understand the word this way. All translations of post-biblical Hebrew and Aramaic are my own unless otherwise noted. All translations from Tanakh (the Hebrew Bible) are from the New Jewish Publication Society translation (1999) unless otherwise noted.

M. Lockshin (✉)
York University, Toronto, ON, Canada
e-mail: lockshin@yorku.ca

Mishnah, the Talmuds, and the contemporaneous midrash collections, the foundational texts of what we know today as "rabbinic Judaism")—will help determine if this attitude is rooted in those early times.

THE BIBLE AND HATRED OF JEWS

As the books of the Hebrew Bible were written by many authors over many centuries, it is difficult to generalize about "the biblical attitude" to any issue. Nevertheless, the nearly total absence of references to hatred of Jews and/or Judaism in the Bible is telling.[2]

Biblical authors have a variety of attitudes to gentiles (Eisen 2011). Many passages in the Bible project a universalistic worldview, suggesting that gentiles can and often do live good and meaningful lives. The prophet Malachi, for example, quotes God as saying: "For from where the sun rises to where it sets, My name is honored among the nations, and everywhere incense and pure oblation are offered to My name; for My name is honored among the nations ..." (Malachi 1:11).

Other passages portray the gentiles, or at least many gentiles, as cruel and immoral. In the opening chapters of his book, the prophet Amos lists the shortcomings of Israel's ancient neighbors and the Jews themselves. But Amos never hints that Israel's neighbors have any more animus toward the Israelite state and toward Jews than they do toward any other nation. Amos identifies gentile cruelty toward Judah and Israel but he also speaks of gentile cruelty toward other nations. For example, he severely chastises the king of Moab for violating basic moral standards when he "burned the bones of the king of Edom [a gentile] to lime" (Amos 2:1).

Other books of the Bible describe some gentiles as behaving cruelly or defiantly to Jews. For example, in the book of Samuel, the Philistine Goliath defies or perhaps curses and abuses the Jews and their God when challenging the Jews to provide a champion (I Samuel 17). In the book of Kings, the Rabshakeh (a high official sent by the king of Assyria) tells the inhabitants of Judea, "Don't listen to [King] Hezekiah [of Judah] who misleads you by saying, 'The LORD will save us'" (2 Kings 18:32). The Bible understands that the Philistines and the Assyrians attack the Israelites—just as they attack other peoples—to advance their own interests. They are not portrayed as having any particular hatred for Jews or Judaism. In the heat of battle, an effective way to insult an enemy is by insulting its gods. When the northern kingdom of Israel falls to the Assyrians and when the southern kingdom of Judah falls to the Babylonians, the Bible does not portray this as Jew-hatred.

---

[2] Some scholars insist that the religion practiced in the days of the Hebrew Bible must be called "the Israelite religion," and not Judaism, and that the word Israelites, not Jews, should be used for its practitioners. Since this essay is about Jewish self-perceptions, and since traditional Jews feel that the religion they practice is the same religion as that of their biblical ancestors, I am using the words "Judaism" and "Jew."

To the contrary, Jeremiah describes it as divine retribution. In 27:4–6, he says: "Thus said the LORD of hosts, the God of Israel...It is I who made the earth, and the men and beasts who are on the earth, by My great might and My outstretched arm; and I give it to whomever I deem proper. I herewith deliver all these lands to My servant, King Nebuchadnezzar of Babylon." Similarly the Assyrians, cruel as they may have been, are also seen as fulfilling God's will when they destroy the northern kingdom (2 Kings 17:7–23). The enslavement of the Jews in Egypt, which in later years, as we shall see, was understood by many Jews as a manifestation of hatred of Jews, is not described as such in the Bible.

Only in one of the latest books of the Hebrew Bible, the book of Esther, can we find an incident that conforms to what many of us think of as antisemitism. When Haman is offended because Mordechai refuses to bow down to him, presumably for Jewish religious reasons, Haman decides to take revenge on the entire Jewish people, telling the king:

> There is a certain people, scattered and dispersed among the other peoples in all the provinces of your realm, whose laws are different from those of any other people and who do not obey the king's laws; and it is not in Your Majesty's interest to tolerate them. If it please Your Majesty, let an edict be drawn for their destruction .... (Esther 3:8–9)

On the personal level, an insult from one Jew leads Haman to plot against all Jews. And on the political level, Haman argues that the Jews' allegiance to their own laws causes them to be disloyal to the laws of the state.

Early Exegesis of Esther

The history of Jewish exegesis of this passage shows a good deal about how later Jews viewed gentile attitudes toward the Jewish people. Jews in medieval times did see gentile hatred of Jews as a pervasive phenomenon requiring explanation. In Barry Walfish's study of how medieval Jews read the book of Esther, he categorizes their interpretations of Haman's hostility to the Jews into social, religious, economic, or political understandings (or some combination of these factors) (1993, pp. 143–55).

But what about before the medieval period? The Jews who composed the Septuagint version of Haman's words (c. 100 BCE) made his speech more aggressive. As Peter Schäfer summarizes the Septuagint reading:

> ... the Jews are a "hostile" people who are "opposed" in their laws to "any other people". Moreover, they are the only people who are in the state of military alertness "always and against everyone," who follow with their laws a foreign way of life, and who finally "commit, ill-disposed toward our affairs, the worst evil deeds." (1997, p. 208)

Two centuries later, in the works of Josephus, Schäfer finds even clearer evidence of the belief that the alleged fundamental hostility of Jews toward gentiles was the cause of (at least Haman's) hatred of Jews. According to Josephus, Haman told the king:

> that there was a certain wicked nation scattered throughout the habitable land ruled by him, which was unfriendly and unsocial and neither had the same religion nor practiced the same laws as others, "but both by its customs and practices it is the enemy of your people and of all mankind." (1958, 11: pp. 212–13)

Schäfer concludes that these texts show that some Jewish authors understood that the essence of the animus toward Jews in the Greco-Roman world was "the allegation of *amixia*, 'unsociability,' and of a [Jewish] way of life that is hostile to and, therefore, dangerous to all humankind" (1997, p. 208). According to Schäfer, Greek texts confirm that these Jewish authors correctly understood the thinking of many of their Gentile neighbors.

THE CLASSICAL RABBIS AND GENTILE HATRED OF JEWS

A few centuries later, the most famous restatement in rabbinic literature of Haman's accusations and arguments has a different emphasis. The Talmud reconstructs a conversation between Haman and King Ahasuerus, based on ostensible hints from Esther 3:8. The king tells Haman that he is worried that the Jewish God might intervene on their behalf as in past eras of history. Haman retorts that the Jews have become lax in their observance of Jewish law, so God's intervention is not to be feared. Here, Haman's "antisemitism" is explained, but in a way that allows the rabbis to rebuke their Jewish audience for its lax observance at the same time.

Haman continues: "Should you argue that you [the king] receive benefit from them, it is not the case. They are like mules, producing nothing." The heart of Haman's accusation follows, in the same verse: the Jews' "laws are different from those of any other people." The Talmud expands on this:

> They won't eat from our food, won't marry our women and won't allow their women to marry us. "They do not obey the king's laws": They spend all their time [shirking responsibilities and making excuses like] "today is the Sabbath" or "today is Passover."[3] "It is not in Your Majesty's interest to tolerate them": They eat and drink and revile the king. If a fly were to fall into the wine cup of any one of them, they would throw away the fly and drink the wine. But if Your Majesty were to touch the wine cup of one of them, they would throw the wine on the ground and would not drink it.[4] (*b. Megillah* 13b)

---

[3] I have translated the difficult Aramaic phrase, *demafqei lekhulah shattah beshahi pahi* according to Rashi's explanation in his commentary here.

[4] Alluding to the rabbinic rules of *setam yeinam*, which would require a Jew to throw away wine touched by an idolater.

In these texts, as in many others, the rabbis claim that gentile hatred of Jews is a direct and even understandable result of the Jews observing Jewish law. It is somewhat shocking that the classical rabbis seem to blame the observance of *mitzvot* [the religious rules of Judaism], the very essence of their Judaism, for gentile animosity to Judaism. But how significant was this hatred of Jews in the classical rabbis' worldview? To answer this, we must first consider what they thought about gentiles in general.

The Rabbis and Gentiles

If generalizing about "the biblical attitude" to an issue is difficult, determining "the rabbinic attitude" to almost anything is even more so. Classical rabbinic works span the first six centuries of the first millennium and were produced in a number of countries where Jews lived under various gentile governments—some friendly, others decidedly not. Adding to the sheer quantity and variety is the problem of knowing what opinion to rely on: a passage in rabbinic literature often juxtaposes several viewpoints on an issue without coming to a resolution.

Some rabbinic statements about gentiles are positive (e.g. Sifra 13:11). From time to time the rabbis also mention the teaching that all human beings are created in the image of God (e.g., *m. Avot* 3:14). But many other rabbinic statements show a very low opinion of non-Jews. Some rabbis taught that God had in fact offered the Torah to the other nations, but they rejected it since they felt that rules of the Torah—such as refraining from murder, theft, and adultery—went against their essential nature. Thus the gentile nations rejected even the seven Noahide commandments, which the rabbis saw as the basic rules of decency that were supposed to govern all humans (*Mekhilta, Ba-hodesh* 1). It is likely that many rabbis agreed with the assessment of the author of the Book of Jubilees, who, as James Kugel explains, feels that "Israel's holiness means first and foremost that Israel belongs to an order of being different from the order of being of other humans so that Israel is, in effect, wholly different, the earthly correspondent to God's heavenly host" (1996, p. 27). In the twentieth century, Rabbi Abraham Isaac Kook (1865–1935) wrote that the difference between the souls of Jews and gentiles is greater than the difference between the souls of humans and animals (1956, p. 156). Many classical rabbis presumably felt similarly.

Accordingly, their expectations of gentiles were low. They often expressed concern that gentiles might harm Jews. I believe, however, that the rabbis' low expectations of gentiles were not because they saw gentiles as inherently and predictably antisemitic, but rather because they felt that gentiles, who lacked the humanizing influence of the Torah, were simply not to be trusted.

In addition to statements and parables, some rabbinic laws reflect this fear of gentile violence. Unless witnesses were present, the rabbis ruled that a Jew should not be circumcised by a gentile (*t. Avodah zarah* 3:12), a Jew should not have his or her hair cut by a gentile barber (*m. Avodah zarah* 2:2), and a Jewish woman should not use a gentile midwife (*t. Avodah zarah* 3:3). Unpleasant as these attitudes may be to contemporary sensibilities, it does not seem that what the rabbis feared was hatred of Jews specifically. Rather, gentiles were suspected of wanting to kill or harm anyone, not Jews specifically (cf. Y. Cohen 1975, p. 46).

ROME AND ROMANS

Many of the classics of rabbinic Judaism, including the Mishnah (the first post-biblical code of Jewish law) and the Jerusalem Talmud (an expansion of and elaboration on the Mishnah), were produced in the land of Israel under Roman occupation, which was often, but not always, brutal. We might expect the rabbis' attitude to these people to be particularly negative, but here, too, a range exists.

What the Rabbis Thought of the Romans

As Nicholas de Lange has written: "The amount of [rabbinic] preaching on this theme [the relationship between the Jews and the Romans] is enormous, but the lessons drawn from the texts are by no means uniform. They cover the whole range of attitudes, from the bitterly antagonistic to the positively enthusiastic, and we are often presented with two or more interpretations side by side" (1978, p. 270).

A well-known story about three rabbis in the land of Israel in the early second century shows an array of opinions:

> Rabbi Yehudah spoke first: "How fine are the things done by this nation [the Romans]! They build markets, bridges, and bathhouses." Rabbi Yose was silent. Rabbi Shimon [bar Yohai] retorted: "Everything they do, they do only for their own benefit. They build markets for their prostitutes, bathhouses to pamper themselves, and bridges to collect tolls." (*b. Shabbat* 33b. Perhaps the Monty Python skit "What Have the Romans Ever Done for Us?" was inspired by this text.)

Another reaction was to exaggerate the extent and the motivations for Roman persecution. Though no one denies that the Romans were often ruthless, many scholars doubt that, as the Talmud claims, the Romans forced Jewish men to have sexual relations with menstruant women in order to cause Jews to transgress Jewish law (*b. Meilah* 17a). Lieberman (1974, p. 215, note 22) writes that the story told here is dubious.

What the Romans Thought of the Jews

The Romans did pass laws restricting some practices of the Jewish religion, especially circumcision. Lieberman argues, though, that the Roman law against circumcision was not drafted with Jews in mind, and its original purpose was definitely not to cause Jews to transgress their religious laws (1974, p. 214). He discusses some cruel acts of the Romans described in rabbinic literature but concludes that even these despicable examples conform to the standard practice of Roman law (*ha-kol keminhag Roma*, i.e., "the entire procedure followed the standard practice of Rome"); they are not to be seen as displaying a specific anti-Jewish animus (p. 218).

Similarly, in discussing Apion and Herod, two Roman-era figures who are often perceived as hating Jews, Shaye Cohen writes: "The former had good reason to dislike the Jews and to oppose their attempts to obtain civic equality, and the latter had good reason to suppress a Jewish rebellion and to forbid the practices of Judaism" (1986, pp. 46–47). In other words, hatred of Jews was probably not the root cause of their anti-Jewish measures. In general, Cohen writes that: "The Greco-Roman world consisted of those who hated Judaism, those who were indifferent to it, and those who loved it" (p. 47).

What the Jews Thought About Roman Attitudes to the Jews

The Romans certainly persecuted the Jews harshly at times and it would not have been surprising had the rabbis concluded that hatred of Jews was inevitable and universal. But they did not. Perhaps they too understood that the issue was more complex. One Talmudic story suggests that, in the rabbis' opinion, the Romans would have liked to kill all the Jews in their empire but did not know how (*b. Pesahim 87b*). But generally the rabbis perceived Roman measures as directed against Jewish law. As Richard Kalmin puts it: "What the rabbis describe as having been prohibited by the Romans, and/or as having been difficult to fulfill during 'the time of danger,' is for the most part what these rabbis view as most precious about Judaism" (2003, p. 22). In other words, the rabbis perceived Roman measures to rule the land of Israel and strike terror into its inhabitants as actions against the Torah, thus perhaps encouraging Jews to feel that adhering to the laws of the Torah constituted resistance. They do not explain why the Romans opposed the Torah but they take that opposition for granted. One text in the Babylonian Talmud may provide a hint. It says that had the Romans known about a specific Jewish law that discriminates against gentiles, they would probably have been even more negatively inclined to the Jews (see the story of the two Romans who were sent to study Torah, *b. BQ 38a*). Like the attitude in earlier times described by Peter Schäfer, they seemed to be able to see their enemies' point of view.

The rabbis write of other factors that led to some Roman anti-Jewish measures. A fascinating story is told to explain why the emperor Diocletian (244–311) took measures against Jews. Diocletian came from a family of low status. In the rabbinic telling, he began life as a swineherd; young yeshivah students used to make fun of him. When he became emperor, he decided to take revenge on the rabbis. He summoned them to appear before him at a time when they would have to desecrate the Sabbath in order to arrive on time. (Again an anti-Jewish measure is presented as opposition to Jewish law.) With the help of divine intervention, the rabbis succeeded in arriving at the emperor's without desecrating the Sabbath. Diocletian chastised them for having made fun of him years ago. They attempted to defend themselves: "We made fun of Diocletian the swineherd, but we are subjects of Diocletian the emperor." Diocletian, though, is given the last word in the story, wisely suggesting to the rabbis that it would be best not to make fun of anyone, even a person of lowly status (*Genesis Rabbah* 63). Thus we see that the rabbis did not present all Roman discriminatory measures as resulting from hatred of Jews but rather as resulting from many factors, even including Roman reactions to Jewish misbehavior.

How Prevalent Is the Hatred of Jews in the Rabbis' Understanding?

I am unable to find evidence in classical rabbinic literature that the rabbis saw gentile hatred of Jews as inevitable and/or universal. In such a vast corpus, it is hard to say with finality that a specific belief is never mentioned. But at least the most commonly quoted traditional texts cited to support it, when closely examined, actually do not make the case.

"It Is a Well-Known halakhah *(halakhah beyadua) That Esau Hates Jacob"*

This quotation (mentioned above) appears only once in classical rabbinic literature, in a discussion about the story of the meeting of the brothers, Jacob and Esau, after many years of separation. Years before, Esau had been very angry, expressing a desire to kill Jacob (Genesis 27:41–2). When the brothers finally meet, the Bible reports that "Esau ran to greet him. He embraced him and, falling on his neck, he kissed him; and they wept" (Genesis 33:4). In a Torah scroll, each of the letters of the Hebrew word *va-yishshaqehu* (and he kissed him) has a dot on it, an unusual phenomenon. The classical rabbis offer two interpretations. Here is how they appear in standard printed texts:

> *Va-yishshaqehu* has dots above it [to teach us] that he [Esau] did not kiss him [Jacob] sincerely. [However,] Rabbi Shimon bar Yohai says: "It is a well-known *halakhah* (*halakhah beyadua*) that Esau hates Jacob. Nevertheless, at that moment he became merciful and kissed him with his full heart." (*Sifre Numbers* 69)

The phrase *halakhah beyadua* is difficult and is otherwise unattested in rabbinic literature. A new scholarly edition of Sifre, based on the majority of old manuscripts, reads "*veha-lo beyadua*," i.e., "Is it not well-known that Esau hates Jacob? Nevertheless …" (Kahana 2011–2015, 1: p. 167; 3: pp. 474–75; see Shochetman 1997). This reading, a more common rabbinic Hebrew locution, takes away some of the force of the saying. But beyond the wording issue, this saying in its original context has nothing to do with the prevalence or inevitability of gentile hatred of Jews. While some rabbinic texts use the word "Esau" as a code for Romans or Christians or even, on rare occasions, for all gentiles (Yuval 2006), here this is not the case. Two rabbis are discussing the proper interpretation of a verse in Genesis that refers to the meeting of two biblical characters, Esau and Jacob. Rabbi Shimon bar Yohai feels that without a doubt, Esau, the biblical character, hated Jacob most of the time; but still, he kissed him sincerely at the moment of their meeting described in Genesis 33.

Sinai and Hatred

The idea in the Talmud that the mountain where the Jews received the Torah is called Sinai "because hatred (*sin'ah*) descended onto the gentiles there" appears in just one passage in the vast corpus of classical rabbinic literature (*b. Shabbat* 89a–b). It has been cited to prove that the rabbis see hatred of Jews as inevitable, even originating at the creation of the Jewish religion. But I believe this explanation of the text is unlikely (Steinsalz 1969, p. 385).

The phrase "hatred descended onto the gentiles there" (*she-yaredah sin'ah le-ummot ha-olam alav*) most likely means that the gentiles' rejection of the Torah and even of the seven Noahide commandments caused them to be hated by God since the text does not mention Jews. In the continuation of the same passage, the name of Mount Horeb (which the rabbis saw as synonymous with Mount Sinai) is explained in a phrase with the identical syntax "destruction descended onto the gentiles there" (*she-yaredah horvah le-ummot ha-olam alav*), and there it certainly means that the gentiles were the recipients of destruction. Other Talmudic passages (e.g., *b. BQ* 38a and Midrash *Tanhuma* [Warsaw] *Shemot* 25) make it clear that the rabbis believed that the gentiles received punishment from God for rejecting the Torah.

The earliest post-Talmudic reformulations of this midrashic statement make it clear that it was not understood as describing hatred of gentiles for Jews, but hatred of God for gentiles. For example, in *Midrash Tanhuma* (dated to the ninth century) this saying is paraphrased as "*har Sinai she-bo nistanneu ummot ha-ʿolam la-qadosh barukh hu venatan lahem epofsim*— Mount Sinai where the gentiles became hated by the Blessed Holy One who brought retribution upon them."[5]

---

[5]This exact wording is found in both editions (Warsaw and Buber) of *Tanhuma Bemidbar* 7. The word *epofsim* is unusual; it is apparently connected to a Greek word for verdict. The Tanhuma's explanation is also found in the later midrash collection *Numbers Rabba* 1:8.

The first time this midrash was used to refer to gentile hatred of Jews appears to be in the twelfth century, by Tuvia ben Eliezer in the collection *Midrash Leqah Tov*. This later understanding has become popular since, but it is not found in classical rabbinic literature.

Vehi she-amedah

Another Jewish text that is often cited to prove that hatred of Jews is universal and inevitable is the *vehi she-amedah* prayer from the *haggadah*, the service read in Jewish homes at the Passover Seder. It reads in part:

> for not just once did somebody try to destroy us, rather in every generation they try to destroy us, but the Blessed Holy One saves us from them. (Silber 2011, p. 17)

This text unambiguously describes hatred of Jews and attempts to destroy them as phenomena that continue throughout all generations. But neither the words nor the sentiment can be found in any classical rabbinic text. Most of the *haggadah* consists of texts from the Bible, the Mishnah, the Talmuds, and the early collections of midrash. But *vehi she-amedah* is a post-Talmudic addition to the *haggadah*.[6]

AFTER THE CLASSICAL RABBINIC PERIOD

The classical rabbis did not teach that hatred of Jews was inevitable and universal. This was not because they had a high opinion of gentiles. We have seen a good deal of evidence that they did not. And yet, even the rabbis who lived under cruel Roman occupation did not believe that all gentiles hated Jews. Certainly, the rabbis who composed the Babylonian Talmud and lived in relatively tolerant Sassanian Persia (Secunda 2014) did not believe and did not teach that "in every generation they try to destroy us." They had no term for "hatred of Jews." In later Hebrew, we find the common term *sinat yisrael*. But the earliest use of this term that I can find is in the ninth century.[7]

At some point after the classical rabbinic period, Jews started to teach that gentile hatred of Jews was inevitable and universal. The post-Talmudic prayer *vehi she-amedah* from the Passover *haggadah* ("in every generation they try

---

[6] The prayer is found in the writings of a number of the *geonim*, including Rabbi Saadiah Gaon (882–942). It has been found in the oldest full *haggadot* to survive, but these are post-Talmudic. See Rovner (2000), Fleischer (2012, pp. 47–49), Kohen (1997, pp. 164–67), and E. D. Goldschmidt (1960, pp. 73–79). According to E. D. Goldschmidt (p. 79, note 6), the prayer is not found in all the old manuscripts.

[7] Midrash *Tanhuma* (Buber) *Balak* 11. A search through the vast amounts of rabbinic literature available through Bar Ilan University's electronic "Responsa Project" (Version 25+) yields 47 mentions of the term, but none in the hundreds of volumes from before the ninth century.

to destroy us ...") caught on quickly and, perhaps due to the centrality of the Passover Seder in establishing Jewish beliefs and values, had a wide influence. The fact that Rashi (1040–1105) included (a presumably incorrect version of) Rabbi Shimon bar Yohai's obscure remark about Esau's hatred of Jacob in his very popular Bible commentary certainly led to its wide circulation.

Other sources also show this change in post-Talmudic times. In the Midrash Tanhuma collection, generally dated to the ninth century, the Jewish people say to God, "Master of the universe, see how the idolaters oppress us. They have no activity other than sitting and plotting against us" (*Tanhuma Toledot* 5). In that same collection, we find hatred of Jews read back into the story of the Israelites in Egypt: "People from all seventy nations lived in Egypt but they enslaved only the Israelites" (*Tanhuma Va-yetze* 7). In a prayer composed at the end of the eleventh century, the author describes the Jews as being "oppressed and enslaved by every nation" (S. Goldschmidt 1965, p. 48).

Turning to Bible commentators, Rabbi Moses ben Nahman (1194–1270) reads the story of the enslavement of the Israelites in Egypt as one of attempted genocide (Commentary to Genesis 15:14). Rabbi David Kimhi (1160–1235) explains that in Genesis 15, God grants Abraham a vision that hinted to Abraham "that in every generation the nations of the world attempt to exterminate the Jews but God saves them" (Commentary to Genesis 15:11), thus reading the *vehi she-amedah* prayer back into the first book of the Bible.

This change seems to have taken place at some point between the seventh and tenth centuries. Beginning then and continuing until the twentieth century, virtually all the Jews of the world lived either in Christian or Muslim countries. Although a tolerated minority group in those countries, they had a lower status and fewer rights than the majority group and were occasionally subject to expulsions, forced conversions, violence, or worse. Before that period, Jews often lived in more cosmopolitan societies where the dominant religion was not monotheistic and where the Jews were one of many minority groups. Was it the experience of being the only minority group that led Jews to believe that their lower status must be a function of a specific hatred of Jews? Or did the situation of Jews truly become worse in Christian and Muslim countries than it had been in polytheistic ones? Either way, the perception that "in every generation they try to destroy us" became a significant part of Jewish self-understanding.

This even led to the assumption in some Jewish circles that any violence of a gentile toward a Jew, whatever the motive, was actually an act of anti-Judaism. Edward Fram and Verena Kasper-Marienberg (2015) show that the Jews of Frankfurt in the late eighteenth century referred to Jews who were killed by gentiles as "martyrs," even though they knew, in one case, that a certain murder was the result of an argument over an unpaid debt or a quarrel of same-sex lovers. Even a Jewish woman who murdered another

Jewish woman and was subsequently executed by the gentile authorities for the crime (standard procedure for murderers) was described by other Jews as having died a martyr's death.

Conclusions

Most of the discussions in rabbinic literature about hatred of Jews and anti-Jewish measures were related to Jewish law, which was, for the rabbis, the essence of Judaism. Some texts asserted that the particularistic aspects of Jewish law—the fact that non-Jews were not equal to Jews in the halakhic system—were what caused anti-Jewish animus. Unlike modern observers, the rabbis were not averse to blaming the victim, saying that Jews and Judaism were understandably hated because of particularistic Jewish laws and attitudes. The classical rabbis were hardly the last Jews in history to make that argument.

Neither the Bible nor classical rabbinic Judaism teaches that the hatred of Jews is universal and inevitable. However, for approximately the last 1400 years this has been a common Jewish perception.

References

Amar, Shlomo. n.d. http://haravamar.org.il/ פרשת-ושלח/157-הלכה-בידוע-עשו-שונא-ליעקב/ על-הפרשה/בראשית Translated by M. Lockshin.

Cohen, Yehezkel. 1975. "The Attitude to the Gentile in the Halacha and in Reality in the Tannaitic Period." PhD. diss. [In Hebrew]. Hebrew University of Jerusalem.

Cohen, Shaye. 1986. "'Anti-Semitism' in Antiquity: The Problem of Definition." In *History and Hate: The Dimensions of Anti-Semitism*, edited by David Berger, 43–48. Philadelphia: Jewish Publication Society.

de Lange, Nicholas. 1978. "Jewish Attitudes to the Roman Empire" In *Imperialism in the Ancient World*, edited by P. Garnsey and C. Whittaker. Cambridge: Cambridge University Press.

Eisen, Robert. 2011. *The Peace and Violence of Judaism: From the Bible to Modern Zionism*. Oxford: Oxford University Press.

Feinstein, Moshe. 1980. *Responsa Igrot Moshe*. Vol. 2. New York.

Fleischer, E. 2012. *Statutory Jewish Prayers: Their Emergence and Development* [In Hebrew]. Edited by S. Elizur and T. Beeri. Jerusalem: Magnes.

Fram, Edward, and Verena Kasper-Marienberg. 2015. "Jewish Martyrdom Without Persecution: The Murder of Gumpert May, Frankfurt am Main, 1781." *AJS Review* 39: 267–301.

Goldschmidt, E. D. 1960. *The Passover Haggadah: Its Sources and History* [In Hebrew]. Jerusalem: Mossad Bialik.

Goldschmidt, S., ed. 1965. *Seder ha-selihot ke-minhag polin ve-rov ha-kehilot be-eretz yisra'el*. Jerusalem: Mosad Harav Kook.

Josephus, Flavius. 1958. *Antiquities of the Jews*. Translated by Ralph Marcus. Cambridge, MA: Harvard University Press.

Kahana, Menahem, ed. 2011–2015. *Sifre on Numbers: An Annotated Edition*. 5 vols. [In Hebrew]. Jerusalem: Magnes.
Kalmin, Richard. 2003. "Rabbinic Traditions About Roman Persecutions of the Jews: A Reconsideration." *Journal of Jewish Studies* 54 (1): 21–50.
Kohen, Yekuti'el Zalman. 1997. *The Haggadah of the Geonim and Maimonides* [In Hebrew]. Jerusalem: Otzar Ha-poskim.
Kook, Abraham Isaac. 1956. *Orot* [In Hebrew]. Jerusalem: Mossad Harav Kook.
Kugel, J. 1996. "The Holiness of Israel and the Land in Second Temple Times." In *Texts, Temples and Traditions: A Tribute to Menachem Haran*, edited by Michael Fox et al. Winona Lake: Eisenbrauns.
Lieberman, Saul. 1974. "On Persecution of the Jewish Religion" [In Hebrew]. In *Salo Wittmayer Baron Jubilee Volume*, edited by Saul Lieberman and Arthur Hyman, vol. 3. Jerusalem: American Academy for Jewish Research.
Rovner, Jay. 2000. "An Early Passover Haggadah According to the Palestinian Rite." *Jewish Quarterly Review* 90 (3/4): 337–96.
Schäfer, Peter. 1997. *Judeophobia: Attitudes Toward the Jews in the Ancient World*. Cambridge, MA: Harvard University Press.
Secunda, Shai. 2014. *The Iranian Talmud*. Philadelphia: University of Pennsylvania Press.
Shochetman, E. 1997. "A *Halakhah* that is not *Halakhah*" [In Hebrew]. *Sinai* 120: 184–86.
Silber, David, trans. 2011. *A Passover Haggadah: Go Forth and Learn*. Philadelphia: The Jewish Publication Society.
Steinsalz, Adin, ed. 1969. *Talmud*. Jerusalem: Israel Institute for Talmudic Publications.
Tanakh. 1999. Philadelphia: Jewish Publication Society.
Walfish, Barry. 1993. *Esther in Medieval Garb: Jewish Interpretations of the Book of Esther in the Middle Ages*. Albany: SUNY Press.
Yuval, Israel Jacob. 2006. *Two Nations in Your Womb: Perceptions of Jews and Christians in Late Antiquity and the Middle Ages*. Berkeley: University of California Press.

CHAPTER 22

Zionism

Scott Ury

INTRODUCTION

Zionism emerged as a political movement in late nineteenth-century Eastern and Central Europe in the context of "the Jewish question"—debates in different countries about what place Jews were to have in modern societies and nation-states. Key figures such as Leon (Yehuda Leib) Pinsker, Theodor Herzl, Vladimir (Ze'ev) Jabotinsky and others helped shape the movement and bear the moniker "Zionist" due to their common understanding that "the Jews" constituted a separate nation and their demand that "the Jews" of Europe relocate to Palestine or some other land where they would enjoy autonomy, if not sovereignty (Shumsky 2018). Despite such commonalities, these and other Zionist ideologues differ from each other in many respects, not the least of which is the place and interpretation that they assign to antisemitism and its relationship to Zionism. For some Zionist figures like Rabbi Abraham Isaac Kook or Ahad Ha'Am (Asher Ginsberg), antisemitism is subordinate to questions regarding the role of religion, language, or culture (Mirsky 2014; Zipperstein 1993). For others, in particular, those who viewed it primarily as a political project, antisemitism is inextricably linked to the very nature of and justification for Zionism.

In this essay, I will analyze six Jewish intellectuals and scholars whose thinking exemplifies the recurrent, strange, and, at times, befuddling dialectic of

---

Parts of this essay appeared in Ury (2018).

S. Ury (✉)
Department of Jewish History, Tel Aviv University, Tel Aviv, Israel
e-mail: scottury@tauex.tau.ac.il

confrontation and influence between two ostensibly contradictory ideologies, Zionism and antisemitism. Through this analysis, I will argue that various studies of antisemitism published over the past century and a half not only illustrate the different ways that key thinkers have imagined, researched, and written about antisemitism. These studies also highlight the underlying relationship between each author's respective understanding of antisemitism and its impact on their interpretation of the very nature, history, and fate of "the Jews."

My selection of thinkers—drawn from among the most prominent proponents of Zionism as well as influential scholars who identified with it—not only reveals the extent to which specific interpretations of antisemitism often served as precursors to the development of Zionist thought but also how this dialectical relationship influenced the manner in which antisemitism was, in turn, understood, studied, and discussed in both the public and the academic realms. Indeed, the current study of antisemitism cannot be grasped fully without recognizing its longstanding connection and deep indebtedness to Zionist conceptions of the Jewish past, present, and future. In this and other ways, the works discussed in this essay also demonstrate the degree to which the lines separating the scholarly study of antisemitism from public debates regarding the phenomenon are often blurred.

This point becomes particularly apparent when one considers the influence that contemporary social and political concerns continue to have on academic studies of antisemitism. Of course, the study of antisemitism is not the only scholarly field in close conversation with current political or social considerations. Indeed, many of the same dilemmas that confront scholars of antisemitism plague a number of fields, in particular those connected to the politics of identity and the demands—both explicit and implicit—of affiliated community members and institutions. In these and other cases, scholarly research and contemporary concerns repeatedly intersect and interfere with one another through the implementation of key concepts—like antisemitism and Zionism—that are simultaneously academically accurate and politically loaded. Moreover, while some may claim that such moments of confluence are problem-free, many of the examples discussed in this chapter demonstrate the extent to which the study of antisemitism has long been influenced by popular notions regarding "the Jews," their history, their dilemmas, and their fate. The ongoing intersection and interference between public debates and academic research regarding antisemitism remains one of the biggest challenges facing scholars of antisemitism today.

The Die Is Cast? Pinsker's Anger, Herzl's Designs

One of the earliest examples of Zionist political thought, *Auto-Emancipation*, was published anonymously in German in 1882 by the former adherent of the Jewish Enlightenment (*Haskalah*) and longtime advocate for Jewish integration into European society, Leon (Yehuda Leib) Pinsker. To be sure, Pinsker did not employ the term Zionism (it would not be introduced into the lexicon until the next decade). However, his clarion led directly to the establishment of the Lovers of Zion (*Hovevei Zion*) movement in the Russian Empire and neighboring regions, and, soon thereafter, the establishment of a series of Jewish agricultural settlements in Ottoman Palestine. Pinsker's pamphlet was structured around the realization that antisemitism—or Judeophobia as he would refer to it—was an indelible psychological-social disease and that the only viable solution available for "the Jews" was to dedicate themselves to "the sacred work of national regeneration" ([1882] 1975, p. 101). The impetus for Pinsker's treatise was the wave of anti-Jewish violence that swept the southwestern provinces of the Russian empire in 1881–1882, some two years after the German journalist Wilhelm Marr helped popularize the term "antisemitism." Spirited in nature and enticing in its rhetoric, Pinsker's manifesto would eventually attain canonical status as it bound antisemitism to Zionism through a series of axioms that forged a deep bond between the two concepts. Its central tenets are critical for understanding contemporary conceptualizations of antisemitism as well as the ongoing, potentially counter-intuitive, connection between these two turn-of-the-century ideologies and their respective movements.

The first of Pinsker's fundamental axioms was that "the Jews" would never become full, equal members of European society. Rejecting over a hundred years of Enlightenment ideology and practice, Pinsker maintained that no level of linguistic adaptation, cultural integration, or political loyalty would ensure the Jews' entry into European society. Alluding to traditional religious themes of dispersion and punishment, Pinsker surmised that the Jews: "Are everywhere as guests, and nowhere *at home*" ([1882] 1975, p. 76). Fated to lives on societies' margins, "the world saw in this people [the Jews] the uncanny form of one of the dead walking among the living" (p. 77). The recurrent confrontation with the image of "the Jews" as "a dead man," in turn, stirred fears "of the Jewish ghost" (pp. 83, 78). According to Pinsker, who was trained as a physician at the University of Moscow, Judeophobia was not only "a psychic aberration," but over time it had become an incurable hereditary social disease that had been "transmitted for two thousand years" (p. 78).

As a result, antisemitism had been transformed from a social curse into a "blind natural force" and Jews had little choice but to "reconcile ourselves, once and for all, to the idea that the other nations, by reason of their eternal, *natural* antagonism, will forever reject us" (pp. 80, 91). Confronted with a cruel fate of liminality and hostility, Pinsker urged his Jewish readers to embrace their inner (Jewish) nation. "The constantly growing conviction that we are nowhere at home" led to the conclusion that "we finally must have a *home*, if not a *country* of our own" (p. 94). And, thus, Pinsker, the founder of political Zionism, would conclude that "Judaism and Anti-Semitism passed for centuries through history as inseparable companions" (p. 79).

A generation later, Theodor Herzl's confrontations with social, political, and popular antisemitism—in Vienna amid the rise of Karl Lueger and in Paris during the Dreyfus Affair—led him to a set of political principles that were strikingly similar to Pinsker's. Although he had earlier advocated a range of far-reaching solutions to the "Jewish Question," including mass conversion to Catholicism, the rise of modern political leaders and movements with openly anti-Jewish agendas in turn-of-the-century Central and Eastern Europe convinced Herzl of antisemitism's permanent nature. As he would note in a personal letter to Albert Rothschild from 1895: "Anyone who thinks that agitation against the Jews is a passing fad is seriously mistaken. For profound reasons it is bound to get worse and worse" (1960, vol. 1, p. 190).

While Pinsker's pessimism bound him to a fate of separation, Herzl's optimism led him to promote a strategy in which antisemitism and the ensuing "misery of the Jews" would serve as the very motor that would lead to the transformation of "the Jews." Enamored with technology as well as the prospects for social engineering, Herzl likened antisemitism to a powerful, unstoppable force that simply awaited the proper engineer to guide its (negative) energies in the right direction. As he states in his 1896 blueprint for political Zionism, *The Jewish State*:

> Everything depends on our propelling force. And what is our propelling force? The misery of the Jews. Who would venture to deny its existence? We shall discuss it fully in the chapter on the causes of Anti-Semitism. Everybody is familiar with the phenomenon of steam-power, generated by boiling water, lifting the kettle-lid...Now I believe that this power, if rightly employed, is powerful enough to propel a large engine and to dispatch passengers and goods. ([1896] 1993, p. 8)

Much like Pinsker, a seemingly eternal antisemitism not only led Herzl to embrace Zionism but, as part of this process, it also transformed his understanding of what "the Jews" were. As he notes in *The Jewish State*: "We are one people - our enemies have made us one...." (p. 27). For both supporters of antisemitism and adherents to Zionism, the two opposing ideologies repeatedly converged at the moment of confrontation when antisemitism was understood as "a national question" and "the Jews," in turn, were perceived as a separate nation—one of the basic components of late nineteenth-century social and political thought. Commenting on the potentially strange and awkward relationship between antisemitism and Zionism, Herzl did not shrink before the potential reaction of liberal opponents of Zionism (including many Jews) who maintained that "Jews" were strictly a religious community. Embracing fundamental aspects of the reigning discourse of nationalism, he confessed in *The Jewish State*: "It might more reasonably be objected that I am giving a handle to Anti-Semitism when I say that we are a people - one people ..." (p. 17).

Jabotinsky's Inferno: The "Antisemitism of Things" and the Call for Jewish Evacuation

While Pinsker and Herzl helped create Zionist ideology and politics in turn-of-the-century East Central Europe, it was up to a later generation of Jewish leaders to implement these and related ideologies in the new nation-states that arose in the region after the collapse of the Austro-Hungarian, Russian, and Turkish empires. Of the many Jewish figures active between the two World Wars, Vladimir (Ze'ev) Jabotinsky remains one of the most widely recognized and oft-celebrated representatives of Zionist politics and thinking. Born in Odessa and comfortable in a number of languages and cultures from Russian to Italian, Jabotinsky's understanding of the dilemmas that plagued European Jewry echoed many of the points raised by Pinsker and Herzl. It also reflected the growing centrality of integral nationalism in Poland and other states in the region. In this and other ways, Jabotinsky's analysis of antisemitism and its relationship to Zionism represents another link in the ongoing dialectic between the two ideologies. As Jabotinsky wrote in a 1907 letter to the Zionist leader Menachem Ussiskhin regarding the "nationalities problem" and its influence on the state of European Jewish society and the development of Zionism, "I also want to understand the anti-Semites, in particular their policies regarding the middle class. In that realm, they are specialists" (1992, p. 59).

Like Pinsker and Herzl before him, Jabotinsky was convinced that the path of legal emancipation was illusory and that Jews ought to abandon any hope of achieving or maintaining civic equality. Increasingly concerned with the fate of Europe's largest Jewish community in interwar Poland, Jabotinsky argued that legal means would do little to alleviate the suffering of the country's three million Jewish citizens or the millions of Jews residing in neighboring nation-states. As he would caution in *The War and the Jew*, which was published posthumously in 1942, "I warn my fellow-Jews (if they still need the warning, which I doubt) that equal rights are, at best, a very perishable kind of goods, infinitely prickly, to be handled and used with caution, moderation and tact" (p. 116).

Jabotinsky maintained that the problem wasn't antisemitic politicians or their noxious ideas (what Jabotinsky poignantly referred to as "the antisemitism of men") but, rather, the fundamental conditions of Jewish society across East Central Europe. Pointing to what he would define as "the antisemitism of things," Jabotinsky argued that the demographic, economic, and social nature of Jewish life in East Central Europe, in particular, and in the Jewish Diaspora, more generally, condemned Jews to generations of suffering. Moreover, while the "Antisemitism of Men" was prone to fluctuation, "the Antisemitism of Things" was "steady, constant and immutable, and therefore much more formidable" (1942, p. 78). Alluding to the influence of "three generations of Jewish thinkers and Zionists" in his testimony to the British Royal Commission on Palestine in 1937 (the Peel Commission), Jabotinsky emphasized the "conclusion that the cause of our suffering is the very fact of the Diaspora, the bedrock fact that we are everywhere a minority" (1986, p. 560). Similar to Pinsker's warnings some fifty years earlier, Jabotinsky maintained that the Jews' strange state of diaspora existence made them "the most abnormal of peoples and therefore the most unfortunate" (p. 561).

Pinsker's influence on Jabotinsky did not end with their common understanding regarding the "abnormal" nature of Jewish life in the Diaspora. In light of his conclusions about the permanent nature of the "antisemitism of things," the Jews' abnormal state of existence, and the illusory character of equal rights, Jabotinsky called for the "evacuation" of millions of Jews from East Central Europe to the Middle East. While Jabotinsky's call for the Jews' "evacuation" was opposed by a range of Jewish leaders in Poland, many in the Polish nationalist camp agreed, in principle, with his position. In fact, some even maintained that the agreement between these ostensible opponents regarding the Jews' "evacuation" from Poland (regardless of each parties' specific motives) might help lay the foundations for future cooperation between Jabotinsky's Revisionist Zionist camp and those on the Polish right. As Jabotinsky noted in *The War and the Jew*: "Any assertion that the cancer of antisemitism can be cured in its principle breeding zone, East-Central Europe, by the ointment of 'equal rights' without a preliminary exodus of the bulk of the Jews, is empty, thoughtless and harmful twaddle" (1942, p. 121). According to Jabotinsky, the founder and leading figure of Revisionist Zionism, "[m]ass evacuation is the only remedy for the cancer of Jewish distress" (p. 124).

Jerusalem Scholars of Antisemitism: Politics, History, Narrative

The post-WWII era witnessed the discourse regarding antisemitism pass from the contentious realm of national politics to the hallowed halls of academia. Despite the wide range of scholarship on antisemitism published over the past seventy-five years, research on antisemitism over the past generation or two has—to a large extent—embraced an interpretation strikingly similar to the one advanced by early advocates of the Zionist solution to "the Jewish Question." This approach was adopted by several influential scholars at the Hebrew University of Jerusalem whose research on these questions absorbed and implemented many of the central assumptions and postulates advocated by Pinsker, Herzl, and other Zionist figures. Important studies on the topic by seminal scholars of Jewish history like Shmuel Ettinger and Jacob Katz reflect this scholarly trend and demonstrate the extent to which many of the same tensions between antisemitism and Zionism that characterized early Zionist analyses of "the Jewish Question" influenced later scholarly studies of antisemitism. This methodological transition from political analyses to academic works also demonstrates the extent to which practitioners in both the political and the academic realms often took part in the same intellectual discourse regarding antisemitism, its origins, and its potential resolution.

One of the key figures in this transition from political interpretations of antisemitism to academic analyses of the phenomenon was the Kiev-born,

Israeli scholar of Jewish history Shmuel Ettinger. Although he wrote on a wide range of topics, Ettinger published a number of studies on antisemitism that adopted and reinforced many of the themes that were central to the traditional Zionist interpretation of antisemitism including the long history of anti-Jewish prejudice, the recurrent abandonment of "the Jews" by their neighbors, and the ongoing link between antisemitism and Zionism (1978). A dominant figure in Israeli academia for decades, Ettinger helped shaped the way that generations of scholars understood, researched, and wrote about antisemitism.

One of Ettinger's central points was that anti-Jewish prejudice was historically continuous and, therefore, unlike any other form of ethnic or religious hatred. Openly positioning himself in direct contradistinction to prominent (Jewish) scholars in post-war North America such as Hannah Arendt and Theodor Adorno, Ettinger criticized those "psychologists, sociologists and historians who view anti-Judaism (*sinat yisrael*) as a phenomenon with wider, general implications" (1980, p. 11). Ettinger believed that the cardinal sin of such studies was that their approach treated the Jews as "a minor if not random factor" in the historical process and that they were not at all concerned with "how to evaluate it [anti-Semitism] as part of the history of the Jews" (p. 17). According to Ettinger, such comparative or universalist studies of antisemitism "completely miss the point" (p. 17). In an essay on the connection between antisemitism and the Holocaust, Ettinger clarified his position regarding the historically continuous nature of antisemitism—which helped determine its uniqueness—as well as its central place in the course of Jewish history. "The Holocaust is intimately connected to the phenomenon of antisemitism, which accompanied the Jewish people over its history for thousands of years; this hatred is a unique phenomenon in the history of relations between national and religious collectives" (1992, p. 258). For Ettinger and many other Israeli scholars of his time, antisemitism was deemed to be as historically continuous and as unique as the people that it helped mirror and shape, "the Jewish People" (1978, pp. 210–11, 225). Moreover, as a historically unique phenomenon, antisemitism could not be compared accurately to any other form of ethnic or religious prejudice or hatred.

Composed in the heat of the Cold War, Ettinger's understanding of antisemitism was directly informed by his growing preoccupation with Soviet Jewry. In a series of essays on the topic that liberally intertwined historical research, contemporary concerns, and personal interests, Ettinger repeatedly emphasized the historical continuity of antisemitism. "Soviet anti-Jewish propaganda relies on the classical anti-Semitic motifs derived from nineteenth-century Russian antisemitic literature, European anti-Semitic literature and a flavoring of elements of current affairs" (1988, p. 52). Moreover, despite periodic displays of tolerance, Ettinger warned—similar to Pinsker and Herzl—that antisemitism was not only "deeply rooted in the Russian heritage" but that it could easily "be activated among the various strata of society" (1983, p. vi).

Ettinger's critique of the Soviet Union was exacerbated by a personal sense of betrayal. As a young immigrant student in Jerusalem in the 1940s, Ettinger was a dedicated member of the Palestine Communist Party and many observers maintain that his writings on Soviet Jewry should be seen as part of his own transition from Soviet darkness to Zionist light. As part of this process, Ettinger repeatedly pointed to antisemitism as proof of the fundamentally duplicitous and corrupt nature of the Soviet experiment. Writing about the Holocaust as well as larger anxieties of social and political abandonment, Ettinger would declaim: "The Holocaust years uncovered the bitter truth about the Soviet 'brotherhood of peoples,'" and helped expose many of the underlying similarities between the Soviet Union and Nazi Germany (1983, pp. vii, xiv).

Little seemed to expose the Soviet Union's corrupt nature more than the regime's anti-Zionist campaigns. According to Ettinger, anti-Zionism in the Soviet Union after the 1967 Arab–Israeli War was little more than a fig-leaf designed to camouflage traditional anti-Jewish sentiments. "The main expression of antisemitism in the USSR today is through a propaganda campaign which can be called 'The Struggle Against Zionism'" (1988, p. 49). Nor was his understanding of this phenomenon limited to the Soviet Union. In a caustic Hebrew pamphlet that was published in 1985 by a division of the Israeli Ministry of Education and Culture, Ettinger charged that hostility toward Israel on the part of many members of "the New Left" was simply another chapter in the long, irrepressible history of antisemitism. "A new situation has arisen that integrates antisemitic instincts and tendencies that were temporarily suppressed due to the Holocaust and liberal education into the war against so-called racism and anti-Zionism" (1985, p. 7). Although they were separated by over a hundred years, two world wars, the rise of the Soviet Union, the creation of the State of Israel, and the Cold War, Ettinger and Pinsker shared a common language and a common worldview.

A colleague of Ettinger's for decades, few scholars have influenced the study of Jewish history more than Jacob Katz. Born in Hungary, Katz received his doctorate at the University of Frankfurt in 1935, relocated to British Palestine soon thereafter and began teaching at the Hebrew University in 1949–1950. His use of traditional Jewish sources to uncover various aspects of social history represented a turning point in the way that Jewish history was studied and his scholarly impact remains palpable to this day. While Katz's early research focused on developments within the Jewish community, much of his later work dealt with relations between Jews and non-Jews, including the study of antisemitism (1973, 1980). Moreover, while Katz was widely recognized for his intellectual independence and creativity, his approach to the study of antisemitism often mirrored traditional Zionist interpretations of "the Jewish Question." Much like Pinsker, Herzl, and others, Katz pointed to an integral if not endemic antisemitism in European society as the main factor leading to the collapse of Enlightenment visions of Jewish–Christian rapprochement. Although Katz's removed academic style differed greatly from the spirited engagement that characterized many of the other authors discussed in this essay, his belief in a deeply embedded, if not potentially eternal, hostility toward Jews as well as his emphasis on the ultimate, if not predestined, collapse of the different attempts to create a new, rational society across eighteenth- and nineteenth-century Europe mirrored many of the central points addressed in earlier works.

Originally published in Hebrew in 1958, Katz's seminal work *Tradition and Crisis* revolved around the pivotal role played by the construction of a "neutral society" in late eighteenth-century Central Europe that would create a space in which Jews and Gentiles could meet, interact and befriend one another "as equals" (1993, pp. 214–25, esp. 221). According to Katz, the "neutral society" would serve as the incubator for a new era characterized by rational thinking, Enlightenment ideals, and civic equality for Europe's Christians and Jews. A generation later, in his study *Out of the Ghetto*, which examined Jewish emancipation in a number of Central European countries, Katz revised his understanding of this key concept by referring to the failure to create a "semineutral" society in Enlightenment Europe (1973, pp. 42–56). The ostensibly minor addition of this four letter preface to his core concept reflects Katz's growing doubts regarding the nature of European society and the potential for the construction of a framework that would ensure Jewish emancipation and equality in the region. Thus, while social integration and civic emancipation may have been noble endeavors, they were doomed to fail due to the enduring nature of anti-Jewish hostility. Katz notes that the new "social communion" between Jews and non-Jews "can scarcely be said to have achieved the abstract model of a neutral society conceived by the propounders of the Enlightenment" (p. 54). Throughout this study, Katz pointed to a deeply rooted hostility toward Jews that repeatedly prevented their integration into European society. According to Katz, "the bulk of the population...hardly ever overcame its reservations against the Jewish variant in their society" (p. 217).

European society's persistent ambivalence regarding "the Jews" and the contradictions embedded deep within the various plans for their integration into European society lay at the core of Katz's next major work, a history of antisemitism *From Prejudice to Destruction* (1980). In this study, Katz argued that despite the many efforts to promote Enlightenment ideals and rational thinking, large parts of European society remained deeply, if not inherently, hostile to the Jews' presence (pp. v, 324). Embracing an approach that antisemitism had a long, continuous history, Katz concluded that: "modern anti-Semitism turned out to be a continuation of the premodern rejection of Judaism by Christianity" (p. 319). The interpretation of antisemitism that was as universal as it was eternal was reinforced in this study by Katz's methodological decision to examine the collapse of the Enlightenment promise and the rise of antisemitism in a number of central European countries: Germany and France, Hungary and Austria. Across the continent, the Jews' of Europe encountered a deep undercurrent of hostility that had its roots in Europe's dominant religious faith, Christianity.

While Katz's prodigious oeuvre was far more tempered and academic than the passionate analyses of Pinsker, Herzl, Jabotinsky, and even Ettinger, *From Prejudice to Destruction* actually ends on a particularly engaged, contemporary note regarding the extent to which the State of Israel already (in 1980) served as the primary focus for present-day antisemitism. Pondering the current state of affairs, Katz bemoaned the fact that the "Jewish state" had become the "target of constant attack" and that "in the ideological expression of these attacks, anti-Semitic motives are routinely intermingled." Adopting a tone that emphasized the eternal nature both of antisemitism and of the Jews, as well as the ongoing dialectic between antisemitism and Zionism, Katz seems to echo, consciously or not, Ettinger's conclusions regarding the nature, history, and future of antisemitism. "Since anti-Jewish animosity has always trailed the path of Jewish history, and the last phase of it is characterized by the creation of the Jewish state, the new metamorphosis [of antisemitism] is hardly surprising" (p. 327).

Toward a New Orthodoxy? The Historiographical Antecedents of "the New Antisemitism"

Many of the points raised in earlier studies of antisemitism are central to the scholarship published by the most prolific and influential scholar of antisemitism over the past thirty years, Robert S. Wistrich, also of The Hebrew University of Jerusalem. Through a series of lengthy studies, Wistrich helped refine, revive, and reaffirm traditional Zionist interpretations of antisemitism and their place in the study of Jewish history and society. In fact, Wistrich's work is so influential that many contemporary scholars in Europe, Israel, and North America embrace much of his oeuvre without questioning its underlying assumptions, interpretations, or conclusions (Porat 2011, pp. 93–94; Rosenfeld 2013, pp. 525–29). More than any other scholar, Wistrich has helped integrate traditional Zionist interpretations of Jewish history, society, and fate into the study of antisemitism.

Like Pinsker, Herzl, and others, Wistrich maintained that antisemitism is nothing less than "the longest hatred," one that originated in ancient times, has continued, albeit in different permutations, to the present, and whose demise seems far from imminent (2010, pp. 3–13, 17–21, 104–6). Pointing to these and other ostensibly unique aspects of antisemitism, Wistrich noted in his 2010 tome—whose title embraces its overall argument—*Lethal Obsession: Anti-Semitism from Antiquity to the Global Jihad*, that: "There has been no hatred in Western civilization more persistent and enduring than that directed against the Jews. Though the form and timing that outbursts of anti-Jewish persecution have taken throughout the ages have varied, the basic patterns of prejudice have remained remarkably consistent" (p. 79). Not only has antisemitism continued from ancient times to today, but its unprecedented historical longevity and continuity demonstrate how impervious it has proven to various interventions (p. 13). Although some of his early work criticized sweeping analyses of the phenomenon, Wistrich's later studies present antisemitism as a historically continuous and unique, if not a practically ineradicable, phenomenon.

Another point made by early Zionist thinkers, key historians of the Jews, and Wistrich are his comments regarding the nature and collapse of the Enlightenment promise. Paralleling Pinsker, Herzl, and others, Wistrich wrote repeatedly about the Jews' abandonment or betrayal by their former allies, particularly those on what Wistrich (and other scholars) refer to rather loosely as "the Left." Wistrich's 2012 volume, *From Ambivalence to Betrayal: The Left, the Jews, and Israel*, discusses at length the ostensible hypocrisy of the European, North American, and even the Israeli (Jewish) Left. Focusing on how "the Left" has betrayed "the Jews" through its support for the Palestinian cause and its calls for the dissolution—or at the very least the radical reconstruction—of "the Jewish State," Wistrich's rhetoric is merciless and his anger visceral. "The advocacy by a broad section of the contemporary Left of such *defamatory* propositions is a betrayal of its own egalitarian principles and supposed respect for democratic values" (p. 3).

A third key point shared by earlier thinkers discussed above and Wistrich is the link between Zionism and a growing anxiety, if not a palpable fear, of antisemitism. The same tension-filled dialectic between antisemitism and Zionism that shaped the thinking of many early Zionist thinkers remains critical for Wistrich and other contemporary observers, academic, communal, and those who wear both hats. For Wistrich and other scholars, this connection is best illustrated by the prevalence of "The New Anti-Semitism" and the manner in which this latest iteration of "the longest hatred" focuses its bile on the State of Israel as "the collective Jew" (Wistrich 2010, pp. 5–6, 34–35; 2012, pp. xi–xv, 17). Turning his attention to current political debates regarding Israel and the Middle East, Wistrich declares that: "The 'new' anti-Semitism involves the denial of the rights of the Jewish people to live as an equal member within the family of nations. In that sense contemporary anti-Semitism above all targets Israel as the 'collective Jew' among nations" (2012, p. 1). As Wistrich notes in *Lethal Obsession*: "Anti-Zionism has never been completely identical to anti-Semitism, but some thirty years ago it began to fully crystallize as its offspring and heir. At times it even seems like its Siamese twin" (2010, p. 62). Try as they may disavow and disown one another, antisemitism and Zionism continue to conflict, contradict, and influence one another.

Antisemitism and Zionism Between the Academic and the Public Realms

The ongoing dialectic between antisemitism and Zionism in both the public and the academic spheres raises a myriad of fascinating questions for scholars, students, and observers of both phenomena. First, does the contemporary centrality of the traditional Zionist interpretation of antisemitism and the accompanying fate of "the Jews" represent the result of empirical findings, deeply-seated ideological and political predispositions, or an odd coupling of both? Moreover, can the study of antisemitism simultaneously serve both the academic ideal of scholarly research and the collective needs—both real and existential—of a specific ethno-religious community, "the Jews"? These and related dilemmas have led many to ask whether or not there is anything that scholars can (or should) do to isolate the study of antisemitism from contemporary concerns and to return the study of anti-Jewish animus to a protected, neutral academic space. At the same time, others will maintain that there is little that one can do to ensure such a divide, and that Pinsker, Herzl, and other observers were alarmingly prescient in their observations regarding the longstanding, befuddling, and, at times, strange relationship between antisemitism and Zionism.

References

Ettinger, Shmuel. 1978. *Ha-antishemiyut ba-ʿet ha-hadasha: pirkei mehkar ve-ʿiyun*. Tel Aviv: Moreshet.

Ettinger, Shmuel. 1980. "Sinat-yisra'el be-retzifut historit." In *Sinat Yisra'el le-doroteha*, edited by Shmuel Almog. Jerusalem: Merkaz Zalman Shazar.

Ettinger, Shmuel. 1983. "Introduction." In *Anti-Semitism in the Soviet Union: Its Roots and Consequences*, edited by Shmuel Ettinger and Jacob M. Kelman, vol. 3, i–xiv. Jerusalem: Hebrew University.

Ettinger, Shmuel. 1985. "Antishemiyut ve-anti-Zionut ba-dor ha-tsaʿir ba-ʿolam ha-maʿaravi." In *Antishemiyut ha-yom*, 3–9. Jerusalem: Merkaz ha-hasbara.

Ettinger, Shmuel. 1988. "Soviet Anti-Semitism After the Six-Day War." In *Present-Day Antisemitism*, edited by Yehuda Bauer, 49–56. Jerusalem: Hebrew University.

Ettinger, Shmuel. 1992. "Ha-antishemiyut ha-modernit ve-ha-sho'a." In *Historiya ve-historionim*, edited by Shmuel Almog and Otto Dov Kulka, 258–66. Jerusalem: Merkaz Zalman Shazar.

Herzl, Theodor. (1896) 1993. *The Jewish State: An Attempt at a Modern Solution of the Jewish Question*. London: Henry Pordes.

Herzl, Theodor. 1960. *The Complete Diaries of Theodor Herzl*. Edited by Raphael Patai. 5 vols. New York: Herzl Press.

Jabotinsky, Vladimir. 1942. *The War and the Jew*. New York: The Dial Press.

Jabotinsky, Vladimir. 1986. "Evidence Submitted to the Palestine Royal Commission (1937)." In *The Zionist Idea: A Historical Analysis and Reader*, edited by Arthur Hertzberg, 559–570. New York: Atheneum.

Jabotinsky, Vladimir. 1992. "Jabotinsky to Ussishkin, Vienna, Dec. 1, 1907." In *Igrot, 1908–1914*, edited by Daniel Carpi and Moshe Halevy, vol. 1. Jerusalem: Jabotinsky Institute.

Katz, Jacob. 1973. *Out of the Ghetto: The Social Background of Jewish Emancipation, 1770–1870*. New York: Schocken Books.

Katz, Jacob. 1980. *From Prejudice to Destruction: Antisemitism: 1700–1933*. Cambridge, MA: Harvard University Press.

Katz, Jacob. 1993. *Tradition and Crisis: Jewish Society at the End of the Middle Ages*. New York: Schocken Books.

Mirsky, Yehuda. 2014. *Rav Kook: Mystic in a Time of Revolution*. New Haven: Yale University Press.

Pinsker, Leo (Leon). (1882) 1975. "Auto-Emancipation: An Appeal to His People by a Russian Jew." In *Road to Freedom: Writings and Addresses,* edited by Benzion Netanyahu. Westport, CT: Greenwood Press.

Porat, Dina. 2011. "The International Working Definition of Antisemitism and Its Detractors." *Israel Journal of Foreign Affairs* 5 (3): 93–101.

Rosenfeld, Alvin H. 2013. "The End of the Holocaust and the Beginnings of a New Antisemitism." In *Resurgent Antisemitism: Global Perspectives,* edited by Alvin H. Rosenfeld, 521–34. Bloomington: Indiana University Press.

Shumsky, Dmitry. 2018. *Beyond the Nation-State: The Zionist Political Imagination from Pinsker to Ben Gurion.* New Haven: Yale University Press.

Ury, Scott. 2018. "Strange Bedfellows? Antisemitism, Zionism and the Fate of 'the Jews.'" *American Historical Review* 123 (4) (October): 1151–71.

Wistrich, Robert. 2010. *A Lethal Obsession: Anti-Semitism from Antiquity to Global Jihad.* New York: Random House.

Wistrich, Robert. 2012. *From Ambivalence to Betrayal: The Left, the Jews, and Israel.* Lincoln: University of Nebraska Press.

Zipperstein, Steven J. 1993. *Elusive Prophet: Ahad Ha'am and the Origins of Zionism.* London: Halban.

WORKS CITED

AAwP (Archiwum Archidiecezjalne w Poznaniu). Dep. Testium XV, 75v-76.
Abramson, Henry. 1999. *A Prayer for the Government: Ukrainians and Jews in Revolutionary Times, 1917–1920*. Cambridge, MA: Harvard University Press.
Ahmad, Aijaz. 1992. *In Theory: Classes, Nations, Literatures*. London: Verso Books.
Akbari, Suzanne Conklin. 2005. "Placing the Jews in Late Medieval English Literature." In Kalmar and Penslar 2005, 32–50.
AKM (Archiwum Kurii Metropolitalnej). Kraków, Acta Episcopalia 90.
Allen, Gary. 1972. *None Dare Call It Conspiracy*. Rossmoor: Concord Press.
Alperin, Mimi. 1989. "JAP Jokes: Hateful Humor." *Humor: International Journal of Humor Research* 2 (4): 412–16.
Aly, Götz. 1999. *Final Solution: Nazi Population Policy and the Murder of the European Jews*. Translated by Belinda Cooper and Allison Brown. London: Arnold.
Aly, Götz, and Susanne Heim. 2002. *Architects of Annihilation: Auschwitz and the Logic of Destruction*. Translated by A. G. Blunden. Princeton: Princeton University Press.
Amar, Shlomo. n.d. http://haravamar.org.il/ ליעקב-שונא-עשו-בידוע-הלכה-157/ושלח-פרשת/ בראשית/הפרשה-על Translated by M. Lockshin.
Amar, Tarik Cyril. 2015. *The Paradox of Lviv: A Borderland City Between Nazis, Stalinists, and Nationalists*. Ithaca: Cornell University Press.
Améry, Jean. (1971) 2005. "The Birth of Man from the Spirit of Violence: Frantz Fanon the Revolutionary." *Wasafiri* 44 (Spring 2005): 13–18.
Anderson, Benedict. 1983. *Imagined Communities: Reflections on the Origin and Spread of Nationalism*. London: Verso.
Anidjar, Gil. 2003. *The Jew, the Arab: A History of the Enemy*. Stanford: Stanford University Press.
Anidjar, Gil. 2008. *Semites: Race, Religion, Literature*. Stanford: Stanford University Press.
Anidjar, Gil. 2009. "Muslim Jews." *Qui parle: Critical Humanities and Social Sciences* 18 (1) (Fall/Winter): 1–23.

Anonymous. 1920. "Anti-Semitism—Will It Appear in the U. S.?" In *The International Jew*, 55–67. Dearborn: Dearborn Publishing.
Anzaldúa, Gloria. 1990. *Making Face, Making Soul = Haciendo Caras: Creative and Critical Perspectives by Women of Color*. San Francisco: Aunt Lute Foundation.
Appiah, Kwame Anthony. 1992. *In My Father's House: Africa in the Philosophy of Culture*. New York: Oxford University Press.
Arendt, Hannah. 1944. "The Jew as Pariah: A Hidden Tradition." *Jewish Social Studies* 6 (2): 99–122.
Arendt, Hannah. 1963. *Eichmann in Jerusalem: A Report on the Banality of Evil*. New York: Viking.
Arendt, Hannah. (1951) 1973. *The Origins of Totalitarianism*. San Diego: Harcourt Brace Jovanovich.
Arendt, Hannah. 1992. *Hannah Arendt/Karl Jaspers Correspondence, 1926–1969*. New York: Harcourt Brace Jovanovich.
Ariel, Yaakov. 2011. "'It's All in the Bible:' Evangelical Christians, Biblical Literalism, and Philosemitism in Our Times." In Karp and Sutcliffe 2011, 257–85.
Aronson, Michael I. 1990. *Troubled Waters: Origins of the 1881 Anti-Jewish Pogroms in Russia*. Pittsburgh: University of Pittsburg Press.
Asad, Talal. 1993. *Genealogies of Religion*. Baltimore: Johns Hopkins University.
Auerbach, Karen. 2013. *The House at Ujazdowskie 16: Jewish Families in Warsaw After the Holocaust*. Bloomington: Indiana University Press.
Avrutin, Eugene M. 2018. *The Velizh Affair: Blood Libel in a Russian Town*. New York: Oxford University Press.
Azouvi, François. 2012. *Le Mythe du grand silence*. Paris: Fayard.
Badiou, Alain. 2011. "Uses of the Word 'Jew.'" In *Polemics*, translated by Steve Corcoran, 157–256. London: Verso.
Badiou, Alain, and Eric Hazan. 2013. "'Anti-Semitism Everywhere' in France Today." In *Reflections on Anti-Semitism*, edited by Alain Badiou, Eric Hazan, and Ivan Segré, 1–42. London: Verso.
Baer, Yitzhak. 1966. *A History of the Jews in Christian Spain*. Vol. 2. Philadelphia: The Jewish Publication Society.
Bajohr, Frank. 2002. *'Aryanisation' in Hamburg: The Economic Exclusion of Jews and the Confiscation of Their Property in Nazi Germany*. New York: Berghahn.
Balibar, Etienne. 1991. "Is There a 'Neo-racism'?" In *Race, Nation, Class: Ambiguous Identities*, edited by Etienne Balibar and Immanuel Maurice Wallerstein, 17–28. London: Verso.
Balzac, Honoré de. 2006. *Scenes from a Courtesan's Life*. Gloucester: Dodo Press.
Bangstad, Sindre, and Matti Bunzl. 2010. "'Anthropologists Are Talking' About Islamophobia and Anti-Semitism in the New Europe." *Ethnos* 75 (2): 213–28.
Barkun, Michael. 2006. *A Culture of Conspiracy: Apocalyptic Visions in Contemporary America*. Los Angeles: University of California Press.
Baron, Salo W. 1928. "Ghetto and Emancipation: Shall We Revise the Traditional View?" *Menorah Journal* 14 (6) (June): 515–26.
Baron, Salo W. 1946. Foreward to *Essays on Anti-Semitism*. In Pinson 1946, vii–ix.
Bartlett, Robert. 1993. *The Making of Europe: Conquest, Colonization, and Cultural Change, 950–1350*. Princeton: Princeton University Press.
Bartov, Omer. 1998. "Antisemitism, the Holocaust, and Reinterpretations of National Socialism." In *The Holocaust and History: The Known, the Unknown, the Disputed,*

and the Reexamined, edited by Michael Berenbaum and Abraham Peck, 75–98. Bloomington: Indiana University Press.
Baskind, Samantha. 2007. "The Fockerized Jew?: Questioning Jewishness as Cool in American Popular Entertainment." *Shofar* 25 (4): 3–17.
Bauer, Bruno. 1843. *Die Judenfrage*. Braunschweig: Friedrich Otto.
Bauer, Yehuda. 1990. "Antisemitism and Anti-Zionism—New and Old." In *Anti-Zionism and Antisemitism in the Contemporary World*, edited by Robert Wistrich, 195–208. London: Palgrave.
Bauman, Zygmunt. 1998a. "Allosemitism: Premodern, Modern, Postmodern." In *Modernity, Culture and the Jew*, edited by Bryan Cheyette and Laura Marcus. Stanford: Stanford University Press.
Bauman, Zygmunt. 1998b. *Modernity and the Holocaust*. Oxford: Polity Press.
Bayrakli, Enes, and Farid Hafez. 2018. "Co-optation of Islamophobia by Centrist Parties." In *European Islamophobia Report 2017*. Ankara: SETA.
Beck, Evelyn Torton. 1991. "Therapy's Double Dilemma: Anti-Semitism and Misogyny." In *Jewish Women in Therapy: Seen But Not Heard*, edited by Rachel Siegel and Ellen Cole, 19–30. New York: Haworth Press.
Beck, Evelyn Torton. 1992. "From 'Kike' to 'JAP': How Misogyny, Antisemitism and Racism Construct the "Jewish American Princess." In *Race, Class, and Gender: An Anthology*, edited by Margaret L. Anderson and Patricia Hill Collins, 88–95. Belmont: Wadsworth.
Beller, Steven. 2007. *Antisemitism: A Very Short Introduction*. Oxford: Oxford University Press.
Benedict XIV, Pope. 1847. *Benedicti XIV Pont. Opt. Max. olim Prosperi Cardinalis de Lambertinis Bullarium*. 17 vols. Vol. 3/1. Prati: Typographia Aldina.
Benedict, Ruth. 1940. *Race: Science and Politics*. New York: Modern Age Books.
Ben-Itto, Hadassa. 2005. *The Lie That Wouldn't Die: The Protocols of the Elders of Zion*. London: Vallentine Mitchell.
Bergen, Doris L. 1996. *Twisted Cross: The German Christian Movement in the Third Reich*. Chapel Hill: University of North Carolina Press.
Bergen, Doris L. 2010. "Antisemitism in the Nazi Era." In *Antisemitism: A History*, edited by Albert S. Lindemann and Richard S. Levy, 196–210. Oxford: Oxford University Press.
Berger, Benjamin L. 2015. *Law's Religion: Religious Difference and the Claims of Constitutionalism*. Toronto: University of Toronto Press.
Berger, Elmer. 1957. *Judaism or Jewish Nationalism: The Alternative to Zionism*. New York: Bookman Associates.
Berger, Elmer. 1960. "The Old Wolf—In Sheep's Clothing." *Issues* 14 (2) (Spring): 5–7.
Bergman, Shlomo. 1943. "Some Methodological Errors in the Study of AntiSemitism." *Jewish Social Studies* 5 (1) (January): 43–60.
Bergmann, Werner, and Christhard Hoffmann. 1987. "Kalkül oder Massenwahn: Eine soziologische Interpretation der antijüdischen Unruhen in Alexandria 38 n. Chr." In *Antisemitismus und Jüdische Geschichte: Studien zu Ehren von Herbert A. Strauss*, edited by Rainer Erb and Michael Schmidt. Berlin: Wissenschaftlicher Autorenverlag.
Berkovitz, Jay R. 1989. *The Shaping of Jewish Identity in Nineteenth-Century France*. Detroit: Wayne State University Press.

Bernasconi, Robert. 2011. "Nature, Culture, Race." In *The Philosophy of Race*, edited by Paul Taylor, vol. 1, 41–56. New York: Routledge.

Bernasconi, Robert. 2014. "Where Is Xenophobia in the Fight against Racism?" *Critical Philosophy of Race* 2 (1): 5–19.

Bernasconi, Robert. 2019. "A Most Dangerous Error: The Boasian Myth of a Knock-Down Argument against Racism." *Angelaki* 24 (2): 92–103.

Bernstein, Peretz Fritz. 1951. *Jew Hate as a Sociological Problem*. New York: Philosophical Library.

Bernstein, Richard J. 1996. *Hannah Arendt and the Jewish Question*. New York: Polity Press.

Beska, Emanuel. 2014. "Political Opposition to Zionism in Palestine and Greater Syria: 1910–1911 as a Turning Point." *Jerusalem Quarterly* 59: 54–67.

Beska, Emanuel. 2016. "The Anti-Zionist Attitudes and Activities of Ruhi al-Khalidi." In *Arabic and Islamic Studies in Honour of Ján Pauliny*, edited by Zuzana Gažáková and Jaroslav Drobný, 181–203. Bratislava: Comenius University.

Bevir, Mark, and R. A. W. Rhodes. 2010. *The State as Cultural Practice*. Oxford: Oxford University Press.

Bhabha, Homi. 1986. "Remembering Fanon: Self, Psyche and the Colonial Tradition." Introduction to *Black Skin White Masks*, by Frantz Fanon, vii–xxvi. New York: Grove Press.

Bhabha, Homi, ed. 1990. *Nation and Narration*. New York: Routledge.

Bhabha, Homi. 1994. *The Location of Culture*. London: Routledge.

Bhabha, Homi. 2004. "Framing Fanon." Introduction to *The Wretched of the Earth*, by Frantz Fanon, vii–xli. New York: Grove Press.

Bhuta, Nehal. 2012. "Two Concepts of Religious Freedom in the European Court of Human Rights." *EUI Working Papers*, no. 33: 1–19.

Billig, Michael. 1978. *Fascists: A Social Psychology of the National Front*. London: Academic Press.

Billig, Michael. 1987. "Anti-Semitic Themes and the British Far Left: Some Social-Psychological Observations on Indirect Aspects of the Conspiracy Tradition." In *Changing Conceptions of Conspiracy*, edited by C. F. Graumann and S. Moscovici. New York: Springer-Verlag.

Blalock, Hubert M. 1967. *Toward a Theory of Minority-Group Relations*. New York: Wiley.

Blanchot, Maurice. (1969) 1993. *The Infinite Conversation*. Translated by Susan Hanson. Minneapolis: University of Minnesota Press.

Blatman, Daniel. 2011. *The Death Marches: The Final Phase of Nazi Genocide*. Cambridge, MA: Belknap of Harvard University Press.

Blitz, Samuel. 1928. *Nationalism: A Cause of Anti-Semitism*. New York: Bloch Publishing.

Blome, Astrid, Holger Böning, and Michael Nagel, eds. 2010. *Die Lösung der Judenfrage: Eine Rundfrage von Julius Moses im Jahre 1907*. Bremen: Edition Lumiere.

Bloom, Harold. 2005. *Jesus and Yahweh: The Names Divine*. New York: Riverhead Books.

Blumenbach, Johann. 1865. *The Anthropological Treatises of Johann Friedrich Blumenbach*. London: Longman, Green, Longman, Roberts & Green.

Boas, Franz, et al. 1938. *Science Condemns Racism*. New York: New York Section of The American Committee for Democracy and Intellectual Freedom.

Bonfil, Robert. 1994. *Jewish Life in Renaissance Italy*. Berkeley: University of California Press.
Boyarin, Daniel. 1994. *A Radical Jew: Paul and the Politics of Identity*. Berkeley: University of California Press.
Boyarin, Jonathan, and Daniel Boyarin, eds. 1997. *Jews and Other Differences: The New Jewish Cultural Studies*. Minneapolis: University of Minnesota Press.
Boyarin, Jonathan, and Daniel Boyarin. 2002. *Powers of Diaspora: Two Essays on the Relevance of Jewish Culture*. Minneapolis: University of Minnesota Press.
Brenner, Michael. 1996. *The Renaissance of Jewish Culture in Germany*. New Haven: Yale University Press.
Brent, Jonathan, and Vladimir Naumov. 2004. *Stalin's Last Crime: The Plot Against the Jewish Doctors, 1948–1953*. New York: Harper Collins.
Breuilly, John. 1982. *Nationalism and the State*. New York: St. Martin's Press.
Bright, Martin. 2012. "Jeremy Corbyn Calls for Inquiry on 'Pro-Israel Lobby.'" *The Jewish Chronicle*, April 19. https://www.thejc.com/news/uk-news/jeremy-corbyn-calls-for-inquiry-on-pro-israel-lobby-1.32916.
Brod, Max. 1934. *Rassentheorie und Judentum*. Prague: J. A. Verb.
Brown, Colin, and Chris Hastings. 2003. "Fury as Dalyell Attacks Blair's 'Jewish Cabal.'" *Daily Telegraph*, May 4. http://www.telegraph.co.uk/news/uknews/1429114/Fury-as-Dalyell-attacks-Blairs-Jewish-cabal.html.
Brown, Michael, ed. 1994. *Approaches to Antisemitism: Context and Curriculum*. New York: American Jewish Committee.
Brown, Wendy. 2012. "Civilizational Delusions: Secularism, Tolerance, Equality." *Theory & Event* 15 (2): 1–16.
Browning, Christopher. 2004. *The Origins of the Final Solution: The Evolution of Nazi Jewish Policy*. Lincoln: Nebraska University Press.
Brubaker, Rogers. 2008. *Nationalist Politics and Everyday Ethnicity in a Transylvanian Town*. Princeton: Princeton University Press.
Bruns, Claudia. 2011. "Toward a Transnational History of Racism: Wilhelm Marr and the Interrelationships Between Colonial Racism and German Anti-Semitism." In *Racism in the Modern World*, edited by Manfred Berg and Simon Wendt, 122–39. New York: Berghahn.
Bunzl, Matti. 2005. "Between Anti-Semitism and Islamophobia: Some Thoughts on the New Europe." *American Ethnologist* 32 (4): 499–508.
Bunzl, Matti. 2007. *Anti-Semitism and Islamophobia: Hatreds Old and New in Europe*. Chicago: Prickly Paradigm Press.
Brustein, William I. 2003. *Roots of Hate: Anti-Semitism in Europe Before the Holocaust*. Cambridge: Cambridge University Press.
Butler, Judith. 1993. *Bodies That Matter: On the Discursive Limits of "Sex."* New York: Routledge.
Butler, Judith. 2003. "No, It's Not Anti-Semitic." *London Review of Books* 25 (16) (August 21): 19–21.
Butler, Judith. 2012a. "Judith Butler Responds to Attack." *Mondoweiss*, August 27. http://mondoweiss.net/2012/08/judith-butler-responds-to-attack-i-affirm-a-judaism-that-is-not-associated-with-state-violence/.
Butler, Judith. 2012b. *Parting Ways: Jewishness and the Critique of Zionism*. New York: Columbia University Press.
Butler, Rohan. 1941. *The Roots of National Socialism, 1783–1933*. London: Faber and Faber.

Byford, Jovan. 2011. *Conspiracy Theories: A Critical Introduction*. Basingstoke: Palgrave Macmillan.
Byford, Jovan, and Michael Billig. 2001. "The Emergence of Antisemitic Conspiracy Theories in Yugoslavia During the War with NATO." *Patterns of Prejudice* 35 (4): 50–63.
Cahan, Abraham. 1896. *Yekl: A Tale of the New York Ghetto*. New York: D. Appleton.
Calabi, Donatella. 2016. *Venice, the Jews, and Europe, 1516–2016*. New York: Rizzoli.
Calo, Zachary R. 2014. "Constructing the Secular: Law and Religion Jurisprudence in Europe and the United States." In *EUI Working Papers*. European University Institute: Robert Schuman Centre for Advanced Studies.
Campos, Michelle. 2011. *Ottoman Brothers: Muslims, Christians, and Jews in Early Twentieth-Century Palestine*. Stanford: Stanford University Press.
Carby, Hazel. 1988. "It Jus Be's Dat Way Sometime: The Sexual Politics of Women's Blues." In *Gender and Discourse*, edited by Alexandra D. Todd and Sue Fisher. Norwood: Ablex Publishing.
Carmichael, Stokely, and Charles. V. Hamilton. 1967. *Black Power: The Politics of Liberation in America*. New York: Random House.
Carynnyk, Marco. 2011. "Foes of Our Rebirth: Ukrainian Nationalist Discussions About Jews 1929–1947." *Nationalities Papers* 39 (3): 315–52.
Césaire, Aimé. (1955) 2000. *Discourse on Colonialism*. New York: Monthly Review Press.
Cesarani, David. 2004. *The Left and the Jews/The Jews and the Left*. London: Labour Friends of Israel.
Chaouat, Bruno. 2016. *Is Theory Good for the Jews?* Liverpool: Liverpool University Press.
Chatterjee, Partha. 1993. *The Nation and Its Fragments: Colonial and Postcolonial Histories*. Princeton: Princeton University Press.
Chazan, Robert. 1980. *Church, State, and Jew in the Middle Ages*. New York: Behrman House.
Chazan, Robert. 2011. "Philosemitic Tendencies in Medieval Western Christendom." In Karp and Sutcliffe 2011, 29–48.
Cheyette, Brian. 1993. *Constructions of "the Jew" in English Literature and Society: Racial Representations 1875–1945*. Cambridge: Cambridge University Press.
Cheyette, Brian, ed. 1996. *Between 'Race' and Culture: Representations of "the Jew" in English and American Literature*. Stanford: Stanford University Press.
Cheyette, Bryan. 2003. "Neither Excuse Nor Accuse: T.S. Eliot's Semitic Discourse." *Modernism/Modernity* 10 (3) (September): 431–37.
Cheyette, Bryan. 2012. "A Glorious Achievement: Edward Said and the Last Jewish Intellectual." In *Edward Said's Translocations: Essays in Secular Criticism*, edited by Tobias Döring and Mark Stein, 74–97. New York: Routledge.
Cheyette, Bryan. 2014. *Diasporas of the Mind: Jewish and Postcolonial Writing and the Nightmare of History*. New Haven: Yale University Press.
Cheyette, Bryan. 2017. "Against Supersessionist Thinking: Old and New, Jews and Postcolonialism, the Ghetto and Diaspora." *Cambridge Journal of Postcolonial Literary Inquiry* 4 (3): 424–39.
Cheyette, Bryan, and Laura Marcus, eds. 1998. *Modernity, Culture and "the Jew."* Stanford: Stanford University Press.
Cheyette, Bryan, and Nadia Valman, eds. 2004. *The Image of the Jew in European Liberal Culture, 1789–1914*. London: Vallentine Mitchell.

Chomsky, Noam. 1983. *The Fateful Triangle: The United States, Israel and the Palestinians.* Boston: South End Press.
Chynczewska-Hennel, Teresa. 2003. *Marius Filonardi (1635–1643).* Vol. 1, *Acta Nuntiaturae Polonae.* Cracow: Academia Scientiarum et Litterarum Polona.
Clark, Natasha. 2017. "Labour Poster Row." *The Sun,* June 7. https://www.thesun.co.uk/news/3746401/labour-supporting-banner-showing-theresa-may-wearing-star-of-david-earrings-removed-after-complaints-of-anti-semitism.
Cohen, Naomi Wiener. 1951. "The Reaction of Reform Judaism in America to Political Zionism (1897–1922)." *Publications of the American Jewish Historical Society* 40 (4) (Spring): 361–94.
Cohen, Robin. 1997. *Global Diasporas: An Introduction.* New York and London: Routledge.
Cohen, Shaye. 1986. "'Anti-Semitism' in Antiquity: The Problem of Definition." In *History and Hate: The Dimensions of Anti-Semitism,* edited by David Berger, 43–48. Philadelphia: Jewish Publication Society.
Cohen, Yehezkel. 1975. "The Attitude to the Gentile in the Halacha and in Reality in the Tannaitic Period." PhD. diss. [In Hebrew]. Hebrew University of Jerusalem.
Cohn, Norman. 1967. *Warrant for Genocide: The Myth of the Jewish World Conspiracy and the Protocols of the Elders of Zion.* London: Secker & Warburg.
Coleman, Clarence. 1964. "U.S. Rejects the 'Jewish People' Concept." *Issues* 18 (6) (Fall–Winter): 2–6.
Collins, Patricia Hill. 1990. *Black Feminist Thought: Knowledge, Consciousness, and the Politics of Empowerment.* New York: Routledge.
Confino, Alon. 2014. *A World Without Jews: The Nazi Imagination from Persecution to Genocide.* New Haven: Yale University Press.
Connolly, William E. 2006. "Europe: A Minor Tradition." In *Powers of the Secular Modern,* edited by David Scott and Charles Hirschkind, 75–92. Stanford: Stanford University Press.
Cooper, Julie. 2015. "A Diasporic Critique of Diasporism: The Question of Jewish Political Agency." *Political Theory* 43 (1): 80–110.
Cooperman, Bernard Dov. 2016. "What If the 'Ghetto' Had Never Been Constructed?" In *What Ifs of Jewish History,* edited by Gavriel. D. Rosenfeld, 81–102. Cambridge: Cambridge University Press.
County of Allegheny V. American Civil Liberties Union. 1989. 492 U.S. 573.
Cousin, Glynis, and Robert Fine. 2015. "A Common Cause. Reconnecting the Study of Racism and Antisemitism." In *Antisemitism, Racism and Islamophobia,* edited by Christine Achinger and Robert Fine, 14–33. London: Routledge.
Craps, Stef. 2013. *Postcolonial Witnessing: Trauma Out of Bounds.* New York: Palgrave Macmillan.
Crouzet-Pavan, Elisabeth. 1991. "Venice Between Jerusalem, Byzantium, and Divine Retribution: The Origins of the Ghetto." *Mediterranean Historical Review* 6 (2): 163–79.
Cubitt, G. 1989. "Conspiracy Myths and Conspiracy Theories." *Journal of the Anthropological Society of Oxford* 20 (1): 12–26.
Dahlmann, Hans-Christian. 2013. *Antisemitismus in Polen 1968: Interaktionen zwischen Partei und Gesellschaft.* Osnabrueck: Warsaw GHI.
Dean, Carolyn J. 2010. *Aversion and Erasure: The Fate of the Victim After the Holocaust.* Ithaca: Cornell University Press.

de Lange, Nicholas. 1978. "Jewish Attitudes to the Roman Empire" In *Imperialism in the Ancient World*, edited by P. Garnsey and C. Whittaker. Cambridge: Cambridge University Press.

Deutsch, Aladar. n.d. Untitled Manuscript. Jewish Museum of Prague. Archives. File no. 60295.

Diderot, Denis. (1772) 1927. "On Women." In *Dialogues*, translated by Francis Birrell. London: Routledge.

Diesendruck, Zevi. 1946. "Antisemitism and Ourselves." In Pinson 1946, 41–48.

Dirlik, Arik. 1994. "The Postcolonial Aura: Third World Criticism in the Age of Global Capitalism." *Critical Inquiry* 20: 328–56.

Disraeli, Benjamin. 1844. *Coningsby; Or, The New Generation*. Vol. 2. London: Henry Colburn.

Disraeli, Benjamin. (1847) 1904. *Tancred*. London: R. Brimley.

Dobkowski, Michael. 2015. "Islamophobia and Anti-Semitism." *CrossCurrents* 65 (3): 321–33.

Dohm, Christian Wilhelm. 1781. *Ueber die bürgerliche Verbessung der Juden*. Berlin: Friedrich Nicolai.

Dohm, Christian Wilhelm. 1957. *Concerning the Amelioration of the Civil Status of the Jews*. Cincinnati: Hebrew Union College-Jewish Institute of Religion.

Drumont, Édouard. (1886) 1994. *La France juive: Essai d'histoire contemporaine*. Vol. 1. Beyrouth: Edition Charlemagne.

Dühring, Eugen. 1875. *Cursus der Philosophie als streng wissenschaftlicher Weltanschauung und Lebensgestaltung*. Leipzig: Koschny.

Dühring, Eugen. (1881) 1997. *Eugen Dühring on the Jews*. Brighton: Nineteen Eighty-Four Press.

Dumitru, Diana. 2015. *The State, Anti-Semitism, and the Holocaust: Romania and the Soviet Union*. New York: Cambridge University Press.

Dundes, Alan. 1991. "The Ritual Murder or Blood Libel Legend: A Study of Anti-Semitic Victimization Through Projective Inversion." In *The Blood Libel Legend: A Casebook in Anti-Semitic Folklore*, edited by Alan Dundes, 336–76. Madison: University of Wisconsin Press.

Duneier, Mitchell. 2016. *Ghetto: The Invention of a Place, the History of an Idea*. New York: Farrar, Straus and Giroux.

Edelstein, Alan. 1982. *An Unacknowledged Harmony: Philo-Semitism and the Survival of European Jewry*. Westport: Greenwood Press.

Eidelberg, Shlomo. 1996. *The Jews and the Crusaders: the Hebrew Chronicles of the First and Second Crusades*. Hoboken: KTAV Publishing House.

Eisen, Robert. 2011. *The Peace and Violence of Judaism: From the Bible to Modern Zionism*. Oxford: Oxford University Press.

Eisenbach, Artur. 1991. *The Emancipation of the Jews in Poland, 1780–1870*. Edited by Antony Polonsky. Translated by Janina Dorosz. Oxford: Blackwell.

Eisenberg, Ellen. 1998. "Beyond San Francisco: The Failure of Anti-Zionism in Portland, Oregon." *American Jewish History* 86 (3) (September): 309–21.

Eisenmenger, Johann. 1711. *Entdecktes Judenthum*. Königsberg: n.p.

Eley, Geoff, and Ronald Suny, eds. 1996. *Becoming National: A Reader*. New York: Oxford University Press.

Elukin, Jonathan. 1992. "Jacques Basnage and *The History of the Jews*: Polemic and Allegory in the Republic of Letters." *Journal of the History of Ideas* 53: 603–31.

Elukin, Jonathan. 2007. *Living Together, Living Apart: Rethinking Jewish-Christian Relations in the Middle Ages.* Princeton: Princeton University Press.
Elukin, Jonathan. 2015. "Christianity and Judaism; Christians and Jews." In *The Routledge History of Medieval Christianity 1050–1500,* edited by R. N. Swanson. London: Routledge.
Elukin, Jonathan. 2017. "Post-Biblical Jewish History Through Christian Eyes: Josephus and the Miracle of Jewish History in English Protestantism." In *The Jew as Legitimation: Jewish-Gentile Relations Beyond Antisemitism and Philosemitism,* edited by David J. Wertheim, 103–16. Cham, Switzerland: Palgrave Macmillan.
Elukin, Jonathan. 2018. "Shylock, the Devil and the Meaning of Deception in *The Merchant of Venice.*" *European Judaism* 51 (2): 44–51.
Endelman, Todd. 1991. "Jewish Self-Hatred in Britain and Germany." In *Two Nations: British and German Jews in Comparative Perspective,* edited by Michael Brenner, Rainer Liedtke, and David Rechter, 331–36. Tubinden: J.C.B. Mohr.
Endelman, Todd. 2001. "In Defense of Jewish Social History." *Jewish Social Studies* 7 (3): 52–57.
Endelman, Todd. 2015. *Leaving the Jewish Fold.* Princeton: Princeton University Press.
Engel, David. 2009. "Away from a Definition of Antisemitism. An Essay in the Semantics of Historical Description." In *Rethinking European Jewish History,* edited by J. Cohen and M. Rosman, 30–53. Oxford: Oxford University Press.
Engelking, Barbara, and Jacek Leociak. 2009. *The Warsaw Ghetto: A Guide to the Perished City.* New Haven: Yale University Press.
Ettinger, Shmuel. 1978. *Ha-antishemiyut ba-'et ha-hadasha: pirkei mehkar ve-'iyun.* Tel Aviv: Moreshet.
Ettinger, Shmuel. 1980. "Sinat-yisra'el be-retzifut historit." In *Sinat yisra'el le-dor-oteha,* edited by Shmuel Almog. Jerusalem: Zalman Shazar.
Ettinger, Shmuel. 1983. Introduction to *Anti-Semitism in the Soviet Union: Its Roots and Consequences, III,* i–xiv. Jerusalem: Hebrew University.
Ettinger, Shmuel. 1985. "Ha-antishemiyut ve-antitzionut ba-dor ha-tsa'ir ba-'olam ha-ma'aravi." In *Antishemiyut ha-yom,* 3–9. Jerusalem: Merkaz ha-hasbara.
Ettinger, Shmuel. 1988. "Soviet Anti-Semitism After the Six-Day War." In *Present-Day Antisemitism,* edited by Yehuda Bauer, 49–56. Jerusalem: Hebrew University.
Ettinger, Shmuel. 1992. "Ha-antishemiyut ha-modernit ve-ha-sho'a." In *Historiya ve-historionim,* edited by Shmuel Almog and Otto Dov Kulka, 258–66. Jerusalem: Merkaz Zalman Shazar.
Fanon, Frantz. 1952. *Black Skin, White Masks.* Translated by Charles Lam Markmann. New York: Grove Press.
Fanon, Frantz. 1961. *The Wretched of the Earth.* Translated by Constance Farrington. New York: Penguin Books.
Fanon, Frantz. 1967. *Toward the African Revolution: Political Essays.* Translated by Haakon Chevalier. New York: Grove Press.
Fein, Helen. 1979. *Accounting for Genocide: National Responses and Jewish Victimization During the Holocaust.* New York: Free Press.
Feinstein, Margarete Meyers. 2010. *Holocaust Survivors in Post-War Germany, 1945–1957.* New York: Cambridge University Press.
Feinstein, Moshe. 1980. *Responsa Igrot Moshe.* Vol. 2. New York.

Feldman, David. 2017. "Islamophobia and Antisemitism." In *Islamophobia: Still a Challenge for Us All (a 20th-Anniversary Report)*, edited by Farah Elahi and Omar Khan, 78–81. London: Runnymede.
Ferrari, Silvio. 1988. "Separation of Church and State in Contemporary European Society." *Journal of Church and State* 30 (3): 533–47.
Fine, Robert. 2006. "The Lobby: Mearsheimer and Walt's Conspiracy Theory." www.EngageOnline.org.uk, March 21. https://engageonline.wordpress.com/2006/03/21/the-lobby-mearsheimer-and-walts-conspiracy-theory-robert-fine.
Finkielkraut, Alain. 2003. *Au nom de l'autre: Réflexions sur l'antisémitisme qui vient*. Paris: Gallimard.
Finlay, W. M. L. 2005. "Pathologizing Dissent: Identity Politics, Zionism and the Self-Hating Jew." *British Journal of Social Psychology* 44 (2): 201–22.
Finlay, W. M. L. 2007. "The Propaganda of Extreme Hostility: Denunciation and the Regulation of the Group." *British Journal of Social Psychology* 46 (2): 323–41.
Finlay, W. M. L. 2014. "Denunciation and the Construction of Norms in Group Conflict: Examples from an Al-Qaeda-Supporting Group." *British Journal of Social Psychology* 53 (4): 691–710.
Fischer, Eugen. 1938. "Rassenenstehung und älteste Rassengeschichte der Hebräer." *Forschungen über das Judentum* 3: 121–36.
Fischer, Lars. 2007. *The Socialist Response to Antisemitism in Imperial Germany*. Cambridge: Cambridge University Press.
Fishman, Louis. 2011. "Understanding the 1911 Ottoman Parliament Debate on Zionism in Light of the Emergence of a 'Jewish Question.'" In *Late Ottoman Palestine: The Period of Young Turk Rule*, edited by Yuval Ben-Bassat and Eyal Ginio, 103–23. New York: I.B. Tauris.
Fleischer, E. 2012. *Statutory Jewish Prayers: Their Emergence and Development* [In Hebrew]. Edited by S. Elizur and T. Beeri. Jerusalem: Magnes.
Flowerman, Samuel. 1949. Introduction to *Rehearsal for Destruction: A Study of Political Anti-Semitism in Imperial Germany*, by Paul Massing, xiii–xiv. New York: Harper.
Forth, Christopher. 2004. *The Dreyfus Affair and the Crisis of French Manhood*. Baltimore: Johns Hopkins University Press.
Fram, Edward, and Verena Kasper-Marienberg. 2015. "Jewish Martyrdom Without Persecution: The Murder of Gumpert May, Frankfurt am Main, 1781." *AJS Review* 39: 267–301.
Frankel, Jonathan. 1991. "The Soviet Regime and Anti-Zionism: An Analysis." In *Jewish Culture and Identity in the Soviet Union*, edited by Yaacov Ro'i and Avi Beker, 310–54. New York: New York University Press.
Frankel, Jonathan. 1997. *The Damascus Affair: "Ritual Murder," Politics, and the Jews in 1840*. Cambridge: Cambridge University Press.
Frantz, Constantin. 1844. *Ahasverus oder die Judenfrage*. Berlin: Wilhelm Hermes.
Fredriksen, Paula. 2008. *Augustine and the Jews: A Christian Defense of Jews and Judaism*. New York: Doubleday.
Freedland, Jonathan. 2004. "Is Anti-Zionism Anti-Semitism?" In *Those Who Forget the Past: The Question of Anti-Semitism*, edited by Ron Rosenbaum, 422–37. New York: Random House.
Freedman, Jonathan. 2008. "Antisemitism Without Jews: *Left Behind* in the American Heartland." In Lassner and Trubowitz 2008.
Freud, Sigmund. 1939. *Moses and Monotheism*. New York: A. A. Knopf.

Freud, Sigmund. 1964. "If Moses Were an Egyptian." In *Moses and Monotheism: An Outline of Psycho-Analysis and Other Works*. London: The Hogarth Press and the Institute of Psychoanalysis.

Freund, Ismar. 1922. *Der Judenhaß: Ein Beitrag zu seiner Geschichte und Psychologie*. Berlin: Philo Verlag.

Friedländer, Saul, ed. 1992. *Probing the Limits of Representation*. Boston: Harvard University Press.

Friedländer, Saul. (1997) 2007. *Nazi Germany and the Jews*. 2 vols. New York: HarperCollins.

Friedman, Marilyn. 2014. "Jewish Self-Hatred, Moral Criticism, and Autonomy." In *Personal Autonomy and Social Oppression: Philosophical Perspectives*, edited by Marina Oshana. New York: Routledge.

Friedman, Marilyn. 2015. "Authenticity and Jewish Self-Hatred." In *Authenticity, Autonomy and Multiculturalism*, edited by Geoffrey Brahm Levey, 184–202. New York: Routledge.

Fulbrook, Mary. 2013. *A Small Town Near Auschwitz: Ordinary Nazis and the Holocaust*. Oxford: Oxford University Press.

Gager, John. 1983. *The Origins of Anti-Semitism: Attitudes Toward Judaism in Pagan and Christian Antiquity*. New York: Oxford University Press.

Galili, Ziva, and Boris Morozov. 2006. *Exiled to Palestine: The Emigration of Zionist Convicts from the Soviet Union, 1924–1934*. London: Frank Cass.

Gates, Henry Louis, ed. 1986. *"Race," Writing, and Difference*. Chicago: University of Chicago Press.

Gates, Henry Louis. 1991. "Critical Fanonism." *Critical Inquiry* 17: 457–70.

Gay, Peter. 1978. "Hermann Levi: A Study in Service and Self-Hatred." In *Freud, Jews, and Other Germans: Masters and Victims in Modernist Culture*. New York: Oxford University Press.

Gelber, Mark. 1985. "What is Literary Antisemitism?" *Jewish Social Studies* 47 (1): 1–20.

Geller, Jay. 1992. "(G)nos(e)ology: The Cultural Construction of the Other." In *People of the Body: Jews and Judaism from an Embodied Perspective*, edited by Howard Eilberg-Schwartz, 243–62. Albany: SUNY Press.

Gellner, Ernest. 1983. *Nations and Nationalism*. Oxford: Basil Blackwell.

Gergel, N. 1951. "The Pogroms in Ukraine 1918–1920." *YIVO Annual of Jewish Social Science* 6: 237–52.

Gessier, Vincent. 2010. "Islamophobia: A French Specificity in Europe?" *Human Architecture: Journal of the Sociology of Self-Knowledge* 8 (2): 39–46.

Gilman, Sander. 1985. *Difference and Pathology: Stereotypes of Sexuality, Race, and Madness*. Ithaca: Cornell University Press.

Gilman, Sander. 1986. *Jewish Self-Hatred: Anti-Semitism and the Hidden Language of the Jews*. Baltimore: Johns Hopkins University Press.

Gilman, Sander. 1991. *The Jew's Body*. New York: Routledge.

Gilman, Sander. 1997. "Decircumcision: The First Aesthetic Surgery." *Modern Judaism* 17: 201–10.

Gilman, Sander. 2017. "The Case of Circumcision: Diaspora Judaism as a Model for Islam?" In Renton and Gidley 2017, 143–64.

Gilroy, Paul. 1998. "Not Being Inhuman." In *Modernity, Culture and "the Jew,"* edited by Bryan Cheyette and Laura Marcus, 282–97. Stanford: Stanford University Press.

Gilroy, Paul. 2000. *Against Race: Imagining Political Culture Beyond the Color Line.* Cambridge, MA: Belknap of Harvard University Press.
Ginaite-Rubinson, Sara. 2005. *Resistance and Survival: The Jewish Community in Kaunas, 1941–1944.* Oakville: Mosaic.
Gingrich, Andre. 2005. "Anthropological Analyses of Islamophobia and Anti-Semitism in Europe." *American Ethnologist* 32 (4): 513–15.
Gitelman, Zvi. 1990. "The Evolution of Soviet Anti-Zionism: From Principle to Pragmatism." In *Anti-Zionism and Antisemitism in the Contemporary World*, edited by Robert Wistrich, 11–25. London: Palgrave.
Glenn, Susan. 2006. "The Vogue of Jewish Self-Hatred in Post-World War II America." *Jewish Social Studies: History, Culture, and Society* 12 (3): 95–136.
Goetschel, Willi, and Ato Quayson. 2015. "Jewish Studies and Postcolonialism." *The Cambridge Journal of Postcolonial Literary Inquiry* 3 (1): 1–9.
Goldhagen, Daniel J. 1996. *Hitler's Willing Executioners: Ordinary Germans and the Holocaust.* New York: Alfred A. Knopf.
Goldmann, Felix. 1920. *Vom Wesen des Antisemitismus.* Berlin: Philo Verlag.
Goldschmidt, E. D. 1960. *The Passover Haggadah: Its Sources and History* [In Hebrew]. Jerusalem: Mosad Bialik.
Goldschmidt, S., ed. 1965. *Seder ha-selihot ke-minhag polin ve-rov ha-kehilot be-eretz yisra'el.* Jerusalem: Mosad Harav Kook.
Goldstein, Phyllis. 2012. *A Convenient Hatred: The History of Antisemitism.* Brookline: Facing History & Ourselves.
Golub, Jennifer. 1992. *Japanese Attitudes Towards Jews.* New York: Pacific Rim Institute of the American Jewish Committee.
Goodman, Martin. 2007. *Rome and Jerusalem: The Clash of Ancient Civilizations.* New York: Vintage.
Gottlieb, Susannah Young-ah, ed. 2007. *Hannah Arendt: Reflections on Literature and Culture.* Stanford: Stanford University Press.
Goulévitch, Arsene de. 1962. *Czarism and the Revolution.* Hawthorn: Omni Publications.
Grafton, Anthony, and Joanna Weinberg. 2011. *"I Have Always Loved the Holy Tongue:" Isaac Casaubon, The Jews, and a Forgotten Chapter in Renaissance Scholarship.* Cambridge, MA: Harvard University Press.
Grayzel, Solomon. 1933. *The Church and the Jews in the XIIIth Century: A Study of Their Relations During the Years 1198–1254.* Philadelphia: The Dropsie College.
Grayzel, Solomon. 1962. "The Papal Bull *Sicut Judaeis*." In *Studies and Essays in Honor of Abraham A. Neuman*, edited by Meir Ben-Horin, Bernard D. Weinryb, and Solomon Zeitlin, 243–80. Leiden: Brill.
Greenberg, Clement. 1950. "Self-Hatred and Jewish Chauvinism: Some Reflections on 'Positive Jewishness.'" *Commentary* 10 (January): 426–33.
Greiffenhagen, M. 1972. "Emanzipation." In *Historisches Wörterbuch der Philosophie*, edited by Joachim Ritter, vol. 2, 448–49. Basel: Schwabe.
Gribetz, Jonathan. 2017. "The PLO's Rabbi: Palestinian Nationalism and Reform Judaism." *Jewish Quarterly Review* 107 (1): 90–112.
Grish, Kristina. 2005. *Boy Vey! The Shiksa's Guide to Dating Jewish Men.* New York: Simon Spotlight Entertainment.
Gross, Jan. 2006. *Fear: Anti-Semitism in Poland after Auschwitz.* New York: Random House.

Grossman, Marshall. 1989. "The Violence of the Hyphen in Judeo-Christian." *Social Text* 22 (Spring): 115–22.
Groves, Beatrice. 2015. *The Destruction of Jerusalem in Early Modern English Literature*. Cambridge: Cambridge University Press.
Gruen, Erich S. 2002. *Diaspora: Jews Amidst Greeks and Romans*. Cambridge, MA: Harvard University Press.
Guibbory, Achsah. 2010. *Christian Identity, Jews, and Israel in Seventeenth-Century England*. Oxford: Oxford University Press.
Günther, Hans. 1927. *The Racial Elements of European History*. New York: E. P. Dutton.
Haase, Amine. 1975. *Katholische Presse und die Judenfrage. Inhaltsanalyse katholischer Periodika am Ende des 19. Jahrhunderts*. Verlag Dokumentation: Pullach bei München.
Halbertal, Moshe, and Avishai Margalit. 1998. "Idolatry and Betrayal." In *Idolatry*, 9–36. Cambridge, MA: Harvard University Press.
Halliday, Fred. 1999. "'Islamophobia' Reconsidered." *Ethnic and Racial Studies* 22 (5): 892–902.
Halpern, Israel. 1945. *Pinkas va'ad arba aratzot*. Jerusalem: Mosad Bialik.
Hamas. (1988) 2004. "The Covenant of the Islamic Resistance Movement." In *Israel in the Middle East*, edited by Itamar Rabinovich and Jehuda Reinharz, 2nd ed., 430–37. Waltham: Brandeis University Press.
Hamas. 2017. *A Document of General Principles and Policies*. http://hamas.ps/en/post/678/a-document-of-general-principles-and-policies.
Hammerschlag, Sarah. 2010. *The Figural Jew: Politics and Identity in Postwar French Thought*. Chicago: University of Chicago Press.
Hart, Mitchell Bryan, ed. 2011. *Jews and Race: Writings on Identity and Difference 1880–1940*. Waltham: Brandeis University Press.
Harvey, Elizabeth. 2003. *Women in the Nazi East: Agents and Witnesses of Germanization*. New Haven: Yale University Press.
Heine, Heinrich. 1981. "*Reisebilder*." In *Sämtliche Schriften*, edited by Klaus Briegleb, vol. 4. Frankfurt: Ullstein.
Helly, Denise. 2012. "Islamophobia in Canada? Women's Rights, Modernity, Secularism." In *Recode Working Paper Series*, 11. http://www.recode.fi/publications: European Science Foundation.
Herder, Johann Gottfried. 1803. *Outlines of a Philosophy of the History of Man*. Vol. 2. Translated by T. Churchill. London: J. Johnson.
Herf, Jeffrey. 2006a. "Convergence: The Classic Case. Nazi Germany, Anti-Semitism and Anti-Zionism during World War II." *Journal of Israeli History* 25 (1) (March): 63–83.
Herf, Jeffrey. 2006b. *The Jewish Enemy: Nazi Propaganda During World War II and the Holocaust*. Cambridge, MA: Belknap of Harvard University Press.
Herf, Jeffrey. 2016. *Undeclared Wars with Israel: East Germany and the West German Far Left, 1967*. Cambridge: Cambridge University Press.
Herzl, Theodor. (1896) 1993. *The Jewish State: An Attempt at a Modern Solution of the Jewish Question*. London: Henry Pordes.
Herzl, Theodor. 1960. *The Complete Diaries of Theodor Herzl*. Edited by Raphael Patai. 5 vols. New York: Herzl Press.

Heschel, Susannah. 1995. "Configurations of Patriarchy, Judaism, and Nazism in German Feminist Thought." In *Gender and Judaism: The Transformation of Tradition*, edited by T. M. Rudavsky, 135–54. New York: New York University Press.

Heschel, Susannah. 2008. *The Aryan Jesus: Christian Theologians and the Bible in Nazi Germany.* Princeton: Princeton University Press.

Heschel, Susannah. 2011. "Historiography of Antisemitism Versus Anti-Judaism: A Response to Robert Morgan." *Journal for the Study of the New Testament* 33 (3) (March): 257–79.

Hess, Jonathan M. 2000. "Johann David Michaelis and the Colonial Imaginary: Orientalism and the Emergence of Racial Antisemitism in Eighteenth-Century Germany." *Jewish Social Studies* 6 (2): 56–101.

Hess, Moses. 1918. *Rome and Jerusalem.* New York: Bloch.

Hesse, Isabelle. 2016. *The Politics of Jewishness: The Holocaust, Zionism, and Colonialism in Contemporary World Literature.* London: Bloomsbury Academic.

Hilberg, Raul. 2003. *The Destruction of the European Jews.* 3 vols. New Haven: Yale University Press.

Himka, John Paul. 2011. "The Lviv Pogrom of 1941: The Germans, Ukrainian Nationalists, and the Carnival Crowd." *Canadian Slavonic Papers* 53 (2–4): 209–43.

Himmelfarb, Gertrude. 2011. *The People of the Book: Philosemitism in England, From Cromwell to Churchill.* New York: Encounter Books.

Hirschfeld, Magnus. 1938. *Racism.* London: Victor Gollanz.

Hirsh, David. 2007. *Anti-Zionism and Antisemitism: Cosmopolitan Reflections.* Vol. 1 of *Yale Initiative for the Interdisciplinary Study of Antisemitism Working Papers.* New Haven: Yale University.

Hirsh, David. 2017. *Contemporary Left Antisemitism.* London: Routledge.

Hobsbawm, Eric. 1990. *Nations and Nationalism Since 1780: Programme, Myth, Reality.* Cambridge: Cambridge University Press.

Hoffmann, Christhard, Werner Bergmann, and Helmut Walser Smith, eds. 2002. *Exclusionary Violence: Antisemitic Riots in Modern German History.* Ann Arbor: University of Michigan Press.

Hofstadter, Richard. 1967. *Paranoid Style in American Politics and Other Essays.* New York: Vintage Books.

Horkheimer, Max, and Theodor W. Adorno. 2000. *Dialectic of Enlightenment.* New York: Continuum.

Horowitz, Elliott. 2006. *Reckless Rites: Purim and the Legacy of Jewish Violence.* Princeton: Princeton University Press.

Horowitz, Sara R. 2006. "Anzia Yezierska." In *Jewish Women: A Comprehensive Historical Encyclopedia*, edited by Paula Hyman and Dalia Ofer, compact disc. Jerusalem: Shalvi Publishing.

Horowitz, Sara R. 2008. "Lovin' Me, Lovin' Jew: Gender, Intermarriage, and Metaphor." In Lassner and Trubowitz 2008, 196–216.

Horwitz, Gordon J. 2008. *Ghettostadt: Lodz and the Making of a Nazi City.* Cambridge, MA: Harvard University Press.

Hroch, Miroslav. 1985. *Social Preconditions of National Revival in Europe: A Comparative Analysis of the Social Composition of Patriotic Groups Among the Smaller European Nations.* Translated by Ben Fowkes. Cambridge: Cambridge University Press.

Hsia, Ronnie Po-chia. 1988. *The Myth of Ritual Murder: Jews and Magic in Reformation Germany.* New Haven: Yale University Press.
Hummel, Daniel. 2019. *Covenant Brothers: Evangelicals, Jews, and US-Israeli-Relations.* Philadelphia: University of Pennsylvania Press.
Hunt, Lynn, ed. and trans. 1996. *The French Revolution and Human Rights: A Brief Documentary History.* Boston: Bedford/St. Martin's.
Hutton, Christopher. 2005. *Race and the Third Reich.* Cambridge: Polity Press.
Hyman, Paula. 1995. *Gender and Assimilation in Modern Jewish History: The Roles and Representation of Women.* Seattle: University of Washington Press 1995.
Icke, David. 1999. *The Biggest Secret.* Ryde, Isle of Wight: David Icke Books.
IDLO (International Development Law Organization). 2016. *Freedom of Religion or Belief and the Law: Current Dilemmas and Lessons Learned.* Rome: IDLO.
Iltis, Hugo. 1935. "Der Rassismus im Mantel der Wissenschaft." In *Rasse in Wissenschaft und Politik*, 1–9. Prague: Wahrheit.
Iskowitz, Daniel. 2006. "They All Are Jews." In *You Should See Yourself: Jewish Identity in Postmodern American Culture*, edited by Vincent Brook, 230–52. New Brunswick: Rutgers University Press.
Israel, Jonathan. 1989. *European Jewry in the Age of Mercantilism 1550–1750.* Oxford: Clarendon Press.
Jabotinsky, Vladimir. 1942. *The War and the Jew.* New York: The Dial Press.
Jabotinsky, Vladimir. 1986. "Evidence Submitted to the Palestine Royal Commission (1937)." In *The Zionist Idea: A Historical Analysis and Reader*, edited by Arthur Hertzberg, 559-570. New York: Atheneum.
Jabotinsky, Vladimir. 1992. "Jabotinsky to Ussishkin, Vienna, Dec. 1, 1907." In *Igrot, 1908–1914*, edited by Daniel Karpi and Moshe Halevy, vol. 1. Jerusalem: Jabotinsky Institute.
Janik, A. 1987. "The Jewish Self-Hatred Hypothesis: A Critique." In *Jews, Anti-Semitism, and Culture in Vienna*, edited by Ivar Oxaal, Michael Pollack, and Gerhard Botz. New York: Routledge.
Jensen, Tim. 2011. "When Is Religion, Religion, and a Knife, a Knife—And Who Decides?: The Case of Denmark." In *After Secular Law*, edited by Mateo Taussig-Rubbo, Robert A. Yelle, and Winnifred Fallers Sullivan, 341–64. Stanford: Stanford Law Books.
Jewish Voice for Peace. n.d. "FAQ." https://jewishvoiceforpeace.org/faq/.
Jewish Voice for Peace. n.d. "Our Approach to Zionism." https://jewishvoiceforpeace.org/zionism/.
Jivraj, Suhraiya, and Didi Herman. 2009. "'It's Difficult for a White Judge to Understand': Orientalism, Racialisation, and Christianity in English Child Welfare Cases." *Child and Family Law Quarterly* 21 (3): 283–308.
Joselit, Jenna Weissman. 2001. *A Perfect Fit: Clothes, Character and the Promise of America.* New York: Henry Holt.
Josephus, Flavius. 1958. *Antiquities of the Jews.* Translated by Ralph Marcus. Cambridge, MA: Harvard University Press.
Judaken, Jonathan. 2006. *Jean-Paul Sartre and the Jewish Question: Anti-Antisemitism and the Politics of the French Intellectual.* Lincoln: University of Nebraska Press.
Judaken, Jonathan. 2008. "Between Philosemitism and Antisemitism: The Frankfurt School's Anti-Antisemitism." In Lassner and Trubowitz 2008.

Judaken, Jonathan. 2018. "Introduction." *American Historical Review* 123 (4): 1122–38.
Judge, Edward H. 1995. *Easter in Kishinev: Anatomy of a Pogrom*. New York: New York University Press.
Judson, Pieter. 2007. *Guardians of the Nation: Activists on the Language Frontiers of Imperial Austria*. Cambridge, MA: Harvard University Press.
Kahana, Menahem, ed. 2011–2015. *Sifre on Numbers: An Annotated Edition*. 5 vols. [In Hebrew]. Jerusalem: Magnes.
Kalmar, Ivan. 2001. "Moorish Style: Orientalism, the Jews, and Synagogue Architecture." *Jewish Social Studies: History, Culture and Society* 7 (3): 68–100.
Kalmar, Ivan. 2005. "Jesus Did Not Wear a Turban: Orientalism, the Jews, and Christian Art." In Kalmar and Penslar 2005, 3–31.
Kalmar, Ivan. 2012. *Early Orientalism: Imagined Islam and the Notion of Sublime Power*. London: Routledge.
Kalmar, Ivan. 2016. "Orientalism." In *Encyclopedia of Islam and the Muslim World*, edited by Richard Martin. New York: Macmillan Reference USA.
Kalmar, Ivan, and Derek Penslar, eds. 2005. *Orientalism and the Jews*. Lebanon: University Press of New England.
Kalmar, Ivan, and Tariq Ramadan. 2016. "Anti-Semitism and Islamophobia: Historical and Contemporary Connections and Parallels." In *The Routledge Handbook of Muslim-Jewish Relations*, edited by Josef W. Meri, 351–72. Basingstoke: Taylor & Francis.
Kalmin, Richard. 2003. "Rabbinic Traditions About Roman Persecutions of the Jews: A Reconsideration." *Journal of Jewish Studies* 54 (1): 21–50.
Kaplan, Marion. 1998. *Between Dignity and Despair: Jewish Life in Nazi Germany*. New York: Oxford University Press.
Kant, Immanuel. (1775) 2013. "Of the Different Human Races." In *Kant and the Concept of Race*, edited by Jon M. Mikkelsen, 41–54. New York: SUNY Press.
Karp, Jonathan. 2008. *The Politics of Jewish Commerce: Economic Thought and Emancipation in Europe, 1638–1848*. Cambridge: Cambridge University Press.
Karp, Jonathan, and Adam Sutcliffe, eds. 2011. *Philosemitism in History*. Cambridge: Cambridge University Press.
Katibah, Habib Ibrahim. 1921. *The Case Against Zionism*. New York: Palestine National League.
Katz, Dana. 2010. "'Clamber Not You Up to the Casements': On Ghetto Views and Viewing." *Jewish History* 24 (2): 127–53.
Katz, Ethan. 2015. *The Burdens of Brotherhood: Jews and Muslims from North Africa to France*. Cambridge, MA: Harvard University Press.
Katz, Ethan, Lisa Leff, and Maud Mandel, eds. 2017. *Colonialism and the Jews*. Bloomington: Indiana University Press.
Katz, Jacob. 1964. "The Term 'Jewish Emancipation': Its Origin and Historical Impact." In *Studies in Nineteenth-Century Jewish Intellectual History*, edited by Alexander Altmann, 1–26. Cambridge, MA: Harvard University Press.
Katz, Jacob. 1973. *Out of the Ghetto: The Social Background of Jewish Emancipation, 1770–1870*. New York: Schocken Books.
Katz, Jacob. 1980. *From Prejudice to Destruction: Antisemitism: 1700–1933*. Cambridge, MA: Harvard University Press.

Katz, Jacob. 1983. "Misreadings of Anti-Semitism." *Commentary* 76 (1) (July): 39–44.
Katz, Jacob. 1993. *Tradition and Crisis: Jewish Society at the End of the Middle Ages.* New York: Schocken Books.
Kaya, Ayhan. 2014. "Islamophobia." In *The Oxford Handbook of European Islam*, edited by Jocelyne Cesari, 746–69. Oxford: Oxford University Press.
Kieval, Hillel J. 1994. "Representation and Knowledge in Medieval and Modern Accounts of Jewish Ritual Murder." *Jewish Social Studies: History, Culture, Society* 1 (1): 52–72.
Kieval, Hillel J. Forthcoming. *Blood Inscriptions: Science, Modernity, and Ritual Murder in Fin de Siècle Europe.* Philadelphia: University of Pennsylvania Press.
King, Jeremy. 2005. *Budweisers into Czechs and Germans.* Princeton: Princeton University Press.
Kinzig, Wolfram. 1994. "Philosemitismus Teil I: Zur Geschichte des Begriffs." *Zeitschrift für Kirchengeschichte* 105: 208–28.
Klemperer, Victor. 1998–1999. *I Will Bear Witness: A Diary of the Nazi Years.* 2 vols. New York: Random House.
Klier, John D., and Shlomo Lambroza. 1992. *Pogroms: Anti-Jewish Violence in Modern Russian History.* New York: Cambridge University Press.
Klug, Brian. 2014. "The Limits of Analogy: Comparing Islamophobia and Antisemitism." *Patterns of Prejudice* 48 (5): 442–59.
Knee, Stuart. 1977. "Jewish Non-Zionism in America and Palestine Commitment, 1917–1941." *Jewish Social Studies* 39 (3) (Summer): 209–26.
Kohen, Yekuti'el Zalman. 1997. *The Haggadah of the Geonim and Maimonides* [In Hebrew]. Jerusalem: Otzar Ha-poskim.
Kohn, Hans. 1956. *The Idea of Nationalism: A Study in Its Origins and Background.* New York: The Macmillan Company.
Kook, Abraham Isaac. 1956. *Orot* [In Hebrew]. Jerusalem: Mosad Harav Kook.
Koonz, Claudia. 2003. *The Nazi Conscience.* Cambridge, MA: Harvard University Press.
Kopstein, Jeffrey S., and Jason Wittenberg. 2011. "Deadly Communities: Local Political Milieus and the Persecution of Jews in Occupied Poland." *Comparative Political Studies* 44 (3): 259–83.
Kopstein, Jeffrey S., and Jason Wittenberg. 2013. "Pogrom." In *Enzyklopädie jüdischer Geschichte und Kultur*, Band 4, 572–75.
Kopstein, Jeffrey S., and Jason Wittenberg. 2018. *Intimate Violence: Anti-Jewish Pogroms on the Eve of the Holocaust.* Ithaca: Cornell University Press.
Korey, William. 1989. "The Soviet Public Anti-Zionist Committee: An Analysis." In *Soviet Jewry in the 1980s: The Politics of Anti-Semitism and Emigration and the Dynamics of Resettlement*, edited by Robert Freedman, 26–50. Durham: Duke University Press.
Koselleck, Reinhart, and Karl Grass. 1975. "Emanzipation." In *Geschichtliche Grundbegriffe*, edited by Otto Brunner, Werner Consze, and Reinhart Koselleck, vol. 2, 153–97. Stuttgart: Ernst Klett Verlag.
Kriegel, Maurice. 1979. *Les Juifs à la fin du Moyen Age dans l'Europe méditerranéene.* Paris: Hachette.
Kugel, J. 1996. "The Holiness of Israel and the Land in Second Temple Times." In *Texts, Temples and Traditions: A Tribute to Menachem Haran*, edited by Michael Fox et al. Winona Lake: Eisenbrauns.

Kushner, Tony. 2005. Foreword to *Campaigner Against Antisemitism: The Reverend James Parkes, 1896–1981*, edited by Colin Richmond and Tony Kushner. Portland: Vallentine Mitchell.

Kuru, Ahmet T. 2007. "Passive and Assertive Secularism: Historical Conditions, Ideological Struggles, and State Policies Toward Religion." *World Politics* 59 (4): 568–94.

Kuru, Ahmet T. 2008. "Secularism, State Policies, and Muslims in Europe: Analyzing French Exceptionalism." *Comparative Politics* 41 (1): 1–19.

Laclos, Choderlos de. (1793) 1903. *De l'éducation des femmes*. Paris: Vanier.

Lake, E. 2006. "David Duke Claims to Be Vindicated by a Harvard Dean." *The New York Sun*, March 20. http://www.nysun.com/national/david-duke-claims-to-be-vindicated-by-a-harvard/29380/.

Lamb, Lynette. 1989. "JAP Jokes Are Nothing to Laugh At: Why Should Jewish Women Take the Rap for Our Materialistic Culture?" *Utne Reader*, May/June.

Landes, Richard. 2015. "Proud to be Ashamed to be a Jew: On Jewish Self-Criticism and Its Pathologies." *ISGAP Working Paper Series*, no. 9, April. New York: Institute for the Study of Global Antisemitism and Policy. https://isgap.org/wp-content/uploads/2015/05/Landes_Proud_to_be_Ashamed_Working_Paper.pdf.

Langmuir, Gavin. 1990a. "Anti-Judaism as the Necessary Preparation for Antisemitism." In *Toward a Definition of Antisemitism*, 57–62. Berkeley: University of California Press.

Langmuir, Gavin. 1990b. "Ritual Cannibalism." In *Toward a Definition of Antisemitism*, 263–81. Berkeley: University of California Press.

Langmuir, Gavin. 1990c. "Thomas of Monmouth: Detector of Ritual Murder." In *Toward a Definition of Antisemitism*, 209–36. Berkeley: University of California Press.

Langmuir, Gavin. 1990d. "Toward a Definition of Antisemitism." In *Toward a Definition of Antisemitism*, 311–52. Berkeley: University of California Press.

Laqueur, Walter. 1971. "Zionism and its Liberal Critics, 1896–1948." *Journal of Contemporary History* 6: 161–82.

Laqueur, Walter. 2006. *The Changing Face of Antisemitism: From Ancient Times to the Present Day*. Oxford: Oxford University Press.

Lassner, Phyllis, and Lara Trubowitz, eds. 2008. *Antisemitism and Philosemitism in the Twentieth and Twenty-First Centuries: Representing Jews, Jewishness, and Modern Culture*. Newark: University of Delaware Press.

Lavi, Shai. 2009. "Unequal Rites: Jews, Muslims and the History of Ritual Slaughter in Germany." In *Juden und Muslime in Deutschland: Recht, Religion, Identität*, edited by Jose Brunner and Shai Lavi, 164–84. Göttingen: Wallstein Verlag.

Lazare, Bernard. 1995. *Antisemitism: Its History and Causes*. Lincoln: University of Nebraska Press.

Lehrer, Erica. 2013. *Jewish Poland Revisited: Heritage Tourism in Unquiet Places*. Bloomington: Indiana University Press.

Lenz, F. 1941. "Über Wege und Irrwege rassenkundlicher Untersuchungen." *Zeitschrift für Morphologie und Anthropologie* 39 (3): 385–413.

Leo XIII, Pope. 1884. *Humanum genus*. http://www.vatican.va/content/leo-xiii/en/encyclicals/documents/hf_l-xiii_enc_18840420_humanum-genus.html.

Lerman, Antony. 2008. "Jewish Self-Hatred: Myth or Reality?" *Jewish Quarterly* 55 (2): 46–51.

Leroy-Beaulieu, Anatole. 1895. *Israel Among the Nations: A Study of the Jews and Antisemitism*. Translated by Frances Hellman. London: W. Heinemann.

Lessing, Theodor. 1930. *Der jüdische Selbsthaß*. Berlin: Jüdischer Verlag.

Levene, Mark. 2004. "*Wolf, Lucien (1857–1930)*." In *Oxford Dictionary of National Biography*. Oxford: Oxford University Press. http://www.oxforddnb.com/view/article/38145.

Levy, Richard S. 1975. *The Downfall of the Anti-Semitic Political Parties in Imperial Germany*. New Haven: Yale University Press.

Lewin, Kurt. 1948. "Self-Hatred among Jews." In *Resolving Social Conflicts: Selected Papers on Group Dynamics*, 186–200. New York: Harper.

Lieberman, Saul. 1974. "On Persecution of the Jewish Religion" [In Hebrew]. In *Salo Wittmayer Baron Jubilee Volume*, edited by Saul Lieberman and Arthur Hyman, vol. 3. Jerusalem: American Academy for Jewish Research.

Lipset, Seymour Martin, and Earl Raab. 1978. *The Politics of Unreason: Right-wing Extremism in America, 1790–1977*. Chicago: University of Chicago Press.

Lipton, Sara. 2014. *Dark Mirror: The Medieval Origins of Anti-Jewish Iconography*. New York: Metropolitan Books.

Loeffler, James. 2018. *Rooted Cosmopolitans: Jews and Human Rights in the Twentieth Century*. New Haven: Yale University Press.

López, Fernando Bravo. 2011. "Towards a Definition of Islamophobia: Approximations of the Early Twentieth Century." *Ethnic and Racial Studies* 34 (4): 556–73.

Lowth, Robert. (1787) 1847. *Lectures on the Sacred Poetry of the Hebrews*. 3rd ed. London: S. Chadwick.

Macey, David. 2000. *Frantz Fanon: A Life*. London: Granta Books.

MacKay, Angus. 1972. "Popular Movements and Pogroms in Fifteenth-Century Castile." *Past and Present* 55: 33–67.

Magnus, Shulamit. 1995. "Pauline Wengeroff and the Voice of Jewish Modernity." In *Gender and Judaism: The Transformation of Tradition*, edited by T. M. Rudavsky, 181–90. New York: New York University Press.

Mahmood, Saba. 2005. *The Politics of Piety: The Islamic Revival and the Feminist Subject*. Princeton: Princeton University Press.

Mahmood, Saba, and Peter G. Danchin. 2014. "Immunity or Regulation? Antinomies of Religious Freedom." *South Atlantic Quarterly* 113 (1): 129–59.

Malkiel, David. 2009. *Reconstructing Ashkenaz: The Human Face of France-German Jewry, 1000–1250*. Stanford: Stanford University Press.

Mallison, W. Thomas Jr. 1962–1963. "Zionist-Israel Claims on 'The Jewish People' Are Unconstitutional." *Issues* 16 (7) (Winter): 2–14.

Marr, Wilhelm. 1846. *Das junge Deutschland in der Schweiz*. Leipzig: Verlag von Wilhelm Journay.

Marr, Wilhelm. 1862. *Der Judenspiegel*. Fünfte Auflage. Hamburg: Selbstverlag des Verfassers.

Marr, Wilhelm. 1879. *Der Sieg des Judenthums über das Germanenthum: Vom nicht confessionellen Standpunkt aus betrachtet*. Bern: Rudolph Costenoble.

Marrs, Jim. 2000. *Rule by Secrecy: The Hidden History That Connects the Trilateral Commission, The Freemasons and the Great Pyramids*. New York: HarperCollins.

Marshall, William P. 1996. "Religion as Ideas: Religion as Identity." *Journal of Contemporary Legal Issues* 7 (2): 385–406.

Marty, Eric. 2003. *Bref séjour à Jérusalem*. Paris: Gallimard.
Marx, Karl. 1844. Review of *Die Judenfrage*, by Bruno Bauer. *Deutsch-Franzöische Jahrbücher* 1: 182–214.
Massing, Paul. 1949. *Rehearsal for Destruction: A Study of Political Anti-Semitism in Imperial Germany*. New York: Harper.
Mazower, Mark. 2008. *Hitler's Empire: Nazi Rule in Occupied Europe*. New York: Penguin Books.
Mearsheimer, John, and Stephen Walt. 2006. "The Israel Lobby." *London Review of Books* 28 (6) (March 23): 3–12.
Mearsheimer, John, and Stephen Walt. 2007. *The Israel Lobby and U.S. Foreign Policy*. New York: Farrar, Straus and Giroux.
Meer, Nasar. 2013. "Semantics, Scales and Solidarities in the Study of Antisemitism and Islamophobia." *Ethnic and Racial Studies* 36 (3): 500–15.
Meer, Nasar. 2014. Introduction to *Racialization and Religion: Race, Culture and Difference in the Study of Antisemitism and Islamophobia*, by Nasar Meer, 1–14. London: Routledge.
Meer, Nasar, and Tariq Modood. 2012. "For 'Jewish' Read 'Muslim'? Islamophobia as a Form of Racialisation of Ethno-Religious Groups in Britain Today." *Islamophobia Studies Journal* 1 (1): 35–53.
Meer, Nasar, and Tehseen Noorani. 2008. "A Sociological Comparison of Anti-Semitism and Anti-Muslim Sentiment in Britain." *The Sociological Review* 56 (2): 195–219.
Megargee, Geoffrey. P., and Martin Dean, eds. 2012. *Encyclopedia of Camps and Ghettos 1933–1945*. Vol. 2. Indianapolis: Indiana University Press.
Melson, Robert. 1992. *Revolution and Genocide: On the Origins of the Armenian Genocide and the Holocaust*. Chicago: University of Chicago Press.
Memmi, Albert. 1973. "The Impossible Life of Frantz Fanon." *Massachusetts Review* 14: 9–39.
Mende, Claudia. 2010. "Islamophobia and Anti-Semitism—Mechanisms of Exclusion and Discrimination: Interview with Wolfgang Benz, Head of the Center for Research on Anti-Semitism at Berlin's Free University." *Qantara*. https://en.qantara.de/content/islamophobia-and-anti-semitism-mechanisms-of-exclusion-and-discrimination.
Mendes-Flohr, Paul. 1978. "The Throes of Assimilation: Self-Hatred and the Jewish Revolutionary." *European Judaism: A Journal for the New Europe* 12 (1): 34–39.
Mendes, Philip. 2008. "The Strange Phenomenon of Jewish Anti-Zionism: Self-hating Jews or Protectors of Universalistic Principles?" *Australian Journal of Jewish Studies* 23: 96–132.
Menocal, Maria Rosa. 2002. *The Ornament of the World: How Muslims, Christians, and Jews Created a Culture of Tolerance in Medieval Spain*. New York: Little, Brown.
Meyer, Michael A. 1989. "Antisemitism and Jewish Identity." *Commentary* 88 (5) (November): 35–40.
Meyers Grosses Konversations-Lexikon. 1902. 6th ed. 20 vols. Leipzig: Bibliographisches Institut.
Meyerson, Mark D. 2004. *Jews in an Iberian Frontier Kingdom: Society, Economy, and Politics in Morvedre, 1248–1391*. Leiden: Brill.
Michaelis, Johann. 1783. "Hr. Ritter Michaelis Beurtheilung ueber die bürgerliche Verbesserung der Juden von Christian Wilhelm Dohm." In *Ueber die*

bürgerliche Verbesserung der Juden, edited by Christian Wilhelm Dohm, vol. 2. Berlin: Friedrich Nicolai.
Michman, Dan. 2011. *The Emergence of Jewish Ghettos During the Holocaust*. Cambridge: Cambridge University Press.
Miczynski, Sebastian. 1618. *Zwierciadlo Korony Polskiey*. Cracow: Máciej Jedrzeiowczyk.
Miller, Rory. 2000. *Divided Against Zion. Anti-Zionist Opposition in Britain to a Jewish State in Palestine, 1945–1948*. London: Frank Cass.
Mirsky, Yehuda. 2014. *Rav Kook: Mystic in a Time of Revolution*. New Haven: Yale University Press.
Mosse, George. 1964. *The Crisis of German Ideology: Intellectual Origins of the Third Reich*. New York: Grosset & Dunlap.
Moyn, Samuel. 2014. "From Communist to Muslim: European Human Rights, the Cold War, and Religious Liberty." *South Atlantic Quarterly* 113 (1): 63–86.
Mufti, Aamir. 2007. *Enlightenment in the Colony: The Jewish Question and the Crisis of Postcolonial Culture*. Princeton: Princeton University Press.
Müller-Wille, Staffan, and Hans-Jörg Rheinberger. 2012. *A Cultural History of Heredity*. Chicago: University of Chicago Press.
Myers, David N. 2006. "Can There Be a Principled Anti-Zionism? On the Nexus between Anti-Historicism and Anti-Zionism in Modern Jewish Thought." *Journal of Israeli History* 25 (1): 33–50.
Neumann, Franz. 2009. *Behemoth: The Structure and Practice of National Socialism, 1933–1944*. Chicago: Ivan R. Dee.
Nirenberg, David. 1996. *Communities of Violence: Persecution of Minorities in the Middle Ages*. Princeton: Princeton University Press.
Nirenberg, David. 2013. *Anti-Judaism: The Western Tradition*. New York: W. W. Norton.
Nirenberg, David. 2014. *Neighboring Faiths: Christianity, Islam, and Judaism in the Middle Ages and Today*. Chicago: University of Chicago Press.
Noakes, Jeremy. 1989. "The Development of Nazi Policy Towards the German-Jewish 'Mischlinge' 1933–1945." *Leo Baeck Institute Yearbook* 34: 291–354.
Noakes, Jeremy, and Geoffrey Pridham, eds. 2001. *Nazism, 1919–1945: A Documentary Reader*. Vol. 3. Exeter: University of Exeter Press.
Oberman, Heiko. 1984. *The Roots of Anti-Semitism: In the Age of Renaissance and Reformation*. Translated by James I. Porter. Philadelphia: Fortress Press.
O'Brien, Peter. 2016. "Secularism." In *The Muslim Question in Europe: Political Controversies and Public Philosophies*, 144–98. Philadelphia: Temple University Press.
Ocker, Christopher. 1998. "Ritual Murder and the Subjectivity of Christ: A Choice in Medieval Christianity." *Harvard Theological Review* 91 (2) (April): 153–92.
Ockman, Carol. 1995. *Ingres's Eroticized Bodies: Retracing the Serpentine Line*. New Haven: Yale University Press.
Özyürek, Esra. 2005. "The Politics of Cultural Unification, Secularism, and the Place of Islam in the New Europe." *American Ethnologist* 32 (4): 509–12.
Padovan, Dario, and Alfredo Alietti. 2012. "The Racialization of Public Discourse: Antisemitism and Islamophobia in Italian Society." *European Societies* 14 (2): 186–202.
Parkes, James William. 1969. *The Conflict of the Church and the Synagogue: A Study in the Origins of Antisemitism*. New York: Atheneum.

Parsons, Talcott. 1942. "The Sociology of Modern Anti-Semitism." In *Jews in a Gentile World: The Problem of Anti-Semitism*, edited by Isacque Graeber and Steuart Henderson Britt, 101–122. New York: Macmillan.

Passelecq, Georges, and Bernard Suchecky. 1997. *The Hidden Encyclical of Pius XI*. New York: Harcourt Brace.

Patterson, Orlando. 1985. *Slavery and Social Death: A Comparative Study*. Cambridge, MA: Harvard University Press.

Paulus, H. E. G. 1831. *Die Jüdische Nationalabsonderung nach Ursprung, Folgen und Besserungsmitteln*. Heidelberg: C.F. Winter.

Penslar, Derek. 2006. "Antisemites on Zionism: From Indifference to Obsession." In *Israel in History. The Jewish State in Comparative Perspective*, 112–29. London: Routledge.

Philipson, David. 1894. *Old European Jewries*. Philadelphia: Jewish Publication Society.

Pianko, Noam. 2015. *Jewish Peoplehood: An American Innovation*. New Brunswick: Rutgers University Press.

Pinsker, Leon. (1882) 1975. "Auto-Emancipation: An Appeal to His People by a Russian Jew." In *Road to Freedom: Writings and Addresses*. Westport: Greenwood Press.

Pinson, Koppel S., ed. 1946. *Essays on Anti-Semitism*. New York: Conference on Jewish Relations.

Pius XI, Pope. 1938. *Spiritually, We Are Semites*. Primary Texts On History of Relations. Council of Centers on Jewish-Christian Relations. http://www.ccjr.us/dialogika-resources/primary-texts-from-the-history-of-the-relationship/pius-xi1938sept6.

PLO (Palestinian Liberation Organization). 1968. *The Palestinian National Charter: Resolutions of the Palestine National Council July 1–17*. The Avalon Project: Documents in Law, History, and Diplomacy. http://avalon.law.yale.edu/20th_century/plocov.asp.

Pohl, Dieter. 2007. "Anti-Jewish Pogroms in Western Ukraine: A Research Agenda." In *Shared History, Divided Memory: Jews and Others in Soviet-Occupied Poland, 1939–1941*, edited by Elazar Barkan, Elizabeth Cole, and Kai Struve, 305–14. Leipzig: Leipziger Universitätsverlag.

Poliakov, Leon. 1974. *The History of Antisemitism*. 4 vols. London: Routledge & Kegan Paul.

Popkin, Richard. 1980. "The Philosophical Bases of Modern Racism." In *The High Road to Pyrrhonism*, 79–102. San Diego: Austin Hill Press.

Porat, Dina. 2011. "The International Working Definition of Antisemitism and Its Detractors." *Israel Journal of Foreign Affairs* 5 (3): 93–101.

Porter, Brian. 2000. *When Nationalism Began to Hate: Imagining Modern Politics in 19th Century Poland*. New York: Oxford University Press.

Praag, Bernard. 1951. Introduction to *Jew Hate as a Sociological Problem*, by Fritz Bernstein. New York: Philosophical Library.

Protocols of the Elders of Zion. 1923. Translated by Victor Marsden. London: The Britons Publishing Society.

Prell, Riv-Ellen. 1990. "Rage and Representation: Jewish Gender Stereotypes in American Culture." In *Uncertain Terms: Negotiating Gender in American Culture*, edited by Faye Ginsburg and Anna Lowenhaupt Tsing, 248–68. Boston: Beacon Press.

Prell, Riv-Ellen. 1999. *Fighting to Become Americans: Assimilation and the Trouble Between Jewish Women and Jewish Men*. Boston: Beacon Press.

PSR (Physicians for Social Responsibility). 2015. "Body Count: Casualty Figures After 10 Years of the 'War on Terror' (Iraq, Afghanistan, Pakistan)." https://www.psr.org/wp-content/uploads/2018/05/body-count.pdf.

Pulzer, Peter. 1964. *The Rise of Political Anti-Semitism in Germany and Austria*. New York: Wiley.

Pulzer, Peter. 2003. "The New Antisemitism, or When Is a Taboo Not a Taboo?" In *A New Antisemitism?: Debating Judeophobia in 21st-century Britain*, edited by Paul Iganski, Barry Alexander Kosmin, and Geoffrey Alderman. London: Profile.

Pulzer, Peter. 2005. "Third Thoughts on German and Austrian Anti-Semitism." *Journal of Modern Jewish Studies* 4 (2) (July): 137–78.

Rathenau, Walter. 1965. *Schriften*. Edited by Arnold Harttung et al. Berlin: Berlin Verlag.

Ravid, Benjamin. 1992. "From Geographical Realia to Historiographical Symbol: The Odyssey of the Word 'Ghetto.'" In *Essential Papers on Jewish Culture in Renaissance and Baroque Italy*, edited by David B. Ruderman, 373–85. New York: New York University Press.

Raz-Krakotzkin, Amnon. 2015. "Secularism, The Christian Ambivalence Toward the Jews, and the Notion of Exile." In *Secularism in Question: Jews and Judaism in Modern Times*, edited by A. Joskowitz and E. B Katz, 276–98. Philadelphia: University of Pennsylvania Press.

Reichmann, Eva. 1949. *Hostages of Civilisation: The Social Sources of National Socialist Anti-Semitism*. Westport: Greenwood.

Reitter, Paul. 2009. "The Jewish Self-Hatred Octopus." *The German Quarterly* 82 (3): 356–72.

Reitter, Paul. 2012. *On the Origins of Jewish Self-Hatred*. Princeton: Princeton University Press.

Renan, Ernest. (1855) 1863. *Histoire générale et système comparé des langues sémitiques: 1. ptie. Histoire générale des langues sémitiques*. 4th ed. Paris: Lévy.

Renan, Ernest. (1860) 1894. *The Life of Jesus*. London: K. Paul.

Renan, Ernest, and Shlomo Sand. 2010. *On the Nation and the "Jewish People."* London: Verso.

Renton, James. 2007. "Changing Languages of Empire and the Orient: Britain and the Invention of the Middle East, 1917–1918." *The Historical Journal* 50 (3): 645–67.

Renton, James, and Ben Gidley. 2017. "Introduction: The Shared Story of Europe's Ideas of the Muslim and the Jew--A Diachronic Framework." In Renton and Gidley, 1–21.

Renton, James, and Ben Gidley, eds. 2017. *Antisemitism and Islamophobia in Europe: A Shared Story?* London: Palgrave Macmillan.

Reuther, Rosemary. 1974. *Faith and Fratricide: The Theological Roots of Anti-Semitism*. New York: The Seabury Press.

Reznik, David. L. 2016. *New Jews: Race and American Jewish Identity in 21st Century Film*. London: Routledge.

Riesser, Gabriel. 1831a. *Ueber die Stellung der Bekenner des Mosaischen Glaubens in Deutschland*. Altona: Johann Friedrich Hammerich.

Riesser, Gabriel. 1831b. *Vertheidigung der bürgerlichen Gleichstellung der Juden gegen die Einwürfe des Herrn Dr. H.E.G. Paulus*. Altona: Johann Friedrich Hammerich.

Robbins, Bruce. 1997. "Secularism, Elitism, Progress and Other Transgressions." In *Cultural Readings of Imperialism: Edward Said and the Gravity of History*, edited by Keith Ansell Pearson, Benita Parry, and Judith Squires, 67–87. London: Lawrence and Wishart.
Roberts, John Morris. 1974. *The Mythology of the Secret Societies*. St Albans: Paladin.
Roberts, Mary Louise. 1994. *Civilization Without Sexes: Reconstructing Gender in Post-War France, 1917–1927*. Chicago: University of Chicago Press.
Robertson, Pat. 1991. *The New World Order*. Dallas: Word Publishing.
Romeyn, Esther. 2014. "Anti-Semitism and Islamophobia: Spectropolitics and Immigration." *Theory, Culture & Society* 31 (6): 77–101.
Rose, E. M. 2015. *The Murder of William of Norwich: The Origins of the Blood Libel in Medieval Europe*. Oxford: Oxford University Press.
Rose, Jacqueline. 2007. "The Myth of Self-Hatred." *The Guardian*, February 7. https://www.theguardian.com/commentisfree/2007/feb/08/holdjewishvoices6.
Rose, Paul. 1992. *German Question/Jewish Question: Revolutionary Antisemitism from Kant to Wagner*. Princeton: Princeton University Press.
Rosenfeld, Alvin. H. 2013. "The End of the Holocaust and the Beginnings of a New Antisemitism." In *Resurgent Antisemitism: Global Perspectives*, edited by Alvin. H. Rosenfeld, 521–34. Bloomington: Indiana University Press.
Rosenfeld, Alvin H., ed. 2019. *Anti-Zionism and Antisemitism: The Dynamics of Delegitimization*. Bloomington: Indiana University Press.
Roth, Cecil. 1938. "The Mediaeval Conception of the Jew: A New Interpretation." In *Essays and Studies in Memory of Linda R. Miller*, edited by Israel Davidson, 171–90. New York: Jewish Theological Seminary of America.
Roth, Cecil. 1940. "Marranos and Racial Antisemitism: A Study in Parallels." *Jewish Social Studies* 2 (3): 239–48.
Rothbell, Gladys. 1986. "The Jewish Mother: Social Construction of a Popular Image." In *The Jewish Family: Images and Reality*, edited by Steven Cohen and Paula Hyman. New York: Holmes & Meier.
Rothberg, Michael. 2009. *Multidirectional Memory: Remembering the Holocaust in the Age of Decolonization*. Stanford: Stanford University Press.
Rousso, Henry. 1987. *Le syndrome de Vichy, 1944–198--*. Paris: Seuil.
Rovner, Jay. 2000. "An Early Passover Haggadah According to the Palestinian Rite." *Jewish Quarterly Review* 90 (3/4): 337–96.
Rubin, Miri. 2004. *Gentile Tales: The Narrative Assault on Late Medieval Jews*. Philadelphia: University of Pennsylvania Press.
Rubin, Miri. 2014. Introduction to *The Life and Passion of William of Norwich*, by Thomas of Monmouth. Translated and edited by Miri Rubin. London: Penguin Books.
Ruderman, David. 1997. "The Cultural Significance of the Ghetto in Jewish History." In *From Ghetto to Emancipation: Historical and Contemporary Reconsiderations of the Jewish Community of Scranton*, edited by David N. Myers and William V. Rowe. Scranton: Scranton University Press.
Rupnow, Dirk. 2008. "Racializing Historiography: Anti-Jewish Scholarship in the Third Reich." *Patterns of Prejudice* 42 (1): 27–59.
Ruppin, Arthur. 1906. "Begabungsunterschiede christlicher und jüdischer Kinder." *Zeitschrift für Demographie und Statistik der Juden* 2: 129–35.
Rürup, Reinhard. 1975. "Emanzipation—Anmerkungen zur Begriffsgeschichte." In *Emanzipation und Antisemitismus*, 126–32. Göttingen: Vandenhoeck & Ruprecht.

Said, Edward. 1976. "Arabs, Islam and the Dogmas of the West." *New York Times.* October 31. https://www.nytimes.com/1976/10/31/archives/arabs-islam-and-the-dogmas-of-the-west-arabs.html.
Said, Edward. 1978. *Orientalism.* New York: Vintage Books.
Said, Edward. 1981. *Covering Islam: How the Media and the Experts Determine How We See the Rest of the World.* New York: Pantheon Books.
Said, Edward. 1985. "Orientalism Reconsidered." *Cultural Critique* 1 (Fall): 89–107.
Said, Edward. 2000. *The End of the Peace Process: Oslo and After.* London: Granta Books.
Said, Edward. 2003. *Freud and the Non-European.* London: Verso Books.
Said, Edward. 2004. *Humanism and Democratic Criticism.* New York: Palgrave Macmillan.
Said, Edward. 2006. *On Late Style: Music and Literature Against the Grain.* New York: Bloomsbury.
Salaymeh, Lena. 2014. "Propaganda, Politics, and Profiteering: Islamic Law in the Contemporary U.S." *Jadaliyya*, September 29. http://www.jadaliyya.com/pages/index/19408/propaganda-politics-and-profiteering_islamic-law-i.
Salaymeh, Lena. 2015. "'Comparing' Jewish and Islamic Legal Traditions: Between Disciplinarity and Critical Historical Jurisprudence." *Critical Analysis of Law, New Historical Jurisprudence* 2 (1): 153–72.
Salaymeh, Lena. 2016. "Taxing Citizens: Socio-Legal Constructions of Late Antique Muslim Identity." *Islamic Law and Society* 23 (4): 333–67.
Salaymeh, Lena. 2019. "Imperialist Feminism and Islamic Law." *Hawwa* 17 (2-3): 97–134.
Salaymeh, Lena, and Shai Lavi. "Religion Is Secularized Tradition: Jewish and Muslim Circumcisions in Germany." *Oxford Journal of Legal Studies*, forthcoming.
Samuel, Maurice. 1940. *The Great Hatred.* New York: Alfred A. Knopf.
Samuels, Maurice. 2006. "Metaphors of Modernity: Prostitutes, Bankers, and Other Jews in Balzac's *Splendeurs et misères des courtisanes.*" *Romanic Review* 97 (2): 169–84.
Samuels, Maurice. 2016. *The Right to Difference: French Universalism and the Jews.* Chicago: University of Chicago Press.
Sandauer, Artur. 1985. "On the Plight of the Polish Writer of Jewish Origin in the Twentieth-Century: An Essay which I should not have Written" [In Polish]. In *Pisma Zebrane.* Vol 3. Warsaw: Czytelnik.
Sanos, Sandrine. 2013. *The Aesthetics of Hate: Far-Right Intellectuals, Antisemitism, and Gender in 1930s France.* Stanford: Stanford University Press.
Sartre, Jean-Paul. 1965. *Anti-Semite and Jew.* Translated by George J. Becker. New York: Schocken Books.
Schäfer, Peter. 1997. *Judeophobia: Attitudes Toward the Jews in the Ancient World.* Cambridge, MA: Harvard University Press.
Schechter, Ronald. 2003. *Obstinate Hebrews: Representations of Jews in France, 1715–1815.* Berkeley: University of California Press.
Schiffer, Sabine, and Constantin Wagner. 2011. "Anti-Semitism and Islamophobia—New Enemies, Old Patterns." *Race & Class* 52 (3): 77–84.
Schnur, Susan. 1987. "Blazes of Truth: When is a JAP not a Yuppie?" *Lilith* 17 (Fall): 10–11.
Schmitt, Jean-Claude. 2013. *The Conversion of Herman the Jew: Autobiography, History and Fiction in the Twelfth Century.* Translated by Alex J. Novikoff. Philadelphia: University of Pennsylvania Press.

Schorsch, Ismar. 1972. *Jewish Reactions to German Anti-Semitism, 1870–1914.* New York: Columbia University Press.

Schreiber, Emanuel. 1921a. "Why I Am an Anti-Zionist." *Bnai Brith Messenger*, June 3, 12.

Schreiber, Emanuel. 1921b. "Why I Am an Anti-Zionist." *Bnai Brith Messenger*, September 30, 11.

Schultens, Albert. 1729. *Oratio de linguæ Arabicæ antiquissima origine, intima ac sororia cum lingua Hebræa affinitate, nullisque seculis præflorata puritate: habita quum fasces academicos iterum deponeret.* Frankfurt a/M: Willem Coulon.

Schulz, Hans. 1913. "Emanzipation." In *Deutsches Fremdwörterbuch*, vol. 1, 170–71. Straβburg: Trübner.

Schwab, Raymond. 1984. *The Oriental Renaissance: Europe's Rediscovery of India and the East, 1680–1880.* New York: Columbia University Press.

Schwartz, Seth. 2004. *Imperialism and Jewish Society: 200 B.C.E. to 640 C.E.* Princeton: Princeton University Press.

Scott, Joan W. 1986. "Gender: A Useful Category of Historical Analysis." *The American Historical Review* 91 (December): 1053–75.

Secunda, Shai. 2014. *The Iranian Talmud.* Philadelphia: University of Pennsylvania Press.

Semeniuk, V. A. 1981. *Sionizm v politchestkoi strategii imperializima.* Minsk.

Sereny, Gitta. 1983. *Into that Darkness: An Examination of Conscience.* New York: Vintage.

Shaffer, Emily S. 1980. *"Kubla Khan" and "The Fall of Jerusalem:" The Mythological School in Biblical Criticism and Secular Literature, 1770–1880.* Cambridge: Cambridge University Press.

Shalev, Eran. 2014. *American Zion: The Old Testament as a Political Text from the Revolution to the Civil War.* New Haven: Yale University Press.

Shimoni, Gideon. 1986. "From Anti-Zionism to Non-Zionism in Anglo-Jewry, 1917–1937." *Jewish Journal of Sociology* 28 (1) (June): 19–47.

Shochetman, E. 1997. "A *Halakhah* That Is Not *Halakhah*" [In Hebrew]. *Sinai* 120: 184–86.

Shumsky, Dmitry. 2018. *Beyond the Nation-State: The Zionist Political Imagination from Pinsker to Ben Gurion.* New Haven: Yale University Press.

Sicroff, Albert. 2000. "Spanish Anti-Judaism: A Case of Religious Racism." In *Encuentros and Desencuentros: Spanish Jewish Cultural Interaction Throughout History*, edited by C. Parrondo, M. Dascal, F. Villanueza, and A. Badillos, 589–613. Tel Aviv: University Publishing Projects.

Siegel, Rachel Josefowitz. 1986. "Anti-Semitism and Sexism in Stereotypes of Jewish Women." *Women and Therapy* 5 (2–3): 249–57.

Siegmund, Stefanie. 2006. *The Medici State and the Ghetto of Florence.* Palo Alto: Stanford University Press.

Silber, David, trans. 2011. *A Passover Haggadah: Go Forth and Learn.* Philadelphia: The Jewish Publication Society.

Skenderovic, Damir, and Christina Späti. 2019. "From Orientalism to Islamophobia: Reflections, Confirmations, and Reservations." *ReOrient* 4 (2): 130–43.

Smallwood, Mary. 1970. *Philo Legatio ad Gaium.* Leiden: Brill.

Smith, Scott. 2004. "Constitutional Meanings of Religion Past and Present: Explorations in Definition and Theory." *Temple Political Civil Rights Law Review* 14 (1): 89–142.

Soyer, Francois. 2014. *Popularizing Anti-Semitism in Early Modern Spain and Its Empires.* Leiden: Brill.

Spence, Joseph. 1727. *An Essay on Pope's Odyssey, in Which Some Particular Beauties and Blemishes of That Work Are Considered.* London: Wilmot.
Spencer, Gary. 1989. "An Analysis of JAP-Baiting Humor on the College Campus." *International Journal of Humor Research* 2: 329–48.
Spencer, Herbert. 1851. *Social Statics, or The Conditions Essential to Human Happiness Specified and the First of Them Developed.* London: John Chapman.
Spivak, Gayatri Chakravorty. 1988. *In Other Words: Essays in Cultural Politics.* New York: Routledge.
Stahl, Friedrich Julius. 1858. *Der christliche Staat.* Zweite durchgesehene Auflage. Berlin: Oehmigke.
Steinsalz, Adin, ed. 1969. *Talmud.* Jerusalem: Israel Institute for Talmudic Publications.
Steinweis, Alan. 2009. *Kristallnacht 1938.* Cambridge, MA: Harvard University Press.
Stern, Frank. 1991. *The Whitewashing of the Yellow Badge: Antisemitism and Philosemitism in Postwar Germany.* London: Heinemann.
Sternhell, Zeev. 2016. "The Americans Simply Don't Care About Israel and the Palestinians." *Haaretz online*, August 22. http://www.haaretz.com/opinion/.premium-1.738045.
Stiassny, Wilhelm. 1909. *Anlage einer Kolonie in Heiligen Lande oder in einem seiner Nebenländer.* Vienna: Verlag des Jüdischen Kolonisations-Vereines.
Stöcker, Adolf. 1880. *Das moderne Judenthum in Deutschland, besonders in Berlin.* Berlin: Verlag von Wiegandt und Grieben.
Stola, Dariusz. 2000. *Kampania antysyjonistyczna w Polsce, 1967–1968.* Warsaw.
Stow, Kenneth. 1977. *Catholic Thought and Papal Policy, 1555–1593.* New York: Jewish Theological Seminary Press.
Stow, Kenneth. 1992a. *Alienated Minority: The Jews of Medieval Latin Europe.* Cambridge, MA: Harvard University Press.
Stow, Kenneth. 1992b. "The Consciousness of Closure: Roman Jewry and Its *Ghet*." In *Essential Papers on Jewish Culture in Renaissance and Baroque Italy*, edited by David Ruderman, 386–400. New York: New York University Press.
Stow, Kenneth. 2006. *Jewish Dogs: An Image and Its Interpreters.* Palo Alto: Stanford University Press.
Stow, Kenneth. 2016. "The Roman Ghetto and Its Significance." Unpublished paper.
Struve, Kai. 2015. *Deutsche Herrschaft, ukrainischer Nationalismus, antijüdische Gewalt: Der Sommer 1941 in Westukraine.* Oldenbourg: De Gruyter.
Sullivan, Winnifred Fallers. 2005. *The Impossibility of Religious Freedom.* Princeton: Princeton University Press.
Surkis, Judith. 2006. *Sexing the Citizen: Morality and Masculinity in France, 1870–1920.* Ithaca: Cornell University Press.
Sutcliffe, Adam. 2003. *Judaism and Enlightenment.* Cambridge: Cambridge University Press.
Szobar, Patricia. 2005. "Telling Sexual Stories in the Nazi Courts of Law: Race Defilement in Germany, 1933 to 1945." In *Sexuality and German Fascism*, edited by Dagmar Herzog, 131–63. New York: Berghahn.
Tanakh. 1999. Philadelphia: New Jewish Publication Society.
Taguieff, Pierre-André. 2001. *The Force of Prejudice: On Racism and Its Doubles.* Minneapolis: University of Minnesota Press.
Taguieff, Pierre-André. 2002. *La nouvelle judéophobie.* Paris: Mille et une nuits.

Tareen, Sherali. 2014. "Islam, Democracy, and the Limits of Secular Conceptuality." *Journal of Law and Religion* 29 (1): 206–22.
Tcherikover, Victor. 1959. *Hellenistic Civilization and the Jews.* New York: Atheneum.
Terpstra, Nicholas. 2015. *Religious Refugees in the Early Modern World: An Alternative History of the Reformation.* Cambridge: Cambridge University Press.
Tibi, Bassam. 1993. "Deutsche Ausländerfeindlichkeit - Ethnisch-Religiöser Rechtsradikalismus der Ausländer. Zwei Gefahren für die Demokratie." *Gewerkschaftliche Monatshefte* 44 (8): 493–502.
Tompkins, Jane. 1985. *Sensational Designs: The Cultural Work of American Fiction, 1790–1860.* New York: Oxford University Press.
Trachtenberg, Joshua. 1983. *The Devil and The Jews: The Medieval Conception of the Jew and Its Relation to Modern Anti-Semitism.* Philadelphia: Jewish Publication Society.
Traverso, Enzo. 2016. *The End of Jewish Modernity.* Translated by David Fernbach. London: Pluto Press.
Trivellato, Francesca. 2019. *The Promise and Peril of Credit: What a Forgotten Legend about Jews and Finance Tells Us About the Making of European Commercial Society.* Princeton: Princeton University Press.
Tyzik, T. 1908. "Listów do 'Posiewu.'" *Posiew* 3/4 (January 23): 61.
UNESCO. 1952. *The Race Concept: Results of an Inquiry.* Paris: UNESCO.
Ury, Scott. 2018. "Strange Bedfellows? Antisemitism, Zionism and the Fate of 'the Jews.'" *American Historical Review* 123 (4) (October): 1151–71.
U.S. Congress. 2019. *Anti-Semitism Awareness Act of 2019.* S 852. 116th Cong., 1st sess. Introduced in Senate March 14. https://www.congress.gov/bill/116th-congress/senate-bill/852/text.
U.S. Department of State. 2010. "Defining Anti-Semitism." https://www.state.gov/s/rga/resources/267538.htm.
Valentin, Hugo. 1936. *Anti-Semitism: Historically and Critically Examined.* New York: Viking.
Valman, Nadia. 2007. *The Jewess in Nineteenth-Century Literary Culture.* Cambridge: Cambridge University Press.
van der Horst, Pieter W. 2003. *Philo's Flaccus: The First Pogrom: Introduction, Translation, and Commentary.* Leiden: Brill.
Vincent, Nicholas. 2013. "William of Newburgh, Josephus, and the New Titus." In *Christians and Jews in Angevin England: The York Massacre of 1190, Narratives and Contexts*, edited by Sarah Rees Jones and Sethina Watson, 57–90. Woodbridge: Boydell.
Viswanathan, Gauri, ed. 2001. *Power, Politics and Culture: Interviews with Edward W. Said.* New York: Pantheon Books.
Volkov, Shulamit. 1989. "The Written Matter and the Spoken Word. On the Gap Between Pre-1914 and Nazi Anti-Semitism." In *Unanswered Questions: Nazi Germany and the Genocide of the Jews*, edited by François Furet, 33–53. Schocken: New York.
Volkov, Shulamit. 2006. "Readjusting Cultural Codes: Reflections on Anti-Semitism and Anti-Zionism." *Journal of Israeli History* 25 (1) (March): 51–62.
Volkov, Shulamit. 2011. "Tenu'a be-ma'agal: Heker ha-antishemiut mi-Shmuel Etinger u-hazara." *Tsiyon* 76 (3): 369–79.
von Bieberstein, Johannes Rogalla. 1977. "The Story of Jewish-Masonic Conspiracy: 1776–1945." *Patterns of Prejudice* 11 (6): 1–21.

von Treitschke, Heinrich. 1870. *What We Demand from France*. London: Macmillan.
von Verschuer, Otmar. 1938. "Rassenbiologie der Juden." *Forschungen über das Judentum* 3: 139–54.
Walfish, Barry. 1993. *Esther in Medieval Garb: Jewish Interpretations of the Book of Esther in the Middle Ages*. Albany: SUNY Press.
Webster, Nesta. 1921. *World Revolution: The Plot Against Civilization*. London: Constable.
Weiler, Joseph H. H. 2007. "A Christian Europe? Europe and Christianity: Rules of Commitment." *European View* 6 (1): 143–50.
Weinberg, Gerhard L. 1995. *Germany, Hitler, and World War II*. New York: Cambridge University Press.
Weininger, Otto. 2005. *Sex and Character: An Investigation of Fundamental Principles*. Translated by Ladislaus Lob. Bloomington: University of Indian Press.
Weinstein, Roni. 2000. "'Mevudadim akh lo dehuyim': Ha-yehudim ba-hevra ha-italkit be-tekufat ha-reformatzya ha-katolit." In *Mi'utim, zarim ve-shonim: Kevutzot shulayim ba-historya*, edited by Shulamit Volkov. Jerusalem: Zalman Shazar Center.
Weir, Tood H. 2014. "The Specter of 'Godless Jewry': Secularism and the 'Jewish Question' in Late 19th Century Germany." *Central European History* 46: 815–49.
Weiss, John. 1996. *Ideology of Death: Why the Holocaust Happened in Germany*. Chicago: I.R. Dee.
Weiss-Wendt, Anton, and Rory Yeomans, eds. 2013. *Racial Science in Hitler's Europe, 1938–1945*. Lincoln: University of Nebraska Press.
Wistrich, Robert. 1985. *Anti-Zionism as an Expression of Antisemitism in Recent Years*. Jerusalem: Shazar Library, The Institute of Contemporary Jewry, Vidal Sassoon International Center for the Study of Antisemitism, The Hebrew University of Jerusalem.
Wistrich, Robert. 1992. *Antisemitism: The Longest Hatred*. New York: Pantheon Books.
Wistrich, Robert. 1996. "Zionism and Its Religious Critics in fin-de-siècle Vienna." *Jewish History* 10 (1) (Spring): 93–111.
Wistrich, Robert. 1998. "Zionism and Its Jewish 'Assimilationist' Critics (1897–1948)." *Jewish Social Studies* 4 (2) (Winter): 59–111.
Wistrich, Robert. 2010. *A Lethal Obsession: Anti-Semitism from Antiquity to Global Jihad*. New York: Random House.
Wistrich, Robert. 2012. *From Ambivalence to Betrayal: The Left, the Jews, and Israel*. Lincoln: University of Nebraska Press.
Wistrich, Robert, ed. 2016. *Anti-Judaism, Antisemitism, and Delegitimizing Israel*. Lincoln: University of Nebraska Press.
Wojtyska, Henryk Damian. 1993. *Aloisius Lippomano (1555–1557)*. Vol. 3/1, *Acta Nuntiaturae Polonae*. Rome: Institutum Historicum Polonicum Romae.
Wolf, Lucien. 1904. "The Zionist Peril." *Jewish Quarterly Review* 17 (1) (October): 1–25.
Wolf, Lucien. 1910–1911. "Anti-Semitism." In *Encyclopaedia Britannica*, vol. 2, 11th ed., 134–46. Cambridge: Cambridge University Press.
Wolf, Lucien. 1921. *The Myth of the Jewish Menace in World Affairs: The Truth About the Forged Protocols of the Elders of Zion*. New York: MacMillan.
Wolff, Philippe. 1971. "The 1391 Pogrom in Spain: Social Crisis or Not?" *Past and Present* 50 (1): 4–18.

Wünschmann, Kim. 2015. *Before Auschwitz: Jewish Prisoners in the Prewar Concentration Camps*. Cambridge, MA: Harvard University Press.

Yel, Ali Murat, and Alparslan Nas. 2014. "Insight Islamophobia: Governing the Public Visibility of Islamic Lifestyle in Turkey." *European Journal of Cultural Studies* 17 (5): 567–84.

Yerushalmi, Yosef. 1982. *Assimilation and Racial Anti-Semitism: The Iberian and the German Models*. New York: Leo Baeck Institute.

Yezierska, Anzia. 1920. *Hungry Hearts*. Boston: Houghton Mifflin.

Yezierska, Anzia. 1932. *All I Could Never Be*. New York: Brewer, Warren and Putnam.

Yezierska, Anzia. 1950. *Red Ribbon on a White Horse*. New York: Scribner.

Yezierska, Anzia. 1979. *The Open Cage: An Anzia Yezierska Collection*. New York: Persea.

Young, Robert. 1990. *White Mythologies: Writing History and the West*. New York: Routledge.

Young, Robert. 1994. *Colonial Desire: Hybridity, Culture and Race*. New York: Routledge.

Yuval, Israel Jacob. 2006. *Two Nations in Your Womb: Perceptions of Jews and Christians in Late Antiquity and the Middle Ages*. Berkeley: University of California Press.

Zahra, Tara. 2008. *Kidnapped Souls: National Indifference and the Battle for Children in the Bohemian Lands, 1900–1948*. Ithaca: Cornell University Press.

Zimmermann, Moshe. 1987. *Wilhelm Marr: The Patriarch of Anti-Semitism*. New York: Oxford University Press.

Zipperstein, Steven J. 1993. *Elusive Prophet: Ahad Ha'am and the Origins of Zionism*. London: Halban.

Žižek, S. 2017. Interview on *Channel 4 News* (UK), May 16. https://www.facebook.com/Channel4News/videos/10154845916691939/.

Zweig, Arnold. 1927. *Caliban, oder Politik und Leidenschaft: Versuch über die menschlichen Gruppenleidenschaften dargetan am Antisemitismus*. Potsdam: Kiepenhaeuer.

Żyndul, Jolanta. 1994. *Zajścia antyżydowskie w Polsce w latach 1935–1937*. Warsaw: Fundacja Im. K. Kelles-Krauza.

INDEX

A
Alexandria 38CE. *See* Pogroms
Allosemitism, 109, 205
American Council for Judaism, 44
American Israel Public Affairs Committee (AIPAC), 87
Améry, Jean, 232, 233
Anti-colonialism. *See* Colonialism
Anti-Defamation League (ADL), 32, 48, 87
American Jewish Committee (AJC), 43, 87
Anderson, Benedict, 165
Anti-Judaism (*Sinat Yisrael*)
   antiquity, 18, 21, 217
   early modern, 17, 22, 81
   Middle Ages, 20, 21, 82, 226
   Roman world, 19, 279
Antisemitism
   annihilationist, 129, 174, 182, 183
   Berlin movement, 93
   critique of, 156, 253, 260
   definition of, 4, 9, 14, 39, 134, 154, 218
   in Eastern Europe, 122, 171, 184, 290
   economic, 12
   eternal, eternalist, 7, 125, 30, 32, 36, 134, 233, 240, 290, 295, 296
   in France, 36, 136, 137, 168, 203, 247, 295
   in Germany, 26, 30, 31, 102, 135–140, 142, 149, 168, 176, 180, 181, 184, 249, 295
   historical narratives of, 141
   historiography of, 9, 25, 28, 36, 218, 240, 296
   interdisciplinary research on, 144, 231
   Judeophobia, 32, 36, 134, 253, 260, 263, 289
   medieval, 13, 17, 25, 33, 123
   modern, 5, 6, 10, 11, 13, 14, 16, 26, 29, 35, 36, 54, 66, 93, 131, 295
   nationalism and, 162, 171
   prophetic, 156–158
   racist, 202, 246
   redemptive, 155, 176
   spelling of, 10
   uniqueness (exceptionalism), 143, 293
   World War I, 25, 27, 31, 45, 136, 137
   World War II, 5, 25, 30, 34, 76, 139, 174, 203
   See Nazi; New Antisemitism
Anti-Zionism
   Arab, 41–43, 45–47, 294
   Communist, 41, 42, 47
   Jewish, 42, 44, 45

INDEX

Arendt, Hannah, 33, 35, 36, 139, 148, 182, 232–234, 239, 240, 293
Asad, Talal, 263
Assimilation, 48, 99, 100, 106, 110, 115, 137, 139, 150–152, 166–168, 176, 239, 259
Augustine of Hippo, 67
Autoemancipation, 1882. *See* Leon Pinsker

B

Badiou, Alain, 211, 254
Balfour Declaration, 43, 194
Baron, Salo Wittmayer, 6–7, 126, 127, 201, 230
Barruel, Augustin, 81, 169
Basnage, Jacques, 22
Bauer, Yehuda, 48
Benedict, Ruth, 247, 252
Berger, Rabbi Elmer, 44
Bergman, Shlomo, 140, 141, 143
Berlin movement, 93
Bhabha, Homi K., 165, 229, 237, 238
Bible, 18, 83, 188, 190, 191, 195, 274, 275, 280, 282–284
Bilderberg Group. *See* Conspiracy theories
Blood Libels
  England, 54
  France, 54
  Holy Roman Empire, 59
  Poland-Lithuania, 60
  Kingdom of Poland, 60
  Russian Empire, 61, 62
  Trent, 59
Boas, Franz, 247, 248, 252, 253
Bolshevik Party, 85, 182, 220
Boyarin, Daniel, 44, 206, 210, 230
Boycotts, 178
Butler, Judith, 44, 109, 150, 210, 211

C

Capitalism, 6, 26, 31, 237
Catholic Church, 8, 11, 13, 65, 75, 123, 184
Césaire, Aimé, 232, 233
Chomsky, Noam, 88
Christianity, 116, 129, 148, 156, 167, 175–177, 189, 191–193, 206, 225, 226, 230, 246, 252, 258, 265, 295

Christian state, 100, 101, 265
Church and State, 97, 100, 101, 266
Citizenship, 9, 13, 76, 82, 95–98, 101, 106, 107, 109, 166, 167, 179, 201, 207, 218, 223, 224, 268
Colonialism, 6, 47, 130, 157, 174, 187, 195, 230–235, 237, 239–240, 246
  anti-colonialism, 196, 235, 237
Communism, 6, 42, 46–48, 176, 209, 222
Conspiracy theories
  Bilderberg Group, 80, 83, 84
  as means of explanation, 80, 90
  Nazi, 83
  on the Left, 87, 89
  on the Right, 90
  origins of, 81
  Protocols of the Elders of Zion, 82, 88
  rhetorical style, 80
Conversion
  Conversos (crypto-Jews), 21, 225, 252
Cosmopolitanism. *See* Universalism
Council on Foreign Relations, 83
COVID-19, 80
Crusades
  First, 56, 57, 218
  Second, 56, 57
Cultural anxiety, 19, 22, 27, 33–35, 70, 251, 297

D

Damascus Affair, 1840, 61
Diaspora, 44, 87, 126, 139, 165, 210, 231, 235, 237, 291, 292
  diasporism, 210, 211
Disraeli, Benjamin, 191, 234, 250
Dohm, Christian Wilhelm von, 95–97, 187
Dreyfus Affair, 25–27, 36, 63, 111, 136, 137, 168, 289
Drumont, Édouard, 26, 202
Dühring, Eugen, 102, 249, 250

E

Egypt, 5, 45, 61, 275, 283
Einsatzgruppen, 182, 220

Emancipation, 4, 9, 64, 93–103, 107, 109, 168, 176, 201, 202, 207, 291
  Jewish, 31, 44, 82, 96, 97, 101, 111, 123, 137, 201, 207, 239, 295
  self-, 94, 102
Enlightenment, 8, 32, 35, 61, 82, 107, 109, 110, 157, 162, 166, 187, 207, 218, 258, 263, 288, 289, 294, 297
Esau/Edom, 67, 273, 274, 280, 281, 283
Essentialism, 109, 250
Ettinger, Shmuel, 292–294, 296
Eucharist, 22, 57, 58

F
Fanon, Frantz, 232, 233, 235, 236, 238, 239, 248
Feminism, 116
  feminist studies, 105, 116
Final Solution, 140
Frankfurt School, 31, 33–35, 142, 238
French Revolution, 81, 82, 95, 96, 107, 108, 169, 207
Freemasons, 81, 82, 86, 169
Freud, Sigmund, 33, 34, 148, 237

G
Gager, John, 15, 16, 19, 156
Gender, 9, 105–112, 116, 117, 202, 265, 267
Genocide, 5, 33, 47, 134, 140, 143, 208, 232, 240, 260, 283. *See also* Holocaust
Germany, 4, 11, 21, 26, 30, 31, 59, 62, 82, 93, 95, 97–99, 102–103, 107, 123, 135–140, 142, 143, 149, 168, 175–178, 180, 182–184, 203, 233, 237, 247–249, 251, 262, 294, 295
  West Germany, 47, 208
Ghetto, 9, 11, 122, 124, 127
Goulevitch, Arsene de, 85
Group prejudice, 141

H
Halakhah (Jewish law), 273, 280
Hamas, 46
Harem, 189, 194–196
Hatred, 1, 2, 8, 10, 13, 47, 66, 76, 90, 142, 147, 174, 175, 182, 184, 197, 203, 205, 206, 218, 219, 224–226, 248, 249, 261, 273–284, 293
Hebrew Bible, 15, 151, 190, 274
  Esther, 275
Hebrew University of Jerusalem, 292, 296
Hegel, G.W.F., 148, 191, 192
Hellenistic world, 5, 223
Herzl, Theodor, 287
  The Jewish State, 1896, 290
Hitler, Adolf, 30, 138, 140, 161, 173–179, 196
Hofstadter, Richard, 30, 140, 161
Holocaust
  and genocide, 33
  memory of, 239
  studies of, 229
Homosexuality, 177
Host Desecration, 12, 17, 58, 60, 61
Humor, 115, 155
al-Husseini, Mufti Amin, 45

I
Icke, David, 85
Identity, 14, 20–22, 27, 44, 63, 85, 105, 107, 108, 110, 115, 116, 122, 133, 148, 150–155, 165, 167, 168, 202, 210, 234, 239, 251, 264, 288
Illuminati, 80–82, 86, 169
Immigration, 9, 45, 112, 138, 248, 262
Imperialism, 35, 88, 232, 240, 263
Islam, 46, 189, 191, 196, 210, 258–260, 263, 265–267
Islamophobia, 11, 152, 188, 197, 257–265
Israel, 2, 6–8, 23, 26, 39, 43, 45–47, 86–90, 97, 98, 152, 187, 194, 197, 209, 210, 230, 235, 236, 274, 277–279, 294, 296
  1967 Arab-Israeli War (Six Day War), 294
  See New Antisemitism
Italy, 123, 138, 262
  Early Modern, 122

J

Jabotinsky, Vladimir (Ze'ev), 287, 290–292, 296
Jerusalem, 22, 45, 74, 144, 292, 294, 296
Jesus, 2, 6, 14, 15, 18, 19, 22, 53, 54, 56, 67–69, 72, 74–76, 169, 176, 177, 189, 191–193, 195
Jewish
    Jewish American Princess (JAP), 114, 115, 117
    Jewish-Christian relations, 65–67, 73, 77
    Jewish History, 6, 13, 14, 21, 36, 121, 135, 139, 187, 202, 204, 207, 217, 218, 222, 230, 231, 292–294, 296; Lachrymose conception of, 201
    Jewish Labor Bund, 46
    Jewish Question, 4, 43, 76, 93, 95, 97, 135, 137, 144, 181, 234, 239, 249, 287, 290, 292, 294
    The Jewish State, 1896. *See* Theodor Herzl
    quarter, 72, 121–124, 126, 129, 130, 225
    See Anti-Zionism
Jews, of
    British Mandate Palestine, 43
    East Central Europe, 164, 290, 292
    Ottoman Empire, 42
    Ottoman Palestine, 289
    Poland, 181
    Soviet Union, 47, 182
    United States, 47, 48, 90, 112, 113, 210, 230
Jones, Alex, 82, 85
Judeophobia, 5, 18, 32, 33, 36, 134, 257–265, 268, 289
Judaism
    Rabbinic, 19, 20, 274, 278, 284
Judeo-Christian tradition, 187, 195

K

Kabbalah (Jewish mysticism), 22
Kaiser Wilhelm I, 93, 248, 250
Katz, Jacob, 95, 141–143, 292, 294–296
al-Khalidi, Ruhi, 45
Klemperer, Victor, 175

L

Law, Jewish, 19, 153, 273, 276–280, 284
    kashrut, 70, 71
Lazare, Bernard, 26, 29, 136, 137, 250
The Left, 6, 79, 86–90, 297
    "New Left", 294
Levi, Primo, 232, 233
Lobby, the Israel/Jewish/Zionist, 79, 87, 90
Lueger, Karl, 289
Luther, Martin, 16, 30

M

Marr, Wilhelm, 66, 101, 134, 203, 246, 247, 249, 289
Marx, Karl, 101, 210, 211, 234
Marxism, 34, 36
Masculinity, 106, 108–110
Mearsheimer, John, 88–90
Memmi, Albert, 232, 233, 236, 238
Military industrial complex, 82
Misogyny, 106, 109, 115, 116, 152
Modernity, 14, 26, 27, 30, 31, 35, 36, 66, 74, 105, 106, 108–111, 128, 231, 251
Monmouth, Thomas of, 54, 55, 57
Montagu, Ashley, 247, 248
Moral improvement, 96
Mufti, Aamir R., 234, 239
Muslims, 3, 10, 65, 188–191, 196, 197, 210, 252, 257–265, 267, 268
    Muslim-Jewish Relations, 210

N

National Socialism, 36, 146, 245, 247
Nationalism
    antisemitic, 166, 221
    Arab, 42, 45, 190, 196
    civic/ethnic dichotomy, 164
    Jewish, 43, 126, 235
    nation-state, 36, 162, 167, 168, 231, 239, 261, 287, 291
    national identity, 108, 110, 165, 264
    Polish, 167, 171, 292
Natural rights, 96, 97

Nazi
  antisemitism, 129, 152, 153, 173, 176–178, 180–184, 246, 248, 251
  Germany, 11, 175, 184, 232, 237, 251
  ideology, 140, 180, 181, 233
  law, 175, 179
  party, 28, 178
  system, 31, 173, 174, 180, 182
Nazism (National Socialism), 173–185
New Antisemitism, 6, 210, 211, 253, 296
New World Order, 79, 80, 83

O
Oberman, Heiko, 15, 16, 19
Orientalism, 8, 11, 187–197, 234, 262–264, 268
Ottoman Empire, 42, 45, 61, 164, 189, 194

P
Palestine, 5, 42, 43–45, 47, 74, 75, 102, 153, 180, 187, 194, 196, 222, 231, 287, 291, 294
  British Mandatory, 43
  Ottoman Palestine, 45, 289
Palestinian Liberation Organization (PLO), 46
Parkes, James, 28, 29, 31, 33, 65, 66
Patterson, Orlando, 178
Paul, 15, 19, 66–68
Pedagogy, 8, 9
Persecution, 6, 11, 13, 21, 36, 46, 75, 102, 110, 135, 175, 183, 201, 202, 278, 296
Philosemitism, 8, 11, 109, 201–211
Pinsker, Leon (Yehuda Leib), 102, 287–294, 296–298
  Auto-Emancipation, 1882, 288
Pogroms
  Alexandria, 38 CE, 219, 223–224, 226
  Kielce, 1946, 184
  Kristallnacht, 1938, 180, 181, 218
  Lviv, 1941, 219–222, 226
  in Russian Empire, 1881-1882, 1905-1906, 61, 62, 216–218
  Valencia, 1391, 219, 224–226

Poland
  Independent, 177, 216
  Kingdom of, 60
  Polish-Lithuanian Commonwealth, 58, 72
Pope Innocent III, 68–71
Popular Culture, 59, 115, 117
Postcolonialism, 8, 11, 229–240
  decolonization, 36, 208, 233, 238–240
Protocols of the Elders of Zion. See Conspiracy theories
Purity of Blood Statutes, 246, 252, 253

R
Rabbinic literature, 276, 277, 279–282, 284
Racism
  biological, 192, 252, 253, 262
  racialization, 191, 231, 267
Reformation, 15, 16, 21, 29, 59, 125
  Counter-Reformation, 58, 60
Religion, 17, 19, 21, 43, 44, 64, 67, 74–76, 79, 97, 100, 101, 127, 141, 166, 167, 179, 189, 191, 192, 196, 216, 246, 249–252, 257–259, 263–268, 274, 276, 278, 281, 283, 287
Renan, Ernest, 191–193, 250
Riesser, Gabriel, 97–99, 101
Right-wing, 7, 87, 170, 262
  conspiracy theories, 86
  politics, 86
  radicalism, 101
Ritual murder, 17, 32, 53, 54–64, 218
  accusation of, 56, 59
Robertson, Pat, 83, 85, 86
Robison, John, 81
Rome, 67, 72, 73, 81, 123, 128, 174, 223, 278
Rothberg, Michael, 239, 240
Rothschild family, 85, 86
Russian Revolution, 82, 84, 85, 216

S
Said, Edward, 187–189, 195, 196, 229, 234, 237, 238, 240, 263

Sartre, Jean-Paul, 33, 35, 148, 208, 232, 233
Segregation, 121–126, 128, 246, 252
Self-Hatred, Jewish, 8, 9, 11, 147–159
Shylock, 22
Sinat Yisrael. *See* Anti-Judaism
Social death, 178
Soviet Union, 47, 182, 196, 219, 294
Spain, 9, 21, 54, 123, 126, 210, 225, 246, 252, 253, 262
Stalin, Joseph, 47, 153, 183
Stereotypes, 27, 79, 82, 89, 90, 98, 106, 109, 110, 112–115, 117, 176, 177, 196, 261
  Anti-Jewish, 41, 174

T

Talmud, 26, 61, 99, 274, 276, 278, 279, 281, 282
Theology/theological, 3, 4, 6, 10, 13–16, 21, 29, 33, 48, 57, 58, 66–77, 124, 136, 189, 206, 209, 210, 264

U

UNESCO, 248
Universalism, 43, 206, 207, 222, 247
Usurers, 22

V

Violence, 1, 7, 18, 20, 21, 56–58, 68, 76, 130, 135, 141, 164, 173, 175, 178, 180, 181, 184, 215, 220–226, 261, 277, 283
  Anti-Black, 175
  Anti-Jewish, 9, 216–220, 222, 224, 226, 289

W

Waldman, Morris, 43
Walt, Stephen, 88–90
Weber, Max, 34
Webster, Nesta, 86
White supremacy, 90, 175
William of Norwich. *See* Blood Libels
Wistrich, Robert S., 3, 5, 41, 42, 48, 210, 296, 297
  From Ambivalence to Betrayal: The Left, the Jews and Israel, 2012, 297
  Lethal Obsession: Anti-Semitism from Antiquity to the Global Jihad, 2010, 7, 296
Wolf, Lucien, 26–28, 43, 137
World War I, 27, 36, 45, 136–138, 149, 175, 217
  antisemitism, 25, 27, 31
World War II, 5, 76, 133, 139, 174, 203, 235
  antisemitism, 25, 30, 34

X

Xenophobia, 4, 32, 35, 128, 141, 154, 261

Z

Zionism. *See* Anti-Zionism
  evangelical, 209
  non-Zionist Jews and, 42, 44
Żuchowski, Stefan, 60

Made in United States
North Haven, CT
03 October 2022